BEATING PLOWSHARES
INTO SWORDS

BEATING PLOWSHARES INTO SWORDS

THE POLITICAL ECONOMY OF AMERICAN WARFARE, 1606–1865

PAUL A. C. KOISTINEN

UNIVERSITY PRESS OF KANSAS

© 1996 by the University Press of Kansas
All rights reserved

Published by the University Press of Kansas (Lawrence, Kansas 66049), which was organized
by the Kansas Board of Regents and is operated and funded by Emporia State University, Fort
Hays State University, Kansas State University, Pittsburg State University, the University of
Kansas, and Wichita State University

Library of Congress Cataloging-in-Publication Data

Koistinen, Paul A. C.
    Beating plowshares into swords : the political economy of American
warfare, 1606–1865 / Paul A. C. Koistinen.
        p.   cm. — (Modern war studies)
    Includes bibliographical references and index.
    ISBN 0-7006-0791-9 (alk. paper)
    1. War—Economic aspects—United States—History.   2. United
States—Defenses—History.   I. Title.   II. Series.
    HC110.D4K638   1996
    338.4'76233'0973—dc20   96-26399

British Library Cataloguing in Publication Data is available.

Printed in the United States of America

10 9 8 7 6 5 4 3 2 1

The paper used in this publication meets the minimum requirements of the American National
Standard for Permanence of Paper for Printed Library Materials Z39.48-1984.

For Carolyn

Beat your plowshares into swords, and
your pruninghooks into spears: let the
weak say I *am* strong.

Joel 3:10

. . . and they shall beat their swords
into plowshares, and their spears into
pruninghooks: nation shall not lift
up sword against nation, neither shall
they learn war any more.

Isaiah 2:4

Joel calls for war, Isaiah for peace. I study war
to advance the cause of peace.

CONTENTS

PREFACE

This volume constitutes the first of a five-volume study of the political economy of warfare in America—the means the nation has employed to mobilize its economic resources for defense and hostilities. This volume begins with the colonial years and concludes with 1865; volume 2 will cover the period from 1865 to 1920; volume 3, the interwar years; volume 4, World War II; and volume 5, the years after 1945, essentially the period of the Cold War. In this volume, I set forth the paradigm for the whole study and summarize the contents of the five volumes in Chapter 1.

I approach the political economy of warfare before 1900 from a twentieth-century perspective. All of my previous publications have dealt with the economics of warfare in this century. More specifically, I have traced the origins and development of the so-called military-industrial complex from World War I to the Cold War years. Insights gained from those studies have facilitated my analysis of the political economy of warfare in the nineteenth century and earlier. In turn, working with past wars has added depth to my understanding of twentieth-century trends.

There is a general evolutionary pattern to the political economy of warfare. The preindustrial stage, which includes the Revolutionary War, bore a striking resemblance to what has taken place in the twentieth century, even though the technology of war was unsophisticated. War mobilization had a profound and lasting effect upon the nation in both eras, and civil-military relations were exceptionally tumultuous. The preindustrial and industrial stages, therefore, were ones in which economic mobilization created multiple problems for and threats to the society. That was not the case in the transitional stage between the two stages, exemplified best by the Union during the Civil War. Economic mobilization in that stage was comparatively easy, civil-military relations remained stable, and the postwar legacy of harnessing the economy for hostilities was not great. In short, mobilizing the economy in this stage presented few hazards to the social system. After the Civil War, America entered the industrial stage in which big business, big government, a professional military, and sophisticated weaponry combined to require economic planning during major wars or periods of extended conflict. World Wars I and II and the Cold War cumulatively demonstrate the enormous impact that economic mobilization has had on an advanced industrial society, including the fundamental transformation of civil-military relations.

Analyzing the political economy of warfare also means studying power in America. My previous work on World Wars I and II demonstrates that focusing upon economic mobilization offers a nearly unequaled opportunity to examine the development of society and the relative strength of various social groups and institutions. The demands of war tend to reveal social realities that can remain obscure in times of peace. It is not too much to say that one can make a fairly accurate assessment of the nation's growth, development, and power operations by examining economic mobilization for America's many wars.

Economic mobilization for war is shaped at the national level by the interaction of political, economic, and military institutions and by the sophistication of weaponry. However, there is no general history of economic mobilization for wars of the eighteenth and nineteenth centuries that is systematic in nature and based upon an analytic paradigm. Various publications on wartime economics often become diffuse, selective, or erratic in coverage because they lack a clear definition of exactly what is being studied. Occasional monographs exist on some aspects of economic mobilization at the national level, while others deal with the economics of warfare for localities, states, and regions. Scholars have also examined at great length subjects such as the impact of the Civil War on growth rates of the economy. Additionally, many studies deal with military, economic, political, and technical aspects of warfare. All this work relates to but does not constitute an analysis of the means the nation has employed to mobilize its economic resources for defense and hostilities. Such an analysis requires drawing information from a great many sources in a number of fields.

There is more and better scholarship on the political economy of warfare in the twentieth century, but a great deal remains to be done. For instance, no synthesis of the economics of warfare from the Spanish-American War to the present has been written, and although World War I has been analyzed with sophistication in recent years, the interwar years generally have been neglected. Moreover, economic mobilization for World War II has received little attention since the publication of official histories and memoirs of participants shortly after the conclusion of hostilities, despite the availability of probably the best and the most well-organized document collections for any period in American history. Works of varying quality on the political economy of the Cold War are numerous to the point of being overwhelming, yet an authoritative synthesis of this critical period that draws upon the past to help explain the complexities of the present is missing.

The goal of my multivolume study is to provide scholars and other readers with what is now unavailable: a comprehensive, schematic, and interdisciplinary study of the economics of America's numerous wars from the colonial period to today. In doing so, I demonstrate the impact of the political economy of warfare upon domestic life and what economic mobilization for defense and war reveals about the nature and operations of society. I also seek to enlighten military history by examining in depth and breadth an aspect of warfare that is often ignored or treated in a perfunctory manner. A different perspective leads to different insights and conclusions about civilians, soldiers and sailors, and warfare. If I raise as many questions as I answer, I will have more than accomplished my purpose.

It is also important to point out what I am not doing. I am not studying logistics, tactics, or strategy in any organized way. I touch upon those subjects, particularly logistics, throughout the work but only as they pertain directly to the political economy of warfare or serve to enlighten that subject. I examine, for example, the development and production of small arms, but I do not study their impact upon the battlefield. The same holds true for modern ships of war and airplanes. My focus is on how the nation mobilizes its economic might in order to conduct war, not on the conduct of war itself.

Nonetheless, economic might has played a major role in how the United States has fought its wars. In the preindustrial stage, an underdeveloped economy forced Americans to fight defensive wars of attrition during the Revolution and the War of 1812. Growing economic maturity in the transitional stage allowed the United States to operate offensively during the Mexican War. A decade or so later, the Union relied upon its enormous economic might to overwhelm the Confederacy through a strategy of annihilation. The South bungled its strategy of attrition—in which it sought to win by not losing—largely because it failed to mobilize effectively the region's less-developed economy. The North's strategy during the Civil War anticipated the total wars of the industrial stage in which the nation relied upon its superior economic power to virtually crush the enemy—what Russell F. Weigley calls "the American way of war."

From the colonial period through the progressive era—all of the first volume and parts of the second—I have organized the material to elucidate systematically major economic, political, and military developments along with the state of military technology. By 1917, major institutions had reached maturity and no longer need to be surveyed. Thereafter, I simply update the analysis as additional information is necessary and shift the focus to economic mobilization and preparation for war. Nonetheless, at various logical places throughout the remainder of the work, I briefly recast the analysis according to the pattern of the earlier chapters so as to make the volumes consistent and continuous.

In a work as ambitious as this one, scholarly collaboration is not a choice; it is a necessity. My enormous debt to numerous historians, economists, and political scientists is clearly set forth in the notes. Of particular importance are the "new military historians." In the past few decades, they have broadened the study of the armed forces, defense, and warfare to include most of society and have thus enriched military history and the study of the past in general.

A few words about the notes are in order. Throughout this volume and parts of the second, I employ what I call "cluster noting," which means listing in one note the numerous primary and secondary sources I have relied upon in writing various parts of the analysis. When the analysis depends heavily upon primary documents, as is the case throughout the twentieth century, I return to the more usual note procedure.

I have benefited greatly from the assistance of others in putting this first volume into its final form. My son and daughter, David J. Koistinen and Janice H. Koistinen, combined their excellent critical and copyediting talents to help turn a rough and long manuscript into one that was briefer and more readable. Later, Cecilia M. Shulman proved equally valuable as an assistant. At California State University, Northridge, John J. Broesamle, Ronald L. F. Davis, and Ronald Schaffer read the entire manuscript and provided me with invaluable insights and advice. Finally, the unequaled knowledge and keen analytical skills of Mark Edward Lender and Russell F. Weigley not only caught a number of errors I had made but also required that I rethink, restructure, and rewrite substantial portions of the manuscript. A good part of the review process was guided by the watchful eye and sure hand of Michael Briggs, Editor-in-Chief, of the University Press of Kansas. His enormously capable and dedicated staff—including Susan Schott, Marketing Manager, and Megan Schoeck, Production Editor—then stepped in to accomplish the wonders of converting a manuscript into a published volume.

My debt to all of these people is matched only by my appreciation for their labors and contribution. Needless to say, I, not they, am responsible for all that is and is not said in this book.

Much precedes the review of a manuscript. Without the Oviatt Library at

California State University, Northridge (CSUN), and its interlibrary loan services, I would have been hard-pressed to complete this work. Charlotte Oyer, Donald L. Read, Michael Barrett, and Felicia Cousin worked endlessly on my behalf. For word processing of the various drafts, I appreciate the expertise and good humor of Marcia M. Dunicliffe of the History Department and Pamela Fowell of the School of Social and Behavioral Sciences. Over the years, I have benefited from research fellowships from Harvard's Charles Warren Center for Studies in American History, the American Council of Learned Societies, and the National Endowment for the Humanities. Furthermore, CSUN's History Department, School of Social and Behavioral Sciences, and the university as a whole have assisted me in numerous ways for many years.

This volume is dedicated to my wife, Carolyn Epstein Koistinen. It is a mere token of what I owe her for assistance, support, insight, and love over the years.

1

THE POLITICAL ECONOMY OF WARFARE IN AMERICA

Scholars have begun analyzing warfare and the military with increasing breadth and sophistication, but they have not paid much attention to how America has mobilized its economic resources for war and defense—the political economy of warfare—a subject that is important for a number of reasons. Logistics are basic to warfare and depend upon the nation's ability to marshal effectively its economic might. Over the centuries, economic mobilization has followed a discernible evolutionary pattern that enlightens the study of warfare and the military. Furthermore, how the United States has mobilized its economy reveals a great deal about institutional and power structures. Indeed, the stress and demands of warfare make manifest social patterns that are less evident or obscured during years of peace.

The political economy of warfare involves the interrelationships of the political, economic, and military institutions in devising the means to mobilize resources for defense and to conduct war. In each war, the magnitude and duration of the fighting have dictated *what* the nation had to do to harness its economic power, but prewar trends have largely determined *how* this mobilization took place. Four factors are essential in determining the method of mobilization. The first is economic—the level of maturity of the economy; the second is political—the size, strength, and scope of the federal government; the third, military—the character and structure of the military services and the relationship between them and civilian society and authority; and the fourth is the state of military technology.

Patterns of economic mobilization for war have passed through three major stages over the course of American history. The Revolutionary War, the Civil War, and twentieth-century warfare best characterize these stages, which I have labeled preindustrial, transitional, and industrial. Altering the four factors—economic, political, military, and technological—modifies each stage of

1

mobilization. The factors have seldom changed at the same time or pace, but over time each has had to keep pace with the others so that viable patterns of economic mobilization could be maintained.

STAGES OF ECONOMIC MOBILIZATION

The preindustrial stage of economic mobilization for war extended from the colonial period to approximately 1815 and included the Revolutionary War and the War of 1812. During the American Revolution, economic, governmental, and military institutions were in an embryonic state and were not clearly distinguished from one another. Military technology was rather primitive and varied little from production in the peacetime economy. Hence, economic mobilization involved increasing civilian output and diverting products from civilian to military use in order to supply the armed forces without converting the economy. Nonetheless, to maximize output, comprehensive regulation of the emerging nation's economic life became essential. Yet the undeveloped nature of economic, political, and military institutions not only prevented such regulation from ever working well but also resulted in private and public, civil and military activities becoming inextricably intertwined. Merchants simultaneously served as public officials and military officers while they continued to conduct their private affairs.

The effects of harnessing the economy for war carried over into the years of peace. By highlighting the weaknesses of the Articles of Confederation, economic mobilization helped to create the momentum for the ideas underlying the Constitution. And, during the early national period, intense conflict grew between the factions that became the Federalist and Republican parties over the strength and policies of the national government under the new charter. This strife weakened the federal government and stunted the growth of the armed services, a major source of dispute. Consequently, although the economy was much stronger in 1812 than in 1776 and military technology had changed little during that period, economic mobilization for the War of 1812 did not improve measurably over what it had been for the Revolutionary War.

The second, or transitional, economic mobilization stage extended from 1815 to 1865. During this period, the economy developed enormous productive capacity; it became diversified and quite industrialized, and specialized functions emerged in manufacturing, marketing, banking, and the like, although the size of firms was comparatively small. The federal government was limited in size, scope, and activity, but it was capable of expanding in order to handle economic mobilization effectively and efficiently. Both the army and navy, for their part, had professionalized to the point where they had definable structures and missions. But military technology still had not experienced any dramatic change. Since weaponry remained basic, economic mobilization required only expanding and diverting civilian production, not economic conversion.

Harnessing the economy for war was more readily accomplished in the transitional stage than in those stages that preceded and followed it. The pattern was evident in the Mexican War but was best demonstrated by the Union during the Civil War. Operating under the direction of the president, the War, Navy, and Treasury departments acted as the principal mobilization agencies. They relied on market forces in a strong competitive economy, not on the elaborate regulation of the preindustrial and industrial stages, to maintain economic stability while meeting the enormous demands of war. Moreover, institutional barriers were not breached. In the economic realm, little mixing of activities and personnel occurred among private and public, civilian and military affairs. The only major exception involved the railroads, which had begun to organize modern corporations before hostilities. The telegraph system followed a similar trend.

Union success contrasted sharply with the Confederacy's failure. The South was closer to the preindustrial than the transitional stage. Like the colonies/states during the revolutionary years, the Confederacy experimented with comprehensive economic regulation without much success. Weak economic and political systems consistently undermined the Confederacy's economic mobilization effort and played an important role in the South's defeat.

Modern warfare in the twentieth century represents the third, or industrial, economic mobilization stage. By 1900 the United States had become a mature industrialized nation with a modified capitalist system. Although market forces remained significant in the production and distribution of goods, the administered decisions of several hundred modern corporations exercised strong, at times dominant, influence over the economy's direction. In order to make concentrated and consolidated economic power more responsible to the public and to stabilize an enormously complex economy, the federal government began to act as economic regulator. The growth of huge bureaucracies in the corporate and governmental spheres began to blur the institutional lines between both. Businessmen often staffed the government's regulatory agencies, and, as during the preindustrial stage, the affairs of government and business touched or merged at many points. A government-business regulatory alliance began to emerge during the Progressive Era.

After the Civil War, the military services entered a period of relative isolation in America as the nation became absorbed in industrialization, the threat of

war receded, and the army and navy became intensely involved in professionalizing their functions. A technological revolution in weaponry in the later
years of the nineteenth century, however, drew the civilian and military worlds
back together. The consequences of this revolution were first manifest with
the navy. In order to build a new fleet of steel, armor, steam, and modern ordnance, a production team consisting of political leaders, naval officers, and
businessmen was formed. Although the composition, responsibilities, and
operation of such a team have varied over the years, it has continued to exist.
The army was slower to feel the impact of technology, but it eventually experienced the same needs and formed a relationship with industry and civil
authorities similar to the navy's.

By the eve of World War I, therefore, the federal government, the industrial community, and the military services had developed complex, modern,
and professionalized structures, each dependent upon the others in terms of
national defense. Economic mobilization for World War I (unlike the brief
and limited Spanish-American War) forcefully demonstrated this institutional
interdependence. The quantity and sophistication of military demand meant
that increasing and diverting civilian production was no longer adequate; market forces could not be relied upon. Production had to be maximized and
industries had to be converted in order to manufacture the often specialized
military hardware. Priority, allocation, price, and other controls had to be
introduced, and existing governmental departments and agencies were unequal to the task. New mobilization bodies had to be created, the most important being the War Industries Board (WIB) of World War I. Through the
board, centralized control over a planned economy was established and carried out by representatives of the government, the business community, and
the military. The process obscured institutional lines. Civilian and military,
private and public activities once again combined. For very different reasons
and with quite different results, the first and the third mobilization stages are
strikingly similar.

World War I mobilization left an indelible imprint upon national life. During the interwar years, direct and indirect economic planning patterned after
the WIB was tried. Congress and other governmental bodies repeatedly investigated the methods and consequences of harnessing the World War I economy in order to understand better what had taken place, to prevent future
mobilization abuses, and to head off the perceived threats of modern warfare.
Moreover, close ties between the civil and military sectors of the government,
the industrial community, and other new and old interest groups were maintained in order to design, produce, and procure specialized munitions and to
plan for industrial mobilization. During World War II, a modified form of the

World War I model was used to mobilize the economy for meeting the astronomical and often highly specialized demands of the armed forces and America's allies. With the Cold War following World War II, the nation for the first time in its peacetime history supported a massive military establishment, one that became inordinately expensive because of its size and because of a continuing transformation of weaponry through scientific and technological advancement. As a result, a defense and war "complex" included and affected most private and public institutions in American life.

ELITES AND ECONOMIC MOBILIZATION

Economic mobilization has been carried out largely by political, economic, and, ultimately, military elites. Economic and political elites are closely related and comprise the nation's upper classes. In the late eighteenth and early nineteenth centuries they included merchants, planters and large landowners, and professional elements. As the economy matured, the people involved with banks, railroads, and manufacturing gained importance, and the twentieth-century economic elite is based on the vast corporate and financial community.

Military elites did not work in close association with economic and political elites until the industrial stage. In the preindustrial period, no clear line separated the military from the civilian world. During the transitional stage, both the army and navy distanced themselves from civilians as they began to professionalize and acquire separate identities. But in the industrial stage, military leaders out of necessity had to join their political and economic counterparts in order successfully to mobilize the economy for war.

Elites shaped economic mobilization in a number of ways. The federal executive—or what approximated it during the Revolution—devised and implemented the methods for harnessing the economy for war. Throughout American history, the highest appointed officials in the executive branch have been drawn predominantly from among the nation's wealthy or those associated with them. Moreover, the federal government has turned to the nation's business leaders to assist in economic mobilization. They have acted as temporary or permanent advisers to government mobilizers, served in established or newly created federal agencies with or without pay, or engaged in some combination of these activities.

Harnessing the economy for war has generated a great deal of political controversy in America. Much of the conflict grows from the fact that economic mobilization highlights the nation's most basic contradiction: an elitist reality in the context of a democratic ideology. During years of peace that dynamic contradiction tends to be obscured; during years of war it is magnified by elitist economic mobilization patterns. Excluded interest groups and classes inevitably challenge the legitimacy of mobilization systems run by the few as unrepresentative and as failing to protect larger public interests. This resentment is exaggerated by the widespread aversion to and fear of government at the national level. Moreover, economic mobilization for war elevates the armed services to positions of central importance, which intensifies the strong antimilitary strains in American thought. Opposition to war among nonelites also often leads to adverse critiques of economic mobilization policies. There is a close correlation between antiwar and antielite attitudes.

Controversy over the political economy of warfare has been greatest in the preindustrial and industrial stages. By requiring a form of planning, underdeveloped and highly developed economies have made elites quite visible. Market economics do not have that effect because mobilization agencies combining political and economic elites are unnecessary. Consequently, economic mobilization caused comparatively little political turmoil in the transitional stage.

Mobilizing the economy for the Revolutionary War was tumultuous. For over a quarter of a century after hostilities, the new nation was engulfed in basic political strife involving the nature of government at the federal level under first the Articles of Confederation and then the Constitution. Disputes between Federalists and Republicans became so intense that the former attempted to use the military in settling its differences with the latter. Early in the nineteenth century, the torn and distracted nation drifted unprepared toward a second war with Britain. The consequences of political divisions dating back to the Revolution prevented Americans from effectively mobilizing their economy for the War of 1812.

Conflict over the political economy of warfare in the industrial stage began with the building of a modern navy in the late nineteenth century and has never fully subsided. Mobilizing the World War I economy intensified the discord manyfold, and battles over economic mobilization continued throughout the interwar years. Those struggles enormously complicated the means used for harnessing the World War II economy. During the Cold War years, the dispute over the economics of defense and war grew in prominence and level of sophistication. The number of critics multiplied rapidly and zeroed in on the comprehensive consequences of the so-called military-industrial complex, in effect a weapons-driven industrial policy.

Compared with other periods, the political economy of warfare in the transitional stage was politically placid. The Union's economic mobilization is largely remembered for its corruption, a matter that has been greatly distorted and, more important, that largely ceased after the first year of war. With the market acting as regulator and existing executive departments carrying out economic mobilization functions, the centralized planning of the preindustrial and industrial stages was avoided. Hence, harnessing the Union economy did not emphasize the elitist contours of power at the federal level. Among the states, however, elite mobilization patterns were blatantly evident. The Northern states played an important role in economic mobilization, especially during the first year of war. In every state of the Union, political and economic elites—who also often acted as military elites—combined for purposes of economic mobilization to the point that the public and private spheres became virtually indistinguishable. This development caused few political problems because it only exaggerated during an emergency practices that were standard during peacetime among the states and localities. State and local elites are usually more visible and less troublesome than elites at the national level, partly because they are more familiar to the public and wield less power.

The Confederacy differed in fundamental ways from the Union. It was economically underdeveloped, and the planter-slave system made the South the most obviously elite-dominated section of the nation. To maximize its limited economic strength for fighting a much stronger foe, the Confederacy had to plan its wartime economy. This it did, relying heavily upon the South's commercial and professional elements, transplanted Northerners and individuals from abroad, and officers trained at West Point and Annapolis. Overall, economic mobilization in the Confederacy failed. The planter elite consistently thwarted effective planning efforts both by what it did and did not do. This behavior alienated the Southern white masses and significantly weakened the Confederacy's ability to hold off the advancing Union.

Throughout the course of American history, the role of political, economic, and military elites in economic mobilization for defense and war can be understood fully only within the four-factor, three-stage paradigm. If the preindustrial stage is dated from 1765 to 1815 (instead of including the entire colonial years), it lasted about fifty years, approximately the same duration as the transitional stage. Accelerated physical and economic growth quickly modified institutions and power operations, altering in the process the stages of economic mobilization. Rapid industrialization after the Civil War ushered in the last mobilization stage, one that has had a permanence of sorts. Since the late nineteenth century, political, economic, and military elites have been absorbed in creating and refining planning structures to cope with the ongoing weapons revolution, a revolution that has comprehensively affected how America prepares for and conducts warfare.

PART ONE
ECONOMIC MOBILIZATION FOR WAR: THE PREINDUSTRIAL STAGE

Among the four factors shaping the political economy of warfare in the preindustrial stage, the political structure was the most important in determining the outcome. During the Revolutionary War, the infant economy had great potential but was ineffectively mobilized. Americans began their fight with an existing military system that they adapted for hostilities. Military technology was rudimentary. Working with those conditions, a reasonably strong national government could have devised economic mobilization programs to keep the army adequately supplied most of the time. That did not occur.

The national government was exceptionally weak. It could neither work out sound finances nor regulate the economy to control inflation. Civil/military systems for procuring, transporting, and distributing munitions and supplies operated poorly and were uncoordinated. Economic mobilization, therefore, got off to a bad start and deteriorated as the war stretched out. Conditions became so bad that between 1779 and 1781 the federal government turned major mobilization functions over to the states. Yet the states were unable to handle such responsibilities.

Power returned to the national government in 1781 when a faction headed by merchants who favored a strong central government took control of Congress. The change led to better policies for mobilizing the economy. Through a network extending among the thirteen colonies/states and reaching abroad, merchants had provided the cohesion essential for keeping the economy of the new nation functioning after 1775. Political opposition, however, had frustrated effective merchant control of economic mobilization during hostilities. With political and economic power concentrated in their hands between 1781 and 1783, however, merchants strengthened economic mobilization in the last months of fighting by basing it more directly on their own operations.

Two characteristics of mobilizing the revolutionary economy stand out. First, it was carried out by political and economic elites who differed fundamentally over the importance of keeping the system for harnessing the economy answerable to the public. Their conflict accounts in part for the weaknesses of economic mobilization. Second, the struggle for improved mobilization methods facilitated the effort to create a stronger federal government, which was ultimately sanctioned by the Constitution.

The political economy of the War of 1812 was also basically flawed, and, as during the Revolution, the political factor was the paramount reason. Economic growth was significant between 1783 and 1812. Although the armed services in general remained weak, and military technology changed little, their supply operations improved to some degree. But political disorganization continued. Under the Constitution, the federal government never developed fully because government at that level remained a source of intense and ongoing conflict between and within factions and parties. Elite divisions and democratizing forces remained central to those conflicts. Consequently, the relative weakness of the federal government prevented the nation from effectively harnessing its economy for war.

THE AMERICAN REVOLUTION

COLONIAL BACKGROUND

The political economy of the Revolutionary War was the most complex in U.S. history because the process of warfare indeed created a nation. Before the war, identity and cohesion existed at the local, colony/state, and perhaps regional levels, but not at the national level. Institutions were embryonic or in flux. Mobilizing the political, economic, and military parts to create a national whole and win independence proved extraordinarily difficult and came close to failing.

The emerging nation lacked the strong centralized political structure that is essential for any effective system of economic mobilization. Throughout the years of fighting, the colonies were directed by extralegal revolutionary assemblies; until the Articles of Confederation were ratified in March 1781, the Continental Congresses acted without a lawful base. In contrast, almost all of the states, whose representatives made up the congresses, operated under constitutions or charters adopted during the struggle for independence. The states, therefore, not the national congresses, held legal authority to the degree that it existed. Exceptionally weak, the national government lacked an executive structure; Congress acted in both an executive and a legislative capacity. Most critically, Congress relied upon the states for raising revenue and mobilizing troops, sharing with the states the authority to issue paper money, borrow funds, and maintain military forces. The structure that existed before and after the adoption of the Articles of Confederation was a league of states that denied coercive powers to the national government.

The national government's weakness grew from the highly ideological nature of the Revolutionary War. Americans were fighting not only to gain their independence from Great Britain but also to shape a proper political system. What that system would be like was the subject of endless debate, conflict, and even violence among conservatives, moderates, and radicals.

Moreover, the war and mobilization for it almost immediately began to break down the elitist, deferential society that had developed under Britain's imperial system. These political battles were fought out in the states and were reflected in the new constitutions or charters they adopted. Because state governments ranged from conservative to radical, the national government, which had to be based upon the unanimous consent of the states, could be no more than the least common denominator among them. The inevitable result was an exceptionally weak federal government.

At some point, however, ideology had to give way to survival. A weak central government could prevent the success of the revolution against England, a reality that became evident in 1779–1780. Continuing the war effort required a strengthened government; ideology yielded to practicality in 1781 when the so-called Nationalists took control of Congress. Independence was thereby achieved and a conservative trend initiated that ultimately led to the establishment of a more workable political structure under the Constitution of 1787.

In comparison with the political structure, the emerging nation's economic system was relatively strong and less subject to ideology. Mercantilist practices affected the operation of the economy, but market forces were already much more important. In 1775 the thirteen colonies had a dynamic, preindustrial economy with a national product that was nearly 40 percent of Great Britain's and a standard of living that also compared favorably. For well over a century, the colonial economy had been expanding at a rapid pace, pushed by extraordinary population growth and, perhaps more important, by rising exports augmented by coastal trade.[1]

Economic development varied among four regions: New England, the Middle Colonies or States, the Chesapeake area, and the Lower South. New England had a robust economy based on farming, fishing, trading, and some manufacturing.[2] The Middle Colonies/States, principally Pennsylvania and New York, perfected the model of a diversified economy first developed in New England. Grain and grain products accounted for over 70 percent of trade and were supplemented by a wide variety of other goods. Like New England, the Middle Colonies made substantial profits in intercolonial exchange and the shipping business and its invisibles. Here were the best-balanced economies in colonial America and the least disparity in wealth. Long before the Revolution, Philadelphia and New York had surpassed Boston as commercial and financial centers.[3] The vibrant economies of New England and the Middle Colonies duplicated closely the economy of Great Britain and competed with it.

The Chesapeake colonies of Virginia and Maryland matched the traditional mercantilist model much more closely than their Northern counterparts.

Quite early, tobacco became the primary export crop. Merchants in London and later in Scotland supplied credit, bought the planters' crops, and provided a wide range of imports. By 1775 planters had diversified their output to include grain and other products, and they also financed merchant and manufacturing activities that stimulated urban growth, exemplified in the rise of Baltimore and Norfolk. What the Chesapeake economy lacked in economic diversity it made up for in wealth and economic power. These were the richest colonies on a per capita basis, although wealth was distributed much more unequally than in the North. Moreover, the Chesapeake colonies, excluding coastal trade and invisibles, exported more than the New England and Middle colonies combined.[4]

The Lower South, including North and South Carolina, Georgia, and eventually Florida, had the least diverse economy among the colonies. Rice, supplemented by indigo and naval stores, provided for a plantation economy that was tied closely to Great Britain's. The Lower South prospered without diversification, developed cities and a merchant class, or extensive trade contacts with the other colonies.[5]

Viewing the colonial economy as a whole in 1775 reveals three important points. First, a national economy did not yet exist. Regional developments were too disparate for unity, and Great Britain still served as the hub around which the various colonial economies turned. Although exchange occurred among the colonies and was growing steadily in the North, difficulties in transportation created a major barrier to greater integration. During the Revolution, merchant networks replaced the unifying role of Britain.

Second, a society of vast opportunities had a severely skewed distribution of wealth, a reality that goes far in explaining the dynamics of the elitist-democratic duality that shaped the society from its outset. The top 10 percent of the population held over 56 percent of all wealth; the bottom 30 percent had less than one-third of 1 percent; and the remaining 43 percent of wealth went to those who could be defined as a middle class. The richest elements included merchants in the North and planters in the South, both of whom diversified their investments. The principal economic unit, however, was the family farm, and approximately 80 percent of the population was engaged in agriculture. Most were general rather than specialized farmers and produced various goods for the market. Though economic elites dominated the social and political systems, they were increasingly answerable to the people. At least two-thirds of the white population held land or property and thus had the right to vote, and suffrage expanded during and after the Revolution. Yet a growing economy, an ambitious middle class, and vertical mobility tied most of the society to marketplace values and provided the elite with new recruits. As long as elites reflected and responded responsibly to major trends, they remained secure in the world's most open society.

Third, at the end of the colonial period, an economic system existed that would no longer tolerate subordination within the British mercantile empire.[6] To achieve independence, the colonies turned to their military and thus drew upon institutions, ideas, and attitudes that were rich, controversial, and contradictory.

Warfare, or the threat of war, and the military forces to conduct it, were constants in colonial life from the early seventeenth century to the eve of the Revolution.[7] Most colonies originated as military enclaves in the wilderness, threatened by Native Americans and the armies of other European empires. Defense, even survival, depended upon the martial skills in those days; later, aggressive colonial expansion demanded reliable military institutions. From the late seventeenth century through 1763, America was racked by four wars that were extensions of the global conflict between England and France. Only the Peace of Paris in 1763 ended for the time France's role as an imperial power in the Americas and terminated the warfare that had engulfed the colonies for so long.

The colonists had a number of military structures, not just one, since each colony had its own peculiarities. Most colonies, however, shared some common characteristics; early on, they developed a dual military tradition that became explicit during the revolutionary years, with the Continental army serving as a small standing force and the state militia as a reserve.

The militia was basic to colonial military systems.[8] When the colonies were first established and defense was key, most able-bodied men served in the "common militia." Citizen-soldiers provided their own weapons and participated in frequent training, or muster, days. The military hierarchy usually followed a colony's social structure: officers came from the upper strata and enlisted men from the middle ranks and below. As the frontier and the sense of danger receded, the common militia deteriorated. A "voluntary militia" then arose in most colonies, composed principally of better-off men who were devoted to martial values and institutions.

Active or in decline, the militia was essentially a local institution intended for local defense or for maintaining order within a colony. Actually, the common militia seldom functioned as a fighting unit, nor was it intended as such; rather, it served as a reserve pool from which fighting units could be organized. These troops came closest to providing the colonies with standing armies. If a colony alone, or in conjunction with other colonies or Great Britain or both, required troops for operations beyond its borders, a special expedition was usually formed, militia districts within a colony providing a quota of men. Volunteers generally filled the ranks, but draftees, substitutes, and hirelings could also serve. The officers could be from the militia or volunteers. At times, volunteer militia or military units unassociated with the militia carried out expeditions or garrisoned frontier forts. Increasingly, the ranks of the active military units came from the lower classes. The better-off could avoid service by providing a substitute, paying a fine, or securing an exemption based on status, occupation, and so forth. The typical expeditionary troops, therefore, were usually poorly motivated and lacked the militiaman's sense of protecting his home. As the British claimed, he was often a poor, unreliable, and undisciplined soldier.

The emerging dual military structure, which set the stage for the militia reserves and the Continental army of the Revolutionary War, led to misconceptions among the British and the colonists. England often mistook low-grade expeditionary troops for the militia, an error that led Britain to underestimate the capabilities of a common militia protecting its home territory. The colonists, on their part, overvalued the citizen-soldier and undervalued the British regulars, basing their opinion on the contentious relations with England during four colonial wars in the late seventeenth and the first half of the eighteenth centuries. When the two sides faced each other as enemies, they would be forced to adopt more realistic views.

The colonists proved to be the more adaptive. They recognized and met the need to modify basically their strongly held notions about the militia and the regulars in order to win on the battlefield. By late 1775 and early 1776 the Continental army already had begun to disintegrate as the vaunted short-term citizen-soldier returned home to the responsibilities and rewards of civilian life, rejecting the discipline, drudgery, and danger of the common solider. With neither the Confederation nor the states able to generate enough recruits, Congress in September 1776 began authorizing a "new model" land force that George Washington had been advocating for months: a central core of long-term, trained, disciplined, and experienced regulars who would be supplemented when necessary by militiamen. After 1776 the Continental army's nucleus was hired, purchased, and directly or indirectly forced into service of three years or more. Those expedients worked because the new regulars, unlike the typical middle-class, propertied militia members, came largely from the lower classes and had few choices. These men included the unemployed, indebted, drifters, criminals, indentured servants, black slaves, captured British soldiers, Hessians, and accused Loyalists. Without them, the Continental army and thereupon the Revolution stood little chance of success.

In 1776, then, the thirteen colonies had an advantage that few revolutionaries possess: an existing military system with established traditions that could be mobilized with speed.[9] That system and those traditions provided the foundation for victory against the world's most formidable military power.

Weaponry during the colonial and revolutionary period was quite unsophisticated. The basic weapon of the line was the early seventeenth-century smoothbore, muzzleloading, flintlock musket with bayonet. Artillery, also smoothbore and muzzleloading, supplemented small arms. The navy used the same arsenal. Moreover, though naval ships had special designs, commercial vessels could be converted for limited combat, raiding, and supply.[10] Transportation, housing, clothing, food, and the like varied little or not at all from civilian usage except for the quantities used.

FIRST NATIONAL PHASE OF
ECONOMIC MOBILIZATION, 1774–1779

For both Britain and the colonies, the Revolutionary War was a protracted war of attrition. The rebelling colonists won their independence by gradually eroding England's will and its ability to continue the conflict, despite its vast economic and military superiority. The Americans succeeded by relying upon their own strength, talent, and zeal and upon the enormous difficulties and repeated miscalculations the British faced in fighting a war so far from home.

Organizing the American economy for the Revolutionary War resembled twentieth-century mobilization strikingly in three ways: first, Americans attempted to regulate comprehensively the wartime economy; second, the merchants, or businessmen, played a critical role in economic mobilization; and, third, the war set precedents for the nation's future political economy. An analysis of the first two categories elucidates not only how the rebellious colonies marshaled their economic strength but also why the Revolutionary War left such an indelible imprint upon the nation's life.

America's attempt to establish broad controls over the revolutionary economy continued past practices. Britain's North American colonies developed under the mercantilist dictum that the economic activities of individuals and groups had to serve the general interests of a nation-state or a self-sufficing empire. To achieve that end, Britain regulated and protected the colonies' trade, finances, agriculture, and manufacturing, beginning in the late seventeenth century. British regulation was supplemented by controls the colonists themselves enacted in all sectors of the economy, including incentives for various industries, wage and price guidelines, and limitations on hours of work. Although the magnitude of regulation tended to decline as the colonies matured, numerous controls remained in effect on the eve of the Revolution.[11]

Necessity dictated extensive regulation of the wartime economy. By declaring independence, the colonists rejected their only source of centralized political authority and lost the economic benefits of membership in the British Empire. Yet they lacked a national government, their economy was underdeveloped and unintegrated, and normal channels of trade and economic assistance were closed. In order to win independence on the battlefield, the colonies had to create a national government capable of conducting a war. That government needed to maximize the nation's economic strength at home and coordinate—even integrate—local, colonial, and regional economies. It also had to secure economic support abroad to replace Great Britain's.

The colonists created a national government when the First Continental Congress met in September 1774. By organizing the Continental Association in October, Congress started to regulate the colonial economy and enacted a measure that can be defined as the first piece of national commercial legislation. Basing their action on past precedents, the colonists intended the association to be a peaceful means of forcing Great Britain to grant their demands. Over a period of eleven months, the association imposed a total embargo on economic intercourse between the colonies and the British Empire and other parts of the world as well. The colonists soon discovered that their economic weapon produced self-inflicted wounds, however. Without foreign trade, the economy faced stagnation, and the colonies were denied the opportunity to stockpile war materiel as the possibility of hostilities increased. Consequently, in 1775 the Continental Congress lifted the embargo on various products and in April 1776 disestablished the Continental Association entirely. The latter action opened colonial ports to all nations except Great Britain and removed many restrictions on American merchants.[12]

The demise of the Continental Association hardly resulted in free trade for the emerging nation. Indeed, the Confederation government regulated a substantial portion of foreign trade throughout the war years. When Congress relaxed the strictures on trade in 1775, it issued directives on products the states should import and export and licensed merchants to engage in specified foreign commerce. These procedures became more formalized in September 1775 when Congress created the Standing Secret Committee of Trade (succeeded by the Committee of Commerce, or Commercial Committee). In conjunction with congressional committees on foreign relations and army and navy affairs, the Secret Committee of Trade managed exports and imports and coordinated federal and state economic mobilization activities where possible.[13]

Wartime domestic commerce was subjected to even greater regulation than foreign trade, especially in the area of finances. In order to support a national government and an army, Congress in mid-1775 began emitting bills of credit, a form of paper money. Beginning with a modest issue of $6 million in 1775, total emissions exceeded $200 million by the end of 1779. Through 1776 the value of the Continental currency remained remarkably stable, convertible to specie almost at par. Beginning in 1777, however, the Confederation bills depreciated rapidly. The conversion rate fell to 4 to 1 in January 1778, then plummeted to 100 to 1 in January and 167.5 to 1 in April 1781.[14]

Revolutionary finances have been the subject of ongoing criticism; nonetheless, there was no other feasible way for Americans to support their fight for independence. Congress was denied the authority to tax and lacked the prestige at home and abroad to borrow in sufficient quantities. Further, the nation was critically short of specie, had no banking or uniform currency system, and had most of its wealth tied up in nonliquid assets. Moreover, the states generally undermined the Confederation's extremely vulnerable financial structure by refusing to generate tax revenue. Absorbed in the often tumultuous process of creating new governments, buffeted by enormous wartime economic dislocations, and facing constituents who had an intense aversion to taxation, state officials were unable or unwilling to tax their citizens before 1780–1781.

The consequences of that failure were threefold. First, the national government was denied an income to support the war effort. For the first two years of hostilities, the states made no contributions. Only steady pressure from Congress beginning in 1777 led them to make small donations, which they raised through various expedients. Second, none of the numerous Confederation issues of paper was taken out of circulation since Congress planned to retire them with tax revenue from the states, which it never received. Third, without taxation, the states themselves turned to the printing press in order to finance militia units and to meet other wartime expenses. Before the termination of hostilities, the states collectively emitted as much paper money as did the federal government.[15]

Had Congress been able to hold the Continental currency in circulation to the $25 million level, either through restraint or by retiring earlier issues, monetary stability might have been possible, but that level was exceeded before the end of 1776. Thereafter, with both the federal government and the states continuing to emit paper with little or no provision for its retirement, rampant inflation became inevitable. Nonetheless, bills of credit kept the nation in the war. One scholar has estimated that federal income between 1775 and 1779, measured in specie, totaled about $55.5 million. Of that sum, state contributions fell under $2 million; foreign assistance, most of which was spent abroad, exceeded $2 million; and domestic borrowing through the sale of loan certificates netted about $6 million. Continental currency totaling about $45.5 million made up the difference.[16]

Americans tried to temper the inflationary pressure generated by the unlimited issue of paper through regulation between 1776 and 1780. Congress first suggested price controls on scarce commodities as early as 1774 and worked with local communities to achieve that end in 1775 and 1776. Thereafter, state governments took the initiative. In 1776 the New England states, after agreeing on a common program at a conference in Providence, instituted uniform controls on wages and prices. When Congress indirectly endorsed the Providence recommendations, the New England states moved closer to their goal of a national regulatory system. Yet those hopes were dashed when no other state completely followed the New England example. Unable to hold the line against inflation from a regional base and chagrined by the uncooperative attitude of the other states, New England abandoned the Providence accords by mid-1777.[17]

New England's efforts within the context of continued economic deterioration spurred Congress into action. Beginning in November 1777, the national legislature attempted to persuade the various states to adopt a comprehensive, national regulatory system that would allow for local and regional differences. Some states willingly went along; most did not. As economic conditions temporarily improved in 1778, the Confederation gave up trying to impose economic controls but resumed the effort in 1779–1780 as the worst phase of currency depreciation set in. Congress was even less effective in the latter years, however, and by February 1780 the movement for economic regulation was dead. Significantly, subsequent regional conferences called to consider the nation's economic plight concentrated on strengthening the federal government instead of on instituting price and wage controls.[18]

Colonial attempts at economic regulation went beyond wage and price controls. Acting either on their own or at the behest of the federal government, almost all the states enacted laws against profiteering, made paper money legal tender, outlawed the manipulation of money standards, and placed embargoes on the interstate or foreign export of scarce products. State and local governments enforced the latter statutes more rigorously than those involving prices and wages. But in general, violators of the numerous regulatory codes were punished more through adverse publicity than through litigation. Between 1779 and 1781, however, as the nation faced its most desperate economic straits, the confiscation or impressment of commodities and services by state or federal authorities became widespread as an enforcement device. That expedient was no more than a drastic extension of military procurement prerogatives; throughout the war years, at both state and federal levels, the various purchasing agencies had the authority to influence market activities by setting prices, wage schedules, quality standards, and so on for the goods they bought.[19]

Federal-state attempts at economic regulation did not fail for lack of public support; indeed, constituents often pressured local, state, and even federal officials to adopt controls. The general public perceived such regulations as carrying on the mercantilist tradition of maximizing the general welfare without unduly favoring any class or interest group. Yet public confidence in government action eroded with accelerating inflation. Few people remained willing to exchange their goods and services at set prices for money that grew progressively more useless.[20] Once the person in the street began to defy the law, the odium against the profiteer lost much of its meaning. As a result, the regulatory enterprise collapsed of its own dead weight. With the federal and state governments continuing to issue paper, economic controls proved futile. Even if currency finance had been properly limited, the regulatory effort would probably have broken down. The emergency required a national system that was beyond the authority and capabilities of the federal government and the cooperative spirit of the states.

PROCUREMENT FOR THE MILITARY

Although currency finance caused wild inflation and necessitated comprehensive economic controls during the revolutionary years, military procurement created the need for it. Supplying the army, and to a lesser degree the navy, consumed the lion's share of federal budgets from 1776 to 1783 and became the biggest business enterprise the former colonies had ever encountered.[21]

Procurement during the Revolution depended more on foreign goods and finance than would ever again be the case.[22] Although statistics are crude, sparse, or unavailable, evidence suggests that the thirteen states produced well under half of their own munitions, uniforms, and textiles from 1775 to 1783.[23] The balance came from privateering and battlefield captures and from foreign trade and aid provided principally by France and to a lesser degree by Holland and Spain.[24]

Outside supply notwithstanding, Americans established a credible manufacturing record for a preindustrial society. It was achieved largely through private production, despite the conviction of some patriots that business placed profits ahead of republican virtue. This suspicion created considerable sentiment at the beginning of the war for supplying the military through public, not private, enterprise. The federal government and some states did engage in the manufacture of munitions and other items, but the percentage of publicly produced goods during the Revolutionary War was slight. Government at all levels lacked the resources, strength, and commitment to undertake a massive manufacturing program. The nation depended on its businesses to provide the wherewithal for war.[25]

Americans entered the war with a firm though limited industrial base that expanded during the conflict. The colonies had considerable leather, leather goods, textile, and clothing industries in 1775, which grew in the following years. They also had a sizable munitions capacity at the outset. Frontier conditions, the militia system, and numerous prerevolutionary wars had resulted in the widespread possession of firearms and had fostered small industries in gunpowder, gunmaking, and artillery manufacture. During the Revolution, the colonists used these facilities to the optimum and provided incentives to encourage private production. Immediately before and during hostilities, the states and the Continental Congress built a number of public foundries, arsenals, and factories for producing munitions.[26]

Without a vigorous iron industry, the colonies' general manufacturing capacity, and especially the fabrication of munitions, would have been severely restricted. By 1775, however, the colonies were producing some 30,000 tons of crude iron, a fourfold increase since 1771 and one-seventh of total world output, ranking America behind only Russia and Sweden. America had more forges and foundries than Great Britain, and it increased the number during the war years. Steel output also grew rapidly; twice as many facilities for making steel were built between 1775 and 1783 as existed in 1750. The substantial pool of blacksmiths and other metal workers in colonial society converted the metal into the demanding civilian and military requirements of a nation at war.[27]

For food, forage, transportation, and other commonplace supplies and accoutrements, the land forces relied almost exclusively upon domestic output. Farmers constituted 80 percent of the population so that agricultural production was substantial on the eve of the Revolution and increased thereafter. Beasts of burden were in ample supply. Although the stock of wagons and boats was not always sufficient for both civilian and military needs, the nation possessed both the material and the experience for building additional capacity. Canteens, belts, tents, cooking utensils, and the like were either provided by private contractors or artisans hired by the military.[28]

Despite the considerable output of the American economy, supplemented by foreign commodities, the Continental army frequently suffered from desperate supply shortages. After the first years of hostilities, the worst deficiencies involved not munitions but food, forage, clothing, shoes, and shelter—supplies that were readily available or easy to manufacture. The system of procurement and distribution, more than that of production, was to blame.

The Confederation government lacked the experience, trained personnel, and all-important centralized structure for effectively administering a large military establishment, let alone for conducting a national, in part international, purchasing program systematically and efficiently. The Continental Congress at first attempted to direct the national army through a series of special committees, the most important being the Secret Committee of Trade. It acted as an elementary economic mobilization agency by directing exports and imports, contracting at home and abroad, distributing supplies, and raising funds. As legislators gradually realized they needed a more effective body, they appointed a Board of War and Ordnance in 1776 and then reorganized it as a Board of War in 1777–1778, made up of congressmen and nonelected members.[29]

Although charged with general administration of the army, the Board of War and its predecessors concentrated upon procurement, particularly that of munitions, but its accomplishments in that area were unimpressive for several reasons. It had only advisory, not executive, powers. Congress responded to the board's recommendations in an agonizingly slow manner. On certain issues, rather than seeking the board's counsel, Congress conducted its own inquiry or appointed special committees to do so. The board's range of activities also often overlapped with those of other congressional agencies created to direct economic and foreign affairs. Furthermore, it operated without established procedures and with constant turnover of personnel. Ultimately, it was unable to maximize its opportunities for leadership because power was dispersed among many members instead of being concentrated in one. In short, like the other subdivisions Congress established to help conduct its affairs, the Board of War was ill-equipped to perform tasks that should have been executive functions with clearly defined and focused lines of authority and responsibility. Consequently, military procurement carried out within the congressional structure was haphazard, improvised, and piecemeal.[30]

Most military buying was done under the auspices of the army itself rather than through Congress. In 1775 the national legislators created a Quartermaster Department and a Commissary General of Stores and Purchases. The latter was responsible for subsistence (feeding the troops) and, until the Office of the Clothier General was established years later, for clothing them as well. Munitions aside, the Quartermaster Department purchased most other supplies and handled transportation, construction, and army manufacturing. Congress organized minor bureaus, like the Hide Department, when it believed that the Quartermaster General's responsibilities had become excessive.[31]

The army's procurement structure was as disorganized as the congressional purchasing system. Inexperience, emergency conditions, and political divisions led Congress to create army bureaus without specifying how they should function. Regulations were codified after, not before, practice, and bureaus were constantly reorganized. Personnel changed as frequently as structure: many supply officers proved unequal to their assignments, some quit out of frustration, and others departed in quest of battlefield glory. At critical points, the supply bureaus operated without a commander or his subordinates.[32]

Command relationships further plagued the army's supply apparatus. The bureau chiefs were directly responsible to Congress, but neither Congress nor its agents, such as the Board of War, ever directed the bureaus in a systematic manner. Although the war stretched out and the military situation deteriorated, General Washington never established effective control over the bureaus. He allowed command relationships in the Continental army to remain obscure, particularly in the supply services. At times, as with the Yorktown campaign, the commanding general directed logistics with good effect, but no commander could supervise the bureaus as a continuing practice. He needed a structure comparable to a modern general staff—a staff that would aid him in directing the bureaus and coordinating their activity with that of the line. No such staff evolved during the years of the American Revolution. Bureaus functioned as units instead of as a whole and remained uncoordinated with the line. Even within the bureaus, lines of authority were confused. The commissary general, for example, lacked the authority to appoint or remove his subordinates because Congress kept that power for itself.[33]

Though procurement for land forces was inefficient and uncoordinated, the navy avoided some of these pitfalls. Because of its small size and simple organization, it never duplicated the congressional supply structure as did the army. Congress created a Naval Committee (later called the Marine Committee and finally the Board of Admiralty) to procure for the navy. That committee was comparable to but better organized than the Board of War. It established regional boards and appointed Continental agents in each state to carry out its activities. The Naval Committee, however, did not escape the general confusion that characterized the Confederation's administrative system.[34]

In several ways, military procurement fed the inflationary flames that ultimately consumed it. By competing with one another for a limited supply of goods, the uncoordinated purchasing agencies drove prices upward. That competitive pressure was multiplied many times over when the thirteen states, and at times Great Britain and France, entered the scramble for supplies. The disjointed federal procurement structure further abetted inflation by encouraging waste, inefficiency, corruption, and unethical, if not illegal, behavior at all levels. Congress spent millions upon millions of dollars without reliable procedures or proper responsibility and audits. Furthermore, purchasing agents could enhance their own fortunes by maximizing, not minimizing, spending because they were compensated on a percentage of expenditures.[35]

The nation's distribution system was even worse than the procurement apparatus. The army did manage to build a respectable number of depots, magazines, arsenals, and warehouses for storing, servicing, and issuing arms and supplies; and in some of those areas its performance improved during hostilities. Nonetheless, there were many deficiencies. Desperately needed supplies frequently remained in warehouses at home or abroad, unaccounted for or the subject of jurisdictional disputes. Supplies were often lost or pilfered in transit or during distribution to the troops because the army did not institute a reliable system of property accountability until 1778.[36]

The defects in distribution appear minor when compared to the inadequacies of the army's transportation system. Next to deficiencies in finance, transportation accounted for more supply shortages than any other factor. With the British navy patrolling the Atlantic Coast, the Continental army relied almost exclusively upon inland transportation. Although rivers were used to a degree, horse- and ox-drawn wagons remained the primary mode for moving goods. Slow even in favorable circumstances, supply trains were retarded by inordinately long supply lines, inadequate or nonexistent roads and bridges, inhospitable terrain, and the hazards of war, obstacles that were compounded because the army had virtually no transportation corps of its own. The Quartermaster Department hired most wagons, trains, and drivers, usually on a short-term basis. Wagons were seldom available in sufficient quantity. Even if they were, there was no assurance that drivers would deliver supplies to the designated place at the scheduled time since they were not subject to military command, and numerous other opportunities for their services existed. During retreats, enormous quantities of supplies were lost because of transportation failures. Hiring drivers and wagons became virtually impossible once the rapid depreciation of paper money began exhausting army funds. Then, and even earlier, forced requisitions had to be adopted. It took herculean efforts to keep supplies moving from spring through fall; during winter the flow of goods nearly ceased.[37]

In spite of pitfalls and deficiencies, the army's logistical system functioned with a measure of success during the first few years of war, when favorable conditions existed. Paper money held its value, supply lines were relatively short, and the population was willing to make sacrifices. The logistical system faltered in 1777 as these conditions changed, and it virtually collapsed by the end of 1779. The winters at Valley Forge in 1777–1778 and Morristown in 1779–1780 stand as a grim reminder of the severity of conditions for the troops.

Nothing affected military procurement more adversely than the runaway inflation. Soaring prices exhausted army funds before supplies could be purchased. Supply agents frequently were unable to accumulate reserves for winter encampment; during winter they were unable to award contracts and prepare logistically for the coming spring campaigns. When the currency depreciated rapidly after 1776, conditions worsened. At times the federal government was unable to buy supplies or hire transportation even when it had funds. Farmers and merchants began insisting on specie or barter for their wares and services. Soldiers suffered as citizens hoarded goods or sold to the French and British for reliable money.[38]

STATE PHASE OF ECONOMIC MOBILIZATION, 1779–1780

By late 1779 the federal financial system had essentially ceased to function, a failure that temporarily ended the Confederation government's ascendant role in economic mobilization. As long as Congress bore the major burden of wartime expenses, its power far exceeded constitutional limits and the desires of many states. When federally sponsored currency finance collapsed, responsibility for the war effort, and with it the focus of power, shifted back to the states.[39]

To keep the nation fighting, Congress adopted a three-part, state-oriented plan for restructuring the nation's finances. In the first phase, which lasted from September 1779 into 1780, Congress pushed the states to retire through taxation the $200 million of nearly worthless Continental currency in exchange for a new federal issue totaling $10 million. The new bills would be shared on a four-to-six ratio by the Confederation government and the states. Congress hoped to avoid renewed depreciation by limiting the new issue to the presumed needs of the economy, by having the states make it legal tender, by relying on the states to use the new bills in place of their own, and by having both the federal government and the states underwrite the new currency. In the second part of the program, Congress called upon the states to pay the army's current salaries and existing arrears. In the third part, with its treasury nearly empty and its procurement system in shambles, Congress requested that the states provision the troops. Each state was allotted a quota of goods—principally food—to deliver to the federal government as a form of requisition. Through this three-pronged system Congress intended to make the states directly pay a larger percentage of the war's costs. Many congressmen believed that the federal procurement bureaucracy was oversized, too costly, and riddled with waste and fraud. By cutting the scope of its procurement operations with specific supplies, the federal government hoped to eliminate these problems and thereby reduce a serious source of inflation.

The three-part program helped the Confederation government through its worst crisis but eventually failed. By assuming partial responsibility for paying the troops, the states lifted a substantial burden from the federal government. The program of specific supplies, however, fell far short of expectations. Supply was uncoordinated with demand, and enormous problems of collection, storage, and transportation prevented provisions from reaching the troops. More seriously, few states met their quotas. In failing to do so, they were not merely willful; continued currency weakness made it enormously difficult to procure goods. The bulk of provisions coming from the states was either impressed or collected from their citizens.[40]

Because the states donated only limited supplies, the federal government could not meaningfully cut back its procurement apparatus. Meanwhile, the Confederation was still desperately strapped for funds. Some financial assistance came from the states, and for a time federal officials used loan certificates in a dubious manner for purchasing. Such expedients, however, came nowhere near meeting federal requirements. As a result, the federal government, assisted by the states, turned to the use or threatened use of force. Most supplies secured by the Confederation between 1779 and the conclusion of active hostilities in 1781 were seized from citizens or surrendered to government officials in exchange for federal or state certificates that were, in effect, receipts. Hardest hit by impressment were the Middle and Southern states where the major campaigns took place. Although reliable figures are unavailable, certificate debt for the federal government alone probably well exceeded $200 million.

Enormous issues of certificate debt torpedoed the federal-state effort to replace the old Continental currency with a new, stable issue. Citizens insisted upon paying their taxes with the certificates that had been forced upon them. Consequently, most of the old currency was not retired, and only a small portion of the new currency was issued. Old and new bills became discredited, and all hope of establishing a reliable currency vanished by the end of 1780. During the first half of 1781, the depreciated federal currency passed out of circulation. Congress abetted the process by recommending that the states repeal the legal tender laws. An era of wartime finance had passed.

For Congress, the states, citizens, and soldiers, the years from 1779 to 1781 were filled with grief. Federal credit fell to an all-time low as the government ceased paying interest on its debt. Troops mutinied or threatened to do so over the lack of food, clothing, shoes, and pay. Citizens grew outraged at the financial chaos, war profiteering, and incessant political infighting, and the widespread impressment of goods and services alienated many. Paradoxically, the government's hand weighed heavy while its grip grew weak. The repeated defeat of American troops and the steady advance of the British army in the South accelerated a spreading national paralysis. Change was essential to regenerate the war effort. The states could not shoulder the burden thrust upon them, and the Confederation government, without basic modifications, could not resume the dominant position it had held within the Union from 1775 to 1779.

SECOND NATIONAL PHASE OF ECONOMIC MOBILIZATION, 1781–1783

The new nation resolved this crisis when a conservative faction, which historians call the Nationalists, gained control of Congress. This group, initially composed of a wealthy aristocracy concentrated in the Middle Colonies, traced its origins to the prerevolutionary imperial crisis. As the relationship between Great Britain and the colonies deteriorated after 1763, the Nationalists sought to settle the controversy without disturbing the colonial status quo. Pursuing that end, they opposed or reluctantly supported the movement for independence. When independence was declared, they favored replacing Britain's stabilizing hand with a relatively strong, conservative national government. Numerous and complex forces acted to frustrate Nationalist ambitions. Most important was the fact that, ideology aside, loyalty existed at the colony or state, not at the continental, level. Furthermore, revolution set off a populist movement in most states that challenged deferential colonial patterns and elitist rule. Local and state governments, not a central one, were considered the proper forums for creating open systems answerable to the majority. Reflecting developments within the states, delegates to the Continental Congress overwhelmingly insisted upon a weak national government and consistently opposed centralizing authority.[41]

Although conservatives remained a political minority for most of the war, the large merchants in the Nationalists' ranks increased their economic hold over the nation after 1775. As Americans cut off economic ties with England, they faced the need to find new sources of trade and financial assistance abroad and to take over British commercial functions at home. The government supervised this readjustment from the outset of the Revolution, but the substantial merchants always played a crucial part. Men of commerce usually filled the slots in the elaborate military supply apparatus. The two principal quartermaster generals from 1775 through mid-1779, for example, were Thomas Mifflin and Nathanael Greene, prominent merchants from Philadelphia and Rhode Island. Jeremiah Wadsworth, a leading Connecticut trader, was among the most important of the commissary generals of purchases. After leaving office in 1779, he became commissary for the French troops in America.[42]

Prominent merchants played an even greater role on the congressional committees, boards, and departments directing foreign and domestic trade and other economic activities. Robert Morris serves as an exceptionally valuable example, and not only because of his prominence. From late 1775 to mid-1777 his private and public activities, which practically merged, are reasonably well documented and dramatically illustrate the less obvious practices that were occurring throughout the nation.[43]

Morris was a partner in the prestigious Philadelphia firm of Willing, Morris & Company. In December 1775 he joined the Secret Committee of Trade and in April 1776 became its chair. Unlike most committees of the Continental Congress, this one lacked geographic balance and was dominated by merchants from the Middle States. Its members generally held pragmatic commercial values rather than the ardent revolutionary ideology of the Eastern faction that controlled the Continental Congress. Additionally, Morris effectively directed the Marine Committee since he was vice-chair, and John Hancock, its chair, was absorbed in his duties as president of the Continental Congress. The Marine Committee oversaw the navy, including the handling of prize cases and other aspects of trade. Simultaneously, Morris was the key member (at times the only member) of the Secret Committee of Correspondence, which directed foreign affairs and handled matters of trade and finance. Morris's power grew when the Continental Congress abandoned Philadelphia for Baltimore under military threat from the British late in 1776 and he remained in the capital. Until the legislature returned in early 1777, Morris controlled the three committees.

From his strategic position on these committees, Morris managed a mercantile network encompassing the colonies, New Orleans, the West Indies, and Europe. The Secret Committee of Trade first awarded contracts to various merchants but later switched to the general agency system. The latter set-up allowed Morris, while serving on the committee, to act as chief agent for exports and imports and to appoint subagents throughout the states and abroad. The Marine Committee functioned with a Continental agent system. On the recommendation of the Marine Committee, Congress appointed Continental agents to provision vessels and handle prizes in ports throughout the states. Each state had at least one agent, and many had subagents if they had more than one port. Frequently, one person or firm served as contractor and later as subagent for the Secret Committee of Trade, as Continental agent for the Marine Committee, and simultaneously conducted private transactions.

At one time or another during the war, all regions were crucial for military supply operations. At the height of the British blockade of New England, for example, the Middle States became the center of trade. When hostilities focused on the latter, the former was opened and the Chesapeake and Southern states became important as well. The exports of the latter two regions, particularly tobacco, rice, indigo, and naval stores, were critical for financing required imports.

Contractors and agents in the various states often became involved in Morris's mercantile empire, for example, John Bradford in Massachusetts, the Silas Deane and Thomas Mumford families of Connecticut, Philip Livingston of New York, David Stewart and Archibald Buchanan of Maryland, the Benjamin Harrison, Sr., faction in Virginia, the firm of Hewes and Smith in North Carolina, John Dorsius of South Carolina, and John Wereat of Georgia. Outside the states, the nation's supply operations involved the Secret Committee of Trade, in some instances the Marine Committee, the Secret Committee of Correspondence (because diplomacy as well as commerce was at stake), and also Congress and various commissions. Morris's agents acted, with varying degrees of power and competence, wherever the new nation had interests. In New Orleans, the enormously able Oliver Pollack operated on a broad base. Representatives were scattered throughout the French, Spanish, and Dutch West Indies, the most important and successful of whom was William Bingham. In the tumultuous commercial and diplomatic maneuvering in Europe, Morris's half-brother Thomas Morris, Silas Deane, John Ross, and William Hodge served in Morris's circle, along with numerous French, Spanish, Dutch, German, and other foreign merchants. For a time, Morris even directed transactions with branches of English, Scottish, and Irish firms.

Morris's worldwide network, like most revolutionary merchant activities, was built on ledger-book considerations and also on the republican revolutionary ideology prevalent in Congress. The entire system was riddled with politics and conflicts of interest that tarnished the name of Morris, the people in his circles, and merchants in general. Though competence, patriotism, capital, and geography figured in selecting contractors, politics was usually key. Almost all contractors had a record of prerevolutionary activity against Great Britain at the local, colony-state, or continental levels. Continental agents usually reflected local and state power groupings, and agents on foreign assignments needed spokespersons in Congress or on commissions abroad. Once appointments to offices high and low were secured, it was standard procedure for contracts and other favors to be awarded to oneself (as was the case repeatedly with Morris), relatives, friends, commercial allies, and so forth. Samuel Ward, the first chair of the Secret Committee of Trade, who had much less power and much more rectitude than Morris, steered contracts as a matter of course to Nicholas and John Brown and Thomas Greene and Nathanael Greene & Company, prominent merchants and traders in his home state of Rhode Island. Henry Knox, chief of artillery, maintained higher standards concerning conflicts of interest than many other officers and merchants, yet he speculated in privateering ventures while on active duty. In 1779 Quartermaster General Greene and Commissary General of Purchases Wadsworth formed a secret commercial partnership with Barnabas Deane—a partnership that made at least some sales to the Continental army.

Merchants combining public and private functions had been accepted behavior in the prerevolutionary era, especially during wartime. The practice existed in Britain, France, and other European countries.[44] More important, the emerging nation needed the experience, talent, connections, and frequently the daring of the mercantile community. Within certain parameters, merchants could therefore set their own terms, although the profit motive and the national interest did not necessarily clash and often complemented one another.

The price for not giving the large merchants their way could be high indeed. Robert Morris left government service under a cloud in mid-1777 over controversies rending the rebelling colonies. In July 1777 the Commercial Committee effectively took over the functions of the Secret Committee of Trade. Congress kept a tight rein on the Commercial Committee, reducing substantially the conflicts of interest that characterized its predecessor. But greater control and accountability were achieved at the expense of initiative and effectiveness. Congressionally directed foreign trade fell off sharply, and overseas supply operations and naval affairs lacked proper direction. This drift ended only when Morris returned to government service as superintendent of finance in 1781. The freewheeling entrepreneurial spirit he embodied appeared to be practically indispensable for the success of revolutionary commerce. Morris insisted upon demanding terms before he would again hold public office, thus acting to legitimize the modus operandi of the Secret Committee of Trade.

By knitting the thirteen states together economically, the American merchants laid the foundations for a national economy. Many of them became convinced that the weak federal government was undermining their achievement. As Nationalists, they believed in a central government strong enough to stabilize society and win the confidence of the propertied elements. In the eyes of the Nationalists, the mobilization program had foundered prior to 1781 because of inadequate federal authority. The propertied elements viewed the growing chaos with a sense of despair; they identified weak and overextended government with mob rule and thought that the nation's mobilization scheme amounted to massive confiscation of property, seeing themselves as the principal victims.

The Radical or Eastern faction that dominated Congress from 1776 to 1780 ignored the Nationalist critique until currency finance collapsed in 1779–1780 and the states were unable to take over the responsibilities of the federal government. This bloc, dominated by New England and supported by key Southern states, stressed republican virtue, sacrifice, and decentralized government as the proper means for achieving independence and organizing society. As their economic politics failed late in the 1770s, they tended to blame the nation's troubles on a merchant community they saw as involved in profiteering, monopoly, and conflicts of interest. Nonetheless, in 1780 power shifted in the Middle States and some Southern states to the Nationalists, and the trend was discernible even in New England. As a result, the Nationalists, with the powerful merchants of the Middle States prominent, took control of Congress in 1781, determined to strengthen the national government.

The Nationalist-dominated Congress rapidly moved to meet the emergency by revamping its executive agencies. Between January and February 1781, the Board of War and other committees and boards were replaced with departments of War, Marine, Foreign Affairs, and Finance. A secretary, or an equivalent thereof, headed each department. These executives were selected from outside the ranks of Congress and exercised ultimate authority over their departments. Never before had Congress willingly delegated so much power to individuals.[45]

Although Congress failed to spell out clearly the functions of the secretary at war, he gradually assumed responsibility for the supply departments and other service agencies. He also advised Congress about the army's status and requirements. General Benjamin Lincoln served as the first secretary at war, and since he took office after the Yorktown campaign, he presided over the army's retrenchment rather than its growth. Nonetheless, the creation of his office was an important step in the evolution of the nation's land force.[46]

The formation of the Department of Finance was by far the most significant step Congress took to resolve the critical conditions it faced. The collapse of currency finance largely accounted for the crisis; without a reformed financial system, the war effort could not continue for any extended length of time. To fill the office of superintendent of finance, Congress almost unanimously turned to Robert Morris. Before Morris would accept the appointment, he insisted that Congress allow him to continue practicing his private business affairs in office, to select the members of his own department, and to dismiss any official who handled public property. Although some delegates were reluctant to grant any person such vast and potentially conflicting powers, a desperate Congress agreed to his terms. The nation needed Morris's prestige within the mercantile community and his unrivaled knowledge of the American economy to revamp its financial structure.[47]

From the time he took office until he left in 1784, Morris served simultaneously as the nation's financier and leader of the Nationalist faction. In that dual capacity, he emerged as the most powerful individual in America after George Washington. Finances touched almost every aspect of domestic and foreign affairs, and Morris never hesitated to extend the scope of his activities and power. In short order, he seized from Congress and the other executive departments the initiative in formulating Confederation policies.

Morris put in a virtuoso performance as the government's financial agent, leading the nation through its most trying ordeal. Before focusing his attention on finances per se, however, he was drawn into army logistics. With state supply continuing to fail, the Continental army faced disaster. To keep it intact, the superintendent of finance devoted a good part of his first four months in office to supply matters. By August 1781 Morris was concentrating full-time on provisioning and transporting the army to the battlefront for the Yorktown campaign. His unequaled access to funds and credit, extensive commercial connections, and superb administrative abilities ensured the logistical support that made the monumental victory at Yorktown possible.[48] Since active hostilities practically ceased thereafter, Morris enjoyed more favorable circumstances than had any previous treasury official. The government was freed from the extreme pressure of military necessity, and budgets dropped as the army began to shrink and went into relatively permanent encampment. Morris even had the opportunity to increase federal revenue through the sale of surplus military property. While expenses dropped, the government's income rose. Between 1781 and 1784, loans from France and Holland reached an all-time high. Additionally, through requisitions and by not including specific supplies and the assumption of some federal debts, Morris persuaded the states to provide the Confederation with more specie-valued money than had ever been the case before. Between 1781 and 1784, Morris spent almost $7 million; nearly $6.5 million came from foreign assistance and state contributions.[49]

Once in office, Morris set as a principal goal restoring the government's credit. To achieve that purpose, he refused to recognize most of the massive

Confederation debt contracted before he became superintendent and took responsibility only for current expenses. Within those limited terms, Morris exercised his generous talents to balance the federal budget and to pay all government expenditures with reliable money.

Even with increased foreign loans, Morris realized that the federal government could not afford to pay for its expenditures in specie. Rather than expending the hard money coming into the treasury, he used it to support the issue of new currency. The Bank of North America was central to that scheme. Morris organized the nation's first modern commercial bank shortly after he took office, and, after some delay, Congress granted the bank a federal charter of incorporation. This institution was in part an outgrowth of the Bank of Pennsylvania, which Morris and others had created to sustain military purchasing after the failure of federal finances. Although a private corporation, the Bank of North America's ownership was initially quasi-public. Because private sources were reluctant to invest in the new venture, Morris used federal funds to purchase more than half of the bank's $400,000 capitalization. The bank floated some commercial loans, but its primary function was to provide short-term credit to the federal government in the form of paper. Morris supplemented the notes of the Bank of North America with notes issued under his own signature and backed by his prestige and private wealth as well as by the general assets of the federal government. Both types of notes circulated nationally at or near par. By creating a reliable paper medium, Morris maximized the utility of limited federal specie and permitted the government to meet expenses before the actual collection of revenue.[50]

Morris cut government expenses as well as stretching government income in his struggle for a balanced budget. For the first time, he introduced strict accountability in the handling of public funds. Simultaneously, he began to whittle away at the unwieldy federal bureaucracy that had proliferated during the previous six years. His most important reforms involved army procurement. He replaced government supply agents compensated on commission with private firms that bid competitively for contracts. The new system probably did not reduce the cost of the government's supplies, but it did lessen administrative outlays by enabling Morris to eliminate the Office of the Commissary General, cut drastically the operations of the Quartermaster Department, and close down numerous military posts, depots, and warehouses. The superintendent of finance also absorbed into his own office the newly created Department of Marine and either eliminated or took over the functions of other army and navy supply agencies.[51]

Morris's procurement reforms ostensibly "civilianized" military supply operations. Actually, that was not the case, principally because during the Revolutionary War the line between the military and civilian worlds was virtually invisible. The nation's small navy varied little in character or function from its collection of civilian privateers. Although the army was more visible as an institution, it too lacked a clear identity. Based on prerevolutionary patterns, a dual military heritage was emerging in America, consisting of militia as reserves and volunteer units for active duty. The Continental army by stages became a fighting force serving for the duration of the war. Whether militia or Continental army, officer or enlisted person, military service for Americans in general was still only an interlude in civilian life.

The lack of permanence and tradition that characterized the line was even more exaggerated for the staff. Citizens, principally merchants, frequently served within the supply bureaus without the formality of uniform or rank. Regardless of their status, merchants moved between civilian and military and private and public pursuits with relative ease.

The state of military technology, as well as the character of the armed services, kept the soldier and citizen nearly as one during the revolutionary years. Army and navy technology was still basic and in most regards close to or the same as civilian use. To illustrate the point, Morris's greatest contribution to the Yorktown success involved providing food and transport for the troops.[52]

Hence, Morris intended his procurement reforms to advance private power at the expense of the government, not civilian power at the expense of the military. Private contractors, the superintendent of finance was convinced, would rationalize supply operations and maximize the flow of goods to the armed services while reducing the size of the distended governmental structure.

The essentially civilian nature of the military services and Morris's supply reforms notwithstanding, the army was still an intensely controversial issue in America. Throughout the Revolution, endless ideological battles raged over the virtues of the militia versus a standing army and the threat of the latter to civilian and republican institutions. In general, the Eastern or Radical advocates of local and state power put their faith in the militia and constantly guarded against any real or perceived military abuses of civilian and democratic prerogatives. Nationalists increasingly favored a standing army, but one securely under civilian authority, to ensure the security of the state. The dual militia-volunteer/standing army tradition of the colonial and revolutionary periods allowed the nation to reach a compromise on this fundamental and inflammatory issue until time and reality dictated a more lasting and certain solution.

By the time he left office, Morris had converted an often corrupt and inefficient bureaucracy into a trim and effective arm of the state. He managed to institute his reforms principally because the war was drawing to a close. That reality created the opportunity for implementing a financial system that was stable and, therefore, that allowed Morris to enforce his decisions.

WAR AND THE AMERICAN POLITICAL ECONOMY

Morris began his duties as superintendent of finance with the immediate goal of restoring government solvency so that the war effort could continue. His long-term ambition, however, involved securing the future of the nation's political economy. The means he used to achieve his limited goal lent themselves to his larger purpose. In addition to the stabilized economy, a balanced budget, a national bank, a reliable national currency, and an efficient federal bureaucracy encouraged the long-term growth and integration of the national economy and won the confidence of the nation's commercial elements. Previously, they had viewed the federal policies of uncontrolled currency finance and comprehensive economic controls as irresponsible, but now they tended to identify their interests with those of the national government. This shift advanced efforts to persuade Americans to adopt Nationalist principles in the conduct of their affairs.

Like all Nationalists, Morris detested the requisition system, which left the federal government at the mercy of the states. To remedy that condition, the superintendent of finance threw his weight behind the Nationalist-sponsored Impost of 1781. Under this proposed amendment to the Articles of Confederation, the federal government would levy a 5 percent duty on all imports. Morris and the Nationalists envisaged the impost as serving political and economic purposes. While providing the Confederation with the funds to conduct its affairs, the impost would also advance national power at the expense of the states by granting the federal government the right to regulate foreign commerce and by giving it an independent source of revenue. To ensure the latter end, Morris proposed a national tax service to collect and distribute the impost that would replace the existing state-dominated system.[53]

Morris's ambitions for the impost became wedded to a more grandiose scheme involving the revolutionary debt. The Nationalists originally insisted upon adoption of the impost as a war finance measure, but as fighting waned after Yorktown, their argument lost its impact. Faced with the prospect of the states rejecting the impost amendment, which was vital to his larger plans for the Union, Morris persuaded Congress to begin liquidating all federal debt and assuming most outstanding state debt in 1782. This action, of dubious legality under the Articles of Confederation, multiplied Confederation

obligations many times over. It also provided the Nationalists with a new justification for federal taxation. Morris vehemently argued that the nation's
credit, as well as its sense of honor and justice, demanded that all new and
old debt be totally funded. In order to do that, the superintendent of finance
insisted that the impost and many other federal taxes had to be instituted.[54]

The consolidation of the revolutionary debt by the federal government
became the linchpin of Morris's grand design for the Union. He fully expected
that the individuals, groups, and states that stood to benefit from expanding
the Confederation's financial obligations would become an effective lobby for
a strengthened national government, including independent federal taxation.
Once the consolidated debt was funded, the various securities that had been
floated during the war and that had depreciated badly would increase in value.
This new wealth, channeled through the national bank and other commercial
institutions, would provide the mercantile community with a substantial
investment fund for advancing economic growth. The paralyzing burden of
debt would thereby be converted into an enormous national asset.[55]

In its short- and long-term features, Morris's grand design anticipated Federalist policies after the ratification of the Constitution. Morris, like his Federalist successors, drew heavily on British experience in formulating his plans
for the nation. The ultimate goal was a dynamic, expanding, yet stable commercial and industrial empire. The moving force behind that empire would
be the enlightened self-interest of the propertied elements, guided and assisted
but not shackled by a strong national government under upper-class control.[56]

Despite its ingenuity, Morris's program was not adopted, chiefly because
the war ended and the Nationalists lost control of Congress. The new nation,
which was still at least four-fifths agrarian, had turned to the Nationalists in
1780–1781 out of desperation more than conviction. When the emergency
lifted, the democratizing tendencies of the Revolution, the fear of centralized
power, and the suspicion of marketplace values remained and were reflected
in the electoral process. By failing to broaden their base of support beyond
the propertied and commercial classes in the Middle States, the Nationalists
invited defeat. Even the New England and Southern conservatives could not
be counted upon as reliable allies, and only partly because of state and regional
particularism. A widespread attitude grew that the Nationalists intended to
force upon the nation the rule of a narrowly based, self-indulgent minority
that failed to appreciate the larger interests of the population.[57]

Morris himself was instrumental in creating a negative image for the
Nationalists. He antagonized and alienated many people by his arrogant use of
power, sense of intrigue, and boundless ambition, qualities that were most
blatantly manifested during the Nationalists' drive to fund the expanding

national debt after the Yorktown campaign. Doggedly determined to secure the passage of federal taxation, Morris misrepresented the nature of foreign credit available to the nation, arranged to have interest payments on the domestic debt cut off to goad creditors into more forceful action, issued an insulting and impossible ultimatum to the states, threatened to resign his office, and, in a desperate maneuver carried out in conjunction with other leading Nationalists, attempted during the Newburgh conspiracy of March 1783 to use the volatile emotions of the disaffected Continental army for partisan goals. Scornful of the masses and impatient with accommodation, Morris often distressed even those people sympathetic to his goals.[58]

In the eyes of their opponents, Morris and his mercantile colleagues were corrupt as well as irresponsible. Morris's return to office in 1781 rekindled past suspicions, and his actions encouraged these concerns. When instituting the private contractor system in military supply operations, for example, the superintendent of finance undermined his own reforms by awarding most contracts to his partners or former partners. The contractors, in turn, drove prices upward by collusive behavior and did not always fulfill their contractual obligations. Throughout the war years, charges of fraud, embezzlement, and malfeasance were constantly hurled at Morris and other merchants in public life. Congress repeatedly investigated their activities. Due to bureaucratic chaos and scant recordkeeping, few of the accusations were proven, but that did not relieve public doubt and scorn. Even if the general population had accepted the Nationalists' emphasis on economic growth, it would probably have questioned whether the mercantile community was worthy to lead in achieving that goal.[59]

Despite public attitudes, the Nationalist defeat in 1783 was only temporary. By consolidating the revolutionary debt in 1782, the Nationalists created the means for achieving their ends. In the postwar years, however, they faced desperation, perhaps even terror, before triumph. Denied revenue, the national government defaulted on its foreign obligations by 1785 and surrendered its domestic debt to the states. The promise of centralized authority disappeared as the federal government lost control of the debt. More and more statesmen and influential citizens became convinced that a permanently weak national government would deny America the advantages of its dearly won independence. Internal growth, a respected place in the world, and, for some, the democratic experiment itself might be threatened. These perceived threats, combined with fear of a growing radical thrust in various states, a general distrust of power at the state level, and a good measure of self-interest, led the New England and Southern conservatives, who had opposed the Nationalists under Morris's leadership, to join the Middle States' elite in an effort to strengthen the national government. Operating from a national base and representing a much larger constituency than the Nationalists of the Revolutionary War, the new coalition, through illegal procedure and shrewd maneuver but in a spirit of compromise, accommodation, and circumspection, wrote and led in the ratifying of the Constitution. Under Federalist leadership, that document provided the legal sanction to implement Morris's grand design for the nation's political economy.

How the colonists mobilized their economy to meet the demands of a nearly total war was shaped, as in all wars, by four factors: the character and structure of the armed services, the state of military technology, the maturity of the economy, and the nature of the political system. The last factor was by far the most significant.

Mobilization was more a civilian than a combined civilian-military effort because the armed services lacked developed, definable identities. From top to bottom, and with few exceptions, the armed services consisted of civilians in uniform, not expertly trained persons with a permanent mission and a professional, corporate sense.

The civilian nature of the nation's fighting forces was reinforced by the basic level of military technology. The supply requirements of the army and navy were so similar to civilian usage that production for the military was possible without fundamentally restructuring the economy. Moreover, civilians or civilians in uniforms could carry out military logistics with little or no training. Americans felt the economic impact of a long war more through the quantity of goods consumed by the military than through a shift in the type of products demanded.

The colonists' vibrant, preindustrial economy was able to produce around half of the war's requirements, with the rest coming from abroad. Primitive modes of transportation, however, limited severely the effectiveness of distribution. Of much greater significance, the colonists relied on paper money to finance the war, an expedient resulting in destructive, runaway inflation.

To control inflationary forces within the context of harnessing the economy for war, Americans tried comprehensive economic regulation by the Confederation and the states. Government at all levels, however, was too weak to achieve that goal; thus, the colonists had to turn increasingly to the merchant community, particularly to the powerful merchants. Members of that community, serving as government officials and businessmen and combining public and private pursuits, had established a network of commercial connections that included all the colonies and that extended abroad. Throughout the war years, merchants used the network to direct economic mobilization. This system had remained more informal than formal until 1781 because of the ideological dispute between the Radical and Nationalist factions. Once the latter won the upper hand in 1781, Robert Morris, as superintendent of finance, led in making merchant control over economic mobilization more direct by changing governmental structures and policies. Necessity waylaid ideology and strengthened the power of a small minority.

This vital point has been made by two careful scholars of the revolutionary period and deserves emphasis. H. James Henderson, in his insightful *Party Politics in the Continental Congress,* argues that in 1779–1780 "the era of the Party of the Revolution had passed, and the day of the technicians had come"; that this transition signaled "the substitution of bureaucracy and order for virtue and enthusiasm under elitist rather than popular auspices."[60] In a similar fashion, Jackson Turner Main, in *The Sovereign States, 1775–1783,* maintains that in the intense debate in America between 1779 and 1781 over how to resolve the comprehensive and growing crisis, two very different solutions were proposed: the majority at the lower end of the economic scale favored continuing but enforcing the existing policies; a wholly new approach was favored by "the larger property owners, those in trade or the professions, the more substantial commercial farmers, creditors, and most public officials including a majority in Congress."[61] Despite spirited efforts, the will of the general population gave way to harsh realities and pragmatic solutions.

The most important observation about economic mobilization for the Revolutionary War is that it played a vital role in shaping the Constitution and the nation's political economy under it.[62] The colonies' parochial past made impossible a centralized government in 1775–1776. Despite its weaknesses, the government under the Articles of Confederation kept the rebelling colonies fighting for five years. The Americans benefited from British blundering, but that does not detract from their accomplishments.[63] Nonetheless, the Revolutionary War and the extraordinary demands it made revealed that regional and class tensions were preventing the thirteen states from achieving unity. Hence, in 1781 the Continental Congress began experimenting with greater centralization to keep the nation fighting in the face of seemingly insuperable odds. Once the war was over, continued divisions set off the movement leading to the Constitution. That new charter grew from the principles of the Articles of Confederation and the actions of the Confederation government, which resolved fundamental issues and conserved representative institutions despite intense partisan conflict.

After, as before and during, the Revolution, the nation was led by an economic, political, and social elite operating within a republican framework.

Since the officers' corps came largely from the same class, the military services acted to buttress, not challenge, elite rule, although it was weighted to the conservative side. The Revolutionary War did not make America into a nation of democratic politics and elitist leadership, but it made that pattern clearly manifest. In the Revolution, and in every future American war, warfare lays bare the power structure of social systems.

3

THE POLITICAL ECONOMY OF
WARFARE: 1790–1815

Mobilizing the economy for the War of 1812 improved upon what had taken place during the Revolution, but the effort was still badly flawed. Between the two wars the economy grew and military technology remained static, conditions that should have led to better economic mobilization. They did not do so because the federal government was weak during hostilities and the armed services, particularly the army, had been kept small and undeveloped between 1790 and 1812.

A reasonably strong federal government did not emerge in the early national period because of intensely ideological disputes between and among Federalists and Republicans over the nature of government and the conduct of foreign policy. These conflicts also slowed the maturation of the armed services. Republicans checked the Federalists' drive for a larger and better military as unnecessary and as a threat to liberty.

The divisions among America's economic, political, and social elite, manifested during the Revolution, continued into the early national period and thwarted institutional growth and stability, particularly in the political and military spheres. Although the relatively conservative officer corps of the army and navy still came from or aspired to elite status, the services were more affected by national trends rather than affecting the trends themselves. Generally, however, economic growth and physical expansion in curious and elliptical ways acted as unifying forces that ultimately cleared the way for the maturation of political and military institutions.

THE POLITICAL STRUCTURE

The national government in the early years of the republic was unstable, subject to almost constant controversy and significant change. The ongoing political disputes involved the operations of the federal government. The authors of the Constitution ended up disagreeing fundamentally about the nature of government under it, and political parties emerged to resolve their differences. That outcome was unanticipated, never fully accepted, and yet practically inevitable for launching the new republic. By 1812, however, over two decades of intense political battle had exhausted the first party system and in the process weakened the national government. Under these conditions the new nation drifted unprepared into war.

The two-party system grew from Alexander Hamilton's drive to create a strong central government during George Washington's administrations in which the executive branch would predominate over the legislative branch and the states.[1] This move gave birth to a Federalist faction that was soon challenged by a Republican faction led by Thomas Jefferson and James Madison. The Virginia leadership was convinced that Hamilton and his circle intended to foist on the nation a centralized, aristocratic form of rule that would subvert the republic. To protect republican principles, they emphasized dispersed power answerable to the general public. The Federalists, for their part, were equally convinced that the rising tide of opposition would bring back the chaos of the years under the Articles of Confederation.

This highly ideological conflict was intensified enormously when the French Revolution turned radical and expansionist in the 1790s. The outbreak of war in Europe in 1793 threatened from the outset to involve the new nation and acted to convert factions into parties. Republicans charged that with the Jay Treaty of 1795, the Washington administration subordinated the nation's sovereignty to Great Britain and rejected the friendship and revolutionary ideology of France. They used opposition to the treaty to extend their reach beyond the core of Southern planters to small farmers and urban workers throughout the nation. The result was embryonic parties for the presidential election of 1796 in which John Adams won as Washington's successor by a close margin.[2] Under Adams, party strife grew and the president faced brutal divisions within his own administration and party. The turmoil became so great that it threatened to extinguish basic liberties and to undo the republic. France was a source of much of the conflict. To defuse the explosive situation, Adams negotiated peace with that country in 1800. Such statesmanship delivered a fatal blow to the Federalist party and ended Adams's political career.

While Adams saved the nation, a vision for the future came from Jefferson and Madison.[3] Without an intrusive, heavy-handed central government, they envisaged an independent republic expanding westward, growing commercially and industrially, and incorporating more and more of the population into the nation's political life. Republican confidence and flexibility led to Jefferson's victory in 1800 and the immeasurably important precedent of a peaceful change of government through the electoral process.

No sharp break occurred with the Federalist past. Although Jefferson moved quickly to reduce federal powers, Hamilton's national bank, for example, continued until 1811. Moreover, Jefferson flexed federal muscles and overlooked constitutional doubts to expand the national borders. When war resumed in Europe in 1803, the president sought to protect American rights by peaceful coercion with nonimportation and then the embargo. The results were economic ruin and the extreme exercise of police powers. An ideology in behalf of peace abroad nearly created civil war at home.

Madison was left to deal with Jefferson's failed foreign policies.[4] Facing enormous challenges without the latter's ability or prestige, the former lost control of the Republican party and allowed the initiative to pass from the executive to the legislative branch. The process was accelerated by the arrival in Congress of a new, postrevolutionary generation of legislators. These nationalist Republicans, such as Henry Clay, John C. Calhoun, and Peter B. Porter, helped push Madison and the moderate Republicans into war with England.

The turbulence of the early national period revealed some basic truths about the new republic. Leadership after the Revolution, as before, was economically and politically elitist. Economic elites became somewhat more diverse in this era as the economy matured, but wealth concentration remained about the same, the richest 10 percent holding close to 60 percent of all wealth, the bottom 30 percent having little, and a substantial middle class of prosperous farmers, smaller merchants, artisans, and the like, holding the rest. This pattern of inequality has remained remarkably stable to the present day.[5] America's wealthy constituted more than an economic and social upper class; they were also a governing class. At the local, state, and national levels, the most powerful and prestigious offices were reserved for the elite. The middle class was represented in government but usually in lesser positions of sheriff and lower houses of legislatures.[6] Yet beginning before, accelerated during, and continuing after the American Revolution, the nation was democratized by the move toward universal manhood suffrage.

An elitist reality encountering a democratic ideology has been and remains a glaring, yet dynamic, contradiction at the center of America's social system. Mastering that contradiction by converting power into authority constitutes the genius of American politics. By embracing democracy, the Republicans broadened their power base and outmaneuvered the Federalists; the latter, by emphasizing the few and the privileged, narrowed their appeal and ensured their demise.

Ultimately, the nation managed its elitist-democratic duality through electoral politics based upon a two-party system. That solution evolved, more than it was created, in the early national years and was at best hesitantly accepted by the elite. Nonetheless, through it the new republic was launched under the Constitution and survived daunting, formidable odds.

THE ECONOMIC STRUCTURE

The American economy in 1812 was stronger in every way than it had been in 1790. Foreign trade stimulated economic growth, which led to urban expansion, greater agricultural output, increased regional and occupational specialization, and ultimately more manufacturing. Economic change resulted in the Republicans beginning to support the economic nationalism of the Federalists.

Federalists sought to advance national economic independence through fostering domestic trade and manufacturing. For Washington, Hamilton, and other advocates of a strong central government, economic independence and national defense were inextricably combined. Economic growth would facilitate supplying an army and navy without foreign assistance.[7] A new nation surrounded by potentially hostile nations and Indians had good reasons to concentrate upon the close relationship between economic and military might. Forced economic growth, however, did not work. New factory production encouraged by the Federalists succumbed during the Panic of 1792 and did not resume until 1808 or later.[8] With that failure, the close association between economic and military might was greatly attenuated, though not completely lost.

Beginning with the European wars in 1793, foreign trade, not domestic commerce, brought lavish prosperity to America. With a few interruptions, the growth continued until 1807. Although imports exceeded exports, re-exports and American ships taking over as neutral carriers led almost to a balance of international payments for the nation between 1793 and 1807.[9] Southern cotton was the most important export in these early years, accounting for 30 percent of goods sold abroad in 1807.[10] Tobacco, rice, and sugar were secondary crops in the South, and together with cotton they stimulated an active internal commerce.[11] Foreign commerce even stimulated markets west of the Appalachians.[12]

Prosperity spread throughout the nation. Merchants, banks, shipbuilders, and a host of services and industries directly or indirectly related to trade grew rapidly. Urban areas expanded, especially leading port cities such as New

York.[13] Rural sections also benefited as growing foreign markets and expanding urban populations enormously increased the demand for grain, flour, meat, livestock, and other foodstuffs. To deal with the bottleneck of a primitive transportation system, New England and the Middle States around 1793 began to improve roads and rivers, build some bridges and short canals, and, most important, introduce and greatly expand turnpikes. By 1815 the major cities of the Northeast were connected with each other and the surrounding countryside. The improvements broadened access to the marketplace, though transportation costs remained high.[14]

The economic boom came to an abrupt halt in 1807 with Jefferson's embargo, however. Modification in that policy provided a measure of prosperity before Great Britain instituted a total blockade during the War of 1812. Between 1808 and 1815, trade seldom exceeded 60 percent of the 1807 peak, and in 1814 it virtually stopped.[15]

The cutoff of foreign trade affected domestic manufacturing. Despite Federalist efforts, industrial output progressed little after the revolutionary period. Manufacturing centered on processing the country's primary products, which required relatively low investments in man-hours and machinery. Hence, the industrial sector included household manufacturing, lumber, grain, textile mills and iron works, and small-scale firms for the output of leather products, glass, and naval stores.[16]

The low levels of foreign trade after 1808 led to a general rise in manufacturing.[17] The impact was especially great for some industries, and cotton textiles stand out in that regard. Unlike most industries, cotton textiles grew and innovated steadily from 1790 until the embargo. Growth accelerated in 1808, leading to the factory system in textiles by 1815 best exemplified by the Waltham complex.[18] Technologically advanced, large-scale production also arose in woolen textiles, the flour industry, some metal-working, and gunpowder output. Indeed, in most important industries, manufacturing units existed around 1815 even if production efficiency had not greatly increased.[19]

The one area in which the United States genuinely innovated instead of adapting foreign advances was in small arms. Here was born in the late eighteenth century the process that would later be called the American System of Manufactures. By 1812, small arms output was already quite advanced.

The birth of the factory system notwithstanding, the size and organization of business activity showed more continuity than change between 1790 and 1815. Individual proprietors carried out most production and exchange. Nonetheless, partnerships and unincorporated companies became quite common in the Northeast. Chartered corporations assumed a new importance, although they were restricted to areas serving the "general welfare," as was the case with turnpikes and waterworks.[20] Almost the entire federal and state banking community also operated under public charters. State banks proliferated with the Republican ascendancy and boomed with the death of the First Bank of the United States and the onset of the War of 1812.[21]

Specialization advanced as the economy grew from 1790 to 1815. Regions began to be distinct in the goods they produced and traded.[22] Occupational specialization went even further. The general merchant declined as financial, commercial, and industrial functions were performed by different businesses.[23] Quite naturally, occupational specialization proceeded most rapidly in the economically advanced Northeast. Outside of urban areas in the South and West it was much more limited.[24] Overall, the period between 1790 and 1815 prepared the way for economic transformation. An integrated national economy was not created, but the groundwork for it was being laid.

America's political economy during these years reflected the realities of economic change.[25] Jefferson moved closer to Hamilton. By 1805 he was advocating a federally sponsored program of internal improvements, and in 1808 Albert Gallatin worked out the details for such a plan. In 1811 the Bank of the United States went down less from opposition to banks than from the desire of agrarian and commercial elements to free state banking systems from national regulation. At best, however, Jefferson, Madison, and even Gallatin were reluctant economic nationalists. That was not the case, however, with the second generation of Republicans such as Clay and Calhoun. In the brief period of intense nationalism following the War of 1812, they fashioned the American System of banks, internal improvements, and tariffs to tie the nation together and to further economic growth.

As more Americans were drawn into the marketplace, the gulf between Federalists and Republicans narrowed. Economic growth disrupted the new republic at the same time that it unified its people. With most of the population either participating in the market or aspiring to do so, the favored position of the elite was less resented by the mass. Hence, economic growth as the new nation's most distinct and continuing characteristic helped to square the contradictory circle of an elite reality within a society increasingly devoted to a democratic ideology.

The economic development of the early national years was not designed to further national security as the Federalists had desired. The major exceptions involved the production of small arms and gunpowder, which owed more to Republicans than to their political rivals. Nonetheless, general economic growth and specialization ensured that the armed services could be better supplied, thereby enhancing the nation's ability to defend itself or to attack others. Economic growth thus related the civilian to the soldier just as it did the commoner to the gentleman. But matters become more complex. Economic growth in fact and fancy has usually been tied to physical expansion, which carries with it the threat of war. That reality created a tense and paradoxical interdependence between America's civilian and military worlds that is nearly baffling in its dimensions.

THE MILITARY STRUCTURE

Military policy was among the most controversial issues facing the nation between 1789 and 1801. It continued as a source of contention in the Republican administrations until the end of the War of 1812. Some basic elements of policy were worked out between 1789 and 1815, but a permanent military system came only later.

After the Revolution, as before, Americans looked unfavorably upon the military as a threat to liberty and a needless expense.[26] Reflecting these views, the Confederation Congress in June 1784 created what became a small standing army to defend the vast frontier against the Indians, Great Britain, and Spain and expanded the force in 1786 to put down Shays's Rebellion. These troops were too few and too slow for meeting the challenges they faced.[27]

Most nationalists deviated from popular sentiment by supporting a strong military and considered such a force essential for maintaining security domestically and on the frontier. Accordingly, Hamilton, advised by Washington and others, in 1783 proposed creating a small standing army backed up by well-trained and closely regulated common and volunteer militia, maintaining arsenals and armories to supply the troops, establishing a military academy to instill professionalism, and building a respectable navy.[28] The Confederation Congress, dominated by advocates of decentralization, ignored the recommendations.

The Constitution tipped the military scales in favor of the centralized government in terms of raising, commanding, administering, and maintaining civilian control over an army even as it continued the nation's dual tradition of a militia and regulars. Authority over these forces was divided between the states and the federal government, and within the latter between the executive and the legislative branches. Naval forces were much less controversial. The Constitution simply gave the federal government the right "to provide and maintain a Navy."[29]

The first national government under the Constitution moved quickly to deal with military matters. In August 1789 Congress created a Department of War as an executive agency to administer the army. Henry Knox, who had acted as secretary at war under the Articles of Confederation, filled the new post. He and several clerks remained as the bureaucratic structure for administering and, under the president, commanding the army for over a quarter of a century. There were no permanent bureaus, such as a Quartermaster Department, to make up what was then considered to be a general staff to assist the secretary of war or the commanding general in fulfilling their responsibilities. Such supply or staff bureaus were created to facilitate various military expeditions, but theory at the time held that a general staff should exist only for a protracted war, which all but precluded planning for hostilities during years of peace.[30]

Congress proceeded cautiously in dealing with the army because of widespread antipathy toward it. The small standing army maintained under the Articles of Confederation was continued and expanded in the early 1790s to deal with aggressive Indian resistance on the frontier. Ideally, this army of regulars was made up of three-year enlistees, but it usually had to be strengthened with state militia and even levies of federal volunteers serving for six months. This hybrid fighting force met with disaster in 1790 and 1791 in expeditions against the Indians. Between 1792 and 1794, however, Gen. Anthony Wayne rigorously trained regulars, supplemented them with state militia, and in 1794 defeated the Indian opposition at Fallen Timbers. Here was the real birth of America's regular army under the Constitution, which also set the pattern for the future land forces—the dual tradition of a core of regulars training and guiding a mass of citizen-soldiers.[31]

The militia was maintained under the Constitution, but it was left unimproved. With the Uniform Militia Act of 1792, Congress continued the obligation of all free, white, able-bodied males between eighteen and forty-five to serve in the common militia. Since control over these citizen-soldiers was left almost entirely in state hands, the nation was denied a uniform militia. Consequently, the military's future depended upon regulars, with citizen-soldiers intended to play a temporary, supplementary role.[32]

Even the regular army's small size and the militia's unstructured nature did not quiet the deep-seated and widespread suspicion of military institutions. Indeed, a crisis involving the army began in 1793 and reached the point of threatening civil war. The cry of armed tyranny arose from the Republicans when Washington and Hamilton led the militia into Pennsylvania to meet the challenge of lawlessness raised by the Whiskey Rebellion in 1794. An infinitely greater military threat resulted from American involvement in the war between England and France that broke out in 1793. Federalists exploited the Quasi-War with France (1798–1800) to push through Congress the Alien and Sedition Acts and to authorize a substantial land force. It turned out to be the nation's only truly political army. Hamilton and Washington carefully selected Federalists for officers, excluding Republicans whenever possible. Hamilton and his coterie were intent upon crushing militarily the Republican opposition during the anticipated war with France. Alarmed by these schemes, Adams overcame formidable obstacles to negotiate an end to hostilities with France and put an end to the High Federalists' exceptionally dangerous military buildup.[33]

The navy was less controversial than the army from 1789 to 1800.[34] In actuality, the new republic got under way without a fleet. Responding to the outbreak of war between England and France in 1793 and the piracy of the Barbary states, Congress authorized the construction of three frigates in 1794, which turned out to be the beginning of America's navy. These ships were under the War Department's direction until Congress created a Navy Department in 1798, composed of a secretary and a few clerks. During the undeclared war with France, Benjamin Stoddert, the first secretary of the navy, expanded the fleet to approximately fifty ships, supplemented by over 1,000 armed merchant vessels. As with the army, an expanding navy was quickly halted when Adams worked out an accord with France. Harbor defenses continued to be built, however. In 1794 Congress voted to erect coastal fortifications at key seaports, construct four arsenals for storing munitions, and create a corps of artillerists and engineers to man the forts. By 1812, twenty-four forts had been built along the Atlantic Coast.[35]

The military threat to civilian institutions had waned by 1800. As Russell F. Weigley observes, the blatant nature of High Federalist intentions may have ensured the subsequent American tradition of a nonpolitical military.[36] The decline of the Federalist party and the rise of the Republicans resulted in very different attitudes toward the military. Nonetheless, before leaving office, the Federalists worked out rudimentary military policies for the coming century, a structure that Allan R. Millett and Peter Maslowski label "a passive defense." The plan included a small regular army that would expand in war with federal volunteers and state militia and a modest navy, which, along with coastal fortifications, would protect the nation's territory and shipping and could be enlarged to raid an enemy's commerce.[37]

No dramatic change occurred in military policy under the Republican administrations of Jefferson and Madison until the threat of war with England necessitated substantive increases in the size of the armed forces.[38] Jefferson's preference for defense through an effective militia led him to seek congressional approval for reforms of the militia system similar to those advocated earlier by leading Federalists, but the national legislature did not cooperate. The president then turned to paring down the land force to approximately 4,000 men and replacing particularly partisan Federalist officers with Republicans. Moreover, in keeping with his preference for peace over war and construction over destruction, Jefferson acted in 1802 to create the U.S. Military Academy at West Point. This institution trained cadets in engineering and science and opened the officer corps to all eligible males, not just the elite. The president, more than his Federalist predecessors, believed that a standing army would be more tolerated and useful if engaged in peaceful, practical pursuits. Hence, he employed the regular army in road building, exploring, and seeking peace with the Indians.

At least in theory, Jefferson's management of the navy approximated his ideal of a citizens' military. His administration moved rapidly to reduce the size of the fleet. Naval expeditions during the Tripolitan War from 1801 to 1805, however, familiarized Jefferson with the use of small gunboats in shallow waters. Convinced that such craft, in conjunction with coastal fortifications, could protect the nation against any enemy, he had hundreds of these vessels constructed. They were cheap to build, could be handled by maritime militiamen with minimal training, and could be used only for defense.

The resumption of European warfare in 1803 denied Republican administrations the peaceful conditions necessary for a small military. The gross violation of America's neutral shipping rights by France and even more so by Britain, and the latter's impressment of American seamen, forced the Republicans to prepare for war as efforts at diplomatic solutions fell short. At Jefferson's recommendation, Congress in 1808 more than doubled the size of the army, allocated $200,000 annually to arm the militia, and approved funds to bolster coastal defenses.

Jefferson's heart was never in military preparations. His quest for peace through the Embargo Act of 1807 captured much more accurately the true Jeffersonian spirit. The failure of this approach produced results that were both ironic and tragic. Jefferson found himself using military force against numerous American citizens whom the embargo had defined as criminals, at times with greater rigor than Federalists had used it against the Whiskey rebels and those led by John Fries in 1799.

Madison faced increasingly dire circumstances without Jefferson's ability. With the embargo repealed and alternate policies failing, the president in 1810 sought to increase the nation's military might. Because of confusion within the administration, Congress waited until 1811 half-heartedly to authorize fewer troops than Madison requested. As a result, on the eve of war in 1812 the army had less than 7,000 men.

The experiences of 1801 to 1812 demonstrated that leaders who were fundamentally ambivalent about the military could not prepare for war. Jefferson was an outstanding, flexible, and adaptive executive, Gallatin was equally talented, and, in the crunch, Madison could also deliver. The decisive issue was not leadership ability but priorities. Neither Jefferson nor Madison, in contrast to Washington and Hamilton, cared enough about the military to give it the time and energy necessary to ensure quality. Their attitude was reflected in their choices of secretaries of war. Both men selected former physicians with limited military experience who were more intent on reducing military expenditures than on achieving military excellence. The Republicans had carried forth Federalist policies for the army and navy more in theory than in fact. No consistent military policy had been implemented between 1801 and 1812, which was a predictable outcome for a society still seriously divided over the nature of government and the military's role in it.

The army officer corps remained unstable and amateur in the early national years. By 1812 it was in an advanced stage of deterioration. Turnover was high, a corporate sense absent, and training slight, which was not surprising since officers circulated freely between the political and military realms, performing many essentially civilian duties in the West as administrators, policemen, and diplomats. Moreover, since the corps reflected reasonably well the nation's elite, it manifested the political turmoil from 1789 to 1815. Nonetheless, change was evident. West Point and the Corps of Engineers were steps in the direction of professional growth, as was the practice of both Federalists and Republicans to ensure geographic balance within the corps. With more officers coming from the middling ranks and a few originating in the lower classes, the corps was also beginning the process of taking on a separate identity.

The navy's officer corps was different. Beginning under the Federalists and coming to fruition with the Republicans, the navy worked out an informal but rigorous system for thoroughly training and professionalizing its officers. Key to that process was careful selection of midshipmen followed by promotion based on the evaluation of commanding officers. Although some officers were from prominent families, most of the new recruits came from the respectable but probably financially struggling middle class. Navy officers, therefore, did not reflect the national elite as closely as their army counterparts. Moreover, since the navy corps had already developed a corporate sense, it was also practically nonpartisan even though, like the army, it performed numerous essentially civilian functions in diplomacy and other areas.

Several circumstances account for the difference between the two services. Following the English tradition, Americans feared the navy less than the army, giving the former more latitude. Of critical importance was the navy's ability to draw upon the nation's premier maritime industry for its civilian and military leadership. Further, officer training and acculturation took place in the controlled and often isolated environment of a ship at sea—conditions that encouraged and provided the experience for independence, initiative, and sound judgment. Predictably, the navy performed well, even superbly, during the War of 1812. By comparison, the army was more than wanting.

SUPPLYING THE MILITARY, 1789–1812

Military supply operations from 1789 to 1812 were rudimentary, usually inefficient, and often corrupt because crucial issues involving supply were not squarely addressed. In supplying the armed services, should the nation rely upon private or public manufacturing or some combination of the two to ensure availability and quality, control profiteering and corruption, and limit military spending influencing decisions for defense and war? Such vital matters were usually approached only tangentially as leaders focused on the more fundamental question of what was the appropriate military system for America. By default and drift, a makeshift public/private system for supplying the armed services evolved, leaving them open to exploitation by the various elements seeking economic and political gain.

The army's supply bureaucracy underwent numerous organizational changes between the Revolution and 1812, none of which established clear lines of authority. In 1785 Congress abolished army supply bureaus such as the Quartermaster Department. From then until the War of 1812, civilians directed procurement and related duties under an awkward system in which, roughly, the Treasury Department handled purchasing and the War Department took care of accounting, storage, and distribution. Superintendent of Finance Robert Morris had initiated the arrangement during the Revolutionary War. Gradually, the War Department gained greater control over its procurement as Treasury Department duties became increasingly nominal.[39]

To handle both emergencies and the day-to-day activities of the frontier posts the War Department created a field staff. The private contractors who handled supply for Gen. Josiah Harmar's expedition against the Indians in 1790 had proved to be disastrous. Congress therefore provided a civilian quartermaster general for the Gen. Arthur St. Clair and Wayne expeditions between 1791 and 1794, an arrangement that was far from ideal in an intensely rank-conscious organization. Nonetheless, it was a step forward as the quartermaster general supervised all matters of supply and transportation and acted as the army's logistical planner—in effect, a general staff function—for the commanding generals. The quartermaster general assembled various civilian subordinates who acted as deputy and assistant quartermasters, commissary general of forage, wagonmaster general, and so forth. Hundreds of boatmen, wagon drivers, and artificers, including carpenters, blacksmiths, harness makers, and saddlers, were hired to operate manufacturing, assembly, and repair facilities. The St. Clair disaster occurred despite the expanded and improved logistical structure because of poor planning, but effective direction contributed significantly to Wayne's success.[40] After the major Indian campaigns ended in 1794, Congress continued a reduced Quartermaster General's Office to oversee supply of forts and stations.[41]

During this period, the War Department took on functions in manufacturing and transport that it had previously contracted out. The Philadelphia Quartermaster Depot emerged as a site for manufacturing uniforms and related products, and the War Department began to assemble boats for inland transportation of supplies.[42] Most important, in 1794 Congress authorized the latter to establish a number of arsenals to manufacture small arms and ammunition. Springfield was selected as the site for the first arsenal in 1794 and Harpers Ferry followed in 1798. These establishments provided muskets to supplement those purchased from private firms. The War Department also procured cannons, shot, and the like under private contract.[43] During the entire period from 1783 to 1812, however, private contractors continued to subsist the troops.

Overall, the Quartermaster General's Office from 1785 to 1812 was badly flawed. The makeshift structure denied officers the opportunity to prepare for war by perfecting the supply organization during peacetime. Nevertheless, good officers could make the office function effectively. Under the Federalists, the leadership was at least fair. It was generally poor under the Republicans, who continued the Quartermaster's Office under a different name and with some modified practices.[44]

Supply for the navy was simpler than for the army between 1789 and 1815. Naval forces were smaller in size and their activities were largely confined to the Atlantic Coast, making procurement and transportation easier than in the frontier regions where the army operated.[45] When Congress authorized the beginnings of a navy in 1794, the Washington administration built its own ships in rented yards along the Atlantic Coast in order to avoid politics and inflated prices. A naval captain served as yard superintendent and exercised general authority over the establishment; the actual building was directed by a naval constructor; the yard clerk received, issued, and accounted for all government property at the site. These three positions were paid by salary. A fourth position, the navy agent, acted as general purchaser for the navy in all ports and was comparable to the army's quartermaster general. He received a commission of 2 to 2.5 percent on all sums expended. The agents purchased everything the navy needed, from cannons and canvas to food and drink.

When expanding the fleet during the Quasi-War with France, Secretary of the Navy Stoddert scrapped the policy of renting facilities and instead acquired land for six navy yards to build, repair, and service ships. The first yard opened in Washington, DC. Through building in these yards and by using private contractors, and with purchases, acquisitions, and gifts, Stoddert in short order multiplied the navy's size manyfold. During his term, he also secured appropriations and located sites for two ship-repair docks, started construction on a naval hospital, purchased timberland for the navy, and initiated policies to encourage the domestic production of strategic goods such as copper and hemp. The bureaucracy was still simple enough that one talented and energetic individual could usher into existence a new branch of the military.

Stoddert's successors, Robert Smith (1801–1809) and Paul Hamilton (1809–1812), made no basic changes in the supply system but operated under an unfavorable attitude from leading Republicans toward the navy.[46] Beginning in 1801, the Republicans returned funds instead of using them to build docks, sold ships, and consolidated the navy's shore staff. Nonetheless, some building was necessary to implement Jefferson's gunboat policy, keep the navy intact, and meet the needs of the Tripolitan War. This low-grade conflict tested Smith's mettle. To support a naval operation thousands of miles away, he sent regular supply ships to the Mediterranean, established supply bases, appointed navy agents in Gibraltar, Naples, Leghorn, Sicily, and Malta, and set up a payment system in London. In general, these foreign supply operations were well executed.

Hamilton, as Smith's replacement, was less talented than his predecessor, but even he made some gains in reforming the buying patterns of ship captains and in the operations of the Washington Navy Yard. Hamilton, like Smith, suffered from the constant Republican squeeze on naval funding. Both men continued Stoddert's policies of encouraging industries key to the navy's welfare and of helping to finance Robert Fulton's experiments with torpedoes and naval mines.

Smith and Hamilton were never commanding figures, and they presided over retrenchment rather than expansion. In 1812 the navy consisted of only eighteen ships; moreover, the shore establishment was badly neglected and supplies were tight or unavailable. A crash program of expansion would be essential amid the press and confusion of war. Nevertheless, both secretaries were key in devising and implementing policies for selecting and training officers that served the navy so well during the War of 1812.

CORRUPTION, INCOMPETENCE, AND NEGLECT
IN MILITARY SUPPLY, 1789–1812

Military procurement, especially for the army, was plagued by corruption and irresponsibility between 1789 and 1812. No system was worse than the subsistence contracts let by competitive bidding. General Winfield Scott protested that "the interests of the contractor are in precise opposition of those of the troops."[47] Even when troops were in garrison or in forts and free of Indian fighting, the contractor was still a deadly enemy to the rear. The prescribed diet was poor and became worse when soldiers had to go on restricted rations and live off the land because of contractor failures. When food was adequate in quantity, it was frequently spoiled and inedible. Other items of supply could also be bad. Clothing often fell apart with the first rain, shoes and boots could not withstand a sustained march, weapons might or might not work.[48]

During campaigns against the Indians, supply and logistical problems could take on nightmarish proportions. With the St. Clair expedition of 1791, the problems, as usual, began at the top. Secretary of War Henry Knox had a reputation as a good field officer, but he was at best a mediocre administrator, and he allowed personal circumstances to compromise his judgment and ethics in contracting for supplies. Facing insolvency in 1791, Knox teamed up with William Duer, from Robert Morris's circle, who had an unsavory reputation because, among other things, of his performance as a military contractor during the Revolution. Yet Knox disregarded integrity and responsibility by awarding Duer the principal contract for provisioning St. Clair's troops. The results were predictable. Duer received sizable advances but repeatedly failed to deliver provisions as agreed or effectively coordinate his operations. The troops ended up living hand-to-mouth and avoided starvation only by luck. Previously, in the Harmar expedition, incompetent and greedy personnel purposely lost horses to Indians because they and their contractor stood to profit. For most expeditions, supply trains were inadequately guarded against Indian raids, resulting in heavy losses.[49]

Army-supervised operations could fare just as badly as those run by private contractors. Samuel Hodgdon, St. Clair's civilian quartermaster general, was an incompetent who caused an unending series of supply and logistical disasters that helped to undermine the campaign. But the public/private supply structure could be made to work, as Wayne and his civilian quartermaster general indicated in their 1794 expedition. After Fallen Timbers, no major military campaigns in the West occurred before the War of 1812. But from 1801 army supply matters if anything worsened under Jefferson's and Madison's policy of neglecting the military.

Navy supply operations were never as bad as those of the army since the navy had a better supply structure and more capable civilian leaders. The Treasury Department was not involved in navy procurement, sparing it from the divided authority that plagued the army.[50] Moreover, in procuring materials for building ships and in their construction, the navy drew upon the nation's outstanding industry, located principally on the Atlantic Coast where transportation problems were not overwhelming and corruption easier to spot than in isolated frontier areas common to the army. Along this line, Jefferson, over protests from Atlantic ports, concentrated all navy yard work in Washington, claiming that he intended to keep an eye on "plunderers."[51]

The navy, however, never faced the army's grave supply difficulties. The latter's transportation problems were staggering since there were only a few roads and bridges for supplying western outposts. Existing ones were usually neglected and often made impassable by the weather and dangerous by unfriendly Indians. Storage presented further problems because the army lacked the facilities and procedures to protect supplies against neglect, weather, and pests.[52] The lack of an effective, reliable system for inspecting goods was another serious liability.[53] Additionally, funding constituted an ongoing threat to effective purchasing. Tight Federalist budgets became even leaner under the Republican administrations. Consequently, prices offered for feeding troops were low and invited abuse, graft, and corruption, a condition exaggerated manyfold by the frequent sale or subletting of subsistence contracts. Not all contractors were unreliable and rapacious, but the system invited such behavior.[54] Moreover, War Department officials and high-level army officers colluded with corrupt contractors. The Terre aux Boeufs scandal of 1809–1810 involving the notorious Gen. James Wilkinson stands out in that regard but is far from an isolated incident.[55]

Problems involving army supply persisted throughout the period despite repeated congressional investigations and administrative shuffling.[56] A number of points shed light on this perplexing situation. First, because of circumstances, the military was the only area of government spending so plagued by venality. Most federal money went to paying interest on the national debt and salaries, leaving little room for waste and corruption. The 38 percent of federal budgets that the armed services received between 1789 and 1811, not including veterans' pensions and other compensation, was nearly unique in that it involved substantial procurement.[57] Moreover, military spending was not subject to the close congressional control imposed on the other executive departments. The armed services had the largest budgets, the most complex structures, and the most urgent and unpredictable mission. Consequently, both Federalist and Republican administrations prevailed upon Congress to appropriate monies for the military in broad categories with considerable discretion left to the secretaries of war and navy instead of the more typical line-by-line budgeting. Furthermore, the greater the threat to national security, the less scrutiny Congress extended over military appropriations. The principle of controlling the military by dividing authority over it between the executive and legislative branches thus broke down, at least in appropriations, before the proverbial ink on the Constitution was dry.[58]

Second, the country was unprepared for efficiently conducting large-scale procurement. Reliably manufacturing, collecting, and transporting military supplies to frontier armies was beyond the capabilities and experience of most businessmen the government hired.[59] Even the best merchants who were ably led during the Revolutionary War performed unevenly.[60] After independence, most merchants avoided military contracting because of the controversy surrounding it, poor and capricious payment, and so forth. Consequently, the army was often forced to turn to mediocre procurement officials and private contractors who performed poorly and engaged in endless chicanery. The Navy Department, in contrast, performed much better because its supply operations called upon the shipbuilding and shipping industries, in which the nation had great strength, and upon the urban mercantile and manufacturing communities. Stoddert's merchant background served him well, and even the less energetic Republican secretaries of the navy did a passable job.[61]

Third, the armed services had not yet made much professional progress in developing their own institutions, training their own personnel, and inculcating in their officers a corporate sense for guarding the military's interests, growth necessary for supplying the military while minimizing abuse. Merchants had performed army supply functions since colonial days with the mixed results apparent in Robert Morris's operations during the Revolutionary War. Combining military procurement and unchecked marketplace values almost inevitably produced rapacity. Merchants constituted a substantial part of the nation's elite, and their attitudes and activities shaped private and public values, a reality that helps to explain the nation's high tolerance for corruption in military supply during the early years of the republic. Clear lines separating the armed services from the business world were essential for protecting the former.[62]

Even mature military structures could not prevent the millions of dollars spent by the armed services from being influenced by political and commercial interests. The Federalists distributed naval construction and located bases from New Hampshire to Virginia to gain as widespread support for the navy as possible. Naval contractors, forest reserves, and the like were selected with the same purpose in mind.[63] Washington brushed aside the objections of a military engineer and two secretaries of war to pick Harpers Ferry as the site for an arsenal despite its deficiencies.[64] Similarly, Jefferson probably had more in mind than limiting corruption when he concentrated all navy yard activities in Washington. Such an outcome served the economic interests of the fledgling city and the South even though the site was inappropriate for the navy's principal supply center. Practically any growing city in the West, such as Pittsburgh, Cincinnati, and St. Louis, received a large stimulus from merchants and others contracting for or producing goods to meet the military's frontier demands, and they could be relied upon to support continued army expenditures.[65] Hence, decisions about military supply were in part shaped by political and economic considerations even when spending for the armed services was relatively small.

The years from 1789 to 1812 were not seminal ones for the political economy of defense in America. The nation was too absorbed in numerous controversies involving the armed services to focus seriously on matters of supply. Still, the subject received some attention, and consensus appeared evident on several points: private contracting as it operated was unacceptable; the military required greater control over its supply system; and the operations of the Philadelphia Quartermaster Depot and the national arsenals indicated the possibilities of public production for the armed services. Nonetheless, matters of military supply during these years were determined more by drift than design. The War of 1812 underscored the importance of materially providing for the armed services and created conditions for reform in that area.

THE WAR OF 1812

America was deeply divided over the War of 1812; not again until the Vietnam conflict would war with another country create such discord.[66] Dissent climaxed in New England, where the states withheld manpower and resources from Washington, traded with the enemy, and threatened to leave the Union at the Hartford Convention. Since New England was one of the most economically and politically mature regions of the nation, its actions grievously harmed the American war effort.

Republicans also acted to divide the nation. Factionalism grew greatly in the party at the end of Jefferson's second term, primarily over Madison as the president's successor. Once in office, Madison's struggle to avoid hostilities was enormously complicated by continuing party fragmentation.[67] Declaring war against Great Britain in 1812 quieted but did not end divisions among Republicans.[68] Those divisions and conflict between the two parties weakened the country's political structure and its ability to conduct the war. Consequently, the War of 1812 resembled more the chaos of the Revolutionary War than the order of the Union during the Civil War.

War finance illustrates the point. The government badly bungled the effort. Total government war spending was around $119.5 million. Internal taxes covered only about 9 percent of that figure with the tariff and miscellaneous sources accounting for an additional 34 percent, producing $51 million in overall war revenue. The remaining $68.5 million had to be borrowed at very unfavorable terms. Without an adequate banking structure, even handling government accounts became an ordeal. These factors combined with high wartime demand to feed inflationary pressures, which pushed wholesale prices up between 40 and 50 percent.[69]

Prewar patterns set the stage for this dreary outcome. For differing reasons, Federalists and Republicans joined forces in thwarting Secretary of the Treasury Albert Gallatin's attempts beginning in 1807 to raise tariffs and introduce internal taxes to strengthen the nation's ability to finance a possible war.[70] Gallatin received an even greater blow when Senate Republicans in 1811 killed the Bank of the United States (BUS) over his and the president's objections. The bank acted as the federal government's fiscal agent, holding deposits, paying bills, and transferring funds throughout the nation. Moreover, the BUS was a source of credit for the government, its notes circulated as national currency, and it acted to police and assist state banks.[71] The death of the BUS and the outbreak of war led to state banks growing from 88 in 1811 to 246 in 1816 and a threefold increase in note circulation based on less than a doubling of specie reserves, a sure recipe for inflation.[72]

Without a national bank, the Treasury Department had to rely upon state banks to handle wartime finances, which proved to be a chaotic, even disastrous, arrangement. By 1814 the government was dealing with ninety-four banks because most banks would not accept freely the notes of other institutions. Federal bookkeeping became a nightmare, and the government was unable to pay its bills in some states or easily transfer funds from other states to do so.[73]

This makeshift system broke down in 1814. Facing diminishing reserves and a run on scarce specie, banks outside New England suspended specie payments in August and September. Henceforth, the government could neither demand taxes in specie nor sell bonds to raise it. It had to take whatever paper was offered, which reduced drastically the real value of receipts from taxation and borrowing.

The federal government tried to ease financial pressures by augmenting revenue, but its efforts were never enough. Congress finally increased and expanded import duties in July 1812. Receipts rose in 1813 but then dropped off as American trade declined. In July and August 1813 Congress enacted a program of direct and indirect taxes, and with financial conditions deteriorating, the nation's legislators raised and broadened taxes in December 1814 and January 1815. The taxes brought in less than $4 million in 1814 and under $7 million in 1815. Expenditures far exceeded revenue throughout the war years, with 1813 and 1814 being the worst.[74]

The huge shortfall in revenue forced the government to borrow. Between 1812 and 1815 Congress authorized the Treasury to sell government bonds totaling $81 million. They were difficult to move. Only the first issue sold at par, with the rest going for 88 cents or less on the dollar. Most bonds were purchased by banks and wealthy citizens in the Middle States since New England boycotted the loans and the West and South were short on capital. The government received payment in depreciated bank notes and deposits that created the basis for more bank paper and further increased inflationary pressure. As the Treasury periodically approached insolvency, the government reverted to issues of short-term Treasury notes that resembled the paper currency of the Revolutionary War. Between 1812 and 1815 Congress authorized issues totaling $55.5 million, although the maximum in circulation at one time was $18 million. Some of these notes were used as money and also fed inflation. The government ended up receiving the equivalent of $34 million in specie for wartime obligations of $80 million because its securities were discounted and purchased with depreciated paper.[75]

Matters went from bad to worse in May 1813 when the very able Gallatin was driven from office by his numerous Republican enemies and replaced by William Jones and then by George W. Campbell, both of whom proved unequal to the job. Able fiscal leadership returned only when Alexander J. Dallas took office in October 1814.[76]

Overall, war finances were better than during the Revolution. Yet the record was poor, given the national government's authority to tax, raise customs receipts, borrow, and create and regulate banks, powers it generally lacked during the Revolution. Expanded federal authority over the economy remained largely unrealized because political divisions within and between the political parties weakened government. Politics, more than economics, made for a dismal wartime financial record.

Raising manpower for the armies proved to be equally difficult. Politics added to the perennial woes of coaxing men into service. When the United States declared war in June 1812, the nation had slightly under 7,000 regulars scattered along the frontier and the coastline. But by then Congress had authorized a formidable force of over 35,000 federal regulars, 50,000 federal volunteers, and 100,000 men in the state militia.[77]

The size of the wartime militia far exceeded the original call. Nearly 400,000 men served for under six months and another 60,000 over six months. Some militiamen acquitted themselves well, such as New York's forces under Gen. Jacob Brown. More often than not, however, poorly trained and equipped state troops fled before the enemy. Bitter opposition from the states to federal use of their troops exacerbated the militia's inherent weaknesses. New England, with some of the best units, usually repudiated federal calls for troops on constitutional and political grounds. Militiamen from all states claimed constitutional protection in refusing to cross into Canada even in the midst of battle. To defend the capital against advancing British troops, the District of Columbia and neighboring states fielded a paltry 6,000 men. Militia units generally were effective only for short-time service and even then only when commanded by generals such as Brown, William Henry Harrison, and Andrew Jackson, who knew how to win their confidence.[78]

Federal volunteers never exceeded 30,000 since the Madison administration did not push the program because of constitutional scruples. Volunteers were defined as militia by law, with possible limitations on their service. The administration would neither ignore the law nor reclassify the volunteers as federal troops so as to enhance their use.[79]

Without a reliable militia and with only limited numbers of volunteers, the Madison administration depended primarily upon regulars, which turned out to be a risky venture. In the first year of war, only 20,000 of the 35,000 prescribed five-year regulars signed up. To stir enlistment, in 1813 the term of service was dropped from five years to one, the enlistment bounty made more generous, and the authorized size of the force expanded to 60,000. The changes brought in more troops but never up to the quotas set. At the beginning of 1814 the number of regulars may have fallen to the shockingly low level of under 12,000. To complicate matters, troops served for twelve or eighteen months, five years, or the duration of war, depending upon the law under which they entered federal service.[80]

These realities severely limited operations. Early in 1814 Congress desperately and repeatedly passed legislation to fill the ranks of the regular army but with only modest success. After the destruction of the nation's capital, the suspension of specie, and Monroe's elevation to the office of secretary of war, Congress appeared ready for radical measures to get the needed troops. Monroe insisted that a 100,000-man army was essential for defending the coast and invading Canada and that such a force required national conscription.

Predictably, Congress rejected this extreme proposal, electing instead to up the land bounty for enlistees without much promise of better results. Within a few weeks, the Peace of Ghent made the point moot.[81]

Several points stand out in this desperate manpower situation. The militia was not a dependable fighting force. Commanders such as Harrison were necessary to make the state-based system work. More important, a few months of intense, quality training could turn raw recruits into effective soldiers, as Gen. Winfield Scott established at Chippewa and Lundy's Lane. Huge standing armies were unnecessary. Finally, militia, volunteer, or regular troops could never be better than the officers who trained and commanded them. A reliable national army required a system for training and maintaining a high-quality officer corps.[82]

Logistics during the War of 1812 manifested the same weaknesses that had existed since the Constitution and even earlier. Transportation continued to present the greatest difficulties. As in the past, however, supply limitations contributed to military failures but did not prevent successes. Moreover, navy shipbuilding on the Great Lakes and Lake Champlain proved an extraordinary success.

Congress reformed the army's supply system between March and May 1812. Although flawed, the changes were a major step in the right direction. By ending the Treasury Department's involvement in military supply, they concentrated control in the hands of the armed services and established a structure in peacetime that could be adapted for war. The nation's legislators established three supply departments: a Quartermaster's Department to procure general supplies; an Ordnance Department to handle arms, ammunition, and related items; and a Commissary General of Purchases to execute War Department buying. Vague and contradictory statutes overlapped jurisdictions and created confusion, however. Generally speaking, the Commissary General of Purchases bought goods and the other two departments received, transported, and issued them. But so many exceptions were made and conflicting orders issued that no clear supply structure existed during the war years. Like so much of the war effort, improvisation and emergency conditions dictated action more than structure and plan.[83] The reforms failed to create a Subsistence Department; hence, the liabilities of the private contractor were continued. The practice came under such persistent and withering criticism that in 1813 and 1814 Congress was preparing to create a commissariat, but the war ended before that occurred.[84]

Congress followed up on these changes in March 1813 by creating what it called a General Staff. This body was intended to assist the secretary of war in administering his department and included the adjutant and inspector generals, the quartermaster general, the commissary general of ordnance, the paymaster, an assistant to the topographical engineer, and others. These officers resided in Washington and served as the permanent managerial staff for the War Department.[85]

An improved supply structure and a General Staff could not compensate for weak leadership. Madison's first secretary of war, William Eustis (March 1809–January 1813), paid more attention to the details of procurement than to the larger military issues, which added to the problems caused by the aged and mostly ineffective generals Madison selected to lead the army.[86] Growing failure everywhere forced Eustis out and led to his replacement by John Armstrong (January 1813–September 1814). He performed better and left a legacy that included legislation setting up the General Staff and an officer selection process that got rid of many misfits and elevated competent officers such as Brown, Scott, and Jackson. Moreover, he wisely divided the nation into nine military administrative districts to stabilize chaotic conditions instead of attempting centralized control in the midst of war. Regrettably, Armstrong's negatives matched his positives. He constantly plotted to advance his own political fortunes and those of his faction, and he was compulsively drawn to the battlefield where his presence detracted from the war effort. The loss of the capital to the British led to Armstrong's replacement by Monroe (September 1814–March 1815), who seemed to be the leader the department needed, but the war ended before he could take full control.[87]

Leadership in the three newly established supply departments was also wanting. Two quartermasters general lacked either the initiative or the ability to handle effectively their critical roles. Good-to-mediocre talent staffed the two other supply offices. Few left an outstanding record because of personal limitations and the fragmented nature of the supply system. Still, various officers below the chiefs performed excellently and were key to wartime supply operations.[88]

The supply picture improves when the record of war production is considered, especially in the case of weaponry. In sharp contrast to its capacity during the Revolution, the nation was largely self-sufficient in munitions. By 1812 the arsenals at Springfield and Harpers Ferry produced up to 12,000 muskets a year in addition to ammunition, gun carriages, and bayonets. Although musket output dropped off thereafter because of a model change, an ample reserve supplemented by private production ensured a reasonable supply of this basic weapon. Private musket production received a critically important stimulus when Congress in 1808 appropriated $200,000 annually to arm the militia. This measure led to the nation's first long-run arms contracts and created a large arms industry. Private contractors manufactured pistols and cannons as well. Iron was ample to meet wartime demand since the industry continued to grow after the Revolution.[89]

A new industry provided for the country's gunpowder needs. Until the early years of the nineteenth century, the nation had relied almost exclusively on Great Britain for this vital product. By 1810, however, the United States was practically self-sufficient. Some 200 gunpowder mills in sixteen states produced an estimated 1.5 million pounds in that year. The most important manufacturer was E. I. Du Pont de Nemours & Company of Delaware, which began production in 1803. By doubling its capacity during the war, the company manufactured at least half the nation's black powder for the armed services, privateers, and commercial accounts. From the outset, as with firearms and ordnance, the government subsidized Du Pont through orders, high prices for "remaking" powder purchased elsewhere, and other favorable treatment.[90]

The production of clothing was centered at the Philadelphia Depot. Output was improved through a system introduced in 1812 in which 3,000 to 4,000 workers cut cloth for uniforms, let them out to be sewn, and then inspected the finished product. At this facility, supplemented by smaller operations in other parts of the country, up to 3,000 uniforms could be manufactured per week. The army was attempting to duplicate the Philadelphia establishment in Albany when the war ended. Ample cloth should have been readily available since American capacity was considerable and expanding. The textile industry was centered in New England, however, where hostility to the war was greatest and cooperation with Washington the worst. Manufacturers preferred to sell in the rising civilian market rather than to the army. As a result, at least one-quarter and probably more of the cloth bought for the military during the war came from abroad, and the government ended up at times with inferior products.[91]

Shoes, tents, blankets, pots, stoves, entrenching tools, and other army gear were either made by army artisans or acquired through contract. These items were relatively easy to produce since materials and labor were readily available.[92]

Although supplies ranging from weapons to clothing were usually adequate in amounts and quality, protests about severe shortages arose constantly in the army. The problem was in distribution and grew out of a larger failure of planning. The supply bureaus, and especially the Commissary General of Purchases, were unable during hostilities to devise and implement effective methods for property control, including requisition, issue, and inventory. Without a proper system, even shipping the right goods became an ordeal. Much worse, waste, loss, and fraud were rampant as excess supplies were ordered, goods were abandoned, troops discarded equipment and had to be resupplied, and stocks were regularly misplaced or sold as surplus. Military commanders commonly treated depots as sources of unending plenty. If regular channels proved inadequate, they could purchase on the market. Such practices were encouraged by the absence of a reliable system of recordkeeping. Beginning early in 1813, the supply bureaus, the War Department, and Congress struggled to improve the system but without much success.[93]

In the Northwest, transportation constituted the main logistical problem. To supply Gen. William Hull and then General Harrison in 1812 and 1813, goods came from Philadelphia and Pittsburgh and, whenever possible, Ohio and Kentucky. British control eliminated the Great Lakes as a water route. Some rivers and waterways were usable but often flowed the wrong way, were too low in the summer, and could be sledded upon in the winter only when fully frozen. Thus only the tortuous land routes were usually left: hundreds of miles through wilderness on indescribably bad or nonexistent roads, past such obstacles as the notorious Black Swamp of northwestern Ohio. Often only packhorses rather than horse- or ox-drawn wagons could be used. Nearly intractable transportation problems were made many times worse by nonperforming provisions contractors, competing supply agencies driving prices sky-high, officers pocketing funds for critical services, the government providing inadequate or conflicting directions, and units failing to coordinate their activities.[94]

Yet military success still turned more on the quality of command than on the quality of supply. Hull surrendered a fort at Detroit in 1812 well supplied with ammunition and provisions. Somewhat over a year later, Harrison defeated the British and their Indian allies at Thames under conditions worse than those faced by Hull. His logistical staff had been cut and his inadequately lodged troops were short on rations and other items. Unlike Hull, Harrison took the initiative. He asked the citizens of Cincinnati and other towns for provisions when army supply failed and used his troops during the winter to prepare and distribute provisions for the battles ahead.[95]

Since transportation was the principal limiting factor for supply in the Northwest, the Northeastern front should have experienced much better supply conditions. The Niagara area was much closer to the economically advanced sections of the nation and easier to reach overland. Weapons, stores, supplies, and materiel from Philadelphia, New York, Boston, Springfield, and elsewhere were funneled through Albany to the Northern frontier. Yet provisions contracts regularly failed, supplies and weapons arrived late and in insufficient quantities, quality was often execrable, and delayed preparations for winter left troops to face severe weather in linen jackets and improper quarters.[96]

The basic problem in the Northeast was inexperienced and poor leaders. Military units in the Northwest had gained supply experience through Indian campaigns and by maintaining frontier posts, a background missing in the

Northeast. More important, an untried supply structure staffed with generally undistinguished officers was unequal to the challenge. In the Northeast, as in the Northwest, however, quality officers such as Brown and Scott overcame egregious supply failures to acquit themselves well.

The South suffered neglect throughout the war. In trying to defend Washington in summer 1814, Gen. William H. Winder had to assume every role from commander to messenger but had no idea where to buy weapons and supplies. New Orleans was starved for federal funds. Civilian employees went unpaid for months and landlords threatened to toss government goods out of rented warehouses for lack of payment. In his campaigns against the Indians, Gen. Andrew Jackson received little support and had to finance troop provisions himself or rely on private contractors to do so. With Jackson neglecting to requisition goods for the defense of New Orleans, local citizens ended up providing needy troops with clothing and other supplies.[97]

The navy's supply problems were different from those of the army and probably less traumatic. As with the army, the navy entered the War of 1812 less prepared than for any future conflict. But in a sense the navy faced hostilities with greater confidence and abilities. Its officers, unlike the collection of revolutionary relics heading the army, were generally in their thirties, had been well trained, and were tested effectively by the Quasi- and Tripolitan wars. Secretary of the Navy Hamilton served without distinction until December 1812, but his replacement, William Jones (January 1813–December 1814) was qualified for the job through his revolutionary experience as a privateer and long years as a ship owner. Although not without flaws, Jones ably carried out his responsibilities and was the Republican's best secretary of the navy to date. He proved an excellent hands-on manager, cutting costs while improving output and showing a good eye for strategy. Despite his reform efforts, the department remained unchanged except that naval officers replaced civilians as heads of the navy yards.[98]

Although the navy entered the war unprepared, its efficient supply system adjusted readily to the demands of hostilities. At the outbreak of war, the navy consisted of 18 ships and 165 of Jefferson's revered gunboats, only 63 of which were commissioned; the rest were in storage or needing repair. By the war's end, there were 75 ships and 240 gunboats, barges, and other small craft. Though not vast, building and maintenance programs were impressive, given the neglected state of the yards, the lack of dry docks, and the depleted reserves of all supplies, especially ordnance. Personnel, including marines, increased from 5,900 in 1811 to 10,700 at the end of 1814. Besides the six navy yards, the service also had various stations and other facilities stretched out along the Atlantic and Gulf coasts and on lakes Ontario, Erie, and Champlain.[99]

Despite various victories and successes at sea, most of the navy was confined to the humdrum duty of defending America's coastline and ports. Over 60 percent of the navy's wartime manpower served on flotillas and ships of war bottled up by the tight British blockade. The navy organized and supplied this costly and demanding effort with only limited support from New England, the heart of seafaring activity, which placed an additional strain on all aspects of navy supply.[100]

The navy performed most remarkably on the Great Lakes. The United States needed to control these lakes, Lake Champlain, and the St. Lawrence River to invade Canada and capture Montreal. The British had to dominate them to invade the United States through New York or the Mississippi Valley.[101] Since neither nation mastered these crucial waterways, a stalemate ensued. That standoff prevented an American defeat, and the navy played a key role in achieving this critically important end. The first step in that direction occurred when Capt. Isaac Chauncey, the American naval commander for the region, engaged Britain's Sir James Lucas Yeo in a naval-building race on Lake Ontario that started in 1812 and continued through 1814. Since neither established a clear advantage and both lacked fighting instincts, the two held each other at bay.[102] With the critical center in effect frozen, action moved to the periphery. On Lake Erie, in the second step, Lt. Oliver H. Perry destroyed the British fleet commanded by Robert H. Barclay in September 1813, ending any British threat to the Northwest and the Mississippi Valley. The final act came on Lake Champlain. Sir George Prevost's invasion of New York was cut short in September 1814 by his own timidity and by Commandant Thomas Macdonough's mauling of the British flotilla under Capt. George Downie at Plattsburg Bay.

Building the lake fleets constituted the outstanding American logistical feat of the War of 1812. The task facing both sides was extremely difficult because construction took place in the wilderness, entailing horrendous transportation problems. American supply lines were somewhat shorter and therefore easier to maintain. Shipbuilding, supplemented whenever possible by captured, converted, and purchased vessels, occurred on a grand scale and involved huge men-of-war, substantial frigates, and brigs, schooners, and lesser vessels. The smallest fleet on Lake Erie consisted of only two brigs and the usual collection of smaller vessels. It was built in a remarkable effort directed by Capt. Daniel Dobbins and Noah and Adam Brown. An elaborate supply line ran from Philadelphia to Pittsburgh to the lake. Early in 1814 the extraordinary Brown brothers moved their operations to Vergennes, Vermont, a shipbuilding center on Lake Champlain. In a few months, they constructed nearly a dozen ships and gunboats and repaired others to strengthen Macdonough's makeshift fleet.

The largest building program took place at Sackett's Harbor, Chauncey's headquarters on Lake Ontario. Chauncey's exceptional talents for organization and logistics, along with the superb skills of his builder Henry Eckford, permitted the construction of ten vessels mounting 16 to 74 guns in addition to the unlaunched 110-gun *New Orleans*. The principal supply line for this wilderness naval station ran as far south as New York City.

Chauncey had the total confidence of Secretary Jones and the full support of the department's supply structure, which facilitated the enormous stream of supplies, equipment, artisans, sailors, and marines flowing to the Northern lakes as the navy built and maintained ships and facilities using timber from the surrounding forests. Whenever possible, the service used water routes, but a great deal of materiel was hauled overland during the winter freeze or in the summer on parched ground.

Of the navy's 10,700 men in October 1814, 3,250 served on the lakes. Jones estimated that 7,000 would be needed in 1815 when England was expected to redirect the flow of soldiers and sailors to the American front after the fighting ceased in Europe. The nation would have had extreme difficulty mustering such forces. Service on the lakes was extremely unpopular because of the harsh and primitive conditions, and much of the navy operated with a skeletal staff due to recruitment problems. The Navy Department had stripped the coastal fleet of men and equipment in order to staff the North. The effective decommissioning of many of the coastal defenses permitted widespread British raiding on the Atlantic Coast. Secretary Jones and his naval commanders took enormous political heat because of the relatively undefended state of the coast, but they never wavered from their commitment to defending the critical Northern border.

Chauncey orchestrated the logistics of the Northern lake campaigns, but his genius did not encompass battlefield skills. One scholar compares him with the Civil War's Gen. George B. McClellan: both were great builders and organizers but not fighters.[103] Chauncey saved his command and avoided military disaster because Jones tolerated his timidity and because his British counterpart, Yeo, was equally reluctant to risk his fleet. When the critical battles did take place, Perry and Macdonough proved equal to the challenge, but only after Chauncey provided them, against all odds, with what Charles O. Paullin calls the "instruments and sinews of war."[104] The accomplishment seems even greater since the principal sources of supply were in the Northeast, where New England actively aided the enemy and the other states were unenthusiastic about the war. The navy also managed to minimize competition with the army, which was building boats to transport troops, because the two services used the same builder to supervise their frantic construction projects.

The numerous logistical failures during the War of 1812 grew from the larger limitations of the nation's civilian leadership. There was never a well-defined strategy, only general notions about defensive and offensive operations, which precluded effective planning for supply and left too much to improvisation and even chance.

The weakness started at the highest level and was also ultimately resolved there. Madison's leadership was generally wanting. But the president's abilities grew during hostilities, and he brought in new secretaries of war and navy to improve the conduct of the war. More important, despite the setbacks, the president never panicked. That modest nobility of character steadied and encouraged the nation during repeated crises.[105] Through perseverance the nation held off the world's leading military power in a war of attrition, forced a peace settlement that retained the status quo, and humbled and destroyed what had become a party of treason at home. In the final analysis, Madison's leadership withstood the test of war.

The four factors shaping the political economy of warfare explain the confused economic mobilization for the War of 1812. The weakness of the effort grew chiefly from the political area and its effects upon civil-military relations rather than from the economic structure or the technology of war.

The economy had advanced considerably since the Revolution. Consequently, the nation was able to produce almost all supplies for the armed services, even in the demanding areas of weaponry and gunpowder, either through private or public sources or a combination of the two. Transportation remained a problem, but effective leadership could overcome that obstacle, as the Navy Department demonstrated in its supply operations around the Great Lakes. Since the technology of war was still relatively unsophisticated, the stress on the economy came from greater demand, not from the need for economic conversion. Therefore, the existing executive structure, and particularly the Treasury, War, and Navy departments, handled mobilization without the need for new agencies.

The existing executive departments generally failed to handle economic mobilization well because the strengthened federal government provided for in the Constitution had not adequately matured. In part, time and experience were essential for new governmental systems to work well. However, basic disputes between and within the Federalist and Republican parties over the nature of government and the nation's foreign policy contributed significantly to the federal government's weakness. Those intense differences became most divisive before and during the war, with a number of adverse consequences for economic mobilization. States alienated by the war—primarily but not exclusively in New England—defied Washington's call for men, supplies, and money. Further, the Treasury Department's efforts soundly to finance the war were undermined. Most comprehensively, civil-military relations were fundamentally affected. The armed services had been kept small and undeveloped because of the extreme controversy surrounding them, leaving the War and Navy departments, the most important mobilization agencies, unprepared for hostilities.

The War Department faced the most strain because it was larger, grew faster, and had the greatest responsibility. With the militia unreliable and regulars hard to recruit, the army had enormous difficulty in raising troops. Moreover, it had to rely upon a new, untried, and flawed structure for supplying and administering vastly expanded forces in the midst of hostilities. Not surprisingly, the army's overall wartime performance was poor. The Navy Department did much better as a military and mobilization agency because it was less controversial than the army and it drew upon the strength of the formidable maritime industry. Its responsibilities were fewer, its prewar structure superior, and its wartime leaders better.

Many of the same national divisions that had kept the military services small and undeveloped before hostilities had also led to the nation's drifting into war in a shocking state of unpreparedness. Hence, much of the criticism of the Republican military policies is ahistorical at best, illogical at worst.[106] Without a reasonable level of unity, the new nation was unable to devise fully coherent and consistent foreign or military policies. The outcome of the war acted to temper the nation's intense ideological divisions and freed it for nearly a century from involvement in international warfare. Under those more stable conditions, the nation was able to work out for the armed services more mature policies and structures.

PART TWO
ECONOMIC MOBILIZATION FOR WAR: THE TRANSITIONAL STAGE

Mobilizing the economy for war was easiest in the transitional stage and was generally carried out well. Economic, political, and military institutions matured during this period, and military technology did not change in any fundamental way. Thus the existing executive departments could handle economic mobilization, relying upon market forces. There was neither the need for elaborate regulatory mechanisms nor the widespread practice of businessmen serving simultaneously as private citizens and public officials or military officers, as had occurred in the preindustrial stage and would occur again in the industrial stage.

During the antebellum period, the economy, and particularly industry, grew rapidly but remained rigorously competitive. Both the army and navy began to professionalize and to develop a corporate sense. Although the optimal size, scope, and strength of the federal government continued to be a source of dispute, Washington had substantial real and potential powers, especially in the case of the executive. Those powers were enhanced by a vigorous two-party system that channeled growing democratic forces in a still essentially elitist society.

The consequences of these developments for the political economy of warfare were evident during the Mexican War. President James K. Polk directed the war from Washington with the War, Navy, and Treasury departments acting as mobilization agencies; the economy met all requirements without strain or regulation; and the military services performed with exceptional skill.

During the long and nearly total Civil War, the Union dwarfed the efforts achieved in the Mexican War. The Northern states carried much of the burden of economic mobilization in the first year of hostilities. Abraham Lincoln's administration had to rebuild the federal government, which had

71

become debilitated by a decade of sectional strife. Once Washington had its house in order, however, the War, Navy, and Treasury departments gradually worked out the policies for managing war mobilization under the general guidance of the president. The North's strong economy supplied the enormous demands of war without difficulty and, except for the railroad and telegraph systems, with the market as regulator.

Since the Confederacy actually remained in the preindustrial stage, its methods of economic mobilization varied substantially from those of the Union. Underdevelopment forced the South in effect to plan its economy, an approach that produced some brilliant achievements but many more shortcomings—notably unsound finances, poor management of transportation, and inadequate tapping of resources outside the South. Mobilizing the Southern economy was a general failure, one that contributed significantly to the defeat of the Confederacy.

Economic mobilization was among the most important challenges faced by the Union and the Confederacy. It is, therefore, an excellent gauge of political leadership. After the first year of hostilities, the Lincoln administration made no major missteps in harnessing the economy. In contrast, the Jefferson Davis administration never mastered the means for economic mobilization and began to lose control of the process no later than mid-1863. The difference between the two sections stemmed largely from the nature of an elitist system operating within a democratic framework. That of the North was reasonably representative, flexible, and responsive; the South's, however, was increasingly exclusive, inflexible, and unresponsive. Political parties helped both to shape and reflect those realities. Accordingly, in the Union, the Republican and Democratic parties thrived; in the Confederacy, political parties in general disappeared. In form, therefore, the Union and the Confederacy shared political traditions and institutions; in substance, they differed massively.

4

THE POLITICAL ECONOMY OF WARFARE: 1815–1860

Economic mobilization for the Mexican War (1846–1848) was as accomplished as the effort for the War of 1812 was flawed. Indeed, harnessing the economy for America's offensive, but limited, war against Mexico anticipated the Union's outstanding performance during the Civil War. Nearly ideal conditions for economic mobilization emerged during the transitional stage for the political economy of warfare, extending from around 1815 through 1860. Political, economic, and military institutions matured while the technology of war remained relatively static. Thus Washington could mobilize the economy by using existing governmental agencies instead of creating new ones and by relying on market forces instead of expanding governmental regulation. Recasting the argument, political, economic, and military elites perfected and professionalized their structures so that they could be effectively and easily interrelated for purposes of war mobilization during a period when military technology was still relatively unsophisticated.

THE POLITICAL STRUCTURE

The federal government, particularly the executive branch, grew in size and strength between 1815 and 1860. Numerous and ongoing political controversies prevented Washington from fully and consistently developing and exercising its powers, however. Nonetheless, Andrew Jackson and James K. Polk demonstrated that strong presidents could make the federal government work effectively.

Americans experienced a short interlude of glowing nationalism after 1815. Presidents James Madison and James Monroe embraced the Federalist program of stimulating and regulating national economic growth through Henry

Clay's American System, and Secretary of State John Quincy Adams led in giving the nation a continental reach. The Panic of 1819 and the ensuing depression, combined with the slavery issue raised by Missouri's statehood, put a quick end to this superficial sense of unity and confidence. Thereafter, interest-group, class, and sectional differences, complicated by ethnicity, culture, and religion, divided Americans. Rapid and unsettling economic and physical growth was the root cause of this discord—discord that was magnified significantly by democratization.[1]

The two-party system was crucial for holding the nation together in the storm of change. With the first party system undermined after 1815 and another one not yet established, America approached political paralysis by 1824. Jackson's election in 1828 gave birth to the Democracy, made up of disparate groups favoring limits on national government.[2] The president's bank war,[3] rhetoric against internal improvements, and efforts to reduce tariffs combined to create in the 1830s a vigorous opposition in the Whig party.[4] In time, the two parties helped to unify the divided nation because they were national in scope with support in all regions and among all classes. Although they differed over political economy, the Whigs dedicated to federal activism in furthering economic growth and the Democrats taking a dimmer view of such initiatives, the two parties agreed on basic matters. Both were relatively conservative, stressing entrepreneurial capitalism, social mobility, and political democracy. Moreover, over time both parties adopted a pragmatic, opportunistic stance, emphasizing different views in different parts of the country to satisfy their constituents. Points of conflict between the parties diminished as the Democrats in the 1840s became more supportive of the national government's promoting economic growth.[5]

The unifying role of parties began to break down in the 1850s as slavery became a burning issue that, unlike political economy, could not be compromised. That development ultimately destroyed the second party system and created the third, in which regional parties dominated. The bonds of union were lost, plunging the nation into sectional strife and civil war.[6]

Political parties, democratization, and elite rule interacted dynamically during the antebellum period. Richard L. McCormick designates the years from the 1830s to the end of the nineteenth century as the "party period in American history." During those years, in contrast to the periods before and after, parties dominated the political process in terms of mobilizing voters and shaping governmental policy. Political parties, therefore, acted as a bridge between the electorate and government. These were modern, mass-based political parties designed to channel electoral numbers and energy as universal white-male suffrage spread. Here was born the characteristic nineteenth-century politics of hoopla, showmanship, oratory, and demagoguery, which turned out an average of 75 percent of eligible voters in presidential elections.[7]

Mass-based political parties acted to maintain rather than to threaten elite rule—no mean feat. The so-called Age of the Common Man saw sharpening class lines and probably the most extreme economic stratification the nation has ever experienced.[8] Under these more challenging circumstances, the party system kept viable America's elitist-democratic duality by co-opting or marginalizing parties of dissent and allowing the two major parties to obscure basic issues, position themselves in the ideological center, and uphold the status quo.[9] As a result, between 1815 and 1860 political parties and government from the local to the national level generally continued to be dominated by the wealthy and by individuals in prestigious occupations.[10] At the highest levels of the national government, elite representation varied according to party, administration, and stage of economic development.[11] The same pattern occurred in regions, states, and localities as elites by necessity adjusted to a society of almost perpetual change in order to maintain their rule. When elites failed to adapt to major trends in society or divided over them, the outcome could be catastrophic, as documented by the Civil War.

During the party period, the federal executive could be strong even though that was not usually the case. Congress often predominated at the national level, and local and state governments were more active because their populations were more homogenous, enabling them to adjust to the needs of a limited geographical area. Nonetheless, prestige and power were shifting to Washington as the nation grew and governmental responsibilities increased. The two parties reinforced this trend. Although they reached down to the local, state, and regional levels, their ultimate aim was to control government at the federal level. Increasingly, the political parties focused on the four-year cycle of electing the president. Throughout the period the executive departments also grew in size and bureaucratic sophistication.[12] Thus, a strong, determined president could not only assert national over state power but could also take the initiative from Congress at the federal level, an outcome that transpired under Andrew Jackson.

These trends were of the greatest importance for the political economy of warfare. Successfully mobilizing the economy required a strong president leading a powerful national government. Polk came close to filling that bill. Abraham Lincoln, by mastering both party and government, met the demands even more successfully during the Civil War.

THE ECONOMIC STRUCTURE

Economic growth throughout the nineteenth century was high and sustained. As a result, by 1840 the United States was roughly equal in terms of per capita and total product to Great Britain and France, the leading economic powers of Europe.

Unlike in the past, domestic, not foreign, commerce propelled the economy forward between 1816 and 1860. Initial market expansion occurred principally within sections, not among them. After 1840, as the nation's economy reached higher levels of development, intersectional trade became increasingly important as a motor of growth. This trade expanded gradually and created a greater degree of sectional specialization, although the adjustment was not complete before the Civil War. Though never monolithic, cotton predominated in the South; wheat, corn, and livestock in the West; and commerce and industry in the Northeast. The latter region, where urban centers were growing rapidly, was the linchpin of this intersectional trade.[13] Only after the Civil War would industrialization, as opposed to internal commerce, become the principal impetus for growth.[14]

Improvements in transportation and communication played a critical role in the expansion of trade. Between 1790 and 1860 the transportation system was transformed by stages that began with turnpikes,[15] continued with steamboats[16] and canals,[17] and culminated in railroads.[18] Public assistance to the railroads was substantial, totaling one-quarter to one-third of overall outlays before the Civil War. By comparison, the turnpikes and steamboats received only indirect government support, and states built most of the canals. Telegraph systems were also of great importance. Government assistance launched the system in 1844; thereafter, private investors installed 50,000 miles of telegraph lines by 1860, making possible simultaneous communication among all parts of the settled nation.[19]

The transportation and communication developments cumulatively constituted a revolution. They integrated what was probably the world's largest market, freeing it of virtually all barriers to trade. That advance created the basis for promoting both intraregional and interregional trade, increasing the specialization of economic functions, and boosting production of more goods from all regions and sectors of the economy.

Since the nation was still overwhelmingly agrarian before the Civil War, farming played a key role in the growth of the antebellum economy.[20] Between 1800 and 1860 the number of farms and total farm output increased between six and seven times, and in 1860 agriculture accounted for about three-fifths of total commodity output. By then, at least half the agrarian population had become specialized, rather than subsistence or unspecialized, farmers. The growth of cotton culture in the South was the most important agricultural development in the antebellum period. Cotton shaped and dominated the South, ensured the growth of the plantation-slavery system, and provided the nation's principal export commodity for several decades. Northern agriculture had greater diversity and was dominated by the increasingly market-oriented family farm. In the Midwest wheat and corn became the primary crops and livestock-raising assumed a large scale. Older agricultural areas turned to sheep-raising, truck gardening, dairying, and the like and diversified otherwise. Overall, the West grew in conjunction with the Northeast, and the two regions developed deep-seated patterns of economic interdependence. The South, in contrast, maintained an ingrown quality that set the stage for the Civil War.

Despite agriculture's impressive gains, industry was becoming the primary drivewheel of the economy.[21] Agriculture accounted for 72 percent of commodity output in 1839 but only 56 percent in 1859; industry's share rose from 17 to 32 percent over the same period. In the years between 1790 and 1860, the United States was well on its way to becoming a modern, industrial society. Industrialization involved enormous gains in manufacturing productivity, achieved through improved technology, steam as a power source, and the factory system maximizing these advances. The United States had a comparative advantage in primary industries, such as textiles, food, and spirits, which were key to industrialization.

America's premier antebellum industry was cotton textiles. Output of cotton cloth steadily increased between 1815 and 1860. Woolen textiles also advanced but at a much slower rate. Flour and meal, like textiles, could have been high-technology industries beginning in the early nineteenth century, but except for a few urban areas, the industry was scattered and characterized by small mills. A similar situation existed in meat packing. Iron, a basic commodity in which the nation excelled in the eighteenth century, was surprisingly slow to respond to the technological innovation that pushed Great Britain to the forefront. America's iron industry began to increase in size, integration, and technological sophistication only from the 1840s onward.

The nation's industrial development was concentrated in the Northeast. By 1860 that section had over 70 percent of total manufacturing capacity; about 20 percent was in the Midwest and less than 10 percent was in the South. The contiguous states of New York, Pennsylvania, Massachusetts, Ohio, Connecticut, and New Jersey constituted the country's manufacturing belt. The first three alone accounted for roughly half of manufacturing value added and contained the centers of the textile, shoe and boot, clothing, iron, and machinery industries. Yet manufacturing did exist throughout the nation, and the greatest output in some industries, such as flour milling, meat packing, and leather, took place west of the Alleghenies.

The maturing economy further specialized economic functions and benefited from their operations as was clearly evident with financial intermediaries and particularly commercial banks. With the death of the Second Bank of the United States in 1836, followed by the creation of the Independent Treasury System in the 1840s, the national government surrendered commercial banking almost totally to the states and abandoned any attempt at central banking. This retreat resulted in another era of rapid growth in state banks, a further expansion of bank notes, and a bewildering variety of banking regulation.[22] Other financial intermediaries also existed in the first half of the nineteenth century, such as savings banks and insurance companies; however, the investment bank, involved in trading securities, was the most important and grew in tandem with the railroads.[23]

Various other institutional adjustments in the antebellum period also signaled the growing sophistication of the economy. In distribution, for example, the specialized wholesaler replaced the general merchant as an intermediate step to the dominance of the mammoth corporation of the late nineteenth century.[24] And although industry in general had not significantly advanced managerial techniques, the railroads as the first big business introduced and began perfecting the modern corporate form for managing efficiently multimillion-dollar enterprises.[25]

Government in the nineteenth century did not play a major role in the ebb and flow of the economy, principally because its size and operations were comparatively small. Indeed, facing sectional, class, and interest-group conflicts that racked the nation and lacking a mandate for an activist role, Washington became increasingly passive in the exercise of its economic powers in the three or more decades before the Civil War.[26] As federal passivity grew, however, the expenditures of state and local governments increased in the 1830s as they moved to satisfy the needs of an expanding nation. The increase was most evident in internal improvements, especially canal building. States also began to regulate banks, railroads, and insurance companies and sought to improve agriculture.[27]

The American System of Manufactures constituted the nation's most important long-run contribution to the growth of its own and the international economy. This process entailed the mechanized mass production of standardized commodities using interchangeable parts. The system was devised and perfected under the Ordnance Department's direction for producing a limited number of small arms. It then moved to the civilian sector with patent revolvers and rifles and finally tapped mass consumer markets through wooden and brass clocks and other goods.[28]

Two critical matters stand out in the adoption and refinement of the American System of Manufactures. First, as Werner Sombart and other scholars have pointed out, the peculiar nature of military requirements anticipated the demands of industrial society.[29] The armed forces' quest for standardization, uniformity, and regularity in all aspects of their structure and operations preceded similar imperatives from the civilian economy. Second, development of the system required government subsidies. Private manufacturers had neither the capital nor the motivation to pursue on their own the painstaking and expensive effort required. The Ordnance Department, however, wanted high quality and uniform arms with interchangeable parts and was willing to pay to get them. Ironically, the department never required enough weapons to develop the system in terms of economies of scale; that move was left to private firms concentrating on profits.

America's innovations in armament production began at the national arsenals, created at Springfield, Massachusetts, in 1794 and Harpers Ferry in 1798. The arsenals were strongly influenced by the French, who in the late eighteenth century manufactured standardized musket locks with interchangeable parts using hand tools. From 1794 onward, the arsenals, especially the one at Springfield, made important strides toward the American System. Beginning in 1798, however, their work was combined with that of private contractors. With the threat of war with France growing and the arsenals not yet geared up for large-scale production, the War Department contracted with Eli Whitney, among others, for muskets and with Simeon North for pistols. These contracts provided for cash advances which the contractors needed to fulfill their obligations, an arrangement that became a standard department method for underwriting production. Legend aside, North, not Whitney, understood and made major contributions to the mass-production method in his various contracts with the government by dividing labor and inventing special-purpose machinery.[30]

The American System would have evolved slowly and erratically had it been left to individual contractors. Instead, the Ordnance Department between 1815 and the 1840s made its most important contribution to that system by taking charge of perfecting the mechanized mass production of weapons with interchangeable parts. Colonel Decius Wadsworth, the first chief of ordnance, his principal assistants, and a group of West Point–trained officers led the way. In mid-1815 they set a goal of uniform production of the new Model 1816 musket, first by the arsenals and then by all private contractors manufacturing for the War Department. Standardized weapons would simplify supply and train-ing, ensure quality, and facilitate repair.

By 1819 the Springfield Arsenal had made substantial progress toward its goal through a three-step process: first, an elaborate system of gauging for all stages of production and inspection to ensure interchangeable parts; second, the division of labor to facilitate mass output; and third, the use of specialized tools and machinery to achieve full factory production. The three steps evolved at once, not as separate developments. Harpers Ferry had great diffi-culty implementing the transition from shop to factory output, however.

By the mid-1840s the arsenals and private contractors could produce a con-tinuous supply of high quality, uniform small arms with interchangeable parts. In a few decades, Ordnance had laid the foundations of the American System of Manufactures. Private contractors such as North, Thomas Blanchard, and John H. Hall, working with the department and the arsenals, played a criti-cal role in introducing and perfecting the specialized machinery at the heart of the American System. The Ordnance Department was at the center of what Nathan Rosenberg labels "technological convergence."[31] To achieve total uni-formity in small-arms output, the chief of ordnance insisted that the Spring-field and Harpers Ferry arsenals and private contractors establish a fully open relationship on all aspects of operations, machinery, drawings, and patterns; thus, knowledge of the advanced technology was rapidly diffused. The process was accelerated even more by the machine tool industry, which small-arms production had helped to create.

The Ordnance Department completed its major work with private contrac-tors by the 1840s, reducing the number of contracts and finally phasing them out. Before long, many of the original contractors such as North went out of business. Often poor businessmen, they were dependent on Ordnance Depart-ment contracts for long-term solvency. The traditions and methods of the pub-lic/private arms makers were picked up by patent weapons firms such as Colt's Patent Firearms Manufacturing Company, who acted as "crystallizers of [this] nascent technology."[32] Modern production methods were then adopted by the clock, lock, nail, and numerous other manufacturers catering to civilian markets.

Although the Ordnance Department concentrated its modern manufac-turing efforts in small arms, it also made considerable headway in achieving uniformity in artillery output. To do so, the department engaged in research and development in metallurgy, foundry techniques, and explosives as well as applying and adapting the design, gauging, inspection, and production meth-ods established for small arms.[33]

The army also influenced modern management methods, although these accomplishments were much less tangible and important. To achieve and sustain uniformity in arms manufacture, the Ordnance Department pioneered in various modern management methods, such as sophisticated bookkeeping, quality-control techniques, and the use of middle managers, which were systematized in detailed, published regulations. The army's line and staff structure also may have provided a model for the railroads' management innovations in the antebellum years. More directly, between the late 1820s and the 1850s, officers on leave or in retirement from the Corps of Engineers, such as William G. McNeill, helped survey, build, and operate the early railroads. No doubt such men carried the army's organizational structures and management techniques to the railroads and helped adapt them to civilian uses. Whether civilian businessmen would have devised their own methods quickly and efficiently without the army's influence is unclear.[34]

Although the Ordnance Department's advances in weapons production was important for the political economy of warfare, the general growth of the economy was even more significant. Military technology was still relatively basic. Small arms and ordnance were among the few military items requiring a long lead time and special facilities to produce. Most of military demand depended upon the general, not the specialized, capacity of the economy. The overall expansion of the economy, including improvements in transportation, distribution, and finances, ensured that the demand of the armed services could be met during hostilities if the political and military system operated effectively. That development occurred prior to the Mexican War as the armed services grew in size and bureaucratic sophistication along with the federal executive.

THE MILITARY STRUCTURE, 1815–1846

The War of 1812 ended for the foreseeable future the threat of foreign intervention in American affairs, a luxury new to the republic. Hostilities with Indians, small nations, and pirates were relatively minor. During these peaceful decades, the military, and particularly the army, began a professionalizing process that waxed and waned over time but remained permanent. The most prominent and visible changes in the army occurred between 1817 and 1825 under Secretary of War John C. Calhoun.

Calhoun was the department's first secretary of genuine ability, even genius.[35] He has appropriately been compared to Alexander Hamilton at the Treasury. Like Hamilton, Calhoun overwhelmed Congress with reports on nearly every aspect of military operations.[36] His years of experience in Congress and his native executive talents, combined with the palpable need for change and the work of predecessors, enabled Calhoun to implement numerous reforms.[37] The postwar nationalistic fervor also helped. Unlike that of past executives, Calhoun's work had a comprehensive rather than a piecemeal quality.

Calhoun's reforms drew heavily upon the ideas of the new generations of officers who had risen to the middle and upper ranks of the army during the War of 1812, such as Gen. Jacob Brown. The most immediate and important task facing the secretary of war and his aides was expanding and regularizing the General Staff created by statute in 1813 and confirmed in 1816. In 1818 Calhoun secured passage of legislation that reorganized the General Staff according to his views. The eight supply and administrative bureaus, such as the Quartermaster Department and the Office of the Adjutant General (separated from the Inspector General's Office in 1821), were centered in Washington and acted as the apparatus through which the secretary of war managed the army. Of critical importance was the Subsistence Department, which Calhoun created to end the pernicious system of private contractors feeding the troops. A Medical Department was also added. The secretary of war carefully selected bureau heads, won their loyalty, and kept them in charge throughout his years in office. Calhoun or the bureau heads then wrote regulations for conducting bureau affairs, detailed procedures that were ultimately incorporated in the *General Regulations for the Army* and that provided specific rules for governing almost all aspects of army life. One scholar calls the collection "the first comprehensive management manual published in the United States."[38]

Although substantial, the changes did not give the secretary of war command of the fighting forces. To accomplish that end, Calhoun in 1821 ordered General Brown, the army's senior ranking officer, to Washington and designated him commanding general. In theory, Calhoun had created a balanced military organization. The bureaus, acting as a General Staff, provided technical and administrative expertise for managing the army. Through the commanding general, the secretary directed the fighting forces. Thus the secretary of war centralized responsibility and authority over the army, and he in turn answered to the president. Civilian control over the army was ensured.

Prior to the Civil War, theory matched practice only under Calhoun. A commanding figure, he dominated the structure he had created. Both the General Staff and the commanding general looked to him for guidance and to settle any conflict that developed between them. Circumstances changed after 1825, however. Most secretaries of war were weak, inexperienced, or unconcerned about the duties of the office. Consequently, power gravitated to the people managing the War Department on a day-to-day basis: the supply and administrative bureaus and particularly the Adjutant General's Office. This development was undesirable since the bureaus did not act as a corporate body. Instead, concentrating on their specialties, they became virtually independent fiefdoms with staffs who jealously guarded their prerogatives. Over time the bureaus also became nearly invulnerable because their chiefs and other officers served for life in the nation's capital, established close congressional ties, and developed superb bureaucratic skills. The average secretary of war could not control the bureaus and relied upon the Adjutant General's Office to carry out his duties.

Although the bureaus at times fought among themselves and with the secretary of war, their real or perceived rival was the commanding general. The bureaus insisted that they answered only to the secretary of war, not to him, and that their personnel serving with the troops took orders only from the bureau chiefs, not from field commanders. These claims raised vitally important practical and constitutional issues. To command the army effectively, the commanding general had to have authority over both the line and staff—otherwise, he could not reliably carry out his functions. But if the commanding general in fact commanded all branches of the army, he would usurp the authority of the secretary of war as the president's deputy over the land forces, which would be unconstitutional. If the commanding general did not act unconstitutionally, however, his office was in effect useless. The critical matter of command was further complicated because statute law confirmed the secretary of war's authority over the army and even recognized the role of the supply and administrative bureaus but did not set out the powers of the commanding general. The latter's authority and functions were addressed in vague and contradictory ways in various orders, reports, and regulations of the secretary of war, the commanding general, and Congress. Calhoun's rather casual creation of the commanding general's office raised so many fundamental constitutional issues that all interested parties shied away from attempting to resolve them with finality and by law. Practice dictated what the army's senior officer did or did not do.

This solution was unsatisfactory, a fact highlighted by developments between 1853 and 1857. A running feud between Secretary of War Jefferson Davis and Commanding General Winfield Scott led the latter to move his office to New York, commanding only his own staff. In practice, neither the secretary of war nor the commanding general could command the army alone. Relying on compatibility, as had been the case with Calhoun and Brown, meant trusting the nation's fate to chance and opening the way for the bureaus to dominate the army with potentially disastrous results. Strong presidents could make the system work, as occurred during the Mexican and

Civil Wars. Nonetheless, national security required a system that ensured proper command of the army while maintaining the civilian control provided for in the Constitution. Such a structure was not devised until the early twentieth century.

Flaws notwithstanding, Calhoun's reforms created a system of supply and administration that, for the first time, met the army's immediate and long-term needs. Step by step beginning in 1817, military management became increasingly professionalized. The bureaus and various special boards functioned in a way that met the needs of the line despite the inadequacies of command. Regularity, continuity, and predictability improved supply operations immeasurably. Though civilian contractors still had a role in feeding and transporting troops, they were better policed by strengthened bureaus and their numerous drawbacks made less consequential.[39]

Calhoun's reforms also involved the line, and none exceeded in significance his proposal for a skeleton peacetime army. When Congress in 1820 directed the secretary of war to plan for reducing the size of the army, he responded with a report that was perhaps "one of the most important military papers in American history."[40] In it, Calhoun made his proposal for an "expansible army," basing his recommendation on the advice of senior officers and on ideas that reached back to George Washington.

Calhoun insisted that regulars should become the principal fighting force, with the militia reduced to an auxiliary position. To ensure preparedness for war, any cuts in the army's size should be restricted to enlisted men. The officer corps, especially the staff, should be kept at full force, and all wartime formations maintained with reduced ranks. In time of emergency, this army could quickly be expanded two- or threefold with the existing or enlarged number of officers. Such a structure could absorb and professionalize recruits in a relatively brief period of time.[41]

Congress did not adopt Calhoun's plan as such. But he and his advisers made headway because then and in the future the army retained more officers relative to its size than had previously been the case. More important, a secretary of war for the first time had proposed subordinating the role of the militia and elevating the regulars. Calhoun's proposal made sense because Scott had shown the potential of quickly trained recruits during the War of 1812. The ideal of an expansible army became orthodoxy after the Civil War and was adapted in the twentieth century to provide mass armies for fighting abroad.

Calhoun's efforts to rationalize the army/War Department structure turned on the quality of the officer corps. Consequently, the secretary of war played an important role in improving training and fostering professionalism. His most significant contribution involved the U.S. Military Academy (USMA). Captain Sylvanus Thayer became superintendent of the academy just before Calhoun took office. With the latter's full support, Thayer turned a moribund school for training engineers into a high-quality institution for educating cadets for the military profession. Dennis Hart Mahan, whom Thayer had nurtured, played an important part in developing the curriculum. His *Out-Post* (1847) and his student Henry Wager Halleck's *Elements of Military Art and Science* (1846) constituted America's first modern studies of war. The appearance of the *Army and Navy Chronicle* and other periodicals signaled further progress in professionalization. Recognizing that West Point, an under-graduate institution, was only the beginning of reform, Calhoun initiated graduate study, which led him to create the Artillery School of Practice in 1824 and the Infantry School of Practice a few years later. These schools, like the periodicals, did not last long or accomplish all that they might have, but they were the beginning of military modernization.

Under professionalizing trends, the army officers corps took on corporate characteristics that endured throughout the nineteenth century. Long-term service became the norm as system replaced politics in selecting officers. Appointment to West Point was regularized as was the process of evaluating cadets. Though some officers continued to be appointed without USMA training, they were a distinct minority. Moreover, the officer corps became more homogenous. The typical cadet came from the respectable, politically influential middle- and upper-middle-class and, like his navy counterpart, may have been facing diminishing economic security; few came from the ranks of the wealthy business and agricultural interests. Further, the officer corps was becoming increasingly nonpartisan. Army officers continued to interact with civilians in numerous ways, and they turned to politics to advance their own interests or that of their branch or the service as a whole, but they did so as professionals, not as partisans. A military career and battlefield prominence could lead to political office also, but that was an individual choice and accomplishment, not a professional one. Indeed, the acceptance of civilian supremacy became a touchstone of the professional soldier. Overall, the army officer corps took on attributes and attitudes that set it off from the civilian world and gave it a corporate sense.

Between the War of 1812 and the Civil War, then, the army made great strides in professionalization that paralleled and often exceeded similar trends in the political and economic systems.[42] Calhoun's reforms addressed the crucial issues concerning the military in American society: how to raise an army, how to administer and command it, and how to maintain civilian control over it. After the War of 1812 the common militia never again played a significant role in raising mass armies for the nation and virtually ceased to exist. The volunteer militia remained viable but came increasingly under the control of the regulars. An expansible army, in which regulars would serve as cadre for fresh recruits, was slowly becoming a reality in fact, if not in theory.

Calhoun greatly improved army administration, but he did not resolve the matter of commanding the land forces, as the anomalous position of the commanding general indicated. Because of the fundamentally flawed command system and a disappearing role for the militia in raising troops, civilian control of the military did not progress with professionalization. The army was kept relatively small in these years, and a military threat to civilian institutions never arose. Nonetheless, professionalization of the army raised new issues in terms of civil-military relations that Calhoun and his successors did not successfully resolve. The Mexican and Civil Wars exposed some key problems, indicating that further change was essential.

The navy's experience after 1815 both paralleled and diverged from that of the army. It benefited from new administrative structures and growing professionalism. The navy, however, lacked an outstanding leader like Calhoun, its process of professionalization was less accomplished, and it had to cope with more far-reaching technological change than did the army.

The navy, like the army, gained from the nationalistic glow following the War of 1812. In 1816 Congress enacted the first long-term naval building program. Although later modified, it still increased the navy's size and fighting capacity.

Several administrative reorganizations of the navy were of longer lasting significance.[43] The first occurred in 1815, when Congress created the Board of Navy Commissioners. For years, critics had insisted that the secretary of the navy and a few clerks could not effectively run the navy. The War of 1812 made that reality clear. Headed by the senior officer, the Board of Navy Commissioners directed naval procurement, the construction, equipping, and repair of vessels, and other matters of administration. Vagueness in the enabling statute encouraged the board at the outset to claim key command responsibilities. Secretary of the Navy Benjamin W. Crowninshield (1815–1818), forcefully backed by President Monroe, insisted that he alone commanded the navy and restricted the naval commissioners to essentially civilian functions.

Naval administration improved during the years of the naval commissioners (1816–1842). Although some tensions developed among the secretaries, the board, and the line, relations were generally harmonious. The naval commissioners oversaw the expansion of the navy and had all vessels built at the navy yards to ensure quality of construction. The yards began to specialize whenever possible: repairing and equipping ships took place mostly in Boston, New

York, and Norfolk; Washington became a center for manufacturing naval equipment; and so forth. The navy also built two dry docks in Boston and Norfolk. In the late 1830s and early 1840s, the naval commissioners took the first steps toward introducing ships of steam, iron, armor, and modern ordnance.

Among the Board of Navy Commissioners' first reforms was revising naval regulations. Their 1818 edition was so accomplished that it went without further change for over forty years. The commissioners also greatly improved the navy's financial procedures, adopted a system for procuring supplies by contract that reduced malfeasance by contractors, pursers, and naval agents, and reworked the methods for maintaining accounts and making naval estimates.

Ultimately, though, the Board of Naval Commissioners failed because the members were forced into a leadership role for which they were not prepared. After Crowninshield, most secretaries were political appointees without the talent, interest, or background for the office. By default, the Board of Navy Commissioners was left to lead even though it had been created only as an advisory body and depended upon collective, not individual, decisionmaking. Over time, the board became virtually paralyzed by numbing procedures and the lack of personal responsibility, which increasingly left the Navy Department leaderless and confused.

This mounting crisis came to a head in 1841 when the talented Abel P. Upshur (1841–1843) took over as secretary of the navy. He turned to a group of young and progressive naval officers for advice on restructuring the navy. To ensure a proper division of labor and accountability, the secretary proposed to reorganize the department along bureau lines. Congress enacted the system with some revisions in August 1842. The law disestablished the Board of Navy Commissioners and replaced it with five naval bureaus: Yards and Docks; Construction and Repair; Ordnance; Medicine and Surgery; and Provisions and Clothing. At the outset, the second and fifth bureaus could be headed by civilians; in time, all were placed under naval command. The bureaus went through modifications, varying in number from five to eight, but the basic system endured for over a century.

The reorganized administration system improved upon the Board of Navy Commissioners but was still fundamentally flawed. The demise of the naval commissioners ended all collective responsibility. The secretary of the navy became the sole unifying factor in the department, but unlike in the earlier system he acted without the advice of the navy's senior officers. Furthermore, as with the army, the bureaus became a collection of uncoordinated fiefdoms that often came into conflict with each other and with the navy as a whole. An inevitable conflict developed between the staff and the line, a rift that the naval commissioners had avoided in effect by uniting the two. The line viewed the staff as inferior though the staff managed the human and material resources the line needed to fulfill its functions. And interdependence increased as naval technology grew in sophistication.

A more logical organization would have retained the naval commissioners as a General Staff to plan and advise the secretary in directing the navy, including the bureaus. Instead, the navy was left most of the time with an unqualified secretary directing a decentralized structure. Although nothing comparable to the army's commanding general existed to complicate civil-military relations, there was no mechanism for ensuring that the line was competently commanded.

Another major reform occurred in 1845 when Secretary of the Navy George Bancroft (1845–1846) founded the Naval Academy. The navy's outstanding performance during the War of 1812 led to complacency after hostilities and then to professional stagnation in the 1830s. As a result, the service's informal but excellent system for training officers before 1812 broke down. A cohesive corps gave way to one of personal quarrels and warring factions that drove morale to a new low. To deal with this crisis a new group of officers entering the navy after the War of 1812 began working for reform, and their efforts led to the bureau organization. They also insisted upon the need for a naval counterpart of West Point. Congress resisted repeated calls for a naval academy as excessively militaristic, elitist, and unnecessary; however, Bancroft used the Mexican War crisis and bureaucratic stealth to inaugurate Annapolis. Its success and future were in doubt for a number of years, but by 1850 it had instituted a four-year program of study including nautical and more general subjects, which helped lead to a revived navy officer corps whose professional qualities by 1860 matched that of the army. The naval officer corps emerged as more ingrown, isolated, and conservative than that of the army, however.

The various reforms prepared the navy to cope better with the so-called "naval revolution" occurring in steam, iron, ordnance, and armor, categories in which England and France led the United States. Under the guidance of Capt. Matthew C. Perry, the United States started to catch up between 1839 and 1842 when it built two steam frigates. Huge engines and paddlewheels propelled these ungainly vessels, making them slow, extremely vulnerable in combat, and expensive to operate. Captain Robert F. Stockton drew upon the genius of the Swedish engineer John Ericsson to solve the problems with a screw propeller and redesigned steam engines, equipment that operated below the waterline and was relatively safe from attack. The frigate *Princeton* incorporated these advances; built between 1842 and 1843, it was the world's first propeller-driven ship. To counter the newly developed explosive shells, the

United States was also the first nation to authorize the building of a ship plated with iron armor, but the *Stevens Battery,* as it came to be called, never reached completion despite years of effort. The navy did finish a frigate of iron and steam, launching it on Lake Erie in 1843. By the 1840s, the navy was also arming ships with rifled, pivoting guns that fired shells. In 1839–1840, Captain Perry introduced the navy's first school of gun practice on the *Fulton II* and at Sandy Hook and established an experimental battery at the latter location. By 1840 ships also began target practice.

These advances were tentative and did not basically alter the navy of wood and sail. Although the United States inaugurated some key elements of the naval revolution, such as the propeller, it did not exploit them. Most scholars have taken the navy to task for opposition to technological progress. In truth, since the nation's expansionist thrust was mainly inland to the west, a navy that looked outward to the sea was bound to suffer neglect. Naval technology was changing swiftly; for the nation to try to keep up in this area, which was not vital to its defense, would have wasted time, energy, and money. When interests of prosperity and security led America to look outward, priorities changed and the country would benefit from the research and development of other nations in building a modern navy.

THE MEXICAN WAR

The Mexican War (May 1846–February 1848) highlighted the substantial progress the armed services had made since 1815 and the changes still necessary. Army troops were better trained and led than before. Logistical support was also exceptional compared with that of the past. Although assigned a secondary role in the conflict, the navy carried out its responsibilities in an accomplished manner. Furthermore, through public and private production and at times a combination of the two, the nation easily supplied its fighting forces, and it managed to finance the war with relative ease. The fact that the war was brief, limited, and fought against a weak and disorganized enemy facilitated these accomplishments. On the negative side, the war showed that the nation had not perfected a system for raising armies and that military planning and direction were still wanting. Moreover, top civilian and military leaders engaged in political infighting that discredited all the parties involved.[44]

Most of the negative qualities manifested during hostilities arose because the army was in transition from an amateur to a professional status. Methods for mobilizing men were rather crude. According to statistics, about 30,500 officers and enlisted men served in the regular army during the war, and approximately 75,500 saw duty as volunteers or in the common militia. Those figures are probably inflated because mobilization techniques and bookkeeping were simply too rudimentary to permit reasonable accuracy. Washington wisely decided to rely principally on volunteers or volunteer militiamen, not the common militia, to raise troops. In May 1846 Congress authorized the enlistment of 50,000 volunteers. The regular army also grew, ultimately more than doubling its original size of 8,600 men. Initial army growth took place on an expansible basis in which men were integrated into existing units before new regiments were authorized in February 1847. Mobilization policies were poorly executed. Some 12,500 common militiamen were called up, most of whom were unauthorized and unneeded, never saw battle, and caused more problems than they solved. More seriously, President Polk allowed the states or the units themselves to fix the length of volunteer service at one year or for the duration of the war. Most enlistees chose the former, with potentially disastrous results. Scott, for example, halted his drive to Mexico City because the enlistment terms of about one-third of his troops had expired.

Weaknesses in manpower mobilization were symptomatic of a larger reality: no effective military planning had taken place even though war with Mexico had appeared imminent for over a year. Calhoun's General Staff was actually a technical and service staff, not intended for planning. Although Secretary of War William L. Marcy and General Scott exchanged ideas in 1845 on the probability of war and its requirements, they did not share information with the supply bureaus, and the latter failed to act on their own. Consequently, with the outbreak of war, Congress and the president had to decide quickly how to raise troops without the benefit of professional guidelines. Supply operations also started from scratch. In the nation's capital, General Scott became a one-person General Staff as he devised war plans without the benefit of the most basic information. When Scott departed from Washington to command the march from Vera Cruz to Mexico City, "a one-man general staff gave way to none at all."[45] The navy showed the same failures in prewar planning.

Although the government lacked a General Staff, it most assuredly had a commander-in-chief. Polk took control of the military effort because of Secretary of War Marcy's weakness and his own strong personality and conception of the president's constitutional responsibilities. His performance was even more remarkable since he had no military training or specialized knowledge. Combining incredible energy with intelligence and judgment, the president directed almost every facet of the war effort. He set overall military strategy and chose the commanders to carry it out, wrote their orders, and pushed them forward when will and energy flagged. Moreover, he was the first president to act as his own budget officer. Working with the General Staff and Congress, Polk reviewed spending estimates, revised them when necessary, and thereby largely determined the level of wartime appropriations. Polk's supervision did not stop with general policies; he oversaw the most minute details. The president paid particular attention to the operations of the army bureaus, perceiving them to be profligate with funds, casual, and excessively independent. After replacing Secretary of the Navy Bancroft with John Y. Mason, Polk devoted less energy to the navy than to the army. Mason was reasonably strong, quietly competent, and experienced, and the navy had a lesser role in the war.

Polk's extraordinary wartime performance was not without drawbacks. Taking on too many tasks for one person, he paid with his life, dying, probably of exhaustion, shortly after leaving office. The president had assumed so many responsibilities because the army and navy lacked proper general staff and command systems. But even if they had had such an apparatus, Polk might have behaved in the same way. He used his cabinet, in effect, as a war council that reviewed major military decisions and coordinated their implementation. Yet the president always succeeded in bending cabinet members to his will. All in all, then, although Polk explored and demonstrated the power and potential of the president as commander-in-chief, he did little or nothing to improve military command and administration systems.

Ultimately, Polk's domination of the war effort may have contributed to the highest degree of politicization of the military services during hostilities in American history. An intensely partisan Democrat, Polk maneuvered throughout hostilities to ensure that the principal commanders Scott and Zachary Taylor, acknowledged Whigs, did not deprive the Democratic party of sharing in the military glory. On their part, Scott and Taylor, especially the former, had strong political ambitions and constantly gauged the effects of military success on their presidential hopes. As a result, Polk, Scott, and Taylor engaged in petty behavior and unseemly accusations that became public and discredited the offices they held. The three men came from a tradition in which the military and politics mixed easily and naturally, but this attitude flew in the face of the professionalism emerging in the military services, especially the army. Their unbecoming behavior doubtlessly strengthened the impulse toward professionalism among officers who saw the corrupting influence of politics on the military mission.

The positive far outweighed the negative in the military's performance during the Mexican War. Years afterward, Ulysses S. Grant, never known for hyperbole, averred that "a better army, man for man, probably never faced an enemy than the one commanded by General Taylor in the earliest engagements of the

Mexican War."[46] Seasoned by Western campaigns and the extended Second Seminole War (1835–1842), the army also benefited from advances in professionalization. Numerous junior officers had been trained at West Point, and tactical manuals and general regulations helped achieve proficiency and uniformity, which facilitated the regular army's ability to expand by rapidly and effectively training new recruits and absorbing new units. Particularly outstanding during hostilities was the performance of the artillery and engineers. Experience and professional growth made possible Scott's remarkable campaign from Vera Cruz to Mexico City, Taylor's outstanding achievements, and Gen. Stephen W. Kearny's long marches in the West.

Wartime logistics were much more accomplished than during any previous war. Though weaknesses existed, no battle was lost because of supply failures, and strong logistical support contributed significantly to the numerous victories. Calhoun's reforms of the army's supply structure were fully established, tested, and refined by the 1840s and the various bureaus organized rationally by function and usually headed and staffed by experienced officers with many years of service.

The two most important supply bureaus were the Ordnance Department and the Quartermaster Department. Ordnance was exceptionally well organized and commanded. Established regulations governed all operations, ensuring uniformity in weapons and other products.[47] During the war, the department worked closely with private manufacturers to supplement output at the arsenals. In 1847 the arsenals at Springfield and Harpers Ferry turned out nearly 27,000 muskets in addition to components, parts, tools, and related production. Twenty-two other arsenals devoted themselves primarily to manufacturing ammunition for small arms and artillery, producing accoutrements, and repairing and maintaining arms and other equipment. Whatever demand the arsenals could not meet in small arms, private contractors employing mass production techniques could provide. Most of the artillery and much of the ammunition and accoutrements were also supplied by private contractors or through open-market purchasing. Despite the great progress in breech-loading and percussion weapons, the regular army depended on the flintlock musket because Commanding General Scott felt the others had not been adequately tested in the field. Various volunteer units, however, carried the more up-to-date weapons of Hall, Colt, Jencks, and others, which created endless complications in supplying ammunition and carrying out repairs and maintenance. Nonetheless, the American armies never ran short of weapons and frequently benefited from remarkable supply feats. For example, in 1847 Scott's army in Vera Cruz took delivery of forty-nine ten-inch mortars and 50,000 shells only four months after ordering them.

The Quartermaster Department did not face the technological challenges that Ordnance confronted, but as the army's principal supply agency, the scope of the former's responsibilities was vastly greater. To meet the challenge, Gen. Thomas S. Jesup, appointed quartermaster general in 1818, wrote regulations, established procedures, and selected and trained a staff of officers to handle the multiple supply operations in a uniform, efficient manner. A stickler for detail and a strict disciplinarian, Jesup was particularly concerned that all property and money entrusted to the corps be properly accounted for. Never had the Quartermaster Department been in better shape to meet the demands of war.

Despite far-reaching improvement, the supply bureaus still suffered from some major flaws, fragmentation being the biggest drawback. Although the bureaus theoretically operated under the secretary of war, in reality each was independent of him and of the other bureaus. This lack of cohesion probably contributed to the fact that none of the supply bureaus had planned for the emergency. Nonetheless, once war broke out, the supply bureaus rapidly began meeting the challenge of war. Polk's strong leadership provided the coordination and control that the agencies needed but did not receive from the secretary of war.

The supply bureaus' ability to mobilize so quickly stemmed in part from the strength of the American economy. In weapons, the most complex and specialized implements required for war, the nation had ample public and private production capacity. For almost all other items, wartime usage was so close to civilian demand that the requirements of a rather small army in a relatively limited war were easily met without the need to convert facilities, a circumstance that applied in the more economically advanced Northeast as well as in the less developed West and South.

The Quartermaster Department produced a remarkable number of goods at its own facilities, particularly the Schuylkill Arsenal in Philadelphia. Within weeks, the arsenal increased its output of uniforms by tenfold, and by the end of the conflict production had reached 85,000 garments weekly. To relieve the pressure in Philadelphia, a branch facility was created in New York in 1846. As American armies penetrated farther into Mexico, the Quartermaster Department set up clothing factories on foreign soil, although the record of output, quality, and cost did not match that of Philadelphia. The department also began to manufacture tents at the Schuylkill Arsenal during the war years as well as the manufacture of shoes there for the first time. The experiment proved so successful that the army halted private contracting for shoes after the war and made the Schuylkill facility the only producer for peacetime troops.

The supplies the Quartermaster Department did not produce itself it procured, spreading orders across the country when possible. Most army supplies came from the Northeast, but the West also played an active role. Knapsacks, canteens, and cooking equipment were fabricated in Pittsburgh and Cincinnati and shipped to New Orleans. The bulk of supplies for the campaigns of Kearny and Alexander W. Doniphan in the Southwest and northern Mexico were acquired in Missouri and adjoining states by the quartermaster in St. Louis, who then forwarded them to Fort Leavenworth and Santa Fe.

Subsistence operations also went smoothly during the Mexican War. The Subsistence Department stationed officers at the main provision markets in New York, Baltimore, New Orleans, and St. Louis. The War Department facilitated operations by allowing open-market purchasing instead of requiring competitive bidding, which permitted the flexibility essential for feeding troops often on the move in distant regions. The nation's vast agricultural and livestock output eliminated any problems of availability. Doniphan's 6,000-mile anabasis and Kearny's long march from Fort Leavenworth to California required cutting rations and obtaining subsistence from the countryside, however, and the same was true when troops ventured far into Mexico. The army acted to avoid alienating the Mexican farmers so as to facilitate purchasing from them. Nonetheless, provisions still had to be shipped thousands of miles from the United States. The Quartermaster and Subsistence Departments at times set up gristmills, bakeries, slaughterhouses, and so forth to feed the troops.

To aid supply, the army created a string of depots, established in New Orleans (the point of assembly and embarkation for most volunteers), Corpus Christi, Port Isabel, and other points down the eastern coast of Mexico as far south as Vera Cruz, and inland to Mexico City. In the Southwest, supply stations were located in San Antonio, Santa Fe, and California.

With three armies in simultaneous motion at one point, separated from one another and from permanent supply depots by thousands of miles, transportation became key in all logistical operations. Although supplies were generally available in ample quantities, transportation difficulties caused shortages in certain areas. Modern technology nonetheless eased logistical problems. By 1846 telegraph lines linked the nation's capital with New York, Philadelphia, and other Eastern cities and sped the procurement process. Railroads were even more important. Rail lines connected most of the Northeast by 1846 and reached into the Mississippi Valley, facilitating the movement of supplies of all sorts. However, since railroads did not yet go beyond the Mississippi and were limited in the South, thousands of miles of land still separated the troops from major American settlements. In 1845 Quartermaster General

Jesup had recommended constructing a railroad line from the Brazos to the mouth of the Rio Grande. That brilliant suggestion would have permitted a major logistical breakthrough but was not acted upon due to lack of funds and, once war broke out, lack of time.

The steamboat played an enormously significant role in army supply operations. Its importance had been established earlier during the Second Seminole War. For the Mexican War, the Quartermaster Department acquired thirty-five steamships and thirty-eight sailing ships and hired or chartered many other vessels. The steamboats transported supplies and troops on the rivers to Fort Leavenworth, New Orleans, and other ports. Their most original use involved carrying a steady flow of supplies and troops to Taylor's principal base at Camargo, just across the Rio Grande in Mexico. The shallowness of the Rio Grande and other Mexican rivers and tributaries forced the Quartermaster Department to search far and wide for light-draft schooners and similar vessels to meet its transportation needs; it also had some boats built. For transportation operations from the Atlantic Coast to the Gulf of Mexico and within the Gulf itself, the army, albeit with difficulty, bought, leased, and hired sea steamers. Sailing ships executed some of the longest logistical operations during the war, transporting troops, ordnance, camp equipment, and other supplies from New York to California on six-month journeys in late 1846 and early 1847.

By far the most ambitious and impressive logistical operation of the entire war supported Scott's campaign against Vera Cruz. To prepare for it, the Quartermaster Department had the navy design and transport privately built surf boats for an amphibious landing. Ultimately, the navy's Home Squadron joined the army flotilla of some 41 ships off the Mexican coast to constitute an armada of nearly 100 vessels. Despite inclement weather and the demands of a pioneering effort, the army and navy in four hours put ashore 10,000 troops with a two-day ration supply for each without the loss of a man or a boat. Within ten days, enough supplies and equipment, including draft animals and wagons and siege guns weighing over three tons, had been landed to allow Scott to begin his march to Mexico City. On the whole, the expedition proceeded with remarkable ease. Success was facilitated by careful coordination among Scott, Jesup, and Home Squadron commander David Conner.

Transportation on land, not water, caused the Quartermaster Department the most grief. The various campaigns of Taylor and Scott and the long marches of Kearny, Doniphan, and Maj. Gen. John E. Wool required enormous numbers of wagons, harness sets, and draft animals. A number of conditions complicated the inherent difficulties involved. First, the supply of wagons was never enough because expanded canals and railroads had recently reduced their use and availability. A standardized wagon design—advocated but not adopted—would have facilitated repair and allowed the corps to get by with fewer wagons. Second, the demand for horses and wagons would have been eased if American armies had initially accommodated themselves to the readily available and inexpensive mule transport of Mexico. Scott eventually forced his troops to lighten and adapt their loads for such use with excellent results. Third, the army was still plagued with hired teamsters who were often unreliable, incompetent, and destructive to equipment, supplies, and animals. Commanders were unwilling to detail men from the line to take over drivers' duties and Congress did not act on the Quartermaster Department's entreaties for an army teamster corps until March 1847. Finally, too often field commanders failed to submit requirements in a timely fashion, overestimated their needs, or appropriated wagons, draft animals, and key supplies intended for other units. Generally, however, logistics for the Mexican War were commendable compared with the past. The supply and service bureaus, especially the Quartermaster Department, had made great progress in professionalizing their operations.

Although the Mexican War was fought principally on land, the navy's role in the conflict was still important. The Home Squadron, which in time became the largest fleet the United States had ever assembled, maintained a tight blockade of the eastern coast of Mexico and captured and occupied several ports. This move prevented any action by Mexico's diminutive navy, scared off pirates of Mexican and foreign origin, and denied Mexico armaments from abroad. The Home Squadron also protected supply lines and depots, escorted supply ships, and assisted in transporting troops. Its performance for the amphibious landing at Vera Cruz was both crucial and superb. The much smaller Pacific Fleet was also active in blockade activity and, more important, in the military action to seize and hold California.

The Mexican War presented some logistical challenges for the navy, but they were not great. Unlike the army, the navy had years of experience operating in foreign waters; its squadrons traveled throughout the world and were supplied by naval agents in key ports. To service the Home Squadron, the navy began building in Pensacola what would become a high-quality navy yard. More immediately, the navy established its principal station at Anton Lizardo, about twelve miles south of Vera Cruz, where it stored coal for the steamers, general supplies, and water for the fleet. By the beginning of 1847, most logistical problems had been solved. Supply ships operated regularly and in sufficient numbers, though the squadron experienced periodic shortages of basic items throughout the war that stemmed from the same factors plaguing army logistics: slow communications, long distances, and the difficulty of anticipating requirements. The secretary of the navy and the recently created bureaus actually performed reasonably well under the circumstances. Their task was complicated by squadron commanders' and even the War Department's failure to give advance notice of operations.

In terms of operations, the navy at the outset of the war suffered from a lack of shallow-draft vessels necessary for the Mexican coast. It solved the problem by October 1846 through purchasing, capturing from Mexico, and otherwise acquiring various small steamers, schooners, brigs, and the like to constitute a mosquito fleet. The service had more than enough blue-water ships, and four more were completed during the hostilities. Like the army, however, the navy lacked competent pilots and good maps and charts. Manpower also presented serious problems. Although Congress authorized the navy to expand for hostilities from 7,500 to 10,000 men, its numbers never exceeded 8,500. Recruiting was difficult as seamen were drawn to the merchant marine and avoided blockade duty, which was dull and could be dangerous because of tropical diseases and severe and unpredictable storms in the Gulf of Mexico. Nevertheless, the navy fulfilled its responsibilities with the forces available. Moreover, the Marine Corps expanded by over 1,000 men to help the navy occupy various Mexican ports, and 300 men of the corps marched with Scott to Mexico City.

On the West Coast, the navy's fleet was strictly one of sail since no coaling stations existed. Supply was problematic until the very able Thomas O. Larkin became naval agent at Monterey. With the entire Pacific Coast and Hawaiian Islands available for supplies, resourceful leadership provided for basic needs.

Wartime corruption, profiteering, and the like were much reduced from previous conflicts, partly because of the brevity of the war and the greater maturity of the economy. Also of significance, however, was the professionalism in the supply and service bureaus. Their trained personnel, established procedures and regulations, and accounting and auditing practices guarded against the rampant abuses of the past. Wrongdoing, of course, took place. In August 1847 Polk uncovered a situation in which the Quartermaster Department had allowed the Treasury Department and the banking house of Corcoran and Riggs to divert $2 million in a way that allowed the latter to use most of the funds for stock speculation. Little malfeasance marred navy supply, however, since the service procured much less than the army and usually kept a tighter rein on its buying.

Financing the war was also relatively simple compared with efforts in the past. A short war against a weak enemy made that possible, despite divisions over the war at home and the nation's poor credit standing abroad. War costs totaled around $76.5 million. Tariff revenue covered ordinary government expenditures and some wartime spending; the remaining outlays were raised through short- and long-term Treasury issues. In 1846 the government had difficulty selling its paper at home and abroad; but in 1847, with growing prosperity and a promising military situation, Washington easily disposed of its bonds for specie and at above par. The Treasury acted as its own broker in floating loans. Nonetheless, banking houses such as Corcoran and Riggs profited handsomely during the war through commissions and, as transfer agents, by holding and using funds ultimately destined for government contractors and other creditors. These questionable if not illegal practices were furthered by Secretary of the Treasury Robert J. Walker's solicitous behavior in behalf of favored banks.

THE MILITARY STRUCTURE, 1848–1860

No dramatic advances occurred in the military services between the end of the Mexican War and the outbreak of the Civil War. For the army, professionalization continued through improved instruction at home and through American officers studying and reporting on military developments abroad.[48] Jefferson Davis (1853–1857) was the only genuinely talented secretary of war after the Mexican War. Davis advanced the army's professional growth in every way possible, including size, arms, peacetime functions, and war preparation. He failed to make progress only in the constitutionally sensitive area of the relationship between the secretary of war and the commanding general. His inept and weak successor, John B. Floyd (1857–1860), degraded his office and the army by tolerating irregularities and fraud in finances and supply, and by transferring arms to the Southern states as they prepared for disunion.

The army almost tripled in size between 1845 and 1860 because of the newly acquired territory. Accordingly, the overwhelming majority of troops served in the West. Supplying the army in these distant posts proved extraordinarily expensive. To cut costs, the Quartermaster Department phased out most of the army's fleet of ships and stock of wagons and draft animals, choosing to contract with private firms to handle transportation. To economize and to improve reliability and speed, the army used railroad and steamboat routes whenever possible, but that still left hundreds of miles to be covered by wagons. To reduce reliance on wagons, the War Department under Davis became an enthusiastic and active advocate of a transcontinental railroad. To further that end, the army engineers explored and surveyed the four routes that the various transcontinental railroad lines would approximately follow.

Some important advances also took place in the Ordnance Department. In 1855 the army adopted the Model 1855 Springfield rifled musket as the standard infantry weapon. Experimentation and testing continued on the breech-loading and repeating rifles with inconclusive results. Ordnance continued to systematize its collection of twenty-four different types and calibers of guns, howitzers, and mortars as field, siege and garrison, and seacoast artillery. More important, in 1857 the department adopted the Napoleon gun as a general-purpose weapon, which greatly simplified ammunition supply.

Naval progress between 1848 and 1860 was piecemeal and uneven.[49] No outstanding secretary of the navy served during these years. Without proper leadership, positive changes lacked coherence, and some deterioration set in. Also of consequence was the fact that Southerners exercised unusual influence over the navy and favored its expansion to further territorial ambitions in the Caribbean and Latin America and to check British actions against the slave trade.

Nonetheless, various advances occurred. Politics aside, the navy grew to meet the nation's expanding security, diplomatic, and commercial responsibilities. And the transition from sail to steam continued. The bureaus gradually became more professional under the guidance of qualified chiefs who were required to be naval officers, not civilians. Needed reforms were carried out in supply operations and ship construction. Examinations were instituted to select and promote officers in various specialties, the training of officers generally improved as the Naval Academy matured, and enlisted men benefited from a number of programs. Two of the most important reforms involved a retirement list, ridding the service of aged, incapacitated, and incompetent officers while opening up promotions for deserving ones, and "assimilated rank," giving staff officers such as engineers and surgeons rank comparable to those of the line.

The real test of naval modernization involved building, arming, protecting, and servicing the navy's ships. Compared with the fleets of European nations, the American blue-water navy in 1860 was obsolete. It consisted of lightly armed wooden frigates and sloops propelled by sails, with steam-driven propellers only auxiliary. The entire American fleet could not prevail in battle against one European seagoing ironclad built with the latest technology. Although lagging American naval technology was explicable, given the nation's priorities and imperatives, neither civilians nor naval officers seemed to grasp fully the significance of the naval revolution taking place in Europe.[50]

Yet some technological gains occurred. Despite failed attempts to standardize ordnance as Great Britain and France had done earlier, John A. Dahlgren made significant, though halting, advances in the design and manufacture of various guns at the Washington Navy Yard. Additional navy yards were created at Vicksburg and Mare Island, almost all existing yards were modernized so that they could build and repair steamships, and more and better dry docks were constructed.

Still, naval growth and spending continued without clear goals and able leadership, which encouraged waste, misused funds, and corruption. Beginning late in the 1840s, for example, Washington subsidized private shipping companies based on the specious rationale that their vessels could be converted to ships of war during hostilities. Moreover, members of Congress sought spoils for their states and districts in the form of navy yards, dry docks, and the like. By 1859 matters had so deteriorated that the House of Representatives and the navy both investigated the service's supply operations. Revelations led to enhancing naval and diluting civilian power in the navy yards, but entrenched interests and the political parties protected the spoils system and other practices against the full-blown reforms needed to guard the navy's interests and the public's purse.

Events on the eve of the Civil War made clear the degree to which the navy had fallen victim to politics and poor leadership. Secretary of the Navy Isaac Toucey (1857–1861), reflecting the temporizing policies of James Buchanan's administration, did nothing to prepare the navy for the obviously impending rebellion and in fact undermined it by acquiescing in the surrender of the Pensacola Navy Yard, by failing to contest the resignation of 68 commissioned officers who, along with 313 army officers, in effect declared their loyalty to the South, and by other acts of omission.

Just before the Civil War, then, both the War and Navy departments were headed by secretaries at best mediocre, at worst incompetent and corrupt, who undermined morale and discipline, weakened the government they served, and strengthened the proponents of disunion.

The four factors shaping the political economy of warfare—military technology, the economy, civil-military relations, and the political structure—explain both the dynamics of economic mobilization for the limited Mexican War and the various national developments relevant to that effort. Economic mobilization for the brief and relatively undemanding Mexican War was more accomplished than in any previous conflict. Military technology was entering a period of transition, particularly for the navy, but had not yet changed so dramatically that converting the economy was necessary to meet the demands of the armed services during hostilities. Consequently, the War, Navy, and Treasury departments acted as the principal mobilization agencies to procure more, but not significantly different, supplies and goods from the civilian economy. The dynamic American economy, which was growing, diversifying, and specializing in all areas and which had enormous capacity for production and distribution, easily met the growing military requirements through the operation of market forces and without the need for new sources of regulation. Army arsenals and navy yards alone or in combination with private firms efficiently manufactured the more specialized weaponry. Moreover, the war was financed without any major difficulty.

Positive changes in civil-military relations facilitated the economic mobilization process. The beginnings of professionalization in both services improved supply operations along with the military's combat effectiveness and acted to give the army and navy identities increasingly separate from that of the civilian world. These developments assisted Polk in his remarkable, although flawed, role as the civilian commander-in-chief, directing the entire war effort in a nearly modern manner. But they also made the political maneuvering among Polk, Scott, and Taylor during hostilities seem even more incongruous.

Polk's wartime leadership demonstrated that the real and potential powers of the federal government were great. He drew upon those powers in coordinating and focusing the nation's economic and military strength in an unusually effective way. In contrast to the past, the role of the states in mobilization was relatively minor. The president's achievements were remarkable, given the limitations placed upon Washington by growing conflict among classes, interest groups, and sections and by the fragmentation beginning to affect the parties.

Between the Mexican and Civil Wars, Washington's power atrophied more as the nation divided and the second party system was replaced by the third. Nonetheless, a strong president and party could ultimately mobilize the Union's strength to conduct effectively even a long and demanding war, as Polk had done during the earlier, more limited one.

5
ECONOMIC MOBILIZATION
IN THE NORTH

The Civil War ultimately became a contest between the competing strategies of annihilation and attrition. The North set about to crush the South, and the Confederacy attempted to win by not losing. At all times, the Union's overwhelming economic superiority gave the region a great advantage in the conflict. In 1861 the North's real and personal property was three times greater than that of the South, its output of manufactured goods ten times greater, its incorporated banks four times greater in numbers, and its railroad mileage and population three times greater. Moreover, the Union had a practical monopoly on registered ships. These rather crude statistics, however, do not adequately measure the enormous advantage the Union had in every economic sense. The North's transportation and communication systems, economic diversification and occupational specialization, and managerial sophistication had modernized the region in many ways.

Advantages notwithstanding, the North required over a year to work out successful mobilization policies. Abraham Lincoln's administration inherited a federal bureaucracy enervated by decades of sectional conflict and nearly paralyzed by the secession crisis that began after the election of 1860. Throughout 1861 the administration constantly struggled to establish a governmental structure that would enable the North to meet the unending demands of warfare.

The states stepped in to provide the Lincoln administration with the time it needed to rebuild the federal government. For nearly a year, they carried a large portion of the mobilization burden. Studying the states, therefore, is indispensable for understanding fully the Union's political economy of warfare. Focusing upon the Northern states also provides the best opportunity after the Revolution to examine power patterns and especially the interaction of political, economic, and military elites. In nearly every Northern state a rel-

atively small group of economic and professional elites filled the major political and military offices. They were either elected or appointed to these positions or served formally or informally in an advisory capacity. In the East, elite
structures were well established and had generational depth; traveling west,
power systems became increasingly fluid.

Elite power patterns are more visible at the state than at the federal level
because the nation was in a transitional stage. There was a collection of local,
state, and regional economies, not a national one. Since regional governments
did not exist, states constituted the most significant power groupings. As in
the past, a state's economic elite dominated politics, and, with the militia system, the military structure as well. Washington reflected these realities. Political parties gave it a national reach, but those parties were essentially
state-based, making the federal government's grasp weak. War mobilization
forced a vast expansion of national power that otherwise would not have
occurred. After hostilities, Washington predictably lost its artificial dominance.
It regained power naturally, gradually, and permanently in the late nineteenth
and early twentieth centuries as a truly national economy emerged.

The comingling of elites at the national level, unlike in the states, was limited
and could be found only within the railroad and telegraph systems, where business was large, national, or where the modern corporation had appeared. Elsewhere, business was comparatively small, decentralized, and subject to competition, which allowed an artificially expanded national government to use existing
executive departments for mobilizing the economy through market forces.
Moreover, with the army and navy fairly far along in the professionalizing
process, the armed services also avoided an invasion of civilians at the top levels
of supply and command. The mixing of elites that occurred in the states during
the Civil War would not be seen at the national level until the twentieth century when a national, corporate economy existed.

MOBILIZATION BY THE STATES

The War Department was unable to handle Lincoln's call in April and May
1861 for expanding an army of 16,000 to 156,000. Out of necessity, the states
took over a good part of the responsibility.[1] In addition to raising militia and
volunteer units, the states clothed, equipped, and armed the troops and set
up camps and garrisons for them until they were integrated into the force that
became the Union army.

All states made efforts along these lines. The results ranged from outstanding to poor, although supply operations were always rather hectic and

piecemeal and small arms the most difficult to acquire. The New England and Middle States, with most of the nation's manufacturing capacity, did a good job. Massachusetts, New York, and Pennsylvania performed at extraordinary levels. The states of the Old Northwest, with less-developed economies, generally did not do as well, although Ohio was economically advanced and Indiana demonstrated as much vigor as any state in the Union. The new states of the Midwest and the prairie often found it difficult to accomplish as much as states to the east. Some, such as Kansas, Iowa, and Minnesota, were just beyond the frontier stage. Moreover, these states and the Territory of Nebraska faced Indian uprisings, and Kansas had to contend with guerrilla warfare on its eastern border. The border states experienced even harsher conditions. During most of the war, martial law was in effect in Kentucky, Missouri, West Virginia, Maryland, and Delaware, with federal troops ensuring governments loyal to the Union. Most of these states also had to cope with internal strife, guerrilla warfare, and periodic battles between Union and Confederate forces. Regardless of accomplishments, most states approached the tasks suddenly thrust upon them with remarkable vigor and dedication.

Although state mobilization varied enormously during 1861, a number of generalizations are still possible. First, cooperation among the states and regions was limited. Second, governors led in mobilizing the states, but they depended heavily upon the states' economic elites in doing so. Initial mobilization was usually financed by banks and wealthy individuals until the states adapted their finances to wartime conditions and the federal government stepped in. Thereafter, governors regularly turned to elite representatives in fulfilling their numerous tasks. Third, state leadership tapped mass support for mobilization, which was vital in caring for sick and wounded soldiers, looking after the troops in general, and helping to support their families. The U.S. Sanitary Commission (USSC), and to some degree the U.S. Christian Commission (USCC), brought a significant measure of national control to local and state efforts to aid soldiers. Finally, although states continued to play an important part in raising and caring for the troops throughout the war, the government took control of economic mobilization by early 1862.

RELATIONS AMONG THE STATES

Despite regional similarities in the way states responded to the war, there was not much cooperation among them.[2] This trend is understandable in light of the states' rights doctrine and the tendency for states to go their own way before the war. Led by Gov. John A. Andrew of Massachusetts in the early months of the war, New England states coordinated their efforts more than other regions. Even in this case, however, no formal structure for consultation ever existed; and the New England states followed no one leader or state in a lockstep fashion. Although Ohio, Indiana, and Illinois consulted on the future of Kentucky and the defense of the Ohio River, again the efforts were ad hoc.

Governors or their alternates gathered on only three occasions. The first conference took place in Cleveland in May 1861, when representatives of New York, Pennsylvania, and several Western states strategized and prevailed with some success upon the Lincoln administration to prosecute the war more energetically. Andrew engineered the second meeting in Providence, Rhode Island, where the New England governors consulted over the dire state of affairs after Second Bull Run. They called on the president to reshuffle his cabinet and army generals, unsolicited advice that Lincoln ignored. The last governors' conference grew out of the second and was convened in Altoona, Pennsylvania, in September 1862, to devise a strategy to increase support for the administration. In reality, this conference represented a move by Lincoln and Republican moderates to co-opt the radicals and end the growing criticism of Washington manifest at the Providence gathering. Before the meeting convened, Lincoln cut the ground from under his critics with the Emancipation Proclamation. Thereafter, despite endless grumbling and criticism, the governors made no collective effort to pressure the Lincoln administration or to improve the level of communication and cooperation among themselves.

The most effective interstate action was carried out by the Union Defence Committee (UDC) in New York City from approximately April 20 to May 3, 1861.[3] During those weeks, New York's elite directed Union war mobilization when rioting in Baltimore temporarily isolated Washington. The bipartisan UDC was organized by the city's leading businessmen working through the chamber of commerce and included such prominent names as James A. Dix. It had the support of New York City's public officeholders and was at least vaguely endorsed by the governor and high civil and military officers in the Lincoln administration. Within days the energetic committee, among other activities, mobilized the army and navy in defense of the North, conducted elaborate supply operations, acted to secure the allegiance of the border states, undertook intelligence operations, and blockaded Southern ports. Early in May, the UDC presented Washington with better information on the mustering of troops than did the War Department. Throughout these weeks, the committee members in Washington conferred with the nation's highest officials and pushed for greater vigor in mobilization, asserting that unless it was forthcoming, individuals would move on their own.

The Lincoln administration did not long tolerate such challenges to its authority and soon began taking control of the war effort. It worked with the state government to rein in the committee, which for a time defied control from any source. Although the UDC existed until nearly the war's end, its heyday was largely over by the end of May 1861. No other state had a mobilization organization as active, ambitious, and prestigious as New York's UDC, although other cities organized bodies of a similar nature, often called committees of safety. Chicago's Union Defence Committee was the only other private agency of businessmen and wealthy citizens that even came close to matching the New York City group.

The central point remains that although there was some cooperation between the states during the war years it was always quite limited. Confusion and isolation in the capital allowed a private, unofficial agency such as the UDC virtually to take over national mobilization functions for a short time, but its tenure was brief. The administration moved quickly to reestablish its authority so as to check centripetal forces that could have created a chaotic mobilization scheme operating from many centers. Society needed centralized mobilization to conduct a war successfully.

GOVERNORS, ELITES, AND STATE MOBILIZATION

The role of governors and elites in wartime leadership was crucial, and I shall analyze it within the general context of state mobilization by examining the experiences of Massachusetts, New York, Indiana, and Iowa, which are reasonably representative of the North's various regions. Covering all of the states would add little to the analysis and is impractical since information on many of them is still rather sketchy.

The states' chief executive largely determined the nature and tempo of the mobilization process, a factor dictated by several circumstances.[4] Throughout the nineteenth century, governors had gained power at the expense of legislatures through direct election, longer terms of service, fewer restrictions on reelection, the use of patronage, and veto power. This process was accelerated by the emergency of war and the governors' status as commanders-in-chief of the militia. Furthermore, the death of the Whig party, the fragmentation of the Democrats, and the rise of the Republican party in the 1850s strengthened the states as the primary focus of national politics and thus furthered the power and influence of governors, especially in the election of 1860. In carrying out their multiple tasks, governors created or expanded special staffs, relied upon their peacetime assistants, called upon official or unofficial advisers, or pursued some combination of those approaches.

Economic elites played a dominant part in nearly all aspects of state mobilization, primarily to fulfill their responsibilities and to protect their power. Secondarily, they acted from mixed motives, ranging from the high purpose of ending slavery to the narrow desire for maximizing political and economic gain. Whatever the motive, elite leadership was generally effective and played an important role in keeping an often war-weary population committed to fighting.

John A. Andrew, the abolitionist governor of Massachusetts, led the others in his single-minded, spirited, and efficient mobilization effort.[5] Starting in January 1861, he began preparing the state militia for hostilities, collecting ships for transporting men and supplies, and seeing to the defense of Boston Harbor. Within twenty-four hours of Lincoln's call for militia on April 15, two state regiments were en route to Washington.

The state of Massachusetts spent $27 million for war mobilization from 1861 through 1865, and its towns and cities spent nearly as much, bringing the total to about $50 million. Wartime finances presented no extraordinary problems for the Bay State since it had a well-established, efficient taxation mechanism, a high level of economic development, and a sound system of banks and other financial intermediaries. Moreover, as a major center of production for the military during the war, Massachusetts generated substantial wealth and a high level of savings.

Beginning in January–February 1861, the legislature generously supported Andrew's hectic efforts to prepare the state's militia for war and to assist the Union in general. In May 1861, at Andrew's urging, state legislators established a $3 million Union Fund to cover wartime expenses for which Washington would compensate the state; allowed the governor to create additional funding along the same lines up to $7 million; acted to finance through taxation and a sinking fund the state's war debt; exempted state banks from laws restricting their ability to make loans to the federal and state governments or buy their securities; and granted towns the authority to levy taxes to aid the families of soldiers, with provisions for reimbursement by the state government.

Massachusetts was equally diligent in raising troops for the military. It provided close to 160,000 men for both services, including nearly 20,000 for the navy. The state supplied one-fifth of the navy's enlisted men and slightly under one-quarter of its officers.[6]

As Washington took charge of organizing, equipping, and arming troops, Massachusetts generally ceased to supply and equip the volunteers it mustered.

Nonetheless, the state continued to be a major procurement center for textiles, leather products, clothing, and other goods.[7] Furthermore, the Springfield Arsenal remained critically important for research and development on small arms and the Connecticut Valley was the small-arms manufacturing center for the United States.[8] Thus Massachusetts had a reasonable number of small arms compared to other states when the secession crisis erupted in April.

With enormous economic potential and Andrew's dynamic leadership, Massachusetts outpaced most states in war preparedness. Besides mobilizing, arming, and equipping its own men, the state lent supplies and equipment to Maine and other states and retained agents in the nation's manufacturing centers to buy and contract for Massachusetts and for New England in general. It also sent well-financed delegations to Europe to purchase and contract for large numbers of small arms, ordnance, and the like, which it shared with numerous other states.

Elite leadership was evident in all aspects of Massachusetts' mobilization. The state's financial community came forward after Sumter to help fund mobilization, an action typical of what occurred throughout the nation. Boston banks offered the state $3.6 million in unsecured loans, and banks in other cities and wealthy individuals responded similarly.

Governor Andrew was from the state's elite and ably tapped the state's business and executive talent to aid mobilization. When Andrew became governor, an adjutant general and one clerk directed the state militia, a token system soon replaced by a structure that constantly grew in size. Shortly after being inaugurated, Andrew selected four aides as his personal staff to assist him as commander-in-chief of the militia, including Horace Binney Sargent and Henry Lee, Jr. Both men were well-connected members of the Boston elite, and the former had served in the administration of Andrew's predecessor, the conservative Nathaniel P. Banks.

Besides his official staff, the governor relied upon a host of personal advisers, emissaries, and assistants to help him carry out his overwhelming wartime duties. These aides included John M. Forbes, a leading Boston merchant; Francis B. Crowninshield, a prestigious Boston attorney; Ebenezer R. Hoar, a state supreme court justice; George S. Boutwell, a former Massachusetts governor; and Frank E. Howe, a Massachusetts merchant doing business in New York City. Howe became the New York agent for Massachusetts and other New England states. His place of business became known as the New England Rooms and served as a center for meeting the needs of the region and its troops traveling to or from the battlefields.

Logistical operations were becoming modern in terms of the number of supplies involved and the method of moving them. Merchants, manufacturers, railroad managers, and their associates, who had experience in conducting large business operations over long distances, proved invaluable in handling these new demands of warfare. Moreover, the businessmen and attorneys who assisted Andrew in the mobilization effort usually served without compensation. They and others like them resembled the dollar-a-year men who would direct economic mobilization for war in the twentieth century.

New York outdid Massachusetts.[9] It had the largest population and most advanced and diverse economy in the country. Through efficient mobilization, New York contributed more human and material resources to the Union war effort than any other state. Total spending for the war was at least $150 million and probably exceeded $200 million. Actually, most spending took place at the county, city, town, and village levels and was financed through taxation and various forms of borrowing.

New York was even better prepared than Massachusetts to meet the extraordinary financial demands of war since it had become the nation's financial center by 1850. Not only did the state have a rich, powerful, and diverse banking system, but Wall Street was emerging as a genuine center for securities exchange. As in Massachusetts, banks, other institutions, and private citizens made loans to the state for financing mobilization after Sumter. Municipalities throughout the state rallied to the Union cause with money, men, and supplies, but New York City, as the center of wealth, power, and the Union Defence Committee, was the natural hub of activity. New York, furthermore, extended its financial power in behalf of the Union. The state's institutions and citizens were a major source of credit for the federal government throughout the war years.

Unlike Andrew of Massachusetts, New York governor Edwin D. Morgan faced numerous obstacles to war mobilization, including several serious challenges to his authority. The first came from a divided and jealous legislature. This body delayed Morgan's attempts to prepare the militia before Sumter and then forced the governor to share executive authority with a Military Board. With skill and patience, Morgan minimized the damage from this intrusion on his authority. The Union Defence Committee was a second source of difficulty. Welcome and extremely helpful at first, the committee became troublesome when it continued functioning as an independent mobilization body. Morgan quickly squelched the UDC but established clear authority over mobilization only with assistance from Washington. Firmly in control by 1862, the governor led in meeting the wartime needs of the state and the Union. When Horatio Seymour became governor in 1863, political rivalry caused friction between the Republican legislature and the Democratic executive, and major irritation emerged between the governor and Washington. Lincoln managed the problem by maneuvering Seymour into a position in which his ambitions appeared opportunistic and even unpatriotic.

Discord aside, the Empire State more than carried its load in war mobilization. Over the course of the war, more than 500,000 New Yorkers served in the military, exceeding by more than 100,000 the contribution of any other state.[10] And the state paid the significant sum of $150.47 for every man recruited for the Union, including bounties and relief for families.

Like most states, New York faced emergency conditions once Lincoln called for troops after Sumter. Nonetheless, it responded with great rapidity because of its high level of preparedness relative to other states and its greater resources for meeting neglected or unanticipated needs. As was true for the Union in general, small arms were the limiting factor. To make up for the shortage, Governor Morgan and his staff procured 23,000 muskets from the Springfield Arsenal and also bought all the weapons they could at home and abroad. In time, Morgan put together an effective military staff, assisted by regulars on short-term loan to help standardize military procedures. The purchase of military clothing, equipment, and other supplies generally proceeded through competitive bidding. In the wake of a scandal over purchases of "shoddy" uniforms involving Brooks Brothers and state and other officials, proper inspection systems kept contracting abuses to a reasonably low level. At first, New York purchased some goods from outside its borders; within months, however, the state supplied almost all of its own needs.

By mid-August, regular army officers had taken charge of equipping and supplying New York troops. The state's role thereafter shifted to raising manpower and supplying the war effort. Economic strength ensured that New York remained a major source for foodstuffs, armaments, and numerous other products. The state was second to Pennsylvania in ironmaking and second to Massachusetts in the output of textiles and boots and shoes.[11] Two-thirds of the nation's imports and one-third of its exports passed through New York City; only London and Liverpool surpassed it as centers of international trade. Although war at first disrupted the state's prosperity, overall it stimulated manufacturing, thereby increasing wealth and savings.

Morgan was assisted and supported by a collection of elites more impressive than those available to Andrew. The governor, a wholesale grocer whose firm had investments in banking, railroads, public utilities, and state bonds, was a wealthy person with good connections in business and public life. His advisers and assistants included his cousin George D. Morgan, W. M. Evarts, M. H. Grinnell, and George Opdyke, all prominent merchants, and others such as the attorney R. M. Blatchford and the aristocratic gentleman-farmer James S. Wadsworth. To facilitate recruitment after the first flush of patriotism had passed, Morgan organized throughout the state military committees made up of prominent and influential citizens. Moreover, Morgan and his successor had the support of the chamber of commerce, the Stock Exchange, the Board of Currency, the Clearing House, and other similar organizations. The Union Defence Committee was also a New York City creation, and the critically important U.S. Sanitary Commission and U.S. Christian Commission originated in the Empire State. In short, New York's contribution to the Union cause in wealth, goods, and ability was unmatched.

Indiana was one of the important states of the Old Northwest and also the fifth most populous state in the nation.[12] Governor Oliver P. Morton remained in office throughout the war and was among the Union's few outstanding chief executives. Indiana was crucial to the Union because of its large population, agricultural output, and geographic location. Southern Indiana, along with the southern parts of Ohio and Illinois, joined Missouri, Kentucky, and West Virginia in constituting a borderland separating the North from the South.[13] Loyalties and sentiments in this region were profoundly divided and fed a growing Democratic challenge to Republican rule. These conditions gave a raw and raucous quality to Indiana politics typical of the Old Northwest and West in which political violence broke out sporadically or lurked beneath the surface, civil liberties were badly compromised, and dictatorial rule was not a rarity. In the midst of the Civil War, partisanship west of the Mississippi came to resemble combat more than political competition.

Despite the nearly unending strife that rent Indiana throughout the war years, the state more than carried its weight in supporting the war. Total war-related spending approximated $25.5 million. Counties, cities, towns, and villages accounted for over $20.5 million, with approximately $4.5 million going for relief of soldiers' wives and families and the rest spent on bounties. The state government used its part mainly to raise, supply, and arm the troops and to service the debt. As in most other states, a combination of taxes and borrowing at all levels was used to raise funds for war, with borrowing the favored device.

Unlike the New England and Middle States, Indiana was not in a favorable position to finance ordinary, and certainly not extraordinary, expenditures. Reforms in 1855 stabilized a chaotic banking system; but on the eve of war the system was still limited in nature, and there were few other financial intermediaries. Because Indiana had repudiated its internal-improvement debt of the 1840s and fraudulent practices arose in the sale of bonds during hostilities, wartime securities sold at a substantial discount in and outside the state and were difficult to market in any quantity.[14]

The outbreak of war found the state virtually without financial resources. Morton quickly called the legislature into an emergency session and several millions were authorized for mobilization and defense, but that action did not provide the funds the state needed immediately. Consequently, banks, merchants, and others in Indiana stepped in with loans to initiate mobilization, and the governor prevailed upon a New York banking house to advance the state $400,000.

If Indiana finances were shaky before 1863, they became positively bizarre thereafter when Democrats took over the legislature. With Morton and the lawmakers at loggerheads on most issues, the state functioned without legally sanctioned appropriations for two years. Bold, and constitutionally cavalier, Morton operated his own public treasury, borrowing from the federal government, counties, and individuals and institutions in Indiana and New York to finance state operations and to pay interest on the debt. The governor defied court judgments against his unlawful behavior and was vindicated in 1865 when the Republicans took back the legislature and retroactively legalized his activities of the past two years.

Indiana faced even greater initial difficulties in acquiring the arms, equipment, and supplies needed to mobilize the militia and volunteers. The state had fewer than 1,000 serviceable muskets as hostilities approached. When Washington could not provide the weapons the state needed, Morton turned to open-market purchasing. State agents were sent to Canada and the East to buy whatever arms they could obtain. Ultimately, Robert Dale Owen directed the arms-purchasing program, which extended as far as Europe. Owen continued his operations through February 1863, during which time he purchased 30,000 English Enfield rifles and other arms at a price of nearly $.75 million. The federal government paid for most weapons, but Indiana covered part of the expense. Owen, along with others, also purchased large amounts of equipment and supplies.

Although the federal government took over supply operations in August–September 1861, Indiana, under the direction of the efficient but imperious Morton, continued to purchase for Indiana troops and to supply them throughout the war. The state did so to protect its soldiers in the event federal logistics broke down but also because Morton refused to recognize limits on his authority. Along those lines, the governor set up a state arsenal to manufacture ammunition and kept it in operation until April 1864, long after Washington had ample productive capacity.

Morton's furious mobilization activity achieved results at the cost of corruption. The first state commissary general, for example, was Isaiah Mansur, a meatpacker and personal friend of the governor who was forced out of the position through a legislative investigation that proved incompetence, conflicts of interest, and gross malfeasance in office. Comparable conditions existed in the state's Quartermaster Department, and Indiana's agent in New York was involved in a fraudulent scheme involving huge blocks of state bonds.

Raising troops proved much easier than procuring arms, supplies, and financing. Indiana had filled its quota within five days of Lincoln's call for troops and clamored for Washington to accept more men. Over the course of the war, 208,367 Hoosiers served, about 8,500 over the quota. During the first two years of conflict, Indiana raised men for the army without bounties; any financial incentives were intended to support soldiers' families. From 1863 on, the seemingly unending calls from Washington became harder and harder to meet. As a result, localities, but not the state, had recourse to the bounty system along with the threat of a draft. After extended delay and great reluctance, federal conscription was used to raise about 12,000 men in October 1864, the only instance of coercion other than the militia draft in summer 1862.[15]

Indiana experienced substantial growth in agriculture and manufacturing in the 1850s and 1860s and therefore proved to be an important source of supply for the Union armies. Its principal contribution, naturally, was food. The state led all others in the raising of hogs, corn and wheat were major crops, and raising cattle was also significant.[16] Indiana's industries processed mostly food and natural resources.[17]

Governor Morton, an attorney who grew prosperous through railroad litigation, drew upon an elite structure during mobilization that differed from those in New England and the Middle States. Since Indiana was not too far beyond the frontier stage, economic development and wealth concentration were less advanced and entrenched than in the East. Additionally, a chronic shortage of credit in the West meant that Eastern and European capital played a much larger role in state affairs than occurred east of the Mississippi. New York financiers were especially important in Hoosier affairs, particularly the banking house of Winslow, Lanier, and Company. J. F. D. Lanier was from Indiana and long involved in banking and railroad ventures in the state. His New York investment firm had good connections at home and abroad and pioneered in the sale of Western railroad bonds. The governor turned to Lanier and his company repeatedly to help sell state securities, to secure loans and financial assistance to begin mobilization in 1861, and to continue state operations when Morton carried on without legislative appropriations from 1863 to 1865. The Ocean Bank of New York also aided Morton when Confederate troops threatened the Indiana border late in 1862. As the war progressed, Indiana's banking system fashioned in the 1850s served the state well. It was shaped and managed by Hugh McCulloch, who later served as U.S. comptroller of the currency from 1863 to 1865 and finally as secretary of the treasury under Pres. Andrew Johnson.

Morton relied heavily upon the state's economic leaders to facilitate mobilization. He turned to Indianapolis businessmen to fill the key roles of quartermaster and commissary generals in the early months of the war. For buying arms and supplies in the Eastern cities, Canada, and Europe, he called upon men such as Calvin Fletcher, an Indianapolis banker. To head the state's Sanitary Commission, Morton tapped the talents of William Hannaman, a prominent businessman. Throughout the war, the governor proved exceptionally resourceful in raising troops. One element in this success was that, like Morgan of New York and other governors, he depended upon a statewide network of prominent and influential individuals to activate and push forward the enlistment process. Although Indiana's mobilization relied upon elites, they were less wealthy and prominent than those in the Eastern states.

Politically, Iowa stood somewhere between the turbulent states of the Old Northwest and the rather sedate, more securely Republican, and less-developed states of the Midwest such as Michigan, Wisconsin, and Minnesota.[18] Since numerous Southerners lived there, Iowa experienced some of the divisiveness and violence typical of Indiana, Illinois, and Ohio. Moreover, it faced guerrilla warfare in the southern area that bordered on Missouri in addition to Indian attacks to the west and north. Samuel J. Kirkwood, a moderate Republican, was elected governor in 1859 and reelected in 1861. He stepped aside in 1863 for William M. Stone after ensuring the latter's victory by thoroughly intimidating the Democratic opposition through the use of hysteria and the militia.

Compared with most other states, Iowa spent little on the war. Direct state expenditures totaled $1.05 million. The counties spent about $2.21 million for bounties and relief, or $2.74 million if local and private contributions are included. War spending by the government in Iowa thus comes to under $4 million by official statistics, figures that are somewhat low because all outlays are not included for various reasons.

Iowa's war spending was low, especially at the state level, because the state faced dire economic and financial conditions when fighting broke out. The financial panic of 1857 and the subsequent economic downturn hit the Midwest hard, and recovery was much slower than in the East. Bad weather between 1856 and 1858 exacerbated conditions. The outbreak of war caused further economic deterioration by cutting off the Mississippi as an avenue for marketing Iowa's crops. Substantial delays occurred before commodities started to flow eastward to Chicago by rail. One measure of the state's distress is that late in 1861 nearly $400,000 was outstanding in unpaid or delinquent taxes and $103,645 in state warrants was collecting interest because no funds existed to retire them. An inadequate banking system exaggerated

Iowa's economic troubles. A new constitution and legislation in 1857–1858 lifted the state's ban on banks and set up a state bank with fifteen branches and a carefully structured free banking arrangement. The system began operation in the midst of an economic slump, however, and was barely under way when war broke out.[19]

Iowa's military preparedness on the eve of war was even worse than its economy. There was no militia, only a few independent drill companies. The state lacked arms, uniforms, and supplies and had little or no capacity for manufacturing them. Governor Kirkwood pleaded for small arms from Washington in January 1861 but without success. When war started, he sent purchasing agents throughout the nation and personally traveled to New York and Washington on a largely futile hunt for weaponry. Kirkwood finally arranged for the state's meager supply of weapons to be collected, cleaned, repaired, and distributed according to priority. Iowa women and tailors combined their efforts to clothe the first troops in crude uniforms made from skimpy cloth. More than two months passed before Iowa's first regiment left the state.

Lack of funds crippled procurement in Iowa since the state had no liquid assets. As elsewhere, banks, prominent individuals including the governor, and businesses lent money and services or pledged security for loans to raise, train, equip, and transport the first regiments. Kirkwood called the legislature into special session in May 1861 to arrange more permanent solutions. It legalized his mobilization activity and authorized the sale of $800,000 in bonds to cover war costs. The securities proved nearly impossible to sell because most towns and counties had repudiated railroad bonds in the past, and critics charged that the bonds were unconstitutional. By August 1862 Iowa had managed to dispose of only $300,000 of the bonds at a value of $277,320. No effort was made to sell the rest.

Unlike Indiana, Iowa could not tap Eastern wealth during the war. Consequently, the federal government had to take over the financing of mobilization there earlier than in most other states. Iowa equipped and armed only its first three regiments; after that, Washington covered all expenses and also paid the troops from the time they entered the ranks until they were mustered into federal service. Still, supply problems persisted. Because it was so far west, the state's troops often received the weapons other states rejected. Small arms, uniforms, blankets, and equipment were frequently in short supply. Moreover, the state had to equip and arm a Home Guard to protect its border with Missouri and to deter Indian attacks. Though its procurement responsibilities were limited compared with other states, Iowa instituted proper safeguards against malfeasance and fraud. Difficulties notwithstanding, Iowa carried its wartime load. It met all troop quotas and used the draft only once in 1864 to raise fewer than 2,000 men. The state furnished between 76,000 and 80,000 men altogether.[20]

Iowa made some contribution to the Union's economic strength in agriculture, particularly in the output of corn, wheat, and hogs. But production even in those areas was not outstanding, and the state had little to offer in terms of manufactured goods.[21] Generally, Iowa suffered from economic underdevelopment, because of inadequate transportation and banking systems. Nonetheless, as the war continued, the state prospered because of high demand, high prices, and healthy income from taxes. At all levels, Iowa was economically better off in 1865 than in 1861. Revenue sources were sufficient to meet all needs, enabling the state to end bond sales after August 1862.

Iowa's mobilization manifested elite patterns, though the luster, depth, and wealth visible in the East was lacking. Kirkwood, a native of Maryland, had worked in Ohio as a teacher, lawyer, and prosecuting attorney in addition to his involvement in politics. In Iowa, he managed a brother-in-law's farm and flour mill. The governor's nearly indispensable adjutant general was Nathaniel Baker, a Harvard graduate and former governor of New Hampshire. Baker's administrative genius and Kirkwood's energy, decisiveness, and determination largely account for Iowa's overcoming underdevelopment and isolation to contribute modestly to the Union cause. However, many other people joined in facilitating mobilization. Officers of branches of the state bank were particularly important, including Hiram Price of Davenport, also a railroad investor who won election to the House of Representatives in 1862. Additional assistance came from various attorneys, bankers, and merchants, some of whom held political office or served in the military.

Massachusetts, New York, Indiana, and Iowa well represent the range of mobilization activity in the Northern states. They featured temporary financing by banks, the prominent, and the wealthy; a mixed supply record in which clothing and equipment were much easier to manufacture and procure than small arms; and an elite-dominated mobilization process.[22]

A few other observations on state mobilization are noteworthy. Events in the border states did not match those in any of the four representative states, but the models are still useful. Missouri, Kentucky, West Virginia, Maryland, and Delaware resembled the Old Northwest and Midwest states in terms of economic development. Moreover, Missouri was similar to Iowa in that the federal government stepped in very early to finance the state's mobilization. The major difference, of course, was that federal troops or their surrogates intervened to varying degrees in all the border states and oversaw the political and electoral process in most of them throughout the war. The prominent federal role in state affairs naturally favored certain political, economic, and social groups at the expense of others. Nonetheless, with expectable variations, mobilization patterns in the border states resembled those in the rest of the Union.

Additionally, the chief executives of most states fit Duane Lockard's definition of "the businessman's governor," a stage in state governance that lasted from the mid-nineteenth century until the early years of the twentieth century.[23] Business did not control governors and states in some vulgar sense, but the governor usually came from or was affiliated with the business community, and businessmen exercised predominant influence in state affairs. Canal companies, railroad corporations, and manufacturing firms wielded exceptional power and influence as the pace of industrialization quickened.

Andrew of Massachusetts was too idealistic and ideological to fit this paradigm and Kirkwood of Iowa too much the earthy, self-made person for that mold. But Morgan of New York and Morton of Indiana came close to Lockard's definition. Moreover, regardless of the background and pedigree of governors, their civilian and military staff members came principally from the ranks of business, with bankers, merchants, attorneys, and railroad and canal interests heavily represented. Where that was not the case, the staffers were generally young, well educated, well connected, and interested in politics. Such patterns are not surprising. To mobilize a state's financial, material, and human resources under conditions that at least suggested modernity, governors turned to individuals with managerial experience, power, and prestige. The nation's elitist past and the demands of the war allowed few alternatives.[24]

By early 1862 the federal government had fairly well taken charge of equipping, supplying, and arming troops. As that occurred, governors who had acted at the outset of hostilities as independent war ministers were gradually reduced to the status of agents of the War Department, albeit often cranky and petulant ones. Even in their diminished roles, governors and the states they headed performed important mobilization functions in two areas: military manpower and troop welfare. From the opening to the close of hostilities, and even after the federal government imposed a national military obligation with the Enrollment Act of March 1863, the states raised most of the troops in the Union army based on quotas set by Washington.

THE WELFARE OF THE TROOPS

States took a leading role in providing for the welfare of the troops. Although elites usually led in this area, mass support was essential for success. State activity on behalf of troop welfare took place at home and during military operations outside state boundaries. Efforts on the home front were more limited and comparatively uncomplicated.

Home-front activities centered on assisting needy families of volunteers.[25] At the outset, when most people anticipated a short war, family welfare was a major concern only in large metropolitan areas such as New York City. In a protracted war where long-term service was the norm, however, dependent support became an urgent matter. Yet the federal government did little to resolve it. No family allowance existed, troop pay was low, and sending money home was no mean feat. Through the U.S. Allotment System created by Congress in July 1861 (the navy already had a successful program in operation), soldiers could assign all or some of their pay to designated parties, but the system worked poorly. Furthermore, mail delivery was generally unreliable, bank services expensive, and army pay irregular. To give soldiers a dependable, economical means of transferring funds home, various states and organizations such as the U.S. Sanitary Commission set up programs.

Indeed, the burden of providing for volunteers' dependents was left largely to the states. Bounties were initially considered a form of family support. A few states, such as Massachusetts, Vermont, and Ohio, paid dependent support or augmented federal payments to the troops or did both. More commonly, states allowed county and local governments to raise and expend funds for such programs and later made those efforts mandatory, the practice that occurred in Indiana and Iowa. Most mandatory requirements were only enacted in the last months of the war, however. Government aid generally consisted of scheduled payments to families. In Massachusetts, families received a maximum of twelve dollars a month; in one county in Indiana, wives received five dollars a month plus two dollars for each child under ten, and orphans received four dollars. Many states, usually in conjunction with philanthropic organizations, established asylums, sanitariums, homes, and schools for the families of soldiers killed in the war and for disabled veterans and their dependents. Some states established special programs and institutions to meet the needs of sailors, marines, and their dependents. Others took actions such as exempting soldiers' families from taxation and postponing legal proceedings against them. On the whole, however, the direct and indirect contributions of states to the needy families of volunteers were not great. For example, in Indiana, which under Governor Morton was usually a leader in soldier welfare, localities spent $4.6 million on aid for soldiers' families but $15.5 on bounties. Some counties had a ratio of seven to one or higher.

Since government at all levels was not particularly active in supporting soldiers' dependents, private sources assumed much of the responsibility. Relatives, friends, and neighbors were the main sources of relief at first, but that was only an interim solution. As the war stretched out, benevolent organizations assumed a larger role. Churches and the clergy were notably active in this regard, and the Union Defence Committee in New York began financing relief programs as early as April 1861. Most relief work, however, was done by women's groups organized as soldiers' aid societies. Such societies operated, under different names and with varying functions, in practically every village, town, and city. Large municipalities such as New York had ethnic organizations of Irish and Germans, among others. Industrial aid societies, again mostly in large cities, employed soldiers' wives to make clothing and other articles for the troops to increase family income. Most groups, however, began as organizations to help clothe, supply, and feed the first troops in spring 1861, continued to advance the welfare of the state's troops throughout the war, and took on the added duty of providing for needy families. Assistance came in many forms but seldom involved cash payments. Families received contributions of food, fuel, clothing, and other necessities; medical attention was sometimes available; and certain places organized soup kitchens, free markets, and cooperative buying and farming programs. Many rural communities designated contribution days when all residents were expected to donate items for needy families.

Despite this assistance, dependents of soldiers without an adequate income apparently led a precarious existence. Families of volunteers were reported to be living in deplorable conditions throughout the nation. Governments failed to accept responsibility for families in need, and private assistance was piecemeal. Furthermore, though aid to soldiers' families differed from poor relief in theory, that did not occur in fact. Aid was geared to a minimum standard of living, means tests were applied along with strict accountability, and benefits were quickly cut off if the serviceman was discharged or killed. Even then, officials of the U.S. Sanitary Commission protested that over-generous aid programs encouraged indolence and misbehavior among the poor. In short, family assistance was looked upon as a form of charity rather than as a social debt.[26]

State welfare activities on behalf of fighting men were more innovative, ongoing, and generous than for their dependents.[27] Official and voluntary agencies that mobilized the first troops also assisted in feeding, clothing, equipping, and sheltering them in federal camps when the War Department proved unequal to the task. Once the army's supply structure began to function properly, the states cut back their efforts. Nevertheless, the states repeatedly stepped in to help the troops when crises arose. For example, when Gen. Ulysses S. Grant's army in the West ran out of the requisite antiscorbutics in spring 1863, voluntary organizations in the Northwest states set in motion a huge flow of vegetables, dried and preserved fruit, and jellies to the troops.[28]

Beginning in late 1861, some of the most important contributions of the states involved medical and hospital care. The army's Medical Bureau was ill-prepared to serve an expanded regular army, let alone hundreds of thousands of volunteers crowded into makeshift camps. Unsanitary practices led to high sickness rates in the early months of the war. To alleviate this problem, states extended the operations of their own surgeons general to include the federal camps. Additionally, various state groups, usually women's soldiers' aid societies, prepared medical provisions for troops in federal camps. After First Bull Run in July 1861 demonstrated the Medical Bureau's nearly total ineptitude, the states realized the need for increased aid to the Union army. Their response became fully manifest with Shiloh in April 1862, but the pattern was evident for some states even earlier, during lesser engagements. To handle the thousands of casualties, states rushed doctors, nurses, and medical supplies—in effect, surgical teams—to the battle sites. Whenever possible, trains and steamboats transported medical personnel and provisions to the front and evacuated the wounded and dying to nearby medical centers. In many cases, the wounded were sent to their home state for further treatment and convalescence. State assistance decreased as the Medical Bureau improved its operations. Nonetheless, until the war's end, states at a minimum maintained agents with their troops to ensure proper care and to intervene if necessary.

When wounded and sick soldiers could not be brought home, most states implemented programs to ease their pain and speed their recovery at medical facilities near the front. Nurses and cooks were dispatched for long-term service; others supplied food, clothing, reading material and gifts, read to and wrote letters for the soldiers, and did whatever was helpful.

In addition to medical assistance, the states provided services to all troops. They saw to the nonmedical needs of the sick and wounded and also looked after the furloughed and discharged and victims of lost, destroyed, or incorrect records. Numerous state agents, some without pay, worked with volunteer groups to serve the troops in fighting areas and principal cities such as Washington and New York. These agents set up centers providing in an elementary way those services that would later be performed by the USO, Red Cross, American Legion, and Veterans Administration. At their best, these centers offered medical, sleeping, eating, religious, and recreational services (in some instances even for the soldiers' wives, relatives, and friends); assistance with travel, emergency funding, and legal complications; help in dealing with pay, allotments, bounties, pensions, and discharges; and directories for locating wounded soldiers and learning of their condition. Governors, state officials, and agents also demanded that troops held captive by the Confederacy receive proper treatment; sought to get food, clothing, and medicine to them; and facilitated exchanges of prisoners. Many states designed these services only for their own men but most offered temporary assistance to all troops.

The level and quality of services naturally varied greatly with the wealth, political leadership, and esprit of the state involved. For obvious reasons, Massachusetts and New York made great contributions; Kansas and West Virginia ranked very low. Iowa's services were also limited, but Indiana's were among the best. Generally speaking, the Eastern states actively aided their troops but also supported the U.S. Sanitary Commission, even to the point of subordinating their efforts to its own, while providing substantial backing for the U.S. Christian Commission and even the Western Sanitary Commission. States west of the Alleghenies usually did less in quantitative terms because they were less wealthy, had smaller populations, and fielded fewer troops. Nonetheless, the dedication and drive these states brought to assisting the troops often equaled, even exceeded, that in the East. But frontier and agrarian particularism and resentment of the USSC as an Eastern, elite creation made the states west of the Alleghenies much less willing to work with the commission. Consideration of events in Iowa and Indiana demonstrates the complex nature of troop welfare efforts by the Western states.

Among states west of the Alleghenies, Iowa and Indiana provided the lowest and highest level of service for their fighting forces. Iowa's problems stemmed in part from economic underdevelopment, rudimentary transportation and communication systems, and isolation, but the state's political leadership was also lacking. Kirkwood was as concerned about and involved in troop welfare as Andrew of Massachusetts, but the former was not able to maintain centralized control of aid efforts. Stone, his successor, did somewhat better. Beginning in 1861, two organizations in Iowa competed to assist the troops: one based on the women's soldiers' aid societies and the other originating with the governor and principally representing the state's male establishment. The first preferred state-based welfare efforts or working with the Western Sanitary Commission; the second sought to cooperate with the USSC. Competition and recriminations between the two weakened welfare activities. Confused and dispirited by the clash, citizens lost interest in helping the troops or attempted independent aid efforts. In November 1863, as the state's soldiers' relief effort approached collapse, the two organizations compromised and merged into the Iowa Sanitary Commission. Infighting continued with less intensity thereafter as various welfare activists lined up with either the USSC or the U.S. Christian Commission. Better organization permitted the state's aid contributions to increase in 1864 and 1865. Iowa's troops nevertheless suffered from sanitary, dietary, and medical deficiencies, and their needs always exceeded materials the state supplied.[29]

Indiana was as accomplished as Iowa was lacking, largely due to the efforts of Governor Morton. Shrewdly aware that the war and its veterans would shape the political terrain for decades to come, Morton exerted himself to become the most prominent "soldiers' friend." Although the state made unremarkable efforts to aid volunteers' dependents, Indiana outperformed all other states in providing services for the troops through government and voluntary organizations. The entire system became part of the political machine Morton was building, as humane and generous instincts mixed inextricably with opportunism. He frequently visited camps and battlefields, maintained a voluminous correspondence with regimental officers, and directed or closely monitored troop welfare activities. Public relations along modern lines publicized the efforts of the governor and state on behalf of the volunteers. For example, elaborate and highly political receptions in the state capital feted the return home of all troops, from the first volunteers to the last regiments after Appomattox. Other state politicians trying to curry favor with the troops quickly learned that Morton did not welcome competition. Officers of the Union army serving in Indiana who did not please the governor soon found themselves replaced, as did the commanding general of the Army of the Ohio. If Morton could not get his way with officers, he did not hesitate to appeal to the secretary of war or the president. Morton's reputation as the "soldiers' friend" served him well during the war. When the Republicans lost control of the legislature in 1863, he put the Democrats on the defensive by maneuvering to have officers and enlisted men charge them with unpatriotic motives and even treason. To ensure a proper margin of victory for himself, Lincoln, and the Republican party in 1864, the governor brought troops home and prohibited others from leaving the state, fully confident of how they would vote.

Programs organized in the states to maintain the welfare of troops were nearly indispensable. Nonetheless, twenty-four states operating independently, particularly when led by figures such as Morton, could cause problems as well as solve them. State activity had to be coordinated for maximum effectiveness. Since the federal government was unprepared to move forcefully in dealing with troop welfare on a national scale, private organizations took the initiative. The U.S. Sanitary Commission was notable in this regard.

The USSC grew out of the combined efforts of the Women's Central Association of Relief, organized in New York City in April 1861, and several concerned, prominent men of the city who sought to bring some order and direction to the numerous volunteer soldiers' aid societies formed after Sumter.[30] The USSC emerged in June 1861 as an anomalous, mixed commission of men working with the War Department to improve relief, sanitation, and medical care in the army. Although sanctioned by the secretary of war and the president, the USSC was a private, voluntary group with a semiofficial status, not a government agency. The commission drew upon the experience of the British and French during the Crimean War.

The commission found itself from the outset in a nearly impossible position. Fulfilling its goals required working with the army's Medical Bureau, but the bureau was small and its structure ossified.[31] It was grossly unprepared to handle hundreds of thousands of volunteers and had no systems for evacuation and hospitalization in a war that would produce unheard-of levels of casualties. Colonel Clement A. Finley, the surgeon general, was extremely rigid and resistant to change. He bristled at the idea of taking advice from civilians and particularly at putting up with the cold, professional arrogance of USSC president Henry W. Bellows and general secretary Frederick Law Olmsted. Tense relations between the bureau and the USSC took on the characteristics of trench warfare. Progress in upgrading the Medical Bureau's operations was agonizingly slow. The commission gained an important ally when George B. McClellan became commander of the Army of the Potomac and then commanding general. In time, his support combined with that of Lincoln, Assistant Secretary of War Thomas A. Scott, and members of Congress to achieve in April 1862 the USSC's goals of legislation reforming the Medical Bureau and the replacement of Finley with the commission's candidate, William A. Hammond. Relatively young, dynamic, and exceptionally able, the new surgeon general began implementing the changes with a sure hand. Hammond, however, soon antagonized the irascible secretary of war, Edwin M. Stanton. The latter saw Hammond as a tool of the USSC, which Stanton suspected with some justification of trying to take over the Medical Bureau. Stanton forced Hammond out in August 1863 and replaced him with Joseph K. Barnes.

Nonetheless, Hammond and the USSC reworked the Medical Bureau so successfully that the systems instituted for evacuation and hospitalization endured for a century. Precisely gauging the commission's importance in the Medical Bureau reforms is nearly impossible, but the USSC had a hand in most of the restructuring. Overall, the commission's activities fell into three general categories: sanitary work in the camps, hospital and ambulance reforms, and relief and welfare efforts on behalf of the troops.

Unsanitary early army camps presented a major menace to the soldiers' health. The camps were often inappropriately located, overcrowded, and lacking proper arrangements for clean water, latrines, garbage disposal, ventilation, and personal hygiene. Conditions were so bad in the Army of the Potomac that fully one-third of the soldiers were sick in August 1861. The Sanitary Commission addressed these gross deficiencies almost immediately through inspections, reports, and monographs on preventative hygiene and measures to preserve the soldiers' health. Although the work of the commission was rejected at first, many of the reforms it advocated became accepted procedures before the end of 1861. By November of that year the rate of sickness in the Army of the Potomac had fallen to 6.5 percent.[32]

The USSC's work in army hospitals was exceptional. The army had no hospital system to speak of when war broke out. Only a few post hospitals existed, the largest housing forty men. Regimental tent hospitals and facilities improvised in old hotels, barracks, schools, and homes could not meet the needs of the war. Basing their ideas on Britain's accomplishments during the Crimean War, the commission insisted upon and offered designs for inexpensive "pavilion" hospitals that were properly ventilated, with separate wards to prevent the spread of disease and infection. The first such hospital was built in early 1862. By the end of the war, 204 general hospitals existed with a capacity of nearly 137,000 beds. The commission's investigators also helped introduce proper sanitation, antiseptics, and disinfectants in military hospitals. Of critical importance was a series of monographs, written for the Medical Bureau by specialists under the direction of the USSC, on proper surgical methods and the treatment of sick and wounded soldiers.[33] The commission also helped train and supply female nurses, who served under Dorothea L. Dix.

The USSC's contributions to medicine and hospital care were part of a larger system of evacuation and hospitalization designed, perfected, and ultimately implemented for the entire army by Surgeon General Hammond and Jonathan Letterman, medical director of the Army of the Potomac. Under this system, regiments had first-aid or collection stations close to the battlefields, with tented field hospitals about three miles to the rear. Base hospitals were located at main supply depots, and general hospitals conveniently placed throughout the nation. A separate ambulance corps was developed under the Medical Bureau and did not answer to the Quartermaster Department or other army units as had been the case in 1861. Men were carried from battle sites to first-aid stations on litters, to field hospitals by ambulance, and then moved to base and general hospitals, when necessary, by ambulance, train, or boat. The USSC played an important role in founding the ambulance corps and constantly lobbied for an efficient, independent service. More important, the USSC helped inaugurate an evacuation system using steamboats on the Western rivers early in 1862 and took over by default the entire steamer operation during the Peninsula campaign later that year. In 1861–1862 the commission built and turned over to the army special hospital trains. After many bureaucratic snafus, the Medical Bureau succeeded between 1863 and 1865 in having the hospital transports placed under its exclusive control to prevent other military units from seizing its boats and trains.

Overall, the Union posted a good record in sanitation and medical care during the Civil War. Although more than twice as many men died from diseases than from battlefield wounds, there was only an 8 percent mortality rate among the more than 1 million men treated in general hospitals during hostilities. During the Civil War, the Union's sick and wounded had better care than had ever been the case in war before. The USSC made an enormous contribution to that substantial accomplishment.[34]

The USSC is best remembered as a soldiers' relief agency, having assumed large-scale relief work for several reasons. First, the need was great. The War Department was unable to provide sufficient supplies for the large numbers of troops in the early phases of the war. After army supply became regularized, emergencies still arose, and a protracted war created demands among the men that the federal government was simply unprepared to handle. Second, a nationally coordinated effort was essential to meet these needs. Independent local and state efforts produced uneven results that demoralized the army as some troops received more than others. Furthermore, numerous civilians involved in army operations on an irregular basis undermined military discipline. Finally, emphasizing relief maintained the public support that the Sanitary Commission needed to exist. The general population was anxious to participate in the relief of the troops and preferred programs it could see and understand, which was not the case with, for instance, sanitation and medical reforms. By ignoring that reality, the commission was almost forced to shut down late in 1862 when donations lapsed and it ran out of funds. The USSC survived the crisis and became more attentive to public opinion in order to ensure continued support.

In its relief activities, the commission had two principal goals: to create an organization for raising contributions and distributing goods and services in an effective way and to persuade all or most states to cooperate with and subordinate their activities to those of the USSC. The Sanitary Commission was much more successful in achieving the first goal than the second.

The commission's relief work began in 1861 and grew in scope and importance throughout the war. The USSC had a tiered structure to collect resources for relief, with over 7,000 local soldiers' aid societies at the base. Many of these groups had come into existence before joining the Sanitary Commission; they were usually run by women and tied into state and regional organizations. Through the USSC system, tons of supplies were donated, funds collected, and numerous events held to raise money for the cause. Depots and subdepots were maintained in cities throughout the nation as points of collection and distribution. Canvassing agents, bulletins, letters, and advertisements were used to communicate with the thousands of local USSC branches.

Supplies and provisions were distributed according to well-defined rules and procedures for several reasons. For purposes of efficiency, the commission wanted to reinforce, not undermine, military discipline. It also refused to cover for, and thereby encourage, government inefficiency. Help was offered for unanticipated and inevitable shortages, but the USSC would not pitch in where crises resulted from army incompetence or neglect. The commission carefully structured a hierarchy to monitor all hospitals and the condition of troops in camp, on the march, and in battle. During major campaigns such as the Wilderness, the USSC mounted massive supply operations by wagon, rail, and steamboat.

The USSC designated such operations as General Relief. It also had elaborate staffs and structures to handle Special Relief programs for individuals needing assistance but unable or ineligible to get it through the military: discharged, furloughed, sick, and convalescing soldiers; paroled prisoners; and unfortunate men whose records were missing or incorrect.

The Sanitary Commission insisted that all its goods and services be identified as coming from the commission as a federal and scientific organization, motivated solely by priority and need, not from states or localities. The commissioners were so adamant on this point that they refused contributions if donors insisted that the source of gifts be identified or if they specified how assistance was to be used or to whom it should go. Over the course of the war, the USSC collected a total of $25 million in cash, supplies, and services. Clearly, the commission realized its first goal of running an effective relief organization to benefit the Union army.[35]

Its second aim, to bring all relief activities under the umbrella of the USSC, proved more elusive. Several important organizations operated outside the commission's orbit, competing with it, diluting its authority, and weakening its coordinating role. The first was the Western Sanitary Commission (WSC), organized in September 1861 by a group of community leaders in St. Louis to relieve the suffering of sick and wounded soldiers left without hospital care.[36] Throughout the war years it collected and distributed about $4.5 million in supplies and funds, performing west of the Mississippi most of the services the USSC offered in the East. Unlike the USSC, it had no local auxiliaries or agents to facilitate collections, relying instead on word of mouth and newspaper notices. Although most contributions came from the West, the WSC received support from throughout the nation. It was also the first relief organization systematically to offer assistance to Southern refugees and freedmen. From the outset, the USSC unsuccessfully tried to absorb the WSC. Relations between the two were always tense, especially after the WSC began receiving contributions from the East. Various Western states preferred the WSC to the USSC because of its origins, region of operations, and less rigid style.

The U.S. Christian Commission constituted a much more formidable competitor for the USSC.[37] Organized in New York City in November 1861 by evangelical Protestant clergy and laymen, most of whom were active in the Young Men's Christian Association (YMCA), the Christian Commission did not get fully under way until the end of 1862. The USCC had many strengths: it was well connected in the Lincoln administration; included prominent leaders such as Jay Cooke on the executive committee; commanded support among religious, business, and political leaders; and possessed a ready network in the clergy and churches, Bible, tract, temperance, and Sunday school societies, Ladies' Christian Commissions, and YMCA locals.

Although it initially focused on the spiritual welfare of the troops, the Christian Commission, like the USSC, found that material needs had to be addressed to secure the support of soldiers and the home front. Unlike the USSC, it did not work through the army's structure, emphasized healing and comforting the soldier's body and soul over military efficiency, and stressed the value of the layman over the professional. The USCC had paid agents at home and with the troops, but its 5,000 "delegates" formed the core of the organization's strength, some of whom would later become prominent clergymen, evangelists, or social workers. Besides holding religious services and offering spiritual guidance, the delegates and other USCC personnel distributed Bibles, books, pamphlets, writing paper, and various supplies to the troops, read to and wrote letters for them, assisted chaplains and doctors, did battlefield service, set up kitchens, and provided clothing, bedding, and stores to hospitals. Upon returning home, the delegates were unequaled publicists for the good deeds of the USCC. Although the Sanitary Commission and the Christian Commission maintained surface civility, they were always intense and often bitter competitors for volunteers, donations, and loyalty. Before the war ended, the Christian Commission collected donations in cash, supplies, transportation, and advertising worth about $6.3 million.

The USSC faced several other competitors in the relief field. They included the nursing staff of Dorothea Dix, with its often wide-ranging activities; organizations such as the American Association for the Relief of the Misery of the

Battlefields; and a host of individual almoners and other small religious, missionary, and soldiers' aid societies. Although these associations and groups had much less clout than the WSC and the Christian Commission, they still distracted from the centralizing efforts of the USSC.[38]

The states, rather than other voluntary organizations, presented the most significant challenge to the ambitions of the USSC. States in the East, with their industrial development, familiarity with bureaucracy, and recognition of the need for system, were the ones most willing to lend themselves to the Sanitary Commission's direction. This situation was less true in the Old Northwest and the Midwest. Closer to the frontier and agrarian pursuits, these states often bristled at the USSC's insistence upon anonymity and order. They were more comfortable with the operations of the Christian Commission and the WSC, which were based on familiar values and institutions and had less rigid structures. Some Western states, such as Indiana, refused to work concertedly with the USSC; others such as Iowa cooperated only partially with the commission and even then with great division and difficulty. Moreover, almost all states and localities reserved for themselves substantial activities involving the welfare of the troops. At times this relief work constituted a logical extension of caring for the families of troops, a task in which neither the federal government nor the host of soldiers' aid societies became much involved. Therefore, at the end of hostilities, the USSC had not achieved a united front, although it had made considerable progress toward centralizing and coordinating relief activities. Even after the fighting ceased, USSC spokesmen lashed out at state relief efforts as embodying "that obnoxious heresy of State-sovereignty, against which the whole war was directed."[39]

THE LIMITS OF STATE MOBILIZATION

The Sanitary Commission, of course, had a point. But local and state relief activity, which helped to maintain civilian morale and was frequently the center of state and local civic life, also had a legitimate role. Identification often existed at the state and local levels in an agrarian society on the verge of industrialization. Lincoln understood and acted upon this reality, which was basic to his leadership during the Civil War.

The president's response to the Sanitary Commission and the Christian Commission illustrates his extremely sensitive grasp of national dynamics. He was always cool toward the former, in part because the USSC's initial proposals threatened government integrity and could have made it, in Lincoln's trenchant phrase, a "fifth wheel to the coach."[40] The president also disliked the aims and values of leaders such as Bellows and Olmsted, who were a cross between the mugwumps of the Gilded Age and the neo-Hamiltonians of the Progressive Era. Obsessive in their quest to strengthen existing institutions and the state through order, efficiency, and system, these detached professionals revered rule by the elite. During the North's deep despair after First Bull Run, Bellows proposed that preserving the Union required the appointment of a directorate of morally and otherwise superior upper-class males to take over the war effort from vulgar, corrupt, and inefficient elected politicians.

The Sanitary Commission provided method and pedigree to the war effort, but it lacked a feel for the masses, which was also essential to victory. Lincoln was closer to and more appreciative of the Christian Commission, with its evangelical fervor and grassroots and leveling temperament, which reflected the nation's individualism and localism. The president restrained the Sanitary Commission's wilder ambitions while permitting it to impose needed order and at the same time encouraged the warmth and humanity infused by the Christian Commission. Striking the right balance between the two allowed both to contribute to victory.

The USSC was distinct from all other voluntary relief and welfare organizations in that it played a major role in reforming the Medical Bureau. Professionalism in the army's medical service had been far ahead of the civilian sector in the not-too-distant past, but bureaucracy and routine had caused a serious decline in its progressive qualities. Civilian reformers forced recalcitrant army bureaucrats to streamline their organization and to introduce the medical techniques of the Crimean War. The USSC's unique status allowed the Lincoln administration to tap civilian expertise without disrupting the War Department. That precedent would have great import as the economy and professions entered a period of major transformation and would have enormous consequences for national defense and civil-military relations in the future.

Neither the Sanitary Commission nor the states alone could successfully mobilize the North for victory; the federal government had to dominate and centralize, an observation that should not downplay the vital role of the states in mobilization throughout 1861 and into 1862. That effort involved material as well as manpower and relief and welfare activities. Once the government's house was in order, Washington took control of supply but left manpower and the soldiers' welfare to the states. Thus they continued to play an important role, but their sphere of operations constantly shrank. Even in welfare areas, organizations such as the Sanitary Commission ended up coordinating state activity. The Enrollment Act of 1863 further reduced the role of the states, since it essentially made them agents of Washington in raising military manpower. To ensure Union survival, the central government had to tap the spirit and energy of the states while maintaining control over them. That was accomplished. The states retained a strong measure of autonomy in 1865 but lacked the power they had held in 1861. Defeating the Confederacy was a combined federal/state accomplishment, but Washington dominated it.

6
UNION WAR AND
NAVY DEPARTMENTS

The War Department was the basic agency for economic mobilization during the Civil War. The Navy and Treasury departments played important but nonetheless subsidiary roles. Except for manpower, mobilization by the states was always stopgap and supplementary.

A permanent executive department acting as the principal mobilization agency in a major war was a new experience for the nation. During the Revolutionary War, a series of emergency agencies had guided mobilization. The War of 1812 and the Mexican War were relatively brief, undemanding conflicts that the War, Navy, and Treasury departments managed to handle—virtually on their own in the first instance and under James K. Polk's direction during the second.

The Civil War was different. Like the Revolutionary War, it was a major conflict. Unlike the situation during the Revolution, however, existing executive departments were capable of carrying out mobilization, and the economy had grown enormously. The fact that military technology had not advanced much since the Revolution made mobilization easier because economic conversion remained unnecessary. Civil-military relations, though complex, had settled into defined patterns that required some adaptation for war but no basic restructuring.

Economic mobilization during the Civil War therefore required existing departments to acquire the efficiency necessary to muster, supply, arm, and transport millions of men in a long, exceptionally demanding war being fought over thousands of miles of land and water. Once the executive departments reached the requisite level of proficiency, market forces, with a few exceptions, adjusted a still decentralized, competitive economic system to meet wartime demand.

Of the executive departments directing Civil War mobilization, the War Department was the least prepared. The Navy and Treasury departments made some reforms and began functioning efficiently under qualified leadership within a short period of time; the War Department, however, suffered under weak leadership throughout 1861 and did not begin to handle the wartime load well until a competent secretary took charge. By early 1862, however, the War Department was beginning to function effectively. Before the war's end, it had become the largest, most complex, and most accomplished managerial system in the nation's history to that time.

President Abraham Lincoln's role in economic mobilization is instructive. He largely left decisionmaking to the department heads, intervening only when essential, as occurred early in 1862 when he replaced Simon Cameron with Edwin M. Stanton as secretary of war. That change allowed the president to focus on the larger issues of strengthening the national government, building the Republican party, and managing the administration's relations with the states and Congress. Moreover, Lincoln always played an active role in defining and executing Union military strategy that shaped mobilization policies. The president avoided whenever possible involvement in the details of mobilization so as to direct more effectively the overall war effort.

Unlike the pattern unfolding in the states, at the federal level economic elites did not serve simultaneously in public and private capacities. The federal executive was largely staffed by economic and professional elites, but the lines separating political, economic, and military institutions were seldom breached. With the market acting as regulator, efficient executive departments could carry out their responsibilities without calling upon the services of private businessmen, professionals, and other experts. The only exceptions involved the railroad and telegraph systems. To help manage those corporate entities, the War Department brought their executives into its structure, and they often served both as public and private representatives at the same time. This practice also took place to a lesser extent in the Treasury Department's relations with the banking community. Civilians of all sorts, of course, served temporarily in the armed services. Nonetheless, below the secretary level, the army and navy were run by professional officers, usually trained at West Point and, when possible, Annapolis. The mixing of elites so common at the state level would not be duplicated at the national level during wartime until World Wars I and II.

THE WAR DEPARTMENT: THE FIRST YEAR OF WAR

The War Department in 1861 was in an advanced state of decline. James Buchanan's first secretary of war, John B. Floyd, was a Southerner and later a secessionist, who through mismanagement kept the department confused and debilitated. Floyd's successor, Joseph Holt, attempted to repair the damage of his predecessor, but there was little he could do since he served as secretary of war from only January to March 1861. To add to this disarray, over one-third of the department's staff left government service or defected to the Confederacy before and after hostilities commenced.[1]

The secession crisis added to long-run troubles confronting the army and War Department. The perennial problems of command relations and the division between the line and staff precluded effective coordination of departmental and army functions. Moreover, although the various bureaus competently serviced a diminutive regular army in peacetime, they were hardly prepared for the multiplying demands of war.

Lincoln's selection of Simon Cameron as secretary of war in March 1861 compounded the War Department's mobilization problems.[2] Cameron was unfit for the job. His appointment resulted from a political debt and indicated that the president did not appreciate the critical role the War Department would play in mobilizing the nation's human and material resources. But in truth, no past conflict hinted at what would be required during the Civil War. Cameron looked good on paper. He had vast experience in business, finance, and the burgeoning railroad fields and had become deeply involved in politics in Pennsylvania and on the national scene. His background failed to prepare the Pennsylvanian for the secretaryship because he lacked managerial talents and was more a spoilsman than a constructive leader. Failing to grow in confidence and ability as war minister, Cameron was overwhelmed by events.

Raising troops was the most important factor in determining the magnitude and tempo of mobilization throughout the war. In April and May, Lincoln called for expanding an army of slightly over 16,000 to about 156,000. A vast ground swell of patriotic enthusiasm enabled the North to exceed the numbers specified, which set off a chaotic mobilization scramble that did not begin to subside until the end of 1861.

Increasing the size of the ground forces by 140,000 men without planning or advance notice created chaos in an already hobbled War Department. Only a few states had militia units trained, let alone equipped and armed, for service. Although the regular army could handle more than a doubling of its size, increases beyond that caused severe problems. More basically, the department remained confused for months about how, when, and where troops should be raised. Consequently, it fought about these matters with governors and other state officials.

The worst problems involved clothing, equipping, and especially arming the rapidly expanding army. The Quartermaster and Ordnance departments could not be expected immediately to handle a ninefold increase in the number of men they serviced. An efficient secretary working closely with excellent bureau chiefs would have instituted an orderly process of expansion. That did not occur. Cameron did not lead, and the supply bureaus on their own coped with the growing demands with varying levels of activity and competence. In the midst of swirling chaos, the War Department—"the lunatic asylum" according to the capital's grapevine—surrealistically maintained the cumbersome procedures and the leisurely pace of peacetime. Sheer necessity led the states to mobilize and supply most troops in the early months of the war and beyond, thus giving the War Department the opportunity to regroup.

Cameron frequently obstructed his department's adjustment to wartime demands. Ever the politico, the secretary of war treated positions on the department staff as everyday spoils, replacing talented and experienced personnel with political appointees. More serious was Cameron's penchant for delegating supply responsibilities to his cronies and other inexperienced associates. One of the most flagrant examples involved Alexander Cummings, a Pennsylvania newspaper editor and political ally, who had no procurement and little business experience. With the capital cut off from New York from late April to early May 1861, Cameron appointed Cummings as a special agent to purchase goods in New York and forward them to Washington. The appointment was unnecessary because the Quartermaster and Subsistence departments had well-qualified officers stationed in New York. Predictably, Cummings's efforts turned into a fiasco. Operating free of army regulations and without properly accounting for expenditures, he purchased items such as London porter and straw hats.[3]

Cummings was not an isolated case. General and special agents like him operated throughout the nation in 1861, buying and hiring services without regard for rules. They usually purchased through open-market operations and negotiated contracts instead of using the customary competitive bidding. Inexperienced, careless, or lax procurement agents facing greedy or unscrupulous suppliers invited abuse. Such practices might have been justified by critical conditions in the opening months of war but not after mid-1861 when the crisis had passed.

Cameron handled transportation problems better, but here again scandal emerged. The War Department needed long-term assistance with transport and nowhere more so than with the railroads. Regular army officers lacked the expertise to handle this critically important and enormously complex system. Consequently, in April 1861, the secretary of war tapped J. Edgar Thomson and Thomas A. Scott, president and vice-president of the Pennsylvania Railroad, along with Samuel M. Felton, president of the Philadelphia, Wilmington and Baltimore Railroad, to oversee the transportation of troops and supplies. These men performed their tasks remarkably well but diminished their contribution through conflicts of interest and related abuses. Cameron also sought assistance in hiring and buying vessels for water transportation. He selected another friend, John Tucker, a former dry-goods merchant and railroad president, to supervise the effort on the East Coast, an arrangement that also resulted in widespread unethical, if not illegal, practices.

The regular army did not escape Cameron's tenure. Some of the worst corruption occurred in the West from July to October 1861 under the command of Gen. John C. Frémont and his quartermaster, Maj. Justus McKinstry. The influential Blair family was at least indirectly involved, along with a prominent St. Louis retail house and a group of Frémont's friends from California. Almost every aspect of supply and other operations under Frémont, including the purchase of horses and mules, the building of probably unnecessary fortifications and barracks, and contracts and orders for transportation services, was subject to favoritism, bribery, kickbacks, profiteering, and misuse of government funds. Frémont does not appear to have been directly involved in these incredible schemes, but he bore the ultimate responsibility, and he and his wife willingly received gifts and favors intended to win his goodwill. In time the army replaced Frémont, cleaned up the supply mess in his command, and court-martialed and removed Major McKinstry from the service.[4]

Much of the malpractice involving military supply operations at the federal and state levels in the early months of the war was exposed by political rivals of the people in power, enterprising journalists, and congressional and state investigatory bodies. Although the Navy Department and the various states came in for their share of scrutiny, the War Department received the most attention because it conducted the largest operations and its practices involved the greatest abuses. Although various individuals and coteries became targets for exposure, the focus increasingly centered on the secretary of war. To some degree, Cameron became the scapegoat for a situation that no one could have corrected immediately. The War Department was in such a deteriorated state in early 1861 that months, not days or weeks, were required to whip it into shape for administering an enormously expanded army. Furthermore, except for conflicts of interest involving key railroads, Cameron had no personal involvement in the irregular and criminal behavior taking place about him. Nonetheless, the secretary of war's ineptitude and tolerance for corruption account for the ongoing abuse. It was just a matter of time before Cameron was replaced.

Meddling by other cabinet members further complicated matters. Secretary of State William H. Seward moved in on the War Department and acted as if it were part of his domain. Resenting Seward's intrusions, Cameron sought to offset his influence in effect by inviting Secretary of the Treasury Salmon P. Chase to take a part in departmental operations. These encroachments ended only after Cameron left and his successor, Edwin M. Stanton, reclaimed the prerogatives of his office.

The improvement in the War Department's functions (though not in the army supply bureau's) during 1861 resulted largely from the efforts of Thomas A. Scott. Although sharing some of Cameron's proclivity for shady business and political maneuvering, Scott had superb organizational talents. Brought into the department by the secretary of war in late April 1861, Scott concentrated on the railroads and also helped to launch the federal telegraph system. Cameron elevated him to assistant secretary of war in August 1861, when Congress created that position. While continuing to focus on transportation matters, Scott, as assistant secretary in a department with a very weak head, took on a range of duties including the mobilization, supply, and arming of troops and other procurement activities.

Scott's talents could not save Cameron. He had too few assets and too many liabilities to head the most important federal department during wartime. Under continuing pressure, Lincoln jettisoned his secretary of war. Cameron was forced to resign in January 1862 and was later censured by the House of Representatives for procurement abuses. The Senate approved his appointment as minister to Russia as a face-saving gesture.

Despite the negatives, there were some significant accomplishments during Cameron's months in office. Policies were initiated to modernize troop mobilization. The department also began to tap civilian experts to aid economic mobilization. In concert with the U.S. Sanitary Commission, the War Department started to overhaul the Medical Department, and it helped other service and supply bureaus to improve their efficiency. The War Department staff expanded under Cameron, as Scott's appointment to the post of assistant secretary indicates. Indeed, the War Department went through the most troubled phase of mobilization with Cameron in charge. The department inherited by his successor basically retained the same structure for the rest of the war.

Edwin M. Stanton, Cameron's replacement, was the most enigmatic member of Lincoln's administration.[5] A loner, master manipulator, and autocrat, the new secretary of war appeared to have no friends, only allies and enemies. Stanton was from Ohio, had made his mark as an attorney, and had served briefly as attorney general in the Buchanan administration. A human dynamo, Stanton had a knack for administration and a need for order and direction. He was scrupulously honest, in contrast to Cameron, and expected the same standards from those around him. Stanton faced a nearly insuperable task at the outset. He had first to clean up Cameron's mess and then master the department's multiple responsibilities. In struggling to accomplish those goals, he was known to work through the night and expected his staff and subordinates to match his feats.

The War Department took on a new vitality under Stanton that was sustained and that even grew until hostilities ceased. Stanton rapidly began to centralize and expand the department's offices and personnel. To improve general efficiency and to discourage the throngs that had disrupted operations under Cameron, the department closed its doors to all but the military from Tuesday through Friday, with Mondays reserved for the public and Saturdays saved for members of Congress.

No major reorganization of the department occurred under the new secretary, but Stanton did refine operations. He persuaded Congress to add two assistant-secretary positions, for a total of three. To guide his decisionmaking, Stanton consulted regularly with an informal War Board made up of the supply and service bureau chiefs, any field-grade officer in the capital, and, ultimately, his military aide.

Policies and procedures changed quickly. Shortly after taking office, Stanton issued an order requiring that all existing contracts and other business be put in writing and be in accordance with the prescribed standards within fifteen days or face automatic revocation. Thereafter, specific regulations were promulgated for the conduct of all War Department business. Congress strengthened the secretary's hand in mid-1862 by passing legislation to reduce procurement abuses. In March 1862 Stanton created a three-man Ordnance Commission, Joseph Holt, Robert Dale Owen, and Maj. Peter V. Hagner, to review and adjust all ordnance contracts. Working diligently for over nine months, the board saved the army millions and brought new order and efficiency to weapons contracting.[6] Stanton appointed a special investigator to reduce illegal, fraudulent, and corrupt practices in the department through continuous monitoring. He also established a solicitor's office to increase the general effectiveness and legality of departmental affairs.

Stanton's talent and drive quickly brought important changes to the War Department because the service and supply bureaus responded positively to him. Some basic changes had already occurred in bureau leadership and staffing before he was appointed. Montgomery C. Meigs had taken over as quartermaster general in June 1861, other officers of outstanding talent had been appointed, and special assistants were brought in to handle difficult matters. Still, the permanent staffs of most supply bureaus continued to be mature-to-older officers who were dedicated to routine. These bureaus nonetheless performed remarkably well. Their staffs of officers, enlisted men, and clerks grew only modestly from 1861 to 1865, nowhere in proportion to the workload they faced. Yet from late 1861–early 1862 onward, the bureaus carried out their duties with efficiency and usually excellence. The regulations that many civilians damned as red tape protected the public by guiding officials facing unreasonable demands under nearly unbearable tensions.

Most of the procurement scandals in the early months of the war arose from the actions of new or irregular personnel unfamiliar with or contemptuous of military supply procedures. Indeed, congressional committees investigating military procurement in the troubled months of 1861 concluded that only regular army officers consistently did a good and an honest job.

THE QUARTERMASTER DEPARTMENT

During 1861 the War Department's bureaus had to revamp their supply operations largely without direction from above. General-in-Chief Winfield Scott did nothing to guide bureau preparations for hostilities. With his office in New York from 1853 to 1860, Scott had lost contact with supply operations, and age and physical disability prevented him from reasserting authority. When Gen. George B. McClellan moved into the top spot in November 1861, he focused most of his efforts on the Army of the Potomac. For his part, Cameron probably hindered more than he helped the bureaus.

The Quartermaster Department led the process of regeneration. The largest and most important bureau, it was basic to the entire wartime supply effort. Real progress began in June 1861 when Meigs took over as quartermaster general.[7] He slowly reorganized the department between 1861 and 1864 so that it could effectively handle the enormous wartime load. By the end of 1861, department officers in each state managed supply operations and provided troops with standardized clothing, shoes and boots, and equipment. The most fundamental change in the department's organization involved dividing it into nine divisions: clothing and equipage, draft animals, transportation, building, records and correspondence, and the like. Although the Quartermaster Department's staff increased as war responsibilities grew, expansion was never in proportion to the workload, leaving the department chronically short of personnel. An authorized staff of 37 officers was increased only once, in August 1861, to 74; the clerical staff grew from a few to over 200 by the end of 1864.

The Quartermaster Department, like most procurement agencies, operated under laws enacted before hostilities commenced. Those statutes required that all buying be done by contracts based on competitive bids, with negotiations possible if the need was sufficiently great. Open-market purchasing could also take place in an emergency. Because of gross profiteering, fraud, and other forms of malfeasance in military procurement during the first months of the war, Congress between 1862 and 1864 enacted various statutes to check such abuses; but the reforms were never enforced rigorously.

Quartermaster purchasing was based largely on the depot system, which had been evolving since the Second Seminole War (1835–1842), had served the army well in the Mexican War, and had matured during the Civil War. By the end of hostilities, the system consisted of general, advance, and temporary depots. General depots, which handled most procurement, had been established before the war in cities such as New York, St. Louis, and San Francisco; new ones were created during the fighting in such locations as Chicago, Indianapolis, and Detroit. Civil War expenditures were staggering: in 1860 the department disbursed about $6 million; by 1863 spending totaled $240 million. The department spent more than $1 billion over the course of the war, a level of activity around forty times greater than in peacetime.

As a rule, general depots acted as purchasing and distribution centers instead of directly supplying troops in the field. A number of general depots, however, particularly those in St. Louis and Washington, also became the principal services for supplying armies and other military units. The St. Louis depot, under Gen. Robert Allen, the chief quartermaster, was the most impressive in this regard. From headquarters in St. Louis and later in Louisville, Allen supplied all troops in the trans-Mississippi West and Southwest and handled the logistics for Gen. William T. Sherman's campaign against Atlanta. Allen oversaw purchases worth nearly $200 million, about 20 percent of Quartermaster Department expenditures during the war. The Treasury Department did not disallow any of this purchasing when the accounts were settled. Allen exemplified the Civil War Quartermaster Department at its best. In the East, the Washington Depot served as the principal source of supply for the Army of the Potomac and other field forces on the Atlantic Coast.

Advance depots were established as intermediate sources of supply when armies moved beyond the range or the safety of their principal depots. Located so as to be readily accessible by rail or water, some of these secondary depots became enormous operations in their own right. One in Nashville supplied Sherman's army in the Atlanta campaign; another in City Point, Virginia, handled Gen. Ulysses S. Grant's operations against Richmond and became a small city of throbbing activity.

Temporary depots, small in size and established just behind the front lines, were designed to meet the needs of soldiers for a few days and then to relocate. The three-tiered depot system existed in full-blown form only at the end of the war, but its outlines were evident with the outbreak of hostilities. It proved to be exceptionally efficient. At times, supplies were dispatched to the destination of armies on the march, arriving before the troops did as was the case in the last major operations of Sherman and Grant.

The depot system was part of an elaborate Quartermaster hierarchy in which authority became more centralized as the war progressed. Concentrating authority in part grew from the need effectively to control hundreds, even thousands, of Quartermaster officers and staffers at all levels, many of whom were inexperienced and had to be trained on the job. By reserving its limited number of experienced officers for critical and supervisory positions, the department in time built up a very able organization, despite an ongoing struggle to gain rank for its officers commensurate with the responsibilities they carried. The overall quality of the department was such that it even minimized the tensions generated by its officers having to answer to the commanders of the units to which they were attached and to their immediate quartermaster supervisors.

The Quartermaster Department purchased clothing, shoes, blankets, tents, and equipment such as canteens and haversacks. It also bought hundreds of items for construction and repair, along with wood for fuel and straw for bedding. For transport, it procured wagons, ambulances, horses, mules, harnesses, forage, railroad engines, cars, and repair materials. It also bought or leased boats, tugs, and ferries and, in some instances, arranged for railroad transportation.

Clothing was the most pressing matter in 1861. At the outset of hostilities, the department had uniform reserves sufficient only for the regular army of 16,000. While the Quartermaster Department worked frantically in the first months of the war to increase uniform-making capacity, it fell back on temporary expedients, and the states provided uniforms for volunteers, with mixed results. The department purchased ready-made garments whenever it could and relaxed standards on cloth quality and color to speed the manufacture of uniforms. This frenzied buying led to inferior (so-called shoddy) products foisted on the army by unscrupulous contractors and equally bad inspectors. The quartermaster also bought cloth of the requisite grade abroad. Some $400,000 was spent overseas, but those purchases ended in December in response to the protests of domestic firms and the greater availability of American products.

The clothing crisis had passed by the end of 1861, with the uniforms of most troops of good grade and proper color. In 1862 the Quartermaster Department concentrated on getting ahead of immediate demand, but sudden calls for hundreds of thousands of troops, as occurred in July 1862, frustrated this goal. By 1863, however, reserves were adequate, and in 1864 Meigs reported that clothing supplies were plentiful and quality outstanding.

Army uniforms were produced under a public-private arrangement. At the outset, the Quartermaster Department expanded capacity at the Schuylkill Arsenal in Philadelphia, established additional depots in New York, Cincinnati, St. Louis, and Springfield, Illinois, and created "government halls" at lesser depots, such as Louisville, to make clothing and to provide work-relief for the needy wives of soldiers. Some states continued to make uniforms after 1861. Washington provided them with cloth in emergencies, such as during the July–August 1862 call for 600,000 volunteers and militiamen. All garments made by the government were hand-sewn since they were believed to be more durable than machine-sewn products.

Because government facilities could not meet all clothing needs at any time during hostilities, private contractors were used, a new development since the arsenals had produced all uniforms since 1812. At first the Quartermaster Department dispersed its contracts among numerous small firms over a wide area to reduce favoritism and collusion, but this approach proved to be unsatisfactory. In time, the department placed most contracts with large companies of good reputation. These firms, such as Hanford and Browning of New York, were principally located in the big cities of the East, although a few were in the West. The war turned out to be a great boon for ready-made clothing. Army requirements and the introduction of the sewing machine in 1849, which increased labor efficiency at least tenfold, led to mass production in factories. For the first time in the nation's history, the federal government was able to provide its troops with uniforms made exclusively at home.

Textile capacity proved more than adequate to meet the Quartermaster Department's clothing requirements. Textiles, after all, constituted the nation's premier industry, and vast unused facilities existed during the war because of the cotton famine. Lacking raw material, fewer than half of the North's cotton spindles were in use by 1863. Among the firms that continued production, army demand encouraged increased output of hosiery and other knit goods. But the army's greatest requirements involved woolens. The nation's woolen-goods industry was concentrated in New England and the Middle States and had smaller and more dispersed firms than those in cotton. Wartime demand more than doubled the North's consumption of raw wool and led the industry to increase its stock of machinery by 60 percent. The military services purchased nearly 40 percent of the expanded level of output. Since the army's buying favored large firms, woolen manufacturing became further concentrated in the textile states and among the industry's largest companies.

Other items presented varying degrees of difficulty for the department.

Unlike clothing, regulation wool blankets proved to be a problem throughout the war. Extreme shortages occurred at the outset of hostilities, and inferior products were foisted on desperate quartermasters. The situation stabilized within a year, but foreign purchases were essential at all times to compensate for the great deficiencies of domestic production. Duck cloth for the manufacture of tents was in even shorter supply than wool blankets at the outset of the war. The Union solved the problem more by decreasing demand than by increasing supply. Standard large tents were reserved mainly for hospitals; troops depended on the French shelter half. The North procured adequate numbers of knapsacks, haversacks, canteens, pans, and other supplies without major problems after the first year of mobilization. Almost all these items were already being produced for the civilian economy or could be manufactured with only small adaptations in existing facilities.

Next to cloth and clothing, shoes and boots presented the greatest trouble for the Quartermaster Department because of the enormous demand and the difficulty of maintaining quality control. In 1861 footwear, like some uniforms and overcoats, fell apart with minimal usage or when exposed to the elements. Unscrupulous contractors and corrupt or inattentive inspectors were to blame, but these problems largely disappeared after 1861. Footwear was also produced under private-public arrangements. Beginning with the Mexican War, boots and shoes had been manufactured at the Schuylkill Arsenal and continued to be on an expanded scale during the Civil War, but nonetheless the Quartermaster Department had to turn to private contractors. At first the army insisted on hand-sewn footwear, but in time it accepted pegged work, which had become standard on the civilian market, and more important, machine-sewn shoes. The McKay sewing machine, available in 1862, permitted the mechanization of most phases of boot and shoe production, increased worker output up to a hundredfold, and doubled the manufacture of footwear within the year. The footwear industry was centered in Massachusetts, but factories were also located in other large cities in the North.

The Quartermaster Department handled almost all construction projects during the war because they were considered temporary in nature. Building responsibilities were not overwhelming other than for the sudden, huge demand at the outbreak of fighting. The department furnished troops with tools, lumber, and other materials for building barracks and winter quarters. It also supervised the civilian artisans, mechanics, and laborers hired by the army and the builders who constructed the hospitals, depots, warehouses, and other structures required by war. Some building projects, such as those of the Railroad Construction Corps, were under quartermaster supervision more in name than in fact.

Food for the troops was provided by the Subsistence Department, whose operations were close to that of the Quartermaster Department. With a rich agricultural sector, the Union had no basic troubles in feeding its troops. States and localities played a major role in subsisting the troops in the early, disorganized months of 1861. Within a short period of time, however, the Subsistence Department was able to handle the exponentially expanded wartime demand, though states and localities played a role during emergencies and holidays.[8] Ultimately, the department had an administrative and field organization similar to that of the Quartermaster Department. It was a huge operation that reached throughout the nation and was centered in Washington, DC, and Louisville. Most of the buying was done through competitive bidding in the major cities of the East and West, such as New York and St. Louis. The major exceptions were flour and fresh beef: the former was purchased by bidding closer to the troops, and the latter was obtained through negotiated contracts by the block or on the hoof. Like the Quartermaster Department, the Subsistence Department operated many of its own businesses, including cattle slaughtering and meat packing, baking, and vegetable pickling. The department saved millions of dollars by selling meat by-products such as hides and tallow.

Except for the rare occasions when distribution broke down, as at Chattanooga, Northern troops were amply fed. Food was plentiful, though uninteresting, and soldiers generally received enough fresh meat, fruit, and vegetables to prevent scurvy. Canned and dehydrated foods and condensed milk were available but only to a limited degree. Generally, the Union armies were better provisioned than any previous armies in world history.

By tradition, the Quartermaster Department was responsible for all transportation. The railroads provided the department, the army, and the Union their most direct contact with advances stemming from the industrial revolution. Steamboats had been used extensively in the Mexican War but came into their own during the Civil War. To achieve maximum benefit from them, the Quartermaster Department had to institute effective management methods. Despite the modernization of transport, however, horse- and mule-drawn wagons remained basic to most supply operations. Even then, system was necessary for dealing with huge armies in a long war spread over thousands of miles. The more modern the means of transportation, the more the Quartermaster Department's control was diluted by experts and civilians intruding upon soldiers' prerogatives.

Beginning at the simplest level, the Quartermaster Department's transportation responsibilities included procurement of wagons and ambulances. Two- and four-wheel ambulances and carts were necessary in large numbers and were acquired without difficulty once the proper design was agreed upon.[9] Wagons were of paramount importance. Philadelphia was the center of wagon production in the North when the war began. The Quartermaster Department diversified its sources of supply by placing contracts in New Jersey, Connecticut, West Virginia, and other locations as well as in Philadelphia. When time permitted, contracts were let by competitive bid. Sudden increases in demand so typical of the war led to open-market purchasing from the prominent carriage makers, which maintained huge inventories. As with much of wartime output, contractors' efforts to cut costs and maximize profits led to faulty or inferior products. In general, though, the quartermaster experienced few problems with wagons. After years of experience on the rough or nonexistent roads of the West, the army had designed and perfected a sturdy and durable wagon built from standardized and interchangeable parts. Few wagons were ever abandoned. Artisans with proper tools, including portable forges, and an ample supply of axles, wheels, tongues, and so forth kept even the largest army trains moving despite expectable breakdowns and mishaps.

Procuring sufficient draft animals to pull the wagons presented greater difficulties. In the early months of the war, diseased, disabled, and debilitated horses and mules were foisted on the army by middlemen and incompetent or corrupt inspectors and quartermasters. A decentralized, irregular purchasing structure encouraged these abuses. Between 1863 and 1864, the system was almost totally restructured in order to centralize purchasing, establish accountability, and institute harsh punishment for individuals involved in criminal behavior. Under the new system, the army, including the cavalry, was receiving quality horses and mules by the end of 1864.

Army animals too frequently experienced improper care and feeding. Many were needlessly lost through abuse and neglect, particularly before the 1863–1864 reforms, and some suffered from or died of malnutrition. Horses and mules consume enormous amounts of hay and grain, and the difficulties in providing the needed amounts of forage were exaggerated by a decentralized purchasing system that encouraged competition among government agencies. This arrangement drove prices up and opened the way for fraud and monopoly, which interrupted the flow of hay and grain. The problems were made worse by the constant struggle to transport tons of forage. As with most other quartermaster activities, concentrating responsibility improved performance. Forage operations were generally centralized in Washington, DC, for the East and in St. Louis for the West.

Wagon trains distributed supplies from railroad terminals and steamer wharves and remained the principal means for moving military units. At first, both horses and mules were used for wagon transportation, but by 1864–

1865 mules had taken over since they were much more economical and durable. Attempts to institute a corps of military teamsters were rejected during the Civil War, as had been the case in previous conflicts. The Quartermaster Department therefore hired civilians, despite the problems associated with that practice. When civilian teamsters proved unreliable, huge numbers of enlisted men were detailed to the task, and the problems proved manageable.

Much more difficult was the matter of reducing the baggage and supplies armies carried with them. Without regulation, the tonnage became enormous, which slowed down the movement of troops, complicated campaigns, resulted in huge losses of goods and enemy captures, and proved extraordinarily expensive. Reforms began when Lt. Col. Rufus Ingalls took over as chief quartermaster of the Army of the Potomac in July 1862. With the backing of McClellan and Meigs, Ingalls reduced by at least two-thirds the number of wagons in use by excluding luxuries and unnecessary items and determining wagon allotments according to the number of men in a unit.

Ingalls made numerous other reforms. He systematized supply trains by establishing a set order for wagons carrying baggage, ammunition, general supplies, and so forth. Wagons were marked by corps, division, brigade, and contents for easy identification and assignment. After making these improvements, Ingalls focused on the chaos that almost inevitably characterized army movements. Because units proceeded without proper coordination and even on the same routes, horrendous traffic jams resulted in fights between competing officers and men, in broken wagons, and in maimed animals. To correct this situation, Ingalls established an order of march in which all units were coordinated, supply trains were properly supervised by the appropriate quartermasters, and all wagons proceeded according to clearly established rights of way and "laws of the road." The system was extended to the battlefield: wagon trains were kept well to the rear and out of the way of troops, soldiers went to the front with only bare necessities, and wagons brought up supplies as needed and returned with the wounded. In time, Ingalls's reforms were implemented throughout the Union armies. The changes always met resistance and thus occurred with the necessary modifications for region and circumstances. Still, by applying modern management techniques to the oldest of transportation services, the chief quartermaster of the Army of the Potomac increased efficiency immeasurably and saved millions of dollars, fighting resources, and lives.

Water transportation was critical to Union logistics, moving hundreds of thousands of troops and more tonnage than any other mode of transportation.[10] It was particularly crucial in the West, where the Mississippi and other rivers flowed into the heart of the Confederacy. Steamboat operations resembled wagon transportation in the lack of initial organization, but they differed in that the army hired most of the boats it used. Proper management by the Quartermaster Department was critical because there were no large steamboat companies with which the department could contract. Instead, hundreds of small companies or individual owners offered the services of their boats to the army.

Decentralization on the supply side was matched on the demand side. Local quartermasters ordinarily supervised the movements of troops and supplies by water, and each operated according to his own rules. With dozens of officers hiring vessels and proceeding without central direction, endless abuse and inefficiency occurred. Ignorance, indifference, or corruption led quartermasters to pay exorbitant rates, allow boats to sit idle while in service, or delay unloading. This mismanagement cost the government millions of dollars and denied the military vessels that were often in critically short supply.

Reform started in late 1861 when Col. Lewis B. Parsons, a railroad attorney in civilian life, was appointed assistant quartermaster in St. Louis and took charge of rail and water transportation. Parsons experimented with change in St. Louis, and his reforms were then implemented throughout the region when Meigs appointed him chief quartermaster of Western River Transportation in December 1863. His most important innovation was to scrap the existing system of chartering vessels for a number of months and instead to let contracts by competitive bid for moving goods by weight or piece. The incentives created by this arrangement led steamers to carry loads with less turnaround time, saving the government extraordinary sums and greatly increasing efficiency. In fall 1864, Parsons extended his reforms when he became chief of the Rail and River Transportation Division in the Office of the Quartermaster General.

The Quartermaster Department put in an estimable performance on the Western rivers. In addition to extensive hiring, the department purchased vessels, contracted to have steamboats and other craft built, and established its own shipyards to construct vessels of varying sorts. Overall, the department chartered, hired, or impressed some 822 vessels, 635 of which were steamers. It also owned 599 boats, including 91 steamers, 352 barges, and a collection of wharfboats, yawls, and other small boats.

The Quartermaster Department's ocean fleet was even larger than that on the Western rivers. The department chartered and hired 753 ocean steamers, 1,080 sailing ships, and 847 barges. In addition, it purchased or built 183 steamers, 43 sailing vessels, and 86 barges. In the West, the Quartermaster Department called upon civilians for assistance in mobilizing a fleet, but few businessmen played a direct role in army purchasing and leasing. Such was not the case on the East Coast. From the outset of war, the War Department sought the assistance of middlemen in acquiring oceangoing vessels. The practice continued until 1863 and became a source of corruption and controversy.

In May 1861, Secretary of War Cameron tapped his friend John Tucker for a post that became general agent for ocean transportation. Tucker was a dry-goods merchant and railroad president. Although perhaps a person of some integrity, he knew nothing about ocean vessels, was not particularly talented at organization, and could be exploited by others. As a result, his services came at a high price to the government.

Tucker appointed Richard E. Loper, a longtime friend, to acquire vessels for the army. Loper was president of the Philadelphia Steam Propeller Company and owner and builder of many ships. He and a host of agents and sub-agents proved knowledgeable, able, and hardworking in procuring hundreds of badly needed ships for the army, often on very short notice. But Loper and his associates were also grasping and often unscrupulous businessmen. They scrapped the statutory quartermaster practice of obtaining water transportation based on advertisement for the lowest bidder and took a 5 percent commission on all transactions. The former move allowed them to pay exceptionally high rates for daily and monthly charters and to lease vessels they owned or had an interest in to the government. Tucker apparently was not directly involved in the profiteering and abuse, but he turned a blind eye toward it. Stanton, uncharacteristically, focused on Tucker's successes, not his failures, by appointing him assistant secretary in January 1862.

In time, investigations by Congress and others exposed the wrongdoing under Tucker and led him to resign in January 1863. Meigs reasserted his authority over oceangoing transport in 1863–1864 and began the process of reform. Lease rates and practices were restructured to prevent the government from being gouged and to allow the army to buy the vessels it was leasing if that was economical. Moreover, navy officers were detailed to the army for appraising vessels to be chartered or purchased.

The army's pressing need for oceangoing and inland waterway ships created great demand for new vessels. Despite shortages in 1861–1862 and periodic crunches thereafter, the quartermaster's requirements for ships and boats were met. On the Western rivers, where yards did not exist or were insufficient, new ones were quickly set up to produce wooden steamers and even ironclad gunboats. Enough machine shops existed to supply the needed maritime machinery. On the East Coast, the war created a great boom in shipyards. Despite the suddenness of military demand, the limited number of machinery manufacturers, the scarcity of some raw materials, and the shortage of skilled labor, the major shipbuilders were handling all military orders by 1862–1863 and even were constructing vessels for foreign buyers. Moreover, because the North possessed great numbers of civilian ships and boats on the East Coast and Western rivers when war broke out, it could seize that supply for military use until new ships were built.

Once the Quartermaster Department was under way and operating with reformed procedures, no military operations failed because of inadequate water transportation. Indeed, the department's water transportation services played a key part in some of the great Union feats. Outstanding examples on the Western rivers include moving Sherman's 40,000-man army and its equipment some 472 miles from Memphis to below Vicksburg in six days in December 1862. At City Point, Virginia, the base depot of Grant's operations against Richmond in 1864–1865, 40 steamboats, 75 sailing vessels, and 100 barges transported supplies from the North at the height of activity, and daily boats between City Point and Washington carried mail and passengers. The nation had never before seen operations on such a scale, and they were carried out with nearly flawless precision.

THE RAILROAD AND TELEGRAPH SYSTEMS

Railroads constituted the major transportation breakthrough of the Civil War.[11] Having been used in a preliminary fashion during the Mexican War, they took a full role in the Civil War, significantly affecting military logistics.

A partnership of government officials and railroad managers adapted rail lines for war use—a partnership that eroded the barriers between public and private, civilian and military institutions. The alliance was necessary because the railroads could not be handled through competition as could most procurement or through organized demand as was the case with steamboats and other vessels. As the first truly modern business system, the railroads demanded the attention of experts in order to maximize their potential without harming their operations. Fortunately, the nation's top leaders were familiar with the railroad world and recognized these realities from the outset. Cameron's family, for example, held a controlling interest in the Northern Central Railroad, and Stanton had served as a railroad attorney.

Cameron turned to railroad men to assist the War Department shortly after Lincoln's call for volunteer militia in mid-April 1861. He put J. Edgar Thomson, president of the Pennsylvania Railroad, in charge of transporting men and supplies to the capital; Samuel M. Felton, president of the Philadelphia, Wilmington and Baltimore Railroad, acted as Thomson's assistant. Thomson was a leading railroad executive and had been among the pioneers in railroad management on the Pennsylvania Railroad. He and Felton served Cameron and the department well but only for a short period of time. Thomas A. Scott, vice-president of the Pennsylvania Railroad and a close friend, business associate, and political partner of Cameron in Pennsylvania, made the greatest contribution. Although only thirty-seven years old, Scott was a well-connected, experienced, and talented transportation expert. These qualities had led Gov. Andrew G. Curtin of Pennsylvania to select Scott in April as his personal aide for mustering and transporting troops in the Harrisburg area, a responsibility that included control of the railroad and telegraph systems. It practically required an order from Cameron to persuade Curtin to release Scott for federal duty.

Cameron called Scott to Washington late in April to take charge of the railroad and telegraph systems between Washington and Annapolis. Within a month, Scott's authority was extended to cover all railway and telegraph lines the government controlled or might control. In August 1861 Scott was made assistant secretary of war, with explicit orders that all instructions involving the railroads and telegraph systems were to come from his office. This arrangement in effect created a transportation and communication office in the department and in the process limited the Quartermaster Department's broad responsibility over transportation. Although Scott's activities included all War Department responsibilities, he concentrated on the railroads.

Most of his work only laid the foundation for the major progress of 1862 and after; nonetheless, he made substantial contributions. Scott's usefulness, however, was limited by his close association with Cameron and the charges of corruption that always surrounded the latter. The allegations took on even greater importance because Cameron, in directing the railroads from the War Department, relied primarily on managers of the Pennsylvania Railroad like Scott, and purposely excluded John W. Garrett, president of the Baltimore and Ohio Railroad (B & O), and his associates. The Pennsylvania Railroad and Cameron's Northern Central were allied in an intense and bitter competition with the B & O for control of traffic from the West, which predated the war. Garrett and others charged that Cameron and Scott were using the War Department to enhance their interests at the expense of the B & O. The fact that Scott maintained an unsalaried position with the Pennsylvania Railroad after becoming assistant secretary in August 1861 generated further distrust. The catalyst that converted suspicion and rumor into concrete charges of wrongdoing centered on the rates railroads charged the government for military transport under schedules provided by the War Department. Since the army had used the railroads only through competitive bid before the war, any set railroad rates during hostilities would have created distrust.

At the request of the Quartermaster Department in July 1861, Scott had issued a schedule of rates for the shipment of military goods on the railroads that was based on the recommendations made by twenty-one railroad executives in June 1861. The rates were for local runs and produced charges for through traffic that far exceeded ordinary levels, which created a great scramble among railroads for army contracts. With numerous quartermasters and other officers hiring rail services, kickbacks and other forms of corruption resulted. The growing railroad scandal came to the attention of the House Committee on Contracts in December 1861. Once exposed, it was portrayed as outrageous and seemingly documented Cameron's corruption and Scott's ties to it. Few critics accepted the claim of the secretary and assistant secretary of war that the schedule was intended to establish maximum, not set, railroad rates. The episode increased the pressure on Lincoln to rid himself of Cameron.

A wholly new system for regulating the railroads came into being in the first months of 1862 based upon Cameron's and Scott's model but with new personnel and a new legal base. Stanton, replacing Cameron on January 15, 1862, initiated the change. The new secretary moved quickly to reestablish public confidence in the army's railroad operations and to prepare better the War Department for handling the upcoming Union offensive. He established excellent relations with Garrett, assisted in rebuilding the B & O, and made good use of that line. Congress assisted the secretary of war in January 1862 when it passed the Railroad Act, granting the federal government the authority to seize the railroads in order to protect the public interest and to supervise rail transportation of troops, munitions, and supplies. Stanton authored the act in consultation with various members of Congress. In May 1862 the president formally seized all railroads in the United States. Lincoln and Stanton agreed that the government would not physically take over railroads as long as private management cooperated. During the war, the War Department actually took over only a few railroads, even on a temporary basis.

In February 1862 Stanton convened a conference of railroad officers in Washington. A new rate schedule was negotiated that reduced rates considerably and set government tariffs below those paid on regular traffic. Following Stanton's reforms, Quartermaster General Meigs in June 1862 halted the practice of allowing all officers to arrange railroad transportation. Henceforth, only quartermaster officers could contract to transport men and supplies, and they had to ship by the nearest, cheapest, and shortest route. After March 1862 they were guided by the rates Stanton had negotiated with the railroads.

In February 1862 Daniel C. McCallum replaced Scott, whom Stanton had actually eased out of Washington by sending him on an inspection trip to the West. In June 1862 Scott left the War Department to return to the Pennsylvania Railroad. Not sacking Scott was a smart move; he was a gifted railroad expert who had served the government well, and Stanton periodically called upon him for assistance later.

McCallum was a railroad engineer and former superintendent of the Erie Railroad. Along with Thomson, Herman Haupt, and others, he had pioneered modern railroad management. McCallum was commissioned a colonel (later promoted to major general) and was appointed director of the U.S. Military Railroads (USMR). Under the authority of the Railroad Act of 1862, McCallum directed the nation's railroads, including engines, rolling stock, and plant and equipment, in transporting troops and supplies. Although McCallum worked directly under Stanton, all procurement and supplies for McCallum's office were handled by the Quartermaster Department. Meigs attempted to use that leverage to gain control of the USMR and thereby reestablish traditional departmental control over transportation. McCallum did submit reports to the quartermaster general, but the USMR, like Scott's office, remained an independent War Department agency free of Quartermaster control.

The USMR was a mixed military-civilian endeavor. Trainmen, dispatchers, and superintendents were civilians employed by the federal government, and military officers and enlisted men filled the other positions. By the end of the war, the USMR operated over 2,100 miles of track in the South and West with 25,000 men, 199 engines, and 6,330 cars. It laid 641 miles of track, built or rebuilt 137,418 feet of bridge, and spent $42.5 million while taking in receipts of $12.6 million. Before the organization reached peak efficiency, it perfected its system in the Southeast, principally under the direction of Herman Haupt in 1862–1863.[12]

Strictly speaking, McCallum's office had complete authority over all military railroads. Before the new director could take full control of the USMR, however, Stanton called in Haupt to rebuild a railroad between Fredericksburg and Aquia Creek to serve as a principal supply line for Maj. Gen. Irvin McDowell's Army of the Rappahannock. Haupt performed that task so well that Stanton appointed him chief of construction and transportation in the Department of the Rappahannock in May 1862. In that and subsequent positions, Haupt, although technically under the USMR, acted as the head of an independent unit in devising the policies and practices for rebuilding and running the military railroads. Though it was never formalized, McCallum in effect ran the office of the USMR while Haupt directed the field service. Wisely, McCallum never tried to assert authority over his supposed subordinate, allowing the enormously talented but quirky Haupt the latitude he needed for maximum performance.

Haupt was a graduate of West Point who followed a career of railroad and bridge engineering and teaching. He joined the Pennsylvania Railroad in

1847 and served for a time as general superintendent. A close ally of Thomson, the two men restructured the railroad's management system along modern lines.

Haupt had a genius for operating railroads under emergency conditions. Starting from scratch, he put together a team of men, tools, and equipment that became the Railroad Construction Corps, eventually comprising 10,000 persons. The corps was supplied and paid by the Quartermaster Department and fed by the Subsistence Department. For all intents and purposes, it was a civilian organization answerable only to the secretary of war. Haupt was at best a nominal officer: he insisted that only civilians could supervise railroads and preferred civilian and other artisans and laborers to troops on detail.

The feats of Haupt and his corps became legendary and the source of numerous anecdotes. The corps rebuilt railroads and bridges with increasing efficiency, reducing the time required from months to weeks, days, and even hours. Haupt played a key role in all operations but institutionalized an approach of set procedures, well-trained and carefully coordinated teams, standard and custom-made tools and equipment, huge stockpiles of rails and ties, and, wherever possible, portable, standardized, and interchangeable parts, such as bridge trestles. With an ample reserve of supplies, an especially flexible organization, and the ability to anticipate the army's needs, the Construction Corps kept the military railroads operating even in the midst of battles and despite great planned and unplanned damage. The corps also became expert at destroying Confederate railroads. When not working on railroads, the Construction Corps built wharves, storehouses, offices, and hospitals at depots such as City Point, Virginia.

Once a railroad was rebuilt, it had to be run effectively. To smooth the process, Haupt codified some useful rules based on extensive experience. Above all, he insisted that only qualified and properly trained civilians could operate the railroads, a rule that proved difficult to enforce. From 1862 to 1864, Haupt, Meigs, Stanton, and various commanding officers issued repeated orders that trains moved only at the direction of Haupt or his dispatchers: no orders could contradict Haupt and his assistants unless they came from the commanding officer or McCallum, the chief of transportation. By 1863–1864, repeated confrontations and stern enforcement brought home to military officers the simple point that their welfare depended upon a smoothly operating railroad system with which they could not interfere.

Once control of the trains by civilians answering to himself was established, Haupt implemented three other basic regulations. First, supplies were forwarded only when needed. Second, railroad cars had to be promptly unloaded and returned. Finally, all trains ran on established schedules from which they could not deviate without instructions from Haupt or the commanding officer. Extra trains were summoned to handle troops, the sick and wounded, and supplies that missed regular service; otherwise, the railroads would become gridlocked. Railroads run by telegraphic orders were to be avoided since the telegraph network was vulnerable to breakdown, accidents, or enemy action that could halt the entire train system and create havoc. Haupt also established a priority list for use of the railroads, with subsistence first, followed by forage, ammunition, hospital supplies, and troops. He was adamant on the point that no articles for the personal use of officers, individuals, or sutlers could be included on military shipments.

To facilitate smooth operations, the USMR requisitioned locomotives and rolling stock from Northern railroads and their suppliers from time to time. The railroads occasionally protested this action or responded reluctantly, but most firms cooperated. They concurred because they supported the war effort, had exceptionally good relations with Washington, and knew the government had the statutory authority to enforce its will. The War Department also made every effort to maintain friendly relations with the railroads on which it was so dependent. Requisitions were therefore limited in number and based only on genuine need. Moreover, when a railroad line was taken over for military purposes, civilian managers were usually retained, the railroad was returned as quickly as possible to the owners, and any damage was repaired with the characteristic efficiency of the Construction Corps. The government even provided railroads with engines and rolling stock if these were essential for effective operation, as occurred in both the North and the South.

Haupt relied on trial and error to perfect his railroad system. Still, by Antietam in September 1862, it was working reasonably well. The real test came at Gettysburg, where railroad supply under Haupt's direction played a vital role in the Union victory. Beginning on July 1, 1863, Haupt supplied the Army of the Potomac from Baltimore over twenty-nine miles of the Western Maryland, a poorly maintained single-track road without telegraph, water stations, sidings, turntables, or adequate wood. To do so, he ran convoys of five trains each, eight hours apart. By July 3 supplies were being delivered at the rate of 15,000 tons a day, with returning trains, running backward, evacuating 2,000–4,000 casualties daily. The Construction Corps made this feat possible by providing the goods and services that the railroad line lacked. At the same time, Haupt's corps rebuilt lines and bridges to open up another avenue of supply and evacuation by July 4. The USMR placed more supplies in the hands of Gen. George G. Meade during four days of brutal battle than Confederate supply operations provided Gen. Robert E. Lee at Fredericksburg during four months free of fighting.

Haupt's achievement in the East was not matched in the West in the early years of the war. Instead, eclectic, decentralized practices prevailed. Significant change did not begin until fall 1863 when McCallum, assisted by numerous civilian railroad managers, including Thomas A. Scott working out of St. Louis, directed one of the truly remarkable transportation feats of the war. The Eleventh and Twelfth Corps, along with supplies and munitions, were transferred from the Rappahannock River to the Tennessee River within two weeks, to lift the siege against Gen. William S. Rosecrans at Chattanooga. Thereafter, McCallum by slow stages took over the military railroads in the West and implemented a construction and transportation program duplicating Haupt's achievement in the East. By February 1864 McCallum was fully in charge. With the new system, the railroads were able to supply effectively Sherman's campaign against Atlanta using a single railroad line running hundreds of miles through enemy territory and to transfer the Twenty-third Corps from Tennessee to the Atlantic Coast.

McCallum lacked Haupt's charisma and genius but was a better manager and officer. Although a great organizer, innovator, and inspirational leader, Haupt was a loner more than a team player. He was temperamentally unsuited for the army and almost inevitably pushed military authority too far. He clashed with Stanton over a relatively trivial matter, abruptly resigning in September 1863. McCallum then stepped in, using his own abilities and Haupt's system to run the USMR for the nation. In 1864 McCallum established and directed 1,201 miles of railroad in the West, the most extensive and successful USMR operation of the war.

Although the war did not fundamentally alter the railroads, it had a significant impact upon them. Rapid expansion in passenger and freight traffic forced the railroads to operate more efficiently since they were unable to increase their rolling stock and locomotive power and in some cases saw them slightly reduced. Growing demand and lavish wartime profits also encouraged the railroads to introduce or extend the use of steel, as opposed to iron, rails, which proved to be a prudent investment. Moreover, the innovations and methods of the Construction Corps carried over into peacetime years, improving rail and bridge construction. Most important, wartime pressures forced the railroads to work together systematically, particularly in facilitating through traffic, which rose from minor to major significance. Their cooperation transformed rail transportation from essentially a local to a national enterprise.

The public-private, civilian-military system developed to use and extend the railroads during the war years was remarkably successful. Under the USMR, existing rail lines remained in private hands, subject to nominal military control in dire emergencies. At the same time, the government built new lines and ensured service in hostile zones where private companies would never willingly operate. To run this complex system, the War Department was able to tap the best railroad talent. What Cameron initiated, Stanton brought to maturity. Key to Stanton's success was removing tainted leaders such as Scott from authority and using them informally and out of the limelight while putting in charge those with impeccable records and practices, such as McCallum and Haupt. These leaders, along with Stanton's reputation for efficiency and rectitude, gave legitimacy and respect to the USMR and gained for it the indispensable support of almost all railroads and the military.

The same forces that shaped the USMR created the U.S. Military Telegraph (USMT), which is not surprising since the two systems were so clearly related. Indeed, the combining of public and private, civilian and military interests was even greater with the telegraph than with the railroad lines.[13] When Thomas A. Scott came to Washington in April 1861, Cameron assigned him responsibility for the telegraph as well as the railroad system. To assist with the former, Scott assembled a small team of telegraphers from the Pennsylvania Railroad. However, railroad and other duties so absorbed Scott that he was unable to build an effective telegraph organization or begin to establish the necessary controls over the private lines.

In actuality, the USMT was little more than an auxiliary of the North's telegraph companies, the American Telegraph Company and Western Union. Since the federal government made no appropriations for the telegraph service until November 1861, all the interim finances, construction, maintenance, and operation were undertaken by American Telegraph, whose wires reached the capital from the North. E. S. Sanford, president of the company, joined Scott and others in first connecting the key departments in Washington with one another and then establishing contact between them and the various army posts around Washington. Though commendable, this action was inadequate. By the time of First Bull Run, there was no direct line between General McDowell's headquarters and that of Commanding General Scott. Moreover, various regional commanders were setting up telegraph offices and building systems without common policies, guidance, or hookups. This situation created confusion, shortages, and rising prices as government units competed with one another for goods and equipment. Cameron recognized the need for centralized control over the system in the latter months of 1861, and McClellan prodded the secretary of war to act. The commanding general was anxious to establish direct contact with the Union's widely dispersed forces and had been among the first to use the telegraph tactically.

In October 1861 Cameron called Anson Stager to Washington to advise the War Department on telegraph policy. Stager was superintendent of Western

Union and had been assisting civilian and military authorities to manage the telegraph system in Ohio. With some help from Scott, Stager worked out a proposal for what became the U.S. Military Telegraph. The plan gained the approval of Cameron and Lincoln and was implemented with Stager as superintendent, or general manager, of the new agency. It had responsibility for the purchase, transport, and distribution of all supplies necessary to build, maintain, and operate military telegraph lines. It also had the right to priority use of the lines, offices, and equipment of the private telegraph companies and could take possession of their systems in an emergency. To facilitate his work, Stager appointed assistants for each geographic military department. In effect, the USMT was an independent entity serving directly under the secretary of war. Like the USMR, it was essentially a civilian organization. However, since the telegraph office procured and operated through the Quartermaster Department and other War Department subdivisions, Stager and his principal lieutenants were commissioned and appointed assistant quartermasters so they could receive and disperse funds. All telegraphers, centered on the group Scott brought over from the Pennsylvania Railroad, and other USMT personnel remained civilians.

The USMT did not begin to function with maximum efficiency until January 1862 for several reasons. McClellan moved the central telegraph office to his headquarters and used it to help ward off civilian control of his command. Furthermore, Seward assumed control of censorship, which was closely related to the telegraph system, but his department carried it out ineffectively. And the USMT, like the War Department in general, suffered from Cameron's incompetent direction. The situation changed when Stanton took over as secretary of war. He quickly wrestled the USMT's central office away from McClellan and relocated it in the War Department under his own watchful eye. Simultaneously, he had the censorship functions transferred from the State to the War Department. Then, in February 1862, Stanton took possession of all telegraph lines in the United States, doing so in the president's name and citing a law passed by Congress in January 1862 as authorizing the action. Moreover, the secretary of war established a comprehensive and drastic program of censorship. Although Stager continued as superintendent of all USMT lines and offices, Sanford was appointed as military director of telegraphic messages, in effect the Union's censor. The secretary of war tenaciously fought off subsequent efforts to have the USMT's principal office removed from his personal direction, including an attempt by Grant when he became commanding general.

As with the railroads, the War Department's seizure of the Union's telegraph system was more nominal than real. Stager insisted that the telegraph remain in private hands unless management was uncooperative. Few lines were ever physically seized; when they were, management and ownership simply came under military direction for the emergency. With their interests protected and business expanded, the telegraph firms had every reason to cooperate fully with Washington and did so almost without exception. In any case, the telegraph companies ran the wartime agency, supposedly controlling them more directly than did the railroads. Stager and Scott wrote the charter for the USMT. Stager and Sanford, while serving as the top executives of the USMT, maintained their positions as superintendent and president of Western Union and American Telegraph and actively directed and protected their companies. Indeed, Stager, after being appointed general manager of USMT in November 1861, returned to Western Union headquarters in Cleveland to mind the company's business and left much of the responsibility for operating the USMT to the assistant superintendent, Thomas T. Eckert, a former Western Union executive. Eckert's responsibility expanded even further when Stager moved the office of USMT general manager to Cleveland in April 1863.

The USMT/telegraph companies had sufficient power to beat back any challenge to their prerogatives, even one from within the army, as conflict with the Signal Corps proved. The corps traced its origins to Albert J. Myer, who was appointed as the nation's first chief signal officer in 1860, based on his work with signaling flags. Ambitious and innovative, Myer managed to achieve bureau status for the team he led in March 1863. As early as August 1861, Myer proposed that the group that would become the Signal Corps be responsible for electric as well as for aerial signaling. To strengthen the claim, his signal unit began constructing field trains equipped with G. W. Beardslee's frictional and dial telegraph machines, which had an effective range of five to eight miles. The experiment was only partially successful. After corps status was achieved, Myer demanded with increasing firmness that his organization have responsibility for all forms of communication, threatening the autonomy of the USMT. Stager insisted that all telegraph functions be concentrated in the hands of either the USMT or the Signal Corps rather than dividing responsibility between the two. Facing such a choice, Stanton made the only possible decision: he fired Myer and transferred all men and equipment related to electric telegraphy to the USMT. Stanton and other officials agreed on the need to keep the USMT a civilian organization to avoid military interference. Myer's grab for power represented exactly the type of meddling they feared.

Before hostilities ceased, the USMT had between 1,200 and 1,500 operators, line builders, and support staff in addition to the numerous enlisted men and laborers who served with it temporarily. During the war, the agency built over 15,000 miles of lines. As was true with the Railroad Construction Corps, the USMT often advanced with the troops, establishing field lines nearly up to the battlefront under dangerous conditions.

The telegraph system became a powerful instrument of war, more important to communication than the railroads were to transportation. Indeed, the telegraph proved critical to the operations of civilian and military rail systems. Used in a limited way during the Mexican War, the telegraph became indispensable to logistics and command during the Civil War and thus set historical precedents. Without the telegraph system, Lincoln, Stanton, and Grant would have faced insuperable difficulties in effectively commanding the Union's far-flung armies, and the remarkable feats of transferring troops and supplies would have been virtually impossible.

The lines of authority and organizational structure of both the U.S. Military Railroads and the U.S. Military Telegraph were always uncertain and even contradictory. Two related factors created the confusion. The agencies were civilian-military, public-private hybrids that almost inevitably defied clear definition. Moreover, neither the USMR nor the USMT logically belonged in the War Department; they ended up there because no other suitable place existed. This circumstance suggested that as the American economy became larger and more complex and the corporate structure more widespread, the War Department could no longer serve as the basic mobilization agency, as it had since the Revolutionary War. During a major war, new, civilian mobilization agencies would be required to plan and regulate a wartime economy. Thus the military would be properly supplied while the integrity and stability of a corporate capitalist economy were preserved.

THE ORDNANCE DEPARTMENT

Along with the Quartermaster and the Subsistence departments, Ordnance was the big purchasing agency in the War Department. Unlike the other two bureaus, Ordnance's procurement of weapons involved specialized and sophisticated products. By 1840 the Ordnance Department had completed its pioneering work on small arms and methods of producing them.[14] Moreover, after that date the department let no more large, subsidized contracts with private firms for standard infantry muskets, since the Springfield and Harpers Ferry arsenals met the army's immediate and reserve needs. This move led to the demise or reorganization of almost all private arms companies that had come into existence before 1830, such as Simeon North; these were financially vulnerable firms that could not survive without government contracts. A new private arms industry began evolving in the 1830s and was quite advanced by the time of the Civil War. It involved patent arms firms, such as Winchester Repeating Arms Company, which were relatively large, soundly financed, and diversified. They catered primarily to a civilian market and manufactured uniform weapons but without parts that were interchangeable within or among companies.[15] These developments fundamentally affected how the Union armed its troops during the Civil War.

When the Civil War broke out, the Ordnance Department had an authorized strength of forty-five officers.[16] This number was much too low, but Congress stubbornly and inexplicably ignored the bureau's plea for more staff until 1863, when only nineteen more officers were added. The limited number of Ordnance officers could not cover the department's responsibilities: staffing headquarters, directing twenty-eight arsenals, armories, and depots, and being present in the field and at fortifications. Moreover, unlike the Quartermaster and Subsistence departments, Ordnance could not easily train new officers. It was the most technical bureau, with years of training and experience required to master the duties involved. The Ordnance Department also suffered from a shortage of enlisted men; their numbers increased from 450 to around 610 during the war, but that hardly matched the multiplying responsibilities. A similar shortage of clerks existed. The bureau even had to fight for adequate office space throughout hostilities.

Unlike the Quartermaster Department, the Ordnance Department did not have the good fortune of exceptional leadership. Chief of Ordnance James W. Ripley was a sixty-seven-year-old West Point graduate who had unexcelled knowledge and experience in small-arms production. Forty-seven years in the service, however, had made him unimaginative, cautious, and devoted to routine.

After the chaotic months of 1861, the Ordnance Department under Ripley expanded methodically in the face of overwhelming responsibilities. Even a chief of ordnance more bold than Ripley would have found leading the bureau in wartime a frustrating ordeal. Statutes regulated almost all aspects of the bureau's operations, especially in regard to arsenals, armories, and depots. Appropriations were specific and nontransferable.

Detailing officers for maximum benefit was one of Ripley's principal problems, with officers for the field presenting particular difficulties. With so few Ordnance officers available, many units had to fill slots with untrained line officers, answerable to field commanders. This action created numerous problems, which were only partially remedied in May 1864 when all field ordnance officers were placed under the chief of ordnance. Even then the department was left with an undersized and frequently undertrained field staff. To make matters worse, Ordnance constantly lost officers because, more than any other bureau, rank was too low and promotions slow in coming.

The arsenals, armories, and depots presented numerous and growing challenges for Ripley. These establishments tended to operate like little fiefdoms, with their own funding, procedures, statutory protection, and specializations. The Springfield Arsenal concentrated on small arms; others manufactured shells, canisters, gun carriages, and saddles and leather goods. Some facilities were used only for storage, and various Ordnance subdivisions depended upon others for materials and parts. These centers functioned well individually, but they did not coordinate effectively because of inadequate centralization in the Ordnance Department. There were definite limits to what any chief could do since he could not transfer enlisted men or funds among the establishments, and officers were in such short supply that some posts were headed by noncommissioned officers. Existing superintendents and other subdivision heads were often difficult to deal with, at times blaming the executive of Ordnance for adverse conditions that were beyond his control. Even if dissatisfied with arsenal and depot heads, the chief of ordnance often lacked authority over them, or if he did have it, he had sense enough not to interfere with going concerns.

Despite these difficulties, the Ordnance Department expanded successfully to meet the enormous demands of wartime. Few shortages existed by 1862 aside from the standard shoulder arms. Production of ammunition for small arms was truly amazing, exceeding .75 billion rounds with large reserves existing between 1862 and 1865.

Ordnance's greatest single task was supplying millions of troops with small arms, particularly the standard shoulder weapon. In this regard, the department's performance in 1861 was erratic. Shortages were common and foreign weapons filled the gap until public-private production adequately increased. By mid-1863 domestic output had grown to the point that all troops had high-quality weapons. Yet Ordnance is usually judged harshly on the weak record of 1861, not on the remarkable accomplishments of 1862 onward. Among other oversights, critics tend to ignore the fact that producing weapons requires a long lead time.

When war broke out, Ordnance's stock of shoulder arms consisted of about 440,000 rifles and muskets and 4,000 carbines. Approximately 40,000 were the new Model .58 rifles and rifled muskets that had been adopted as the standard shoulder arm in 1855; most of the others were antiquated smoothbore muskets. From this arms stockpile must be subtracted the 60,000 weapons in the Far West that were out of easy access and the 15,000 or so lost to the fire and the Confederates at Harpers Ferry. Still, holdings in state arsenals, which varied in numbers and quality, supplemented the federal government's reserve.

By the time of First Bull Run, most of these weapons had been issued. With the federal government, states, and even some individuals seeking to arm troops, the acquisition and distribution of weapons spun out of control, and a mad scramble for small arms began at home and abroad.

The breakdown was not the responsibility of the Ordnance Department alone. For years, Washington had ignored Ordnance's recommendation that small-arm reserves be expanded greatly. When hostilities erupted, the chief of ordnance's efforts to handle the crisis were frustrated by departmental weaknesses. Moreover, Ripley's superiors undermined his attempt to prioritize arms distribution. He wanted to arm the three-year regulars with the best weapons and distribute the lower-quality guns according to the importance of the units receiving them. Intense political pressure from the states, commanding officers, and others threw off this process, and Ripley simply had to yield at times. When he held firm, Lincoln, Cameron, and other officials often undercut him, and arms were committed and delivered to commanders in the field without Ripley's consent or even his knowledge. These realities prevented Ordnance from keeping the reliable inventory basic to planning, adding to the confusion generated by Cameron's sloppy and irresponsible leadership.

Until public and private small-arms capacity could expand to meet demand, the North acquired desperately needed weapons on domestic and foreign markets. Competing at home and abroad with the states, middlemen, and the Confederacy, Washington purchased some nearly useless and marginal weapons at highly inflated prices. Frantic emergency buying also opened the door to profiteering, fraud, and malfeasance, for which historians and other writers have indicted Cameron, Ripley, and Union economic mobilization in general. Though mostly accurate, the charges are often shrill and fail to point out that most abuses ended in 1861.

With the encouragement of the Lincoln administration, the states began buying weapons on the American market in April 1861 and soon extended their activities overseas. In time, the federal government realized this competition was undermining its purchasing efforts. Cameron urged the states to stop procuring arms and finally ordered them to do so in November 1861; they had fairly well complied by the end of the year.

In contrast to the states, the War Department was late to begin purchasing on the open market. Ripley recommended buying weapons abroad in April 1861 but did not push for action because he, along with the secretary of war and the commanding general, believed that public and private production could expand in time to meet Union needs. The shock of First Bull Run quickly changed their thinking. With the call for troops doubled and an early Union victory not even a fond hope, the War Department late in July began buying small arms in disorderly panic on the home market. This approach predictably did not work well, yielding only around 30,000 muskets and rifles in the first fourteen months of war. Many of the weapons acquired were unfit for military use. Scandals badly marred this domestic procurement drive, commonly involving middlemen who exploited ignorant and overanxious War Department procuring agents. Exchange of the Hall carbines was the most notorious case. With small arms in desperately short supply, Ordnance sold approximately 5,000 Hall weapons in good condition to a middleman for about $3.50 apiece. The guns were altered, passed among different dealers, and sold back to the army several months later for more than $22.00 each. Among others, Simon Stevens, a shady businessman, J. P. Morgan, and probably George Opdyke, the soon-to-be-elected mayor of New York City, had a hand in the operation.[17]

In contrast to the home market, buying and contracting abroad produced a rich lode of weapons. Typical of War Department operations in 1861, foreign purchases took place without centralized direction. Foolishly, the Ordnance Department was bypassed. Cameron and his assistant, working with the president, the secretary of state, and others, in July jumped headlong into the foreign market without consulting Ripley. The chief of ordnance did what he could to strengthen the effort after decisions had been made. Various weaknesses inevitably characterized this irregular approach. First, unqualified agents carried out the buying, and arms brokers received contracts as well, bringing the federal government into competition with itself and driving up prices. Second, no clear policies guided weapons acquisition. Left unresolved were critical matters such as whether Washington would accept second- and third-class, as opposed to first-class, weapons and whether the Union should simply acquire arms or make purchases and let contracts to monopolize capacity and thus deny weapons to the Confederacy. Third, inadequate financing resulted in serious shortfalls, notably the failure to corner the market in English Enfields so as to prevent Confederate purchases. Fourth, the government ignored excellent intelligence on the European scene, which resulted in numerous errors, misjudgments, and misunderstandings. Last, the Union did not send qualified inspectors to Europe to pass on weapons, leaving the matter to overworked ordnance officers in American ports who could not do an adequate job.

Despite these weaknesses, the Union acquired nearly 1.2 million rifles and muskets from Europe in addition to carbines, revolvers, and sabers. "Eighty percent of these [shoulder] arms," according to the most careful scholar of the subject, "were accurate, dependable and of good quality."[18] Of the total, nearly 450,000 were Enfield rifled muskets, a top-quality weapon Ordnance ranked second only to its own Springfield. Among the worst weapons were Belgian, Austrian, and Prussian smoothbores and older guns that were worn, poorly designed, or badly made. Despite an inadequate inspection system, Ordnance turned down many weapons and required alterations in others.

Foreign weapons were critical to the Union during the first two years of war, yet writers on the Civil War have treated them more as a plague than a godsend. Most important in explaining this paradox is the fact that the very worst weapons arrived in 1861 when a panicked War Department bought almost any weapon for sale. These inferior and unserviceable arms permanently tainted the reputation of foreign weapons although they were atypical of Union purchases, and scholars and other writers since then have followed the mistaken notion of contemporaries. By June 1862 the War Department had implemented more orderly and selective procedures. European firms also increased the output and quality of their weapons, and by the end of 1862 troops received only good arms. Foreign purchases ceased by mid-1863 and the Ordnance Department began replacing all but the very best European shoulder arms with the standard Springfield rifled musket.

Though indispensable for the Union cause, foreign weapons created enormous problems for the Ordnance Department. Twenty-five kinds of cartridges were necessary to supply different weapons of varying caliber. Some small arms also came without spare parts, forcing Ordnance to manufacture them or cannibalize some weapons to service others.

Domestic production provided not only the best quality weapons but also uniform ones with interchangeable parts. The Springfield Arsenal led the way in this regard; with Harpers Ferry destroyed, it was the only facility available for public production. Fears of an accident or sabotage at Springfield led Ordnance to begin building an arsenal in Rock Island, Illinois, in 1864, but the facility had not started production when the war ended. Although Springfield did not lead the industry after 1840 as before, it remained an excellent facility. Expansion in production began virtually with Sumter. The growth was facilitated by readily available (though increasingly expensive) skilled labor, raw materials, and machinery in the Connecticut Valley, the nation's small-arms center. In April 1861 the Springfield Arsenal was producing rifled muskets at the leisurely pace of 12,000 per year; between June 1861 and June 1862 output jumped to 110,000; by June 1863 it hit 220,000; and by 1864 it had reached a capacity of 300,000. Ultimately, the arsenal manufactured 802,000 Model .58 rifled muskets during the Civil War.

This quantity was a remarkable feat, and by 1865 Springfield was the largest arsenal in the world in terms of output and size. Quality matched quantity. The Springfield rifled musket was probably the finest weapon of its class. Parts were fully interchangeable, quality control was excellent, and by the end of the hostilities the average cost of the weapon was $11.97.

Ordnance's outstanding wartime record did not stem from public production alone. The department also made extensive use of contractors and subcontractors in the private sector to expand the nation's output of small arms. Subcontracting—by the Springfield Arsenal itself and by large firms such as Colt Patent Fire Arms Manufacturing Company, to which Ordnance let contracts for the .58 rifled musket—played a vital role in wartime output. Firms that in peacetime produced items like tools, machines, and bells during wartime became subcontractors making most parts of the rifled musket. Springfield contracted with firms throughout the Northeast for all musket parts except stocks. The larger arms firms usually subcontracted for only minor parts, but a few hired other firms to make every part of the musket.

Three related points stand out about subcontracting. It was based on uniform weapons with interchangeable parts, which Ordnance's work with private firms in the antebellum years made possible. Second, subcontracting accelerated domestic production and allowed producers, and especially the Springfield Arsenal as the largest subcontractor, to increase output far beyond what plant expansion would allow and to adjust supply readily to fluctuating demand. Third, the fact that firms never before involved in arms manufacture could quite easily produce fully interchangeable parts for the rifled musket testifies to the relative sophistication of the nation's industrial sector.

Private firms under contract with Ordnance produced nearly 650,000 rifled muskets during the war, fewer than Springfield alone produced but still of immense importance. Starting and sustaining private output proved trying. The department let contracts for over 1.5 million weapons, giving a success rate for private manufacturers of only 42 percent. Ripley first let contracts for muskets in early July 1861. The pace became frantic after Bull Run and continued at that level through the year. There was some bribery and other malfeasance in the contracting process, but no fraud per se because firms intended to produce as obligated. Many new and old firms simply could not perform according to contract, however.

The months from July to December 1861 were the shakedown period in relations between the Ordnance Department and private contractors. The department had not had extensive involvement with arms firms since 1840, and the industry had changed fundamentally since that time. By the end of 1861, the department knew fairly well which firms were reliable. The Ordnance Commission, created early in 1862, assisted the department in terminating relations with nonperforming and incompetent firms. Since 1861 was such a difficult time for the War Department in general, Ordnance's special difficulties during those months were to be expected.

Beginning in 1862, Ordnance worked well with private contractors. Ripley and his subordinates understood from the outset that relatively large manufacturing firms with experience in arms-making had the best chance of fulfilling their contracts. The chief of ordnance also appreciated that these firms would encounter unanticipated difficulties that would set back delivery schedules. He was willing to extend deadlines and promise further orders in return for expansions in plants. He also bent rules on manufacturing materials and procedures as long as the quality of weapons was not compromised. Ordnance furthermore accepted minor irregularities without penalty. Ripley proved unbending on only one point, despite loud and long protests from contractors: existing patterns and gauges had to be used as specified without exception. To do otherwise would have provided the army uniform weapons without fully interchangeable parts, sacrificing goals achieved after nearly a half century of effort.

The Ordnance Department's strategy of contracting with many firms ensured that it received the required number of weapons despite the high failure rate. As anticipated, the large firms did best, with the top five companies, including Alfred Jencks and Son and Colt, producing half of all private-sector weapons. By 1863 these firms and others regularly delivered muskets equal in quality to those produced in the arsenal. On the average, arms from private manufacturers cost $19.52, 63 percent higher than the figure for the Springfield Arsenal. Public and private output of the .58 rifled musket totaled nearly 1.5 million. For the first time a number of firms were producing uniform arms with interchangeable parts in massive quantities. The Ordnance Department led the way in this outstanding achievement as primary producer; as source of contracts, model weapons, patterns, gauges, and parts; as adviser and guide to private firms; and as inspector of the finished products.

Ordnance did not perform as well with breech-loading and repeating shoulder arms, a situation that caused the department considerable grief, and arguments about the feasibility of such weapons during the Civil War continue today. Critics charge that the Union could have mass-produced breechloaders and repeaters (and machine guns, especially Gatling guns, according to some) to subdue the South sooner than it did, possibly in two years, if not for Ripley's adamant opposition to these weapons. Such assertions ignore the South's capacity to resist and the stage of development of these guns at the time of the Civil War as well as exaggerating the productive potential of the Union economy. They also manifest a twentieth-century fascination with miracles of production and high-tech weapons. Though Ripley was cautious and strongly biased against most breech-loading and repeating weapons, he does not bear responsibility for a Union failure in small-arms opportunity.[19] Ripley personified Ordnance's nineteenth-century drive to supply all troops with high-quality, uniform, mass-produced weapons with interchangeable parts. Despite numerous obstacles, he consistently, patiently, and flexibly pursued that goal as his first priority.

Ripley did not completely oppose breech-loading and repeating firearms, which were starting to transform the small-arms industry by 1861. Indeed, the army had long experimented with breechloaders, producing and acquiring some of them as early as 1813. Ripley and other conservative ordnance officers believed that breech-loading and repeating carbines were appropriate for the cavalry. But the arsenals did not manufacture such carbines, and Ordnance struggled during the war to get private firms to produce enough of them to arm all mounted troops.

Ripley consistently opposed the newer weapons for the infantry. Significant progress had been made on both breech-loading and repeating rifles, but mass production for military use had not been achieved, principally because of problems with ammunition. Those difficulties would not be fully resolved until shortly after the Civil War through the development of metallic cartridges with a center-detonating device.

Since breechloaders and repeaters were still experimental, Ripley insisted that the Ordnance Department did not have the wherewithal to pursue production on a massive scale. Some twenty-three breech-loading and repeating shoulder arms existed, and at least six could have been considered for adoption. The selection process would have required time, personnel, and effort, which the department could not spare. Had the department ignored existing priorities and emphasized breech-loading and repeating weapons, years would have passed before mass production of truly uniform weapons with interchangeable parts became possible. To pursue the experiment would have necessitated cutting back on public and private production of the Springfield rifled musket. Foreign production of the newer weapons was an option on paper, but it would have been irresponsible in the face of possible war with England and France late into 1862 and would probably have been vetoed by American industry. Through 1862 and into 1863, the Union manufactured breech-loading and repeating weapons by foregoing production of Springfields, often at a ratio as high as six to one. After mid-1863, when private and public production had hit its stride and Ordnance had a reasonably large stockpile of Springfields or their equivalent, breechloaders and repeaters became a genuinely viable option for the first time. Ripley's continued opposition to the newer weapons at this point cost him his job. His successors procured more breech-loading and repeating weapons and initiated procedures to have them adopted as the standard infantry weapon, but the Springfield maintained that distinction at the war's end.

Next to rifles and muskets, the revolver was the most procured weapon in the North. By the time of the Civil War, Ordnance Department arsenals had ceased making revolvers in favor of Colt's patent pistols, which other firms began to match or modify after 1857. Some shortages of handguns occurred early in the fighting, but they were in plentiful supply by 1862–1863. Colt, Remington Arms Company, and the Starr Arms Company manufactured about 90 percent of the nearly 360,000 revolvers procured by the government during hostilities. Miscellaneous producers and foreign purchases accounted for the rest. Ordnance also bought numerous bayonets and sabers.

Artillery was another prime responsibility of the Ordnance Department. By sending officers abroad and encouraging development at home, the department had fairly well achieved parity with other nations in big guns when the war broke out. The old Columbiad was giving way to the improved Rodman and Parrott guns. Ripley wanted uniform batteries, but that goal was never realized. Although the Union had a reasonable number of cannons in 1861, large orders were let in mid-1861, and the Union armies soon had ample quantities of high quality, cast-iron, smoothbore and rifled artillery, including some remarkably large guns. Only artillery for fortifications was in short supply during the fighting. The North made only limited progress on wrought-iron or steel and breech-loading cannons over the war years. Since the Ordnance Department had no foundries, it had to rely on a few private firms to produce artillery and often to carry out experiments and make improvements as well. The biggest foundry was Robert P. Parrott's West Point Iron and Cannon Factory, which was also the largest single contractor of the war, with total revenues of over $4.7 million. Some arsenals did manufacture gun carriages and caissons as well as various kinds of projectiles.

The Ordnance Department also procured gunpowder. Ordnance never manufactured powder despite various proposals for government output, although it worked with Du Pont and other firms in developing and producing what it wanted. Du Pont accounted for approximately one-third of the nation's output in 1860 and remained the largest supplier throughout the war. The Hazard Powder Company of Connecticut was second. With Washington acting to ensure an adequate stockpile of raw materials such as saltpeter, and private industry maintaining up-to-date production facilities, the Union always had ample supplies of gunpowder.[20]

By mid-1863 the department under Ripley had set policies and practices that remained established for the duration of hostilities. Almost all troops were well armed and supplied, and the bureau had generous reserves and the production capacity to meet any sudden surge in demand. Under these conditions, Lincoln and Stanton felt free to remove the chief of ordnance from office. Ripley was never a popular officer, and his effective resistance to breech-loading and repeating weapons, among other factors, led Lincoln and Stanton to decide to replace him as early as spring 1862. They delayed until September 1863 to avoid disrupting the bureau as it was still struggling to fulfill its goals. Though

Ripley remained, his authority was restricted since Assistant Secretary of War Peter S. Watson oversaw the department, reviewed most decisions, and checked some of the chief of ordnance's conservative proclivities.

When Ripley left, Lincoln and Stanton, still concerned about unsettling the department, selected Lt. Col. George D. Ramsay as the new chief of ordnance on the basis of seniority. Ramsay was less talented than his predecessor but more amenable to newer weapons and to directions from above. Under the new chief the department acquired more breechloaders and repeaters. Yet Lincoln and Stanton remained unimpressed with Ramsay's earnest but uninspired and basically conservative qualities. In September 1864 they ignored seniority and appointed Maj. Alexander B. Dyer, the forty-nine-year-old superintendent of the Springfield Arsenal, as the fourth wartime chief of ordnance. The department at last had a leader liberated from the values of the past and anxious to embrace proven and more modern weapons. But before Dyer made any basic changes, the war ended.

After a slow start, the Ordnance Department performed well during the Civil War, particularly in the most challenging area of providing standard weapons for the line. In achieving that goal, Ripley deserves much of the credit.

The Quartermaster, Subsistence, and Ordnance departments handled the overwhelming bulk of Civil War procurement. The other bureaus were more service than supply agencies. In March 1863 the Corps of Topographical Engineers was merged with the Corps of Engineers under the latter title. The Signal Corps achieved bureau status in March 1863, and the Judge Advocate's Office reached that level in July 1862. The Provost Marshal General's Department was a wholly new bureau that handled the draft; the Medical Department, the Adjutant General's, Paymaster General's, and the Inspector General's departments completed the army's complement of staff bureaus, for a total of eleven at the end of the war. All drew some supplies, engaged in procurement, or both, but the amounts were not great compared to the work of the Quartermaster, Subsistence, and Ordnance departments.[21]

ARMY: SUPPLY AND COMMAND, 1862–1865

Once Stanton consolidated and extended the reforms begun under Cameron, the War Department functioned much better in all categories. Of special importance was the matter of requirements. Logistics suffered from the lack of systematic planning during the Civil War. As a result, requirements were estimated, based on the number of troops in the army or expected to be in it, instead of arising from a comprehensive plan. This calculation started when the com-

manding officers of the different geographical departments presented estimates
to the adjutant general; the bureaus, based on consolidated troop figures and
authorized allowances, submitted supply estimates to the secretary of war; and
the latter, in conjunction with the bureaus, adjusted and reconciled the estimates
and forwarded them to the secretary of the treasury, who included them in the
budget proposal to Congress. Congressional figures, accepted by the president,
became the basis for future supply operations. The system was so rudimentary
that its success depended upon the quality of War Department operations in
general and bureau functions in particular. The maturity and experience of longtime bureau personnel proved highly beneficial in this regard. During the tumult
and transition in the War Department in 1861, the bureaus simply multiplied
peacetime estimates by the anticipated number of troops to arrive at respectable
supply figures. When Stanton took over, requirement figures became increasingly accomplished as the secretary of war systematized practices and the bureaus
adjusted to the demands of warfare on a previously unknown scale. Logistical
planning in the Civil War thus turned out to be quite good.[22]

The command structure of the army likewise improved as the war progressed. Despite its improvised quality, the system of command was very effective in the last year of war. Indeed, it anticipated many aspects of Elihu Root's
reforms at the turn of the century.[23]

The command system got off to a bad start in 1861. Secretary of War
Cameron and Commanding General Scott worked reasonably well together,
but the incompetence of the former and the debility and age of the latter precluded sustained effectiveness and encouraged Lincoln's proclivity for actively
directing the war as commander-in-chief. When McClellan became commander of the Army of the Potomac in July 1861, he first established autonomy
from Scott, then took over the latter's position in November 1861, and finally
began arrogating to himself all command authority, including functions that
belonged to the secretary of war and the president. McClellan's reluctance to
fight provided the solution to this threat to civilian control of the military.
Secretary of War Stanton used McClellan's hesitation to reclaim the responsibilities and authority of his own office and to encourage the president to rein
in and in March 1862 to demote the headstrong and arrogant commanding
general. With generals John Pope, Don Carlos Buell, Ambrose E. Burnside,
Joseph Hooker, and others doing little better than McClellan, Lincoln and
Stanton took over by default and jointly acted as commanding general.

These circumstances continued until Ulysses S. Grant became commanding general in March 1864. All army commanders reported directly to him at
his headquarters in the field with the Army of the Potomac. Unlike McClellan,
Grant respected civilian authority over the military and fully recognized that,

as commanding general, he served under the president and the secretary of war. To make the system work more smoothly, former commanding general Henry W. Halleck acted as a chief of staff, with responsibility for liaison between Washington and the line. Lincoln allowed Grant to command under loose, but not neglectful, control from the White House. Potential conflict between the secretary of war and the commanding general was avoided due to the personalities involved. Grant generally was willing to leave supply and staff functions to Stanton; out of respect for him, the bureaus did not balk at orders coming from the commanding general. With a capable officer in charge, Stanton restricted most of his activities to administration of the army and worked through Lincoln when he differed with Grant. Altogether this command structure worked superbly: a careful balancing of civilian and military authority allowed the Union successfully to conduct a nearly total war without threatening civilian control over the army. The only trouble was that this arrangement was based more on personalities than on system.

MANPOWER MOBILIZATION

Mobilizing manpower was a perennial problem for the Union throughout the war.[24] In the early months, the North had to discourage enlistment so as not to exceed the anticipated need for troops and the availability of clothing, equipment, and arms. Moreover, procedures had to be worked out whereby governors acted as agents for the federal government and limited independent recruitment efforts by individuals and groups. Once it was clear that the war would be long, with high casualty rates and repeated defeats, recruitment became increasingly difficult.

To meet its manpower requirements, the Union refined its methods and introduced compulsion. At the outset, the government assigned quotas to the states, first for the militia and later for three-year volunteers. Once the governors had firm control over recruitment, the War Department sought to bring troop mobilization under federal control to make it more uniform, thereby eliminating the governors' role. Of particular concern was the states' practice of meeting their quotas with newly formed units, usually regiments, that allowed men to serve with their neighbors and friends. Though serving the states' interests, this approach harmed the war effort by interfering with organizational continuity. Bloody Civil War battles could reduce regiments by one-half or more. With no method for replacing casualties, regiments had to be consolidated and new ones formed. Furthermore, the state system had no provision for training. It was left to veteran officers, noncommissioned officers,

and enlisted men in the field to introduce new recruits to army life and prepare them for combat.

To address these shortcomings, Cameron in December 1861 ordered into
effect a new recruitment-replacement system designed by Commanding General McClellan. According to the plan, Washington would take over all recruitment functions in January and channel new recruits into existing regiments
according to need. With the governors pushed aside, the War Department in
control, and a replacement system in effect, the North would have a rationalized manpower mobilization program. Before the new system was fully
implemented, however, Stanton shut it down in April 1862, believing the program unnecessary and wasteful of funds. It was the worst blunder of his tenure
in office. High casualty rates at Shiloh and in the Peninsula campaign and the
demands of an expanding war soon forced the secretary of war to arrange a
new call for troops and once again assign quotas to the states. The program
of federal recruitment was reestablished in June 1862 and a replacement system of sorts attempted in 1863. Neither approach worked well, leaving the
states to play a vital role in manpower mobilization throughout the war years.

No voluntary system could mobilize the required number of men after 1861.
Consequently, the national government tried coercion. With state recruitment
lagging during the July 1862 call for over 300,000 men, Lincoln in August
ordered federal conscription for the first time. He based his proclamation on
an obscure provision in the Militia Act of July 1862. According to the president's order, all states failing to fulfill their assigned quotas of three-year volunteers had to make up the deficiency with nine-month drafted militiamen
under regulations prescribed by the secretary of war.

In March 1863 Congress went further, setting up a national conscription
system with the Enrollment Act. In doing so, the nation's legislators ignored
the militia clauses to create for the first time a national military obligation
based upon the constitutional authority "to raise and support armies." This
milestone statute was in effect for the remainder of the war.

The War Department relied upon the year-old Provost Marshal General's
Office to administer the national draft and put the enormously able Col. James
B. Fry in charge. His office reached down to congressional districts throughout the Union via Enrollment Boards made up primarily of military personnel.
The 1862 and 1863 systems both allowed for exemption, substitution, and
commutation. The Enrollment Act placed authority over manpower mobilization squarely in the hands of the federal government, with the states left
out. However, Fry wisely appointed acting assistant provost marshal generals
for all states and some territories. The states remained active in recruitment,
and indeed their cooperation was indispensable for any manpower program.

Since conscription went into effect only when states could not raise sufficient volunteers, the draft encouraged the use of bounties and fed the abuses
associated with the practice. The bounty system was as old as the nation and
had been used to induce men into military service and help support their families. During the Civil War, the federal government used bounties even before
the draft, as had localities and states. Before hostilities ended, the national
government spent over $.5 billion on bounties, and localities and states prob-
ably spent as much or more. While various states and localities mortgaged
their financial futures to mobilize the required manpower, the enticements
offered encouraged desertions and other evils such as bounty jumping and
local, state, and regional draft brokers. These brokers were usually unsavory
or even criminal elements who took more than a generous share of the bounty
money for delivering men for service who were often unfit or undesirable.
Bounties, along with commutation and substitution, helped feed class resentments, which contributed to the antidraft riots that periodically racked the
North. Localities, states, and the national government attempted various
reforms to check the abuses of bounty jumpers and draft brokers, but none
was fully successful. Since the draft was a national system, only a selective service process that was effective and rationalized on a national level could eliminate or reduce the corruption and inequities involved. Such a system was
beyond the will or the capacity of mid-nineteenth-century America.

The draft failed as a means of raising manpower. Of the nearly 2.7 million
men who served for the Union during the Civil War, national conscription
provided only about 6 percent. The indirect effects were much greater: the
threat of the draft proved an effective prod in helping the Union raise the
troops it needed to subdue the Confederacy. Nonetheless, to supplement volunteers and draftees, the North in 1863 began in earnest to recruit black
troops and later even used repatriated Confederates in Union-held territory.

Despite its limitations, the draft as administered by the Provost Marshal
General's Office was an extraordinary innovation at a time when the federal
government did not reach down to the local level. That the system worked as
well as it did testifies to the patriotism of most Northerners, the dedication
of the thousands who staffed the system, and the astute and sensible leadership of Colonel (later General) Fry.

THE NAVY DEPARTMENT

The Navy Department demonstrated greater efficiency than the War Department from the outset of fighting for several reasons. The navy as an institu-

tion stagnated less than the army after the Mexican War. Moreover, it had a smaller role in the Civil War than the army and did not expand to the same degree as the land forces.[25] Further, taciturn Secretary of the Navy Gideon Welles was an exceptionally able administrator, a shrewd politician, and generally a good judge of people who delegated responsibility without losing control. Welles had headed the navy's Bureau of Provisions and Clothing from 1846 to 1849 and hence was familiar with Navy Department operations. He also benefited from first-rate assistants who worked with him to constitute an effective and harmonious leadership team. Congress created the position of assistant secretary of the navy in July 1861. Welles chose for the post Gustavus V. Fox, an Annapolis-trained officer who had retired from the navy to pursue a business career. The assistant secretary was an ambitious, enthusiastic, even impetuous, and indefatigable individual of unusual ability. Fox concentrated on directing the fighting forces, virtually becoming a chief of naval operations. For chief clerk, Welles selected a close acquaintance and fellow journalist from Connecticut, William Faxon. The quietly efficient Faxon acted, in effect, as the department's business manager.

The navy faced significant problems when Welles took over as secretary. Like the army, the navy was demoralized by years of neglect and budget austerity. It had only ninety ships, most of which were obsolete. To make matters worse, half the officer corps had joined the Confederacy. But unlike the War Department, the Navy Department moved quickly to prepare for war. The task of Welles and his assistants was made easier by the fact that the nation had the second largest merchant fleet in the world. As a result, numerous ships could be converted to naval use, experienced civilians could serve as officers and seamen, and facilities existed to construct and equip new vessels. At the end of 1861 the department already had programs well under way for buying, building, and borrowing ships for duty at sea and on inland waterways. Before hostilities ceased, the navy's inventory of ships had grown to 671, including 313 steamers purchased by the navy and 184 miscellaneous vessels received from other executive departments. An additional 179 steam vessels had been built and launched, 55 at naval yards and 124 by private contractors. At the height of activity, the department bought every steamer in Northern ports that was available and that suited its needs. Virtually every major shipbuilder and manufacturer of steam engines was under contract with the Navy Department at some point during the war. This frantic activity resulted in a shortage of skilled labor in the public and private sectors, however, which worsened as the fighting stretched out.

Due to the long experience and great skills of the American shipbuilding industry, the nation had few difficulties constructing wooden vessels. Building such ships did not require advanced technology, but constructing vessels of iron and armor-plating presented problems. No navy yard was prepared to build ironclads or service the largest ships of iron. Few private firms were equipped to construct or outfit such ships, and others were unwilling to make the necessary heavy investments without guarantees of orders to cover the expense. To maximize the supply of iron, steel, and armor, the Navy Department surveyed nearly every facility in the nation during the war. It found the existing capacity inadequate.

The Union responded more slowly than the Confederacy to the advent of armored vessels in naval warfare. Congress authorized Welles to appoint an Ironclad Board to study and make recommendations on the subject in August 1861. After extended deliberations, the hesitant board sanctioned the building of three experimental ironclads—a cruiser, a gunboat, and the vessel that became the *Monitor,* the brainchild of John Ericsson. Proof of the *Monitor's* capabilities in March 1862 was a milestone in experiments involving ironclad vessels that the Navy Department carried out in conjunction with private contractors. The work included various classes and sizes of crafts built both of wood and iron. Elaborate testing was done on engines, valve gears, propellers and shafts, boilers, and fuel for the so-called mastless vessels, and data from Europe as well as the United States was used. In all, sevety-one ironclad vessels, including monitors and other types, were built and in time joined the fleet.

The Navy Department's one major blunder involved light-draught monitors designed for inland waterways. Because of the incompetence of the naval constructor, the negligence or obstruction of the conservative bureau chiefs, discord in the navy's relations with the extremely temperamental Ericsson, and a series of mishaps by Welles and Fox, the department committed to the building of twenty light-draught monitors without first having developed and tested a prototype. The results were disastrous. The vessels were inoperable as built, could not be successfully modified, and cost about $10 million.

The Navy Department's difficulties with ships of iron, armor, and steam propulsion, including the light-draught monitor, stemmed in part from a lack of government facilities. No navy yard was sufficiently large or adequately equipped to handle such projects. Moreover, the Norfolk Navy Yard, one of the largest and best equipped in the department's system, was lost to the Confederacy. Both England and France had greater capacity and technological sophistication in one shipyard than existed in the North's yards combined. Recognizing the inadequacy, Welles in 1862 began pushing for a new and expanded facility with foundries, machine shops, and the like, and favored a location offered by Philadelphia. New England also desired a modern yard, however, and the Navy Department and Congress could not agree on a solution during the war. Thus no new yard was constructed.

Nevertheless, the five Northern navy yards and those later reclaimed from the South did carry their load. They were beehives of building, repair, manufacturing, research, and development, and most expanded to handle the increased wartime activity. Their total work force more than quadrupled, matching the number of artisans and laborers working for the navy in private yards. The New York yard was outstanding for its repair of ships, and New York and Boston served as principal ordnance depots. The Washington Navy Yard, laboratory of the navy's ordnance expert John A. Dahlgren, set standards for all ordnance, tested guns, evaluated inventions, and manufactured ordnance items, including gun carriages and ammunition. During the war, the navy's arsenal of heavy guns and howitzers increased by nearly 150 percent. The newer weapons were often larger than the older ones and patterned after the Parrott, Dahlgren, and Fox models. As with the army, some big guns were rifled, but most remained smoothbore. Also like the army, the navy had relatively few foundries to make its ordnance and offered contracts to any firm that held out genuine promise. The navy purchased gunpowder without difficulty and, like the army, manufactured and purchased millions of tons of projectiles.

Besides the regular yards, the Navy Department maintained various stations, depots, and other facilities in the South to service its fleets. Similarly, on the Western rivers, the Navy Department had a number of yards, ports, stations, and depots to build, buy, convert, repair, and service its fleet of steamers, gunboats, ironclads, and other vessels. Activity on these waterways was so heavy and important that naval officers clamored for the creation of a navy yard in the region. Welles had the matter studied and recommendations for a site were made, but no action was taken before the end of hostilities.

Welles instituted some changes in the bureau structure during his years of service. He led efforts for rationalization that resulted in a congressional reorganization of the system in mid-1862 and included the creation of several new bureaus, of which Steam Engineering was especially important. Welles also selected younger and more efficient, though still tradition-minded, officers for staff positions whenever possible. Despite these developments, the Navy Department's bureau system was fundamentally unaltered when Welles left office. The lack of thoroughgoing change caused problems, particularly in ship design. For example, ships were built and then fitted with ordnance instead of being designed for the ordnance they would carry. Nonetheless, the Navy Department under Welles had an able collection of bureau heads who, according to Charles O. Paullin, "were efficient and painstaking administrators . . . , safe and conservative, rather than brilliant and aggressive."[26]

The Navy Department suffered from some corruption under Welles, but nothing like that in the War Department. A person of integrity and good judgment, the secretary of the navy nevertheless stumbled badly shortly after assuming office. He appointed George D. Morgan, his brother-in-law and cousin of the governor of New York, as agent to purchase ships for the department. Though Morgan did an excellent job, he accumulated about $70,000 in commissions in five months, far above the usual compensation of about $6,000. This episode left Welles open to attacks from numerous political enemies he had made in his otherwise scrupulous and efficient conduct of naval affairs. Only his able handling of the department and the full support of Abraham Lincoln saved him from congressional censure.

When Welles took office, the Navy Department still employed civilian naval agents for much purchasing and the conduct of the navy yards. This practice was part of the political spoils system and involved the department in graft and corruption, which over the years had become almost a science. To the embarrassment of the Navy Department and the Lincoln administration, many of these practices came to light during hostilities, adding to a picture of great wartime corruption. The Navy Department sought to uproot and prosecute such unlawfulness, but only a major change in departmental operations could deal effectively with the problem. The secretary of the navy did introduce some reforms, yet the essential root-and-branch changes never occurred. Still, under Welles's rule, regular paymasters replaced the notorious naval agents, and the bureau system was used to keep the prices bid for new ships and machinery at reasonable levels.

Generally, Welles, with the able assistance of Fox and Faxon, made the awkward bureaucracy he inherited function with unusual vigor. Although its load was nowhere near that of the War Department, the Navy Department's level and range of activity was still substantial. Budgets went from approximately $12 million in fiscal year 1861 to a high of $144 million in 1863; the officer corps grew from 1,300 to 6,700 and the number of seamen from 7,500 to 51,500. Yet the number of Navy Department clerks and draftsmen increased from thirty-nine only to sixty-six. When necessary, Welles created new agencies to assist him in his duties; for example, the Office of Detail in the secretary's office guided the assignment of officers. Welles also set up a mixed civilian-military, navy-army Commission of Conference to assist in strategic matters; a more general commission to deliberate on naval affairs as a whole; and the Permanent Commission, a precursor of the National Academy of Sciences, to advise the department on applications of new technology to warfare.

Because of its small size and limited functions (compared with the army) and because most of its effort went into maintaining a humdrum blockade, the navy's role in the Civil War has generally been slighted. But in addition to the crucial blockade, the navy made substantial and often innovative contributions to the war effort. Basing its actions on the Mexican War and observations of the Crimean War, the navy joined the army in devising amphibious operations that began with the Hatteras Inlet operation in 1861 and concluded with the fall of Fort Fisher in 1865. Moreover, the department designed the vessels and developed the techniques for operations on the Western rivers and other inland waters that were crucial to the Union's victory.

The navy's lack of prestige during the war constantly frustrated Welles, as did his inability to achieve adequate high-level coordination with the army. In part, this failing was of Welles's own doing. Determined to gain recognition for the service he headed, the secretary sent the navy alone on ventures, such as Adm. Samuel F. Du Pont's attempt to subdue Charleston Harbor, where only joint operations with the army could produce success. And Lincoln's tendency to allow each department to operate separately made ongoing coordination among them difficult at best. Personalities also played an important role. The overbearing Stanton so alienated Welles that he had little contact with the secretary of war and the department he headed, an unfortunate state of affairs. Stanton and Lincoln had information on the military situation unavailable to Welles because he was not in the president's inner circle, which often left him operating in the dark. Still, below the cabinet level, army and navy commanders with compatible personalities usually functioned well together when joint action was necessary, as Adm. David D. Porter and generals Grant and Sherman proved.

7

UNION CIVILIAN ORGANIZATION

THE TREASURY DEPARTMENT

The Treasury Department faced the enormous responsibility of financing War and Navy Department procurement.[1] The relative economic sophistication of the Union and the magnitude and cost of the war meant that past conflicts did not provide a guide for the nation's economic leaders in the current crisis. Innovation was imperative. Washington made paper money legal tender, engaged in unprecedented programs to sell government securities nationwide, created a third national banking system and a national currency, began collecting a range of taxes down to the local level that was new to the national experience, and ran up a national debt of unheard-of proportions. These measures, along with highly protective tariff rates, were dramatic departures made possible only by the emergency of war.

Heading the Treasury Department was Salmon Portland Chase. His appointment to the cabinet was a political necessity for Abraham Lincoln and the Republican party because he led the party's radical wing and had been a major contender for the presidential nomination in 1860. Although intellectually gifted and an able administrator, Chase had little experience in financial matters in general and federal finances in particular and was committed to Jacksonian hard money. More troubling was Chase's rigidity and limited promise for growth. Rather pompous, stubborn, and imbued with self-importance and self-righteousness, he proved incapable of devising policies to finance a war of modern proportions. At critical points, Congress had to step in to prevent the economic paralysis of the Union. Lincoln took office with inexperienced and unqualified administrators in the critically important Treasury and War departments. Unlike in Simon Cameron's case, however, others' strengths compensated to some degree for Chase's weaknesses.

178

Both the Treasury Department and Congress by necessity worked closely with the banking community in devising wartime financial policies. In doing so, economic elites moved between private and public institutions in a way that blurred the distinction between the two spheres. Such conditions had existed earlier with the first and second national banks. Andrew Jackson's bank war and the creation of the independent Treasury system had been intended to build secure walls between Washington and the nation's banks. The long and costly Civil War ended permanently the artificial separation. The Treasury Department's relations with banks did not combine public and private interests as overtly as the government did with the railroad and telegraph companies. Nonetheless, those relations are among the few examples at the federal level of economic elites circulating among various institutions in a manner that was commonplace among the states.

Chase faced critical conditions upon taking office. The economic downturn beginning in 1857 was worsened by the secession crisis and had produced an unaccustomed national debt of nearly $75 million by early 1861. More distressing, the Treasury Department could sell securities only at ruinous interest rates after the November 1860 elections. With revenue covering less than 25 percent of escalating expenditures, Chase had to sell $19.6 million of government paper and postpone payment on various debts just to keep the nation solvent until Congress convened in July 1861 and revised finances.

Chase presented to Congress a budget of $320 million for the fiscal year beginning July 1861. He anticipated raising $80 million in revenue and floating bonds for the rest. Congress responded by increasing a few customs duties, levying a direct tax of $20 million on real property in the states, and placing a tax of 3 percent on annual incomes in excess of $800. These expedients produced much less revenue than expected by June 1862, necessitating even heavier borrowing by the Treasury. Congressional acts in July and August 1861 provided for the sale of $250 million in bonds and notes, $50 million of which could be in the form of paper money. The secretary of the treasury used this authority to issue $50 million in noninterest-bearing demand notes and, in addition, virtually forced the leading banks of New York, Philadelphia, and Boston to purchase $150 million in three-year, 7.3 percent notes and other securities in three installments before the end of 1861.

The banks found Chase to be extremely rigid in the sale of the securities. He insisted that they be purchased at par, which, given the uncertainties of war, made them extremely difficult to sell at going interest rates. Even more distressing, Chase refused to interpret broadly a carefully worded provision of the August 1861 act that could have been used to bypass the Independent Treasury Act and permit the banks to hold the $150 million in loans for the Treasury to draw upon like a checking account. Instead, Chase insisted that the banks pay their installments to the government in bullion, which, along with other demands, drew down dangerously their specie reserves. The banks acquiesced because they had no alternative. Their future was tied to the success of the Union war effort, and without their financial support the government's credit would collapse, with disastrous consequences.

Public and bank finances remained on a narrow edge of solvency throughout 1861, vulnerable to any shock that would undermine public confidence. In December 1861 a series of developments forced a reordering of government finances. The North's military situation was particularly gloomy. The *Trent* affair dashed any hopes of selling securities abroad and threatened war with Great Britain. Then Chase's financial report to Congress demonstrated the desperate state of Union finances and the unfitness of the secretary of the treasury to handle the crisis. Chase lowered the estimate of federal revenue for fiscal 1861 from $80 million to $55 million and put anticipated expenditures at $532 million instead of $320 million. To deal with the drastically altered situation, the secretary proposed cuts and reforms in government spending and increases in revenue, with $50 million coming from taxes and another $50 million from other sources. The heart of Chase's report, however, was a call for a national banking system, which he claimed would provide the Union with a national currency, create a dependable market for bonds, and check excessive issues of paper money.

Chase's report directly and indirectly illustrated his attachment to two obsolete financial theories: first, the idea of Albert Gallatin that during a period of hostilities, taxes should pay for normal peacetime expenses and interest on the public debt while borrowing covered the costs of fighting; and second, that the nation's monetary system should be tied irrevocably to specie. A national banking system would further the first end by facilitating lending and the second by giving Washington control over the currency. Both theories might have been relevant for an agrarian past and limited wars, but they invited disaster for a war that was taking on modern proportions. Until First Bull Run, the secretary of the treasury along with most other Northerners could take comfort in the belief that the war would be short. After that major defeat, a long, expensive, and sanguinary war became inevitable, demanding adjustments in thought and policy. Chase's report revealed in stark terms that he could not or would not draw the logical conclusions from Bull Run and respond accordingly. In a conflict on the scale of the Civil War, tax revenue had to cover a larger share of war expenses than Gallatin had believed, if only to soak up consumer buying power and hold back inflation. Although a national banking system had many advantages in the long run, it solved no immediate problems. Chase's report to Congress offered no reasonable plan for financing a long and demanding war.

The accumulating disasters at the end of 1861 set off a run on banks that led them to suspend specie payments in December, with Washington quickly following suit. Chase appeared at a loss about what to do, and his inaction allowed the initiative over financial policy to pass to the nation's legislators. In Congress, particularly the House Ways and Means Committee and the Senate Finance Committee, an especially talented group of bankers, manufacturers, merchants, and attorneys henceforth played a vital role in formulating financial policy. Chase also consulted with an able group of businessmen. The banks of New York, Philadelphia, and Boston naturally had an important say in money and banking matters, and other banking interests throughout the nation made their voices heard. Bankers and businessmen, big and small, were deeply divided over monetary and banking policy, as was the nation at large. Consequently, careful negotiations and compromise were necessary to work out broadly supported wartime financial policies.

Congress' first move in resolving the financial crisis was to approve, after acrimonious debate, the Legal Tender Act of February 1862, a radical departure. Under the act, the federal government for the first time issued authentic paper money that was legal tender for all private and public purposes except payment of tariff duties and interest on U.S. securities. Congress passed the statute based on the argument that it was imperative for expeditiously increasing the financial power of the Union. The act authorized the government to issue $150 million in notes—the infamous greenbacks—that were convertible into government bonds. Once the printing presses started, they were difficult to stop as war costs mounted faster than revenue could be collected or borrowing arranged. The nation's legislators authorized a second issue of $150 million in greenbacks in mid-1862 and a third in early 1863, for a wartime total of $450 million. At Chase's recommendation, Congress in July 1863 ended the convertible feature of the paper money.

Actually, providing a national currency was supposed to be one of the key functions of a national banking system. Congress separated the legal tender provisions from the banking proposal to speed the passage of the former, which was more urgent and in some ways less controversial than the latter. Through the persistence of Chase and over the objection of most banks, a reluctant Congress narrowly passed the National Bank Act in February 1863. The law created a modified free banking system that required each national bank to deposit with the comptroller of the currency federal bonds equal to one-third, but not less than $30,000, of its capital, upon which the bank could circulate national bank notes worth up to 90 percent of the value of the securities. The act provided for reserve requirements and other regulatory devices more stringent than those of most states. Congress liberalized the law in June 1864 in an attempt to attract more banks but without much success. Only a stringent tax on state bank notes enacted in March 1865, to take effect July 1, 1866, ended state banks of issue and led most banks to join the national system. Since this switch did not occur until the end of the war, Chase's scheme of national banks providing a rich and guaranteed market for U.S. bonds did not materialize to a significant degree. That lack of success was also true of his goal to place some centralized controls over the approximately 1,600 state banks that issued about $200 million of bank notes of varying worth and variety. The national banking system proved to be much more important for the future than for the conduct of the war.

Another major innovation of the Civil War years was a federal taxation system more comprehensive than in any previous war, reaching down to the local level. Such practices were quite extraordinary for the time. Washington had abandoned internal taxes after the War of 1812, except for excises on alcohol and tobacco and a few miscellaneous collections, choosing to rely principally on tariff revenue supplemented by income from land sales. That situation and the people's aversion to taxation led politicians to introduce new levies very slowly. Chase recommended relatively light taxation in mid-1861, and Congress responded modestly. The December 1861 financial crisis led Chase to advocate more taxes, but he left both policy and details to Congress. The legislators went far beyond what Chase had envisioned, passing in July 1862, after months of vigorous debate, the nation's most extensive taxation program. This measure was followed by additional taxes in each remaining year of the war, with the taxes in 1864 of particular importance. Congress enacted the first national income tax in 1861 and made it more progressive before the war's end, with a levy of 5 percent on incomes between $600 and $5,000 and 10 percent on incomes above $5,000. A modest inheritance tax was also imposed. Drawing upon past precedents, Congress taxed real property; levied excises on tobacco, liquor, sugar, auction sales, and many other products; placed license taxes on various retailers; covered nearly all legal transactions with stamp duties; instituted levies at various stages of manufacturing and on transportation, advertising, and other services; and reached into an area that had previously been the domain of the states to tax yachts, bank capital and deposits, and dividends. The nation's legislators also pushed up tariff rates from an average of 20 percent on the value of goods in 1860 to between 40 and 50 percent in 1865.

To maximize revenue from these taxes, Congress replaced the office of tax commissioner, created in 1861 and hardly used by Chase, with a commissioner of internal revenue in 1862. This Treasury Department agency divided the country into collection districts, issued regulations, and constantly expanded its force of agents and deputies. Tax evasion occurred, particularly involving liquor and income, but collection was reasonably effective. In 1865, for example, nearly 40 percent of all income tax revenue was collected at the source through withholding from federal employees and from various stock and bond holders. By the war's end, steep taxes on industry were well enforced and accounted for 8 to 20 percent of the costs of all manufactured products. In 1862 internal taxation covered about 10 percent of federal expenditures; by 1864 and 1865 the figure had risen to 25 percent. Taxation had never been so widespread and well enforced, and, for the federal government, had never reached so far into the fabric of the economy. It was a strategy of getting a little from many sources instead of a lot from a few.

Legal tender, taxation, and, to a limited degree, a national banking system played a significant role in wartime financing. But as in past wars, borrowing through the sale of various U.S. securities provided most of the money that kept the Union fighting. Yet the Civil War involved sums never before contemplated and necessitated pathbreaking mass-marketing techniques. Until the Civil War, federal, state, and private security issues were infrequent, small, and sold to the highest bidders, who generally resold all or part of them. This rather informal approach did not work well at the time of secession and war. Throughout his years in office, Chase repeatedly sold government paper maturing in one to three years to meet emergency circumstances. This expedient was undesirable because the short-term notes and certificates kept constant pressure on Washington to refund them and, as legal tender and bank reserves, increased the currency and fed inflation. Long-term bonds were the solution to the Union's nearly insatiable appetite for funds. The Treasury Department, however, lacked the institutions and experience for selling such securities other than in the traditional manner, which did not get the job done.

Jay Cooke & Company, a private banker centered in Philadelphia, devised and implemented mass sales of U.S. bonds. Cooke had proven himself an effective if unorthodox financier early in summer 1861, when he led in selling a $3-million Pennsylvania war loan at par even though the state's credit rating was weak, doing so by tapping a mass market rather than a limited network of banks. His accomplishment received attention in Washington, and Cooke was able to exploit it through political connections. His brother Henry, an Ohio newspaper editor and political operative, belonged to the inner circles of Chase and John Sherman, a senator from Ohio. Through praise, services, and sagacity, Jay Cooke won a place for himself among the secretary of the treasury's advisers on public affairs and also dealt with Chase's personal affairs as investment adviser, lender, and broker. Chase reciprocated in July 1861 by appointing Cooke as one of many subscription agents for selling government issues. As it turned out, Cooke sold over 20 percent of the notes marketed in 1861. Bonds were difficult to sell in the early years of the conflict because of wartime uncertainties and their low returns. Hence, the $500-million issue of the 6 percent, 5–20 bonds (callable in five years, maturing in twenty) authorized by Congress in February 1862 never sold well. Out of urgency and frustration, Chase appointed Cooke as the general and sole agent to market the loan in October 1862, just the goal the private banker had been seeking since 1861.

To sell the bonds, Cooke set up a Union-wide network of some 2,500 sub-agents consisting mostly of bankers; where they were unavailable, he turned to insurance and real estate agents and community leaders. Cooke also appointed hundreds of traveling agents to reach the grassroots. The telegraph and the railroad systems allowed him to stay on top of this vast business enterprise. To stimulate sales, Cooke launched a massive advertising campaign through newspapers, handbills, posters, and the like. He arranged favorable media coverage to convince the public of the soundness of the bonds as an investment and of the public's patriotic duty to support the government and the war effort. The sales network and publicity enabled Cooke to tap a market never before reached. Although banks bought most of the bonds, people from all walks of life and most levels of income and wealth purchased them in denominations as low as fifty dollars. Besides imaginative marketing, the depreciation of the greenbacks, the formation of the national banking system, and the improvement in Union military fortunes made the securities attractive investments. Cooke's organization had sold bonds worth $157 million by July 1863 and $362 million by January 1864.

Cooke's network was efficient as well as effective. Chase limited Cooke's commission to half of 1 percent on the first $10 million and three-eighths of 1 percent thereafter, including all costs. That reduced the banker's profits to around one-sixteenth of 1 percent but still earned his firm a sum of approximately $220,000 in two years, in addition to the prominence, prestige, and contacts throughout the Union that could not be purchased at any price.

Cooke's monopoly generated much envy and criticism. His nontraditional ways had always excluded him from established banking circles, and New York bankers were particularly hostile to his favored position. Democrats and Chase's rivals in and out of Congress also voiced objections to what they saw as an improper and highly profitable arrangement. Feeling the political pressure, Chase in January 1864 terminated the general agency agreement with Cooke. The secretary of the treasury sought to maintain his reputation for rectitude, worried about Cooke's handling of his personal matters, and wanted nothing to interfere with his presidential aspirations. Thereafter, Cooke purchased and marketed some U.S. securities, but the amounts were small and he did so as a banker, not as a government agent.

The sale of bonds all but stopped after Cooke's departure as general agent. Congress authorized a third and fourth loan involving the so-called 10–40s, but those securities and other expedients never succeeded despite Chase's attempts to have the Treasury Department duplicate Cooke's methods. Although increased tax revenue helped the government's finances, Chase had to resort to the sale of short-term notes in order to pay the bills.

Chase resigned as secretary of the treasury in July 1864, and William P. Fessenden, the respected and knowledgeable chairman of the Senate Finance Committee, replaced him. Despite failing health, he was virtually drafted for the post because the Lincoln administration needed his prestige to see the Union through the last phases of the war as expenses rose alarmingly. Fessenden diligently attempted to sell both long- and short-term securities but achieved no great success; massive sales required the techniques and organization Cooke had employed. Yet because Cooke was controversial and would invite attacks on the Treasury Department, Fessenden was extremely reluctant to call on him. Nonetheless, without any reasonable alternative for financing rapidly mounting Union expenses and after failing to put together an agency that combined Cooke's Philadelphia firm with a New York banking house, Fessenden at the end of January 1865 finally gave in.

Cooke headed a campaign to sell the so-called 7–30s authorized in June 1864 and March 1865. He reactivated the organization he had shut down in January 1864, expanded the force of subagents to between 4,000 and 5,000, introduced new techniques such as night offices, and marketed to soldiers and in parts of the South. Between January and July 1865, Cooke's organization sold a total of $830 million in notes and managed to market over $30 million in a single day. Cooke's second sales effort actually took place under Secretary of the Treasury Hugh McCulloch, who replaced Fessenden in February 1865. McCulloch had been the first comptroller of the currency, and Cooke found working with him easier since as a former banker he understood the business.

In retrospect, the Civil War clearly ushered in the modern era of marketing securities. The Union's unprecedented need to borrow billions of dollars created the opportunity for Jay Cooke to pioneer high-pressure, mass-marketing techniques. Variations on his methods became widespread after the war as industrialization hurried forward and modern corporations grew.

Federal spending during the war totaled $3.4 billion. Tax revenue covered about 22 percent of that figure, with the remainder coming from borrowing and the issuance of greenbacks. At its highest point in August 1865, net wartime debt stood at $2.8 billion, equal to nearly one-half of the Gross National Product (GNP).

These financial policies led to strong inflationary pressures, inevitable during the war because of the federal government's enormous demand for goods and services and the monetary devices to which it had recourse. At their wartime peak in January 1865, wholesale prices stood 2.3 times above their level in April 1861; during the worst phase of greenback depreciation in mid-1864, a gold dollar cost $2.62 in paper; and for the war as a whole, the cost of living almost doubled. The principal beneficiary of this inflationary situation was the industrial and business community, which in general reaped uncommonly high and sustained profits. The preeminent loser was the working population. Wages across the board increased only about 50 percent, one quarter the inflation rate, with people at the bottom of the labor ladder suffering more than those in better-paying jobs. Lenders also suffered to some degree from wartime conditions, as did real estate owners and probably farmers. Government at all levels, but particularly at the federal level, was another major victim. Repeatedly, the army and navy found themselves unable to buy in cash or pay their creditors on time because rising prices depleted budgets faster than anticipated and funds were not made available on schedule. Some of the best contractors were driven away because they could not or would not wait long periods to be reimbursed. Thus at times the military had to deal with unreliable companies or with those making inferior products. Moreover, when buying in the open market and contracting without advances, procurement agencies ended up paying higher prices than would have been the case had they dealt in cash or its equivalent. The troops and the families depending upon them for total or partial support also suffered when the government did not meet its payrolls.

Given its economic power, the Union should have been able to finance the war without high inflation rates, and greenbacks were only partially responsible for the situation. Had Washington relied solely on the sale of securities, instead of using fiat money, the debt would have been monetized through greater issue of bank currency and the creation of bank credit with nearly the same results. Earlier and stiffer taxation would have acted to hold down demand and ease inflationary pressures, but the offsetting effect could never have been total.

Chase's financial leadership was basically flawed. The secretary's biggest mistake was in not formulating a long-range program for wartime finances. That gap left the federal government drifting from crisis to crisis with piecemeal policies, a situation that undermined business and public confidence and fed inflationary forces.

Excessive criticism of the secretary of the treasury is unfair, however. The Civil War made unprecedented demands at all levels. Few individuals anticipated the measures that sound financing of the war would require, and deep divisions over the subject abounded in and outside government circles. Talented members of Congress, working with equally gifted members of the business world, groped their way to solutions for major aspects of Union financial policy. They then had to work long and hard in convincing fellow legislators and the public of the wisdom of their decisions. Jay Cooke's imagination and daring engendered so much hostility that Chase felt compelled to drop him, and Fessenden dared use his services only when he was ready to leave office. Although Chase authored few of the financial innovations of the Civil War, they were implemented under him; and by 1865 the Union had a fairly sophisticated program that the war had made both necessary and possible. When Union finances demanded it, Chase ignored his strong convictions and supported paper money, favored tough taxation, and turned the sale of federal securities over to a private banker. At critical points, his backing carried the day for controversial decisions. Thus despite his weaknesses, Chase played a vital role in the clumsy but ultimately successful process of financing the most expensive war to that time.

The administration of the Treasury Department, unlike its financial policies, was accomplished. Next to Navy, Treasury was the most efficient department in the Lincoln administration, and its range and size far exceeded that of the former. Although his conduct was not flawless, as indicated by his compromising relationship with Jay Cooke, Chase was a person of demanding ethical standards. He also recruited a generally high-quality staff that was honest and dependable. Unfortunately, Treasury's administrative quality eroded as Union armies advanced into the South and the department started regulating the region's trade, particularly in cotton. The South's need for goods, the North's hunger for cotton, and the enormous opportunities created by those conditions led to unending corruption about which the Treasury Department did little and, given the magnitude of circumstances involved, probably could not have done much.

The other executive departments did not play an important role in economic mobilization; and Lincoln, unlike James K. Polk, did not use his cabinet as a war council. Nonetheless, the political composition of the cabinet was critical for maintaining Republican unity and commitment to the war effort. In that indirect sense, the entire Lincoln administration was significant in harnessing the economy for war.[2]

Overall, though there was room for improvement, mobilizing the Union's economy was an enormous success. Perhaps better coordination among the

War, Navy, and Treasury departments would have been beneficial, but even that is far from clear. Certainly there is no validity to the assertion of Allan Nevins and Russell F. Weigley that the Union needed a World War I–style War Industries Board or at least an advisory body on statistics and information. Efficient government agencies using market forces in a still rigorously competitive economy proved sufficient. The failed attempt to use what became the National Academy of Sciences as a mobilization agency illustrates the consequences of allowing aspirations to exceed reality.[3] The way a nation mobilizes for war reflects the state of its society, and the Lincoln administration's mobilization methods mirrored the essentially decentralized nature of mid-nineteenth-century America almost perfectly.

CONGRESS

Congress naturally played a critical role in war mobilization.[4] In addition to formulating wartime legislation, both the Senate and the House investigated various aspects of the war effort, the Joint Committee on the Conduct of the War taking the lead. Until the 1940s, historians stressed the divisions and discord between Lincoln and Congress; more recent scholarship emphasizes the positive relations between the two, an interpretation that seems to be more accurate. The relationship between the Lincoln administration and Congress can be characterized as one of constructive tension, in which the two branches of government worked together while each acted to protect and extend its powers.

Congress in 1861 was an old institution dominated by a new party and new leadership. With the South absent and most of the established Whig and Democratic leaders off the scene, the Republican party controlled the national legislature. Though some of its most dynamic members were radicals from New England and the Old Northwest, the party in general represented disparate constituencies, lacked cohesion, and was without strong congressional leadership. At the outset of the war, a majority of the party appeared to share Lincoln's view that the Union must be preserved at all costs but with the least amount of change.

Lincoln's bold acts after Sumter of raising an army, declaring war by blockading the Confederacy, and selectively suspending the writ of habeas corpus without calling Congress into special session until July 1861 received the support of a body usually extremely jealous of its prerogatives. Most Republicans feared a lack of leadership from a virtually unknown president much more than acts that bordered on the dictatorial.

When the Thirty-seventh Congress convened in December 1861, the legislators were still in a cooperative mood, but they were also determined to be more active than they had been in July and August. They felt compelled to act because the war was not going well on either the home or the military front. Army and navy procurement appeared rife with inefficiency and corruption, federal finances were a shambles, and George B. McClellan showed no signs of wanting to fight. Moreover, disquietude was growing within Congress and the nation about arbitrary arrests, the suspension of habeas corpus in some areas, and the use of martial law. Further, Secretary of War Cameron, generals John C. Frémont and Benjamin F. Butler, and other leaders argued that the war should be used to free the slaves and that divisive issue had to be addressed. In short, the Union was suffering from a crisis of confidence in the Lincoln administration's ability to manage hostilities. Congress was determined to restore trust in the federal government as an essential condition for prosecuting the war with vigor.

Congress had actually begun to investigate military procurement as early as July 1861 when the House of Representatives created the Select Committee on Government Contracts.[5] The committee did the bulk of its work in the last half of 1861 and the first half of 1862, continued in existence until 1863, and looked into both important and picayune matters. It focused on the purchase and chartering of vessels by the army and navy on the East Coast and on Frémont's supply operations in the West. The committee's efforts were hurried, its investigations incomplete, its treatment of some witnesses and situations less than fair, and its reports given to self-righteous melodrama and hyperbole, but the investigations substantiated gross irregularities and wrongdoing in War Department supply operations and in Secretary of the Navy Gideon Welles's unusual practices for purchasing vessels. The committee moved to censure both the secretaries of war and navy but succeeded only in the case of the former, an action that seemed to play a significant role in forcing Cameron out of office. Since War Department procurement improved immeasurably under Edwin M. Stanton and the Navy Department's record in that area was always generally good, congressional investigations of military supply operations after 1862 were of no great moment. Nonetheless, Congress required regular reports from the military on supply programs throughout the war and looked closely at some activities. Aware of constant congressional scrutiny, the army and navy maintained a vigilance over procurement that otherwise might have waned.

Largely through Senate leadership, Congress in December 1861 made a much bolder move to bolster its wartime role by creating the Joint Committee on the Conduct of the War. Historians have generally treated the committee harshly, probably in part because they have associated the committee with what occurred during Reconstruction.[6] The committee has been portrayed as the vehicle by which radical Republicans, through ruthlessness and star-chamber tactics, took over the war effort from the president and had their way in most matters. An extremely distorted view of the committee and the Civil War years is required even to approximate this interpretation. Committee hearings and reports do indicate a lack of total objectivity but also a surprising degree of fairness, given the strong emotions generated by the Civil War. Moreover, the committee was much less prone to inflated prose than the House Select Committee on Government Contracts, generally gave the individuals viewed as adversaries a full opportunity to present their cases, conducted reasonably thorough investigations, and reached judgments and historical conclusions that were usually accurate and astute. The committee faltered more in acts of omission than commission. It refused to reach conclusions overwhelmingly warranted by the evidence and did not pursue investigations that were clearly necessary, thus protecting the people who shared its members' convictions. This pattern was especially true for army generals, such as Frémont and Joseph Hooker.

Moderates controlled or at least held swing votes in the Congress that created the committee, and little evidence indicates that the committee had become a renegade. Indeed, in January 1864, the Thirty-eighth Congress reconstituted the Joint Committee and expanded its investigatory scope. Though its personal encounters with Lincoln were often frank and sometimes heated, on the whole the committee and the president were less adversaries than they were public officials who shared common goals but differed over means. The one area of great dispute involved slavery. On that volatile issue, the committee, along with other radical Republicans, acted as a vanguard, pushing Lincoln, the Republican party, and the North toward the abolition of slavery that the war was making inevitable.

The Joint Committee on the Conduct of the War and other congressional committees also served the vital purpose of maintaining the constitutionally prescribed balance of power between the legislative and executive branches, especially in the crucial area of civil-military relations. Congress was willing to ignore some constitutionally dubious executive actions, but it was unwilling to give the president carte blanche in military affairs. Throughout the war, congressional committees insisted on a strict accounting of expenditures by the War and Navy departments. The Committee on the Conduct of the War went much further. It demanded and received from the president and the War Department all documents and other evidence—including orders and communications among the president, secretary of war, chief of staff, and various commanding generals and their subordinates—that it believed necessary to fulfill its congressionally ordained duty of investigating the conduct of the war. Congress recognized no presidential right to withhold information to protect national security, and Lincoln did not propose any. This understanding served pointedly to remind the president and the armed services that they were answerable to the legislature. The committee thus could also reassure the population that an expanded military was being monitored.

The committee, along with others, served the crucial wartime function of checking the rumor mill, even though the Joint Committee and its members actively propagandized for the Union. By investigating the truth, half-truth, or falsehood of various charges, the committee helped maintain the people's trust in government and freed Washington from the damaging effects of wild stories typical of war, which, if left to grow, can be corrosive.

The Joint Committee on the Conduct of the War probably also had a positive influence by strengthening Lincoln's willingness to move forthrightly against generals who would not follow his directions or who failed in their military assignments. In the most important and dramatic case, the president's reluctance to force McClellan's hand dissolved only when Stanton became secretary of war and the Joint Committee launched a formidable attack on the commanding general. Like Stanton and probably most Americans, the committee was biased against West Pointers. Nevertheless, that attitude was safer for both the civilian and military worlds than an attitude of awe and wonder before vaunted military professionals.

On balance, then, the virtues of the Joint Committee on the Conduct of the War outweighed its liabilities. It strengthened Congress in relation to the executive branch and buttressed civilian authority over the military. Both accomplishments facilitated the North's successful prosecution of the war.

Congressional relations with the Lincoln administration in general resembled those between the Joint Committee and the president. The Thirty-seventh Congress of 1861–1863 and the Thirty-eighth of 1863–1865 worked closely with the administration on almost all aspects of wartime policy and compiled an enviable record. Without the assistance of Congress, war finances would have been much worse than they were, if not disastrous. Perhaps the Habeas Corpus Act of 1863 best characterized the nature of executive-legislative relations. In this instance, the two branches of government avoided numerous pitfalls by allowing the Union to maximize internal security while maintaining the rule of law. A somewhat comparable approach was used in crafting the Enrollment Act of 1863.

Despite their differences, Lincoln and the Republican leadership usually pulled together when the interests of party, synonymous to most people with those of the Union, were at stake. That was the case when Democrats maneuvered to take over the speakership of the House at the beginning of the Thirty-eighth Congress and during elections, particularly the presidential election of 1864.

Lincoln's flexibility, however, did not extend as far as allowing Congress to usurp his prerogatives. He made this clear late in 1862 after the Union defeat at Fredericksburg. Key moderate and radical Republican senators, in league with Secretary of the Treasury Chase, attempted to dictate to the president how to use his cabinet and the departure of Secretary of State William H. Seward. By exposing the legislators' intrigue and its possible consequences, Lincoln forced them to back off. The confrontation had some positive results. Congress recognized that it had overreached itself: only the president and his lieutenants, not Congress, could actually conduct a war. Furthermore, by emphatically meeting this challenge to his authority, Lincoln enhanced his stature, strengthening himself and his office for the grave months that lay ahead in 1863 and 1864.

On the whole, then, though never placid, executive-legislative relations were productive. Indeed, passivity would have been a sign of trouble since fundamental issues generated strong emotions throughout the war. To address those issues, Lincoln and Congress joined in an active, usually tense, and sometimes acrimonious partnership that held the Union together and produced victory in a war of unprecedented violence. This political outcome was even more remarkable given the fragmented nature of the Lincoln administration and the divisions and lack of strong leadership among the Republicans in Congress.

FEDERAL-STATE RELATIONS AND PARTY POLITICS

During the Civil War, the national government reestablished its sovereignty in a centralized, as opposed to a decentralized or peripheralized, federalism that most of the Founders had intended for the nation. Sectional discord in the antebellum period had slowly paralyzed centralized federalism, allowing the states to become centers of power. The war for the Union restored the power relations essential for matching the functions of the American system to its form.[7]

Clearly, the Union could not have won the war without the full and dedicated effort of the states and of thousands of local communities. However, control of the war effort at the national level was essential for victory. As the Lincoln administration became increasingly effective, it gradually took back from the states the mobilization functions they had assumed, beginning with troop mobilization late in 1861 and culminating in the Enrollment Act of

1863. In many respects, the Habeas Corpus Act of 1863 was as important as the Enrollment Act in asserting federal authority over the states; and the Legal Tender and National Bank Acts of 1862 and 1863, along with the national income tax and other forms of taxation, also proved to be of crucial importance. More generally, conducting massive logistical operations, beginning to liberate the slaves, and commanding armies of unprecedented size inevitably redirected power toward the capital.

National power over the states was also evident in vital areas not directly related to the war, such as in establishing and subsidizing the intercontinental railroads. More broadly, the federal government permanently reclaimed the active role in political economy, which the South had been instrumental in denying it once sectional discord intensified in the 1830s.

Some of the consequences of the increase in federal power vis-à-vis the states during the Civil War were slow to appear. After the war, federal power contracted, although never to the degree that it had in the decades before the Civil War. Then, toward the end of the century, the government began its transformation into the strong state of the twentieth century.

Centralizing power relations during the Civil War was no mean feat given the disequilibrium in Northern society and politics at the time. If the Lincoln administration had enhanced national power by fiat, it could have disrupted the Union that the president sought to save. An evolutionary process was followed instead, and the continuation of traditional party politics in the North during the war years was basic to it. Lincoln's caution, patience, political instincts, and sense of timing played a crucial role. The power the national government needed to conduct the war gravitated to Washington at the same time that the Republican party was converted from a state- to a nationally based organization. A dynamic interaction between party and the various levels of government occurred throughout the war years.

The Democratic party played an important role in strengthening the Republican party. For the most part, Democrats served as a loyal opposition during hostilities. The threat of losing office to a competing party, made clear in the election of 1862, forced the Republican party to settle its own differences through cooperation and compromise.

Traditional party politics in the North during the Civil War did more than spur the Republican party; it also cemented the Union, as Eric L. McKitrick trenchantly argues.[8] Competition between the parties provided a legitimate outlet for the discontent and numerous grievances generated by the war. It kept the Northern population attentive to public affairs, helping to maintain morale during the long, bloody, and discouraging years of fighting. Competition between the parties also stimulated debate throughout the nation on vital issues, which helped achieve widespread support for wartime policies. Ultimately, it gave voters a genuine choice of leaders. These conditions contributed to the resilience of the North, helping to reconcile the divisive passions, mixed emotions, and moral dilemmas of a civil war. Through party politics the Union succeeded in the hazardous venture of realigning power to make centralized federalism work. In the midst of a terrible war, with habeas corpus suspended, martial law in use, and millions of men under arms, the North remained remarkably open and fundamentally united. Superb presidential leadership, and party politics, played significant roles in that extraordinary achievement.

CIVIL WAR STATISTICS AND ECONOMICS

The economic strength of the North was key to subduing the South by any measure. Comparative statistics show that the Union was far ahead of the Confederacy in every category of economic power. Effective mobilization and the will to win, maintained by resourceful political leadership at the local, state, and federal levels, allowed the North to use its economic superiority to grind down and ultimately defeat the South.

The cost of the war in lives and resources made it one of the most expensive conflicts to that time. One study places war costs at $3.4 billion for the Union and $3.3 billion for the Confederacy. The $6.7 billion total for both sides exceeded the estimated Gross National Product for 1865. In August 1865 Union debt stood at $2.8 billion, equivalent to nearly one-half of the GNP, and the North's spending on the war equaled about 10 percent of the total estimated GNP for the years of hostilities. In comparison, the Revolutionary War took under 5 percent of (roughly estimated) wartime GNP, and the War of 1812 and the Mexican War fell considerably below that figure.[9] Some 4 million men served in the armed forces of the North and South during the Civil War, nearly 13 percent of the population in 1860. There were 600,000 dead and 500,000 wounded; total casualties of 1.1 million equals about 3.5 percent of the 1860 population. In nearly every category but duration, the nation's previous conflicts pale in comparison to the Civil War. Indeed, the Civil War was more indicative of future than of past events. Russell F. Weigley observes that as a major war, the Civil War for Americans overshadowed anything that had occurred in Europe and served as a model for the nation's military leaders in both World Wars I and II.[10]

The North's pattern of economic mobilization during the Civil War more closely resembled the War of 1812 and the Mexican War than the Revolutionary War. The unprecedented demand of the Civil War presented a challenge for the North, but the enormous strength of the economy made it manageable, as did the fact that military requirements were still relatively unsophisticated and did not necessitate any major conversion of the economic system. Once the Lincoln administration began to function with reasonable efficiency and the War, Navy, and Treasury departments perfected their operations to act as the principal agencies for economic mobilization, market forces induced ample war production so that government dictates, regulations, and subsidies were not required. Only the railroad and the telegraph systems, and to a lesser degree war financing, were exceptions.

The extremely controversial issue of whether the Civil War accelerated or retarded industrialization should be addressed. Charles A. Beard began the debate in 1927 by arguing that in defeating the South, the North speeded economic growth by removing the enormous political hindrances to industrialization that the slaveholders had persistently and protectively built up in the decades before the Civil War. Louis Hacker's influential *Triumph of American Capitalism* (1940) buttressed Beard's argument. Since 1960, scholars have been intensely and acrimoniously debating the Beard-Hacker thesis.[11] Several points are in order about their interpretation. First, although the war had a mixed effect upon different sectors of the economy, too little information exists for reliable judgments about the entire economic system. Scholars agree that the 1860s had the lowest decennial growth in manufacturing of any decade between 1840 and 1900. Beyond that point, disagreement abounds, with most arguments based on general or piecemeal information, extrapolations, and speculation. Second, the subject should not be approached solely in terms of econometric measurements. Important institutional developments occurred that cannot be evaluated by statistical aggregates. For example, as Glenn Porter and Harold C. Livesay explain, the war hastened the decline of the middleman and speeded the transition from merchant to industrial capitalism.[12] Moreover, important wartime changes took place in the railroad industry that would accelerate growth and consolidation after the war, the matter of track-mileage aside. Wartime developments also paved the way for further concentration in telegraphy. These two industries experienced a previously unknown level of coordination during hostilities that would continue after the war, and they were not alone. During the fighting, new trade associations were established and existing ones were expanded significantly, including the American Iron and Steel Association, the National Association of Wool Manufacturers, and the National Woolgrowers Association. Furthermore, a generation of Gilded Age entrepreneurs gained invaluable training during the war in the techniques of large-scale manufacturing, transportation, distribution, and finance.

Third, as Harry N. Scheiber argues, policies on tariffs, taxes, and debt during and after the war favored industrialists at the expense of consumers. This trend and high wartime profits aided capital formation in the Gilded Age, thereby contributing to the extraordinary postwar growth rates.[13] Moreover, wartime taxation, borrowing, and money and banking practices transformed the nation's financial policies and institutions, set precedents that were followed for at least half a century, and created a political economy favorable to economic growth and prosperity. Fourth, four years of warfare weakened customs and practices and lifted the vision of many Americans above their local and parochial outlooks, which helped pave the way for the dramatic economic changes of the postwar years. Last, and of enormous importance, the Civil War dealt a crippling blow to America's agrarian tradition. After the war, unlike in those years before it, the commercial/industrial elements had a relatively free hand in the nation's thirty-year rush to industrial maturity. Ultimately, the effects of the Civil War on the nation's political economy must be gauged by consequences in the decades following hostilities, not by immediate developments during the war years alone. Thus, given the information available, Beard and Hacker may be closer to reality in their assessment of the Civil War's impact on the national economy than are their numerous detractors.

8
ECONOMIC MOBILIZATION IN THE SOUTH

The Confederacy was at a great disadvantage in fighting a war of attrition against a much stronger foe determined to annihilate it. The South lacked the Union's deep and diversified economic base. It was essentially an agrarian region shaped largely by the cotton culture, with only rudimentary industry, commerce, finance, and transportation. Consequently, to win independence by holding off the North, the South had to mobilize its resources to the optimum and maximize economic assistance from abroad. Southern leaders failed to achieve either goal, and that reality figured large in the Confederacy's defeat.

The South always faced challenges that dwarfed those of the North. It had to put together a governmental structure and mobilize for war at the same time. Moreover, the Confederacy's limited economic base began to shrink almost from the outset as the North advanced into the border states, the Upper South, and along the Mississippi and increased the effectiveness of the blockade. Over time, the Union's Anaconda Policy tightened a devastating economic and military noose around the South.

Confederate economic mobilization was largely carried out under the direction of Pres. Jefferson Davis. In contrast to Lincoln, Davis became inordinately involved in the details of War Department operations. As in the North, that department was the principal mobilization agency, and its various bureaus achieved a mixed record. Operating under conditions that varied from trying to impossible, the Quartermaster and Commissary departments and the other supply and administrative bureaus performed at least adequately, and the Ordnance Department's efforts were extraordinary. Confederate agencies for mobilizing troops also proved relatively efficient, but exterior circumstances undermined their performance. Although imaginative and innovative in various ways, the Navy Department's overall performance was wanting. In many respects, the toughest task fell to the Treasury Department, which had to devise policies for raising billions of dollars in the capital-short Confederacy in order to pay for the war. From beginning to end, the department could not raise adequate funds, a failure ultimately leading to conditions that wrecked the vulnerable and rather artificial economy of the Confederate states.

While mobilization in the North grew more effective during hostilities, in the South it bogged down. Failure was consequential in a number of critical areas. The Davis administration proved unable to devise financial policies that maintained economic stability. The president and his lieutenants also failed to master a fractured railroad network. Moreover, the South's efforts to run the Northern blockade and to secure financing from abroad suffered from confusion and neglect.

The Confederacy had a limited pool of talent for effectively mobilizing the economy. This is hardly surprising in a society that emphasized agrarian values and whose elite had aristocratic ambitions, a society that relied largely upon the North to market its cotton and handle its economic affairs and that looked down upon industry, commerce, and finance. Relatively few planters distinguished themselves as wartime economic leaders, and their attitudes often prevented the South from using to the maximum the talent it had. For economic mobilization, the Davis administration had to turn to individuals who had experience in business and the professions and, as was the case with the president himself, who had trained at West Point or Annapolis.

From top to bottom—at the local, state, and confederacy levels—elites circulated freely among political, economic, and military institutions during the mobilization process. (This mingling did not occur among the actual fighting forces in the South because the Confederacy matched the Union in terms of professional officers, usually trained at the military academies, running the army and navy.) What took place was reminiscent of practices during the Revolutionary War and resembled contemporary developments in the Union states but was in sharp contrast to the North's mobilization at the federal level. The South differed from the North because its industrial economy was underdeveloped, and the Confederacy was without the commercial specialization and agrarian diversification of the Union. As a result, the South, in effect, had to plan its economy. That meant creating, expanding, and supervising industries and regulating agriculture and internal and external commerce, all of which often required new mobilization agencies. Where the North's strong economy could rely upon the market as wartime economic regulator, the South's weak economy had to depend upon government fiat. Those circumstances broke down the distinctions between private and public, civilian and military institutions, with elites moving among those institutions.

Economic mobilization in the South grew out of harsh realities. It did not stem from any theoretical dedication to state-building, mercantilism, or socialism as some scholars have proposed. The war's legacy for the political economy of the South and the nation was therefore negligible.

The subject of wartime leadership inevitably raises the even larger issue of class dynamics. Tensions, resentments, and divisions among the classes eroded support for the war and played a major role in the defeat of the Confederacy. As a group, the planter elite appeared more concerned with protecting its place, privileges, and slaves than in fighting the war, and the Davis administration too often bowed to its will. This attitude alienated the common people, who were called upon as citizens and soldiers to sacrifice disproportionately for a system of slavery from which they did not benefit. As hostilities stretched out and suffering and privations grew, the white masses began withdrawing their support from the Confederacy, with devastating results. Long before Appomattox, many Southerners had given up on the war.

Class tensions were closely related to the issue of states' rights. It was often in the name of states' rights that the planter elite lashed out at the Davis administration. But the common people also rallied around state leaders who, more than the Davis administration, provided those in need with some relief and protection against the want and caprices of war. Frank L. Owsley's contention notwithstanding, the Confederacy did not die of states' rights. The growing strength of state identity as the war progressed, however, was symptomatic of the Confederacy's inability to maintain the unity essential to hold off an adversary of superior strength.

THE OLD SOUTH: ECONOMIC, SOCIAL, AND POLITICAL

Cotton made the Southern economy distinct.[1] For more than a decade before the Civil War, the South accounted for at least two-thirds of the world's output of "white gold." Most slave states grew some cotton, but the major production took place in South Carolina, Georgia, Alabama, Mississippi, and Louisiana. Other staples contributed to the region's wealth, including tobacco, rice, sugar cane, and hemp. Large plantations with numerous slaves dominated the production of most of these crops.

Despite the prevalence of export staples, the South was largely self-sufficient in food, although it was losing ground to the Middle West in terms of percentage of national output. Diversified agriculture fed the region rather than providing items for exchange with other parts of the nation or foreign countries. Corn was the most important grain cultivated in the South and hogs the key livestock raised there. Nonetheless, Southern wheat and cattle added meaningfully to the region's diet. Mules were the principal draft animals on plantations and farms, though horses were ubiquitous and critical to Southern culture. Dairy farming, truck gardening, and fruit raising were or could be undertaken without difficulty.

The geography of diversified Southern agriculture was critical in the Civil War. Although grains, livestock, and draft animals were raised in all the Confederate states, the major centers of corn, wheat, hogs, horses, and mules were in the Upper South and the border states, particularly Virginia, Tennessee, Kentucky, Maryland, and Missouri; Texas was emerging as the primary cattle state. Once war broke out, most of these areas were quickly lost to the Union.

The South's narrow industrial base was even more detrimental. With about one-third of the nation's population, the South produced only around 10 percent of national industrial output, despite substantial industrial growth in the 1840s and 1850s. Nearly half the leading fifteen industries in the South involved processing agricultural products, including flour and gristmilling, leather tanning, tobacco manufacturing, and sawmilling. Cotton textiles constituted the region's fourth largest industry in 1860 and accounted for one-fifth to one-quarter of national production. Although concentrated in North Carolina, textile mills followed the fall line from Virginia to Alabama. Other leading Southern industries included carriages and wagons; boots and shoes; tin, copper, and sheet-iron ware; woolen goods; saddlery; and bar, railroad, and sheet iron and blacksmithing. Plantation and household production must also be included in the South's industrial output. Plantations throughout the South processed cotton, sugar, rice, and tobacco; and spinning, looming, and similar activities took place on farms.

Southern industrial firms were small in comparison to those in the North, although not necessarily to the West's. Nonetheless, the South had some centers of industry with manufacturing firms of significant size. The leading industrial city was Richmond, which had a considerable variety of manufacturing companies, including the Tredegar Iron Works, one of the nation's largest and most important iron makers. New Orleans was the South's second manufacturing center, specializing in men's clothing, boots and shoes, machinery, steam engines, and a host of other products. Charleston, the third manufacturing metropolis, had firms making most of the major and some of the minor industrial products of the region. The South also had company towns such as Graniteville, South Carolina, where William Gregg diligently supervised a profitable cotton mill. Daniel Pratt set up an even more impressive industrial village at Prattville, Alabama, which produced a quarter of the South's cotton gins and included grist, lumber, and textile mills and a carriage factory.

No industry exceeded the railroads in importance and volume of investment. By 1860 hundreds of millions of dollars had been invested in around 10,000 miles of roads—about one-third of the nation's total mileage. Despite the severe limits of the system, its size indicated that the South was benefiting from the transportation revolution and industrialization.

Its advances notwithstanding, the South was industrially backward compared to the North. Of particular importance was the fact that it did not possess the wherewithal for rapid emergency growth. Aside from some steam engine producers and the elementary output of machine shops, the South depended almost entirely on the North for the machinery to run its factories. It could not make steel, and its capacity for making and fabricating iron was limited in quantity and level of technology. The same was true for copper, lead, tin, bronze, and other metals. Southern railroads for the most part had been built and equipped with Northern products and expertise. In munitions, the South had no facilities for mass-producing small arms, manufactured virtually no powder, and had limited capacity for manufacturing large ordnance. The Tredegar Iron Works was a great asset, but capacity constraints and the shortage of pig iron always limited its output. A shortage of trained management and skilled labor plagued Confederate industry. In short, the South, unlike the North, lacked the extensive industrial base essential for effectively fighting a long and logistically demanding war. Moreover, as with grains, livestock, and draft animals, much of Confederate industry was in the Upper South and border states, within relatively easy reach of Union armies.

The level of commercial and urban development was also much lower in the South than in the North, which limited the region's capacity for economic mobilization. With the exception of New Orleans, the major Southern cities were in the border states or Upper South, and nearly half the Confederate states lacked urban centers exceeding 10,000 people. In addition to the agrarian nature of the South, the region did not develop the rich and varied merchant structure typical of the rest of the nation. Northern merchant houses, acting through middlemen, principally factors, served as intermediaries between planters and the outside world. The middlemen marketed cotton and other crops, sold consumer and capital goods to the plantations, and provided the necessary credit. To a lesser degree, country merchants, neighboring planters, or both performed similar functions for farmers and yeomen producing for the market. Plantation and home production also acted to limit exchange. Thus the familiar institutions of trade and credit were limited outside urban areas and were much less conspicuous than in the North or West. Nevertheless, the larger cities had a full range of merchant operations. By 1860 the South also had a reasonably well-developed system of private and public banks, although it was inferior in numbers and capital to that of the North. In general the South's financial intermediaries lacked the range, variety, and sophistication of their counterparts in the North.

The nature of its economy created a crisis of enormous proportions for the South in 1861. War halted the marketing of export crops on which the economic system was based, cut off badly needed sources of consumer and capital goods, made irrelevant the pivotal economic role of the factor, required financial operations unknown to many Southerners, and threatened the transportation system. Such circumstances would have staggered many economies. Combine those realities with the need to mobilize to the maximum all economic resources to fight a long and total war, and the odds of survival indeed seem slim.

Class dynamics greatly complicated the South's effort to mobilize its human and economic resources.[2] Class relations were paradoxical and, in a strange and exaggerated way, reflected the elitist-democratic duality of the entire nation. The planter and large slave owner dominated Southern life and controlled a grossly disproportionate percentage of the region's wealth. In 1860 the slaveholding element owned 90 to 95 percent of the region's agricultural wealth. Out of a white population of 8 million, there were only 400,000 slaveholders. Expanded to include families, this group had 2 million people, one-quarter of the white population. Large slave owners were even more exclusive: 107,000 owned 10 or more slaves; 11,000 had 50 or more; and only the top 300 families held in excess of 200. Naturally, the large slaveholders were also the large landowners. Most nonslave-owning families were small farmers, of whom 80 to 90 percent owned the land they cultivated. They ranged from subsistence farmers to those fully involved in marketing commercial crops, including cotton. Plantations of different size and farms coexisted in the same regions throughout the South, though large plantations and slaves were concentrated in the most fertile areas of the Lower South. The South's low mountainous areas were devoid of slaves, and the antipathy to planters and the institution of slavery was greatest there.

The class system had been relatively stable for nearly seven decades. As the cotton culture extended westward and the South became increasing prosperous, however, the price of slaves rose dramatically, reducing the number of slaveholders. In 1830, for example, 36 percent of Southern families owned slaves; the figure dropped to 31 percent in 1850 and 25 percent in 1860. Nonslave-owners did not become poorer in the process, but the distance between the yeoman and the planter was growing and the chances of the former rising to the level of the latter diminishing. Nonetheless, the South was a continuum of agrarian elements in which some mobility still existed rather than a bipolar system of planters and yeomen.

The planter dominated the South because his ideology and values were the accepted ones. He set the standards to which others aspired, received the deference of his economic and social inferiors, and returned it with a sense of noblesse oblige; engaged in various forms of economic exchange with his farming neighbors; and benefited from the frequent ties of kinship. Moreover, compared to the rest of the nation, the South was more homogenous in terms of ethnicity, religion, and economic pursuits, and its civilization had become increasingly defined in terms of race. Indeed, racial slavery acted as the social cement of the South, making all white people equal compared to blacks and giving the region its distinctive quality.

Elite domination was obscured by forms of democracy. Beginning in the 1820s, most Southern states reformed under the pressures of Jacksonian Democracy. Universal manhood suffrage became common, many public offices were made elective, and property qualifications for officeholding were reduced or eliminated. These changes reached down to the local level but varied from state to state. In the Lower South, South Carolina maintained aristocratic privileges, but Mississippi stood out for its progressive practices; in the Upper South, North Carolina stayed conservative, but Missouri became exceptionally democratic. Other states fell in between these extremes.

Throughout the South, the legislature was the dominant branch of government, yet the Lower and Upper South differed in certain ways. In the former, the Whig party was virtually eliminated in the 1850s and the Democratic party opposed by the Know-Nothing or American party and other factional elements. In the latter, the Democratic-Whig partisanship continued, although it was stronger in some states than others and most governors were Democrats. The Lower South was also known for extraordinarily high levels of rotation among public officials, with most serving for only one year. That pattern was less true in the Upper South. Legislators from the Lower South were typically middle-aged farmers, planters, and lawyers holding substantial property who had been born in their state or a neighboring one. Legislators in the Upper South had a similar profile, although more lawyers were elected to office. Throughout the South, county and city officials and members of local assemblies resembled state legislators, although they had less wealth and prestige. According to Ralph A. Wooster, the leading authority on the subject, meaningful differences in the South were found more between the East and West than between the lower and upper regions. The seaboard states remained the most conservative; the Southwest states were more receptive to reform.

Several trends of crucial significance stand out in Southern politics. First, state legislatures generally became less representative as the sectional crisis heated up in the decade before the Civil War. Although slave owners were declining as a percentage of the population, their numbers increased in most legislatures, and they held majorities in every state of the Lower South. Second, according to Wooster, although the white masses made their voices heard and could thwart legislation, planters dominated Southern politics, at least indirectly. Besides using their general positions of power and authority, they prevailed by relying on their close ties with those individuals serving at the national level, those holding key positions in state government, and those controlling the Democratic party.

The secession conventions and legislatures of 1860 and 1861 reflected the elite domination of Southern life to an even greater degree. In addition to planters, farmers, and lawyers, many leading public figures participated. In general, the dedication to secession was strongest in the wealthier districts with the greatest concentration of slaves and from those personally involved in agrarian pursuits. The Lower South exceeded the Upper South in its fervor for disunion. Significantly, only three states—Texas, Tennessee, and Virginia—submitted the secession ordinance to a public referendum. Furthermore, once disunion occurred, the fire-eaters stepped aside and more moderate elements sought to construct a confederacy that would maintain unity.

By putting a strain on social systems, war makes manifest their strengths and weaknesses. For the Confederacy, the weaknesses proved fatal as the paradoxes and tensions of the class structure began to fray under stress. The war was fought to preserve a system of slavery that did not benefit the masses and probably harmed them. When the slaveholding elite did not make sufficient sacrifices or provide adequate leadership, the common people began walking away from the war in manyfold ways.

THE CONFEDERATE STATES AND ECONOMIC MOBILIZATION

The role of the states within the Confederacy remains one of considerable uncertainty.[3] Most scholars reject Frank Owsley's dictum that the Confederacy died of states' rights. Nonetheless, the relations between the various states and Richmond were exceptionally complex, and each state's relationship with the Confederate government was different. The major factors influencing the nature of relations between the Confederacy and a state were the state's geographic location, how long the war had been going on, the social and political dynamics within a state, and the mobilization functions that a state assumed. Before examining these particulars, one should be aware of several points. The states were the basic building blocks of the Confederacy. They had seceded individually, their representatives wrote the constitution for the new nation, and that charter guaranteed the "sovereign and independent character" of the states. Nonetheless, the states had to surrender fundamental rights to the Confederacy in order to hold off the Union military and win independence. That reality compounded the complexity of Confederate-state relations.

Geography played a key role in determining to what degree a state subordinated its interests to the Confederacy. No state cooperated more consistently with the Davis administration than Virginia. It remained the South's premier state, became the Confederacy's capital, and had two talented wartime governors. As the northernmost Confederate state, Virginia was the principal military theater and hosted the largest, best-led, and best-supplied army. Had geography put Georgia in Virginia's place on the map, the enormously talented, paradoxical, and perverse Gov. Joseph E. Brown could not have challenged the Confederate government at every turn. The fact that his state's soil was not significantly violated by the Union until very late in the war gave Brown latitude that other states and governors did not possess. Nearly every other state in the Confederacy faced greater actual or potential Union military action in the early years of hostilities; that reality helped maintain Confederate cohesion. Hence, the actions of North Carolina, South Carolina, Alabama, Mississippi, and Florida followed more closely the pattern of Virginia than Georgia. Tennessee also made a valiant effort on behalf of the Confederacy, but its vulnerable geographic position and the Davis government's decision not to make a military stand there left it victim to internal divisions, guerrilla warfare, and Union invasions. By mid-1862, Tennessee had all but ceased to exist as a Confederate state. The trans-Mississippi West was largely left on its own from the start of hostilities, and the fall of Vicksburg in July 1863 isolated it from the rest of the Confederacy. Nonetheless, Louisiana contributed significantly to the Confederate cause and Texas was not far behind. Arkansas was the exception. The state lacked development, quality leadership, and dedication to the South, and before the close of 1862 it was nearly useless to the Confederacy.

Although geography impelled the states to act in concert with the Confederate government, the long duration of the war and social and political tensions within the states pushed them to act in their own interest. As a result, by mid- to late-1863 state cooperation with Richmond was reluctant at best. Military defeat was probable, war weariness was ubiquitous, and resentment toward the Davis government grew over conscription, selecting and promoting civil and military officers, impressment, the suspension of habeas corpus, taxation in kind, and regulation of blockade running. Virginia's favored position also caused problems, as other states felt that their defense was sacrificed to protect the capital state. Perhaps most important, mounting class tensions rent many states.

The war made governors the dominant political force in the states, and they faced increasing difficulty in meeting their duties and controlling their populations as the fighting progressed. In the Lower South, the heavy concentration of plantations and slaves created a dual challenge for chief executives. On one side, planters grew resistant to the use of slaves for war purposes, the suspension of civil rights, and the proliferation of regulations and vented their frustrations under the banner of states' rights. On the other side, the non-slaveholders began rebelling against wartime deprivation and the planters' unwillingness to sacrifice for the cause.

A survey of conditions in states of the Lower South illustrates the problems. Mississippi staggered as early as 1862 and all but collapsed after the fall of Vicksburg in July 1863. Former Whigs returned to office, gangs of draft-dodgers and deserters terrorized communities, and law enforcement agencies and the economy barely functioned.

To the east, Alabama was only slightly better off. The state's third wartime governor, Thomas Hill Watts, assumed office in December 1863 after serving as attorney general in Davis's cabinet in 1862 and 1863. He faced conditions bordering on insurrection. The nonslaveholding areas of the north and southeast had withdrawn their support from the war. Candidates favoring peace had been elected to office at the local, county, and state levels. By the end of 1864, at least half the state's counties were unsafe because soldiers deserting to provide for their families had taken the law into their own hands. Moreover, Alabama, along with Georgia, North Carolina, and Virginia, experienced urban food riots. Watts strove mightily to maintain state support for the war effort but without much success. Just to maintain some credibility, the governor took a states' rights position on numerous points of contention with Richmond.

Georgia remained more stable because of Governor Brown's brilliant balancing act to keep both the upper and lower classes in check. As tensions mounted, Brown increasingly made Richmond the scapegoat for everyone's discontent.

South Carolina resembled Mississippi and Alabama, sharing the conviction that its interests had been neglected before and during Union incursions. By the end of 1864, the state had come nearly full circle, virtually nullifying all critical Confederate laws. Governor Zebulon B. Vance kept North Carolina intact, beat back a formidable peace movement in 1864, and continued to aid the cause of war by adopting tactics similar to Brown's. He constantly challenged Richmond while maximizing the welfare of the masses. The fact that his state had fewer slaves than Georgia made Vance's political juggling act less demanding.

By 1863–1864, therefore, every critical state of the Lower South, plus North Carolina, was experiencing extreme internal divisions that were closely linked to seriously deteriorating relations with the Confederacy. Despite these harsh realities, some of these states continued contributing to the common cause.

Virginia did not suffer the disintegration that occurred elsewhere in the South. Although it had trouble with the mountainous areas and Richmond experienced a food riot in April 1863, Virginia's cohesion was furthered by the fact that the most alienated areas of the state seceded to create West Virginia.

Florida also remained true to the end, but it too had complaints against Richmond, and hordes of deserters disturbed the peace. The state's location on the periphery of the Confederacy and its relative lack of slaves and plantations also contributed to its stability.

The early invasion of Louisiana by Union forces appeared to temper that state's internal divisions. Despite being driven out of New Orleans beginning in April 1862 and facing public discontent, the state government administered its diminished territory effectively, although Louisiana received little aid from Richmond and could not contribute much to the war.

As part of the trans-Mississippi West, Texas was in a position not dissimilar to Louisiana's. Into 1863, it contributed men and supplies to the Confederacy without stint or complaint. Thereafter, disagreements with the Confederacy grew along with the war weariness of the populace. Yet the Lone Star State never insisted upon its point of view to the detriment of the larger Confederate cause. Like Florida, Texas benefited from its location on the periphery of the South and its limited involvement in the plantation-slavery system.

Despite the strain that the duration of the war and intrastate tensions placed upon state-Confederate relations, the states performed functions that were indispensable to the South's struggle for existence. They carried out much of the mobilization effort in 1861 in terms of men, arms, and some supplies and equipment. Thereafter, various states continued to contribute supplies to the Confederate war effort but at a much reduced level. Raising manpower and providing for the welfare of the population became the states' primary role between 1862 and 1865, tasks that grew increasingly urgent and difficult to fulfill as the war stretched out.

At the outbreak of hostilities in April 1861, the South possessed about 150,000 shoulder arms, of which approximately 20,000 were modern rifles. The others were flintlock and percussion muskets, carbines, and miscellaneous weapons. All these arms came from the states because the Confederate government as yet had no arsenals. The states acquired most of these weapons

from the fourteen federal arsenals, armories, depots, and various forts and fortifications seized before and after hostilities broke out. Quite a few states had
tried to build up their stock of militia weapons by petitioning Washington in
1860, and some even tried to get advances for 1861. At the request of the
Confederate War Department, most states transferred the captured weapons to
the Confederacy or used them to arm troops that would be mustered into the
national army.

To bolster the supply of arms seized from federal establishments, the states
engaged in a mad scramble for weapons. Almost all of them appointed agents
to buy whatever arms were available in the North and South, and a few states
sent representatives abroad and engaged in blockade running. The results were
chaotic as prices rose to exorbitant levels, inferior and nearly useless weapons
were acquired, and states at times stole arms from one another. (Virginia was
one of the few states that shared weapons with its neighbors even though its
own supply was low.) Governors were also known to direct sheriffs and con-
stables to search homes for old militia weapons and to demand that citizens
surrender all shoulder arms. Out of desperation, a few states let contracts for
new weapons to shops and foundries and subsidized the creation of new firms,
usually with disappointing results. The efforts turned up relatively few additional shoulder arms. More often than not, states had to use or create arsenals to repair, recondition, and alter old, damaged, and antiquated arms as
well as those intended for hunting or personal use.

By late 1861 the Confederate Ordnance Department was operating efficiently and the states' role in acquiring weapons for the most part ended.
Nonetheless, some states contributed munitions to the Confederacy after
1861. North Carolina helped subsidize the building of a powder mill, Tennessee produced black powder and percussion caps until it was overrun by
Union forces, and Texas manufactured a few cannons and, along with other
states, a fair supply of caps and cartridges.

When seizing federal forts and arsenals, states also acquired ordnance, powder, and other items, which they generally turned over to the Confederacy.
However, states retained some munitions to strengthen key fortifications or
build new ones, such as Fort Henry and Fort Donelson, at Mobile, and along
the exposed North Carolina coast.

Predictably, the matter of arms and munitions generated tension between the
states and the government in Richmond. In May 1861, with the usual level of
acrimony, Governor Brown of Georgia adopted a policy of not allowing any arms
to leave the state (including those owned by individuals) and of trying to reclaim
those already beyond the state's borders. He was equally uncooperative in terms
of ordnance, sulphur, and saltpeter. Even before Vance took over as governor,

North Carolina declined to turn over to Richmond most of the muskets seized at the Fayetteville Arsenal and prohibited the Confederacy from buying or impressing arms in the state. Most states cooperated with the Davis government on seized federal arms, but Alabama and other states retained those they had purchased. Practically every state felt that it had cooperated with Richmond at the expense of its own defense and that the Confederate government was unresponsive to its requirements and overly solicitous of Virginia. As a consequence of such views, Louisiana stopped shipping arms to the Confederacy, Mississippi virtually hijacked Confederate arms, South Carolina loudly protested that it was being neglected, Tennessee despairingly proclaimed that it had been abandoned, and the trans-Mississippi states faced the harsh reality that they were on their own.

State aid for the Confederate army extended beyond weapons. When the Confederate Congress authorized a provisional army of first 100,000 and then 400,000 men, it required soldiers to provide their own uniforms in return for a semiannual commutation payment of twenty-one dollars. Some individuals were able to supply their own clothing; the rest relied upon the states for most of 1861. The states varied in their ability and willingness to shoulder the burden. North Carolina worked out an agreement with Richmond to clothe its troops in exchange for the commutation payments. To fulfill its responsibilities, the state set up a clothing factory in Raleigh, purchased the output of all textile mills in the state, and, when necessary, bought materials at home and abroad. In time both the textile firms and the Confederacy found the agreement wanting, but the state refused to abrogate it. North Carolina's troops consistently were the best clothed in the Confederate armies. In contrast, Arkansas contributed few men, let alone uniforms, to the South. Most states were more similar to North Carolina than to Arkansas. Georgia performed almost as well as the former since Governor Brown insisted on buying clothing, shoes, blankets, and the like for his state's troops even after the Confederacy took over the responsibility. Other states bought, collected, or arranged for the manufacture of clothing, footwear, and supplies. Much of the effort was carried out by local, county, and state soldiers'-aid and voluntary societies. State assistance in the early months of the war also included medicine, food, and supplies of all sorts. The Confederate Quartermaster Department provided most tents and camp equipment, however.

Various states continued contributing to the Confederate effort after 1861, following the lead of North Carolina and Georgia in providing clothing and supplies but on a less dramatic scale. Some states branched out into other areas. For example, Louisiana began efforts to locate strategic metals and to manufacture medicine, and Texas ordered its prison inmates to manufacture cloth for the state and the Confederacy throughout the war.

Soldiers'-aid societies constituted one of the most continuous sources of state assistance. The societies proliferated and were found in nearly every county in some sections of the Confederacy, with churches taking an active role. Philanthropic groups were also helpful, exemplified by the Richmond Young Men's Christian Association. Local and county efforts were uncoordinated in many states, but Georgia, South Carolina, Louisiana, and Alabama had statewide organizations. Those in Georgia and South Carolina did a commendable job of coordination based on substantial public subsidies. North Carolina took such good care of its troops that private organizations at the state level were much less necessary. Other than the Association for the Relief of Maimed Soldiers, which concentrated on providing artificial limbs for the disabled, there were no Confederacy-wide relief associations comparable to the U.S. Sanitary Commission or the U.S. Christian Commission even though the Confederate Congress passed several laws in August 1861 facilitating citizen assistance to the troops. Localism, state particularism, poor transportation and financial systems, limited urban areas, and warfare on Southern soil combined to prevent the rise of national organizations.

The operations of the local, county, and state welfare groups basically fell into four categories. First, they supplied troops with clothing, blankets, footwear, food, and other items to enhance comfort. Often these contributions were supplementary, but at the beginning and end of the war and sometimes in between the aid was a primary source of supply. Second, the welfare groups provided wayside homes for sick, wounded, and furloughed troops passing through local communities. These efforts became increasingly important and absorbed more and more funds as the South's transportation system began to break down, making it difficult to move supplies. Third, the societies assisted in medical care, their efforts ranging from creating hospitals and providing doctors, surgeons, nurses, chaplains, and social workers to supplying medicine, bandages, sheeting, medical instruments, clothing, food, and some luxuries. Since nearly all fighting took place on Southern soil, at one time or another many Confederate homes became temporary hospitals with the inhabitants providing care. Fourth, the soldiers'-aid societies became involved in welfare activities for the families of fighting men. In rural areas, they provided food, shelter, and clothing and in urban areas introduced innovations such as free markets.

Although some soldier assistance was public, with money coming from counties and states, most assistance resulted from private contributions. Many Southerners shared the little they had with the fighting men. Women and some men donated time and labor, businesses contributed money and goods, theater companies gave benefit performances, and cash and supplies were collected at fairs, raffles, and similar events. Putting a value on these donations is nearly impossible. One contemporary estimated contributions in the last three months of 1861 alone at $3 million. Still, welfare efforts in the South lacked the organization and plentitude that characterized similar activities in the North. Moreover, because state identity remained strong in the Confederate war effort, states aided their troops more often and more directly than did those in the North. Discrepancies in the aid provided by different states generated resentment among those persons who received less. Nevertheless, because the South always had less than the North and conditions worsened rather consistently after 1863, charitable efforts proved not only significant but in some instances also nearly indispensable in keeping Southern armies fighting.

The vast expenditures for the military and for relief and welfare put enormous strains on state finances. Only a few states, like Arkansas, had ample financial reserves, and even those resources were usually exhausted quickly. In February 1861 Alabama began using treasury notes, a form of state paper, to finance spending in preparation for war. Almost all other states soon followed suit. By the end of 1862 the Confederate secretary of the treasury estimated that at least $20 million in state notes were in circulation, a figure that probably more than doubled before the war ended. Most states could not sell bonds, although Alabama, Tennessee, and other states forced their private banks to buy issues. Georgia and Texas were among the few states that raised reasonable amounts of revenue through taxation. Several states, such as Georgia and North Carolina, relied upon blockade-running operations, railroads, and other enterprises to increase their income, and Virginia and other states turned to bank loans in emergencies. None of these expedients could avoid ultimate disaster; state finances went under as the Confederacy crumbled in 1864–1865.

Finances aside, the states played a more important long-term role in raising troops for the Confederacy than in supplying and caring for them. Until the first conscription act of April 1862, the states were essential in mobilizing soldiers for the Southern armies. Even after that date, they retained a vital role in raising troops for the Richmond government, arranging for exemptions, and mobilizing and maintaining local troops for home defense who could be called upon for federal service in a crisis.

Relief and welfare constituted another critically important function of the Confederate states. The war left some families in need almost from the outset. As hostilities stretched on, the bulk of the population required assistance because of inflationary pressures; shortages; the operations of speculators, profiteers, and extortioners; taxes in kind; the depredations of friendly and enemy troops; and the loss of breadwinners to the military. Relief measures were usually handled at the local level at first, but that approach quickly proved too limited.

The federal government assisted in relief and welfare work to some degree, but its efforts were minuscule, given the magnitude of the problem. Davis and his cabinet held back from policies such as price controls because they feared further alienating the states, believed that Confederate financing precluded effective regulation of the market, and became increasingly absorbed in the multiplying military crises. Consequently, Richmond's relief activities were piecemeal and indirect, but they included increasing the supply of salt, assisting charitable organizations, and making provisions available to distressed areas at below-market prices. The Confederate government acted more directly at times, as when it temporarily exempted yeomen in hard-hit regions from military service, but such action was rare. Generally, Richmond did little to relieve the suffering of the common people.

The states had to shoulder the burden. At one point or another, most passed legislation intended to control or prohibit speculation, extortion, monopoly, hoarding, and profiteering, and a few states temporarily embargoed the export of food and clothing. These approaches worked poorly at best and usually failed. Measures to limit or prohibit the distillation of alcoholic beverages so as to conserve grain were more successful, as were restrictions on planting tobacco and cotton in order to increase the output of food. Most states also enacted stay laws and other legislation to protect the property of soldiers and their families and to limit or postpone legal action against them. Various states additionally reduced or eliminated the tax burden for men in service and their kin.

Although these indirect approaches were beneficial, direct relief was required. Counties and states, increasingly the latter, at first provided stipends to needy families of soldiers or to those in poverty. As inflation mounted, new methods were tried. Salt, the basic preservative used in the South, was a matter of concern to nearly everyone. Wartime demand and reduced supply priced it out of the range of the common people. To handle the problem, some states purchased salt and sold it to the needy below cost; others contracted with or subsidized private firms, or both, or set up their own works to increase output. Cotton and wool cards were other priority items. Most states purchased the cards at home or abroad or arranged for greater production, then distributed them to the public, at times along with cotton and wool, to help those in need make cloth and clothes. In Texas, Georgia, and some other states, prisons became centers for producing cloth, shoes, clothing, and other goods. States also offered subsidies to private firms or set up government facilities to manufacture turpentine, castor oil, baking soda, and medicines that were given or sold to the people. Louisiana set up a state store that sold food, clothing, footwear, and general goods at subsidized prices.

As starvation became a reality in many areas of the South, states stepped up efforts to distribute provisions. To help feed and clothe the destitute in the last phases of the war, the governor of Virginia brought in food using blockade runners and a special train sent into the Deep South and took over a textile mill from the Confederacy. The breakdown of transportation, finances, and economic structures in general naturally worsened the difficulties of aiding the masses. The influx of refugees from border states and conquered areas increased even further the problems of various states. These unfortunate people generally had to fend for themselves.

It is impossible to say how much the states spent on relief and welfare measures, but some available figures are instructive. Not including county expenditures, Alabama spent $11 million between 1862 and 1865, with $8 million appropriated in the last two years; for North Carolina the figure was $6 million. Georgia's aggregate welfare outlays for the war years almost equaled those for the military.

Without massive state relief and welfare programs, the Confederate home front would have collapsed long before it did. Besides extending a helping hand to the needy and desperate, state aid muted mounting class antagonism. The Southern population watched the elite benefit from the conscription laws; ignore the palpable want around them; resist lending or hiring out their slaves, equipment, and tools for the war; place undue emphasis upon cotton and what it represented; and suffer at most the loss of luxuries. This gulf inevitably caused resentment among the common people toward a social system that tolerated such unequal sacrifice. Harsh deprivation and smoldering class resentments weakened enormously, perhaps fatally, the Confederate war effort despite the attempts of the states and communities to alleviate suffering.

Cooperation among the states never reached a high level after they put together the constitutional structure for the Confederacy. State officials were apparently too absorbed in their relations with Richmond and their troubles at home to be concerned about other states. Various states assisted one another to some degree by providing munitions, provisions, and even troops, and their executives exchanged views, but these contacts were mostly informal and piecemeal.

More formal conferences did occur, however. In July 1862 and August 1863, conferences were held in Marshall, Texas, which directly or indirectly involved the governors of Texas, Louisiana, Arkansas, and Missouri. These meetings, with uncertain results, were intended to confirm the Western states' commitment to the Confederacy and to address matters of finance, economic exchange, and defense. In October 1864 the governors of Virginia, the Carolinas, Georgia, Alabama, and Mississippi met to debate and ultimately to recommend a change in policy involving the use of black troops. Their collective voices may have helped move the Confederacy toward modifying its policies. The governors also addressed other crises facing the South, including the Confederate-state clash over blockade running. Another attempt at state cooperation occurred in January 1865, when William T. Sherman's army entered South Carolina. Despairing of aid from the Confederacy, the governor called upon the chief executives of Georgia and North Carolina to pool their military resources with his, and later with those of Alabama, Florida, and Mississippi, to beat back the enemy and save the Confederacy. Sherman's inexorable advance overrode this desperate proposal.

Clearly, the Southern cause did not go down because of states' rights, although Confederate-state relations were rocky. In 1861 the states provided a good part of the human and material resources for fighting the war, continued their support thereafter, and played a vital role through relief and welfare efforts in keeping the home front going in the face of disaster. The amount of state wartime activity was truly remarkable. Southern states had previously been involved in promoting, regulating, and conducting market enterprise, particularly banking and railroads, but never on the scale of the war years. Along with Virginia, Georgia and North Carolina were among the most innovative and industrious states, even though their interaction with Richmond was the most acrimonious. The states could have contributed more to Southern cohesion had the Davis administration performed better and had the South's war effort been more successful. In the absence of these factors, fragmentation was inevitable. Thus the actions of the states, more than causing it, reflected the collapse of the Confederacy.

9

CONFEDERATE WAR AND NAVY DEPARTMENTS

THE WAR DEPARTMENT

The Confederate War Department was a reconstituted federal department, its main subdivisions usually headed by former U.S. Army officers who were West Point graduates. President Jefferson Davis was also a West Pointer and a former secretary of war.[1] Five permanent secretaries filled the office of secretary of war between 1861 and 1865. The first was Leroy P. Walker, a fire-eating lawyer, jurist, and politician from Alabama who served from February to September 1861. Walker was unknown to the president, without military experience, and selected so as to have an Alabamian in the cabinet. During his seven months in office, Walker inaugurated the department and spent most of his time raising, arming, supplying, and deploying the army. The secretary of war also helped initiate more long-term policies by appointing agents to acquire arms and equipment at home and abroad and by extending enlistments from twelve months to the war's duration. Before Walker left office, the South had fought successfully at First Manassas and had succeeded in raising an army of several hundred thousand.

Despite his accomplishments, Walker was unqualified for his post. Operating without a proper staff or adequate organizational skills and plagued by indecision and procrastination, he was soon overwhelmed. Overwork quickly broke his health, making matters worse. Alarm grew throughout the Confederacy that the secretary of war was jeopardizing the war effort. Davis feared leaving the capital for even a few days out of concern that Walker could not carry on alone. In September 1861 the president replaced him with the Confederate attorney general, Judah P. Benjamin.

Benjamin had emerged by that point as the president's troubleshooter, confidant, and friend. Like Walker, Benjamin lacked a military background.

Nevertheless, enormous talents allowed him quickly to bring order to the department through the proper division of labor and the delegation of responsibility. Yet he did not go beyond those accomplishments to become an effective war minister; he introduced no new programs or policies, merely continuing the work Walker had begun. Moreover, the usually tactful and diplomatic Benjamin adopted an abrupt style that antagonized state executives and leading generals. This curious behavior may have indicated that Benjamin was taking his signals from Davis. Whatever the case, he failed to achieve the necessary harmony among civilians, the military, and the states. Never comfortable with his enigmatic ways and seeking a scapegoat for military losses, the Confederate Congress forced Benjamin from office in March 1862.

George W. Randolph, the third secretary of war, served from March to November 1862. The grandson of Thomas Jefferson, Randolph, unlike his predecessors, had a military background. He had been a midshipman in the U.S. Navy from 1831 to 1837, had played an active role in Virginia's military activities, and then rose to the grade of brigadier general in the Confederate army. By any measure, Randolph was far superior to Walker and Benjamin. He strengthened the department by expanding its work force and by recruiting able persons such as John A. Campbell, a former Supreme Court associate justice, who became assistant secretary. He implemented conscription and introduced innovative and bold policies for impressing supplies, trading with the enemy, purchasing overseas, and managing the railroads. Most significantly, Randolph proved to be strategically astute. Viewing the war from a broad perspective, he saw that protecting the trans-Allegheny West was vital to the Confederacy's military future, requiring decentralized command and concentrated forces to accommodate a war of movement rather than of position. Despite great abilities, Randolph was unable to work with Davis. They reached a breaking point when the president brusquely rebuked the secretary of war for giving an order to a field army without his approval. An indignant Randolph resigned immediately.

James A. Seddon, a Virginia planter and politician, was the fourth secretary. He held the position the longest, serving from November 1862 to January 1865 and proved to be the department's best executive. Although lacking military experience and tact, Seddon was an effective leader, a capable administrator, and an able and aggressive military strategist. Like Randolph, he recognized the importance of the West to the Confederacy. Accordingly, he persuaded Davis to appoint Gen. Joseph E. Johnston as commanding general of the Department of the West with nearly unlimited authority. Ultimately, the secretary's strategic aims were thwarted. Johnston failed to master his command, and the military leaders of the East opposed transferring men and supplies to the Western theater.

Unlike Randolph, Seddon never enjoyed an optimistic climate of Southern victories. In addition to facing repeated Confederate military defeats, Seddon had to wring from constantly shrinking territory the necessary arms and equipment. Yet he proved to be bold and determined in this endeavor. The secretary of war pushed forward with policies of impressing materials, regulating blockade running, and exempting and detailing skilled labor, but Davis blocked his attempts to establish more centralized control over the railroads. All the while, Seddon sought to maximize the mobilization of military manpower in the face of rising desertions.

In pursuing these goals, the secretary presided over a department that had reached maturity by 1863, made up of ten bureaus or subdivisions that included approximately 273 clerks and 8 messengers. Seddon delegated authority easily and relied heavily upon Assistant Secretary of War Campbell and the head of the Bureau of War, Chief Clerk Robert G. H. Kean.

The key to Seddon's success was his relationship with Davis. Before taking office, he and the president were intimate friends, and the relationship withstood the trials of public life. The two men were almost constantly in contact. They held long conferences several times a day and regularly exchanged communications, reports, and correspondence. With few exceptions, the bureau chiefs reported to the president through the secretary of war, and the latter was always privy to all major decisions involving his department and the army. The idiosyncratic president learned to trust his secretary of war, suspended his own judgment at times in favor of the Virginian's, and allowed Seddon to act on his own during Davis's increasing bouts of illness. The secretary of war in turn knew his leader and always cleared all but routine matters with the president.

Seddon came under relentless attack from all quarters as the Confederacy's end approached: as a stand-in for the president, he became the scapegoat. Seddon's role as a lightning rod was widely recognized and won him even greater appreciation from Davis. But even the long-suffering secretary of war had his limits. Sick, worn out, and disgusted by Virginia's attack on the cabinet as a supposed drag on the Confederacy, Seddon resigned in January 1865 over Davis's objections.

The fifth and last secretary of war was John C. Breckinridge, the famous Kentucky politician and soldier. From February to April 1865, Breckinridge acted more as a soldier than as a civilian official, allowing Assistant Secretary of War Campbell to run the department while he prepared for impending defeat and demobilization.

As the principal Confederate mobilization agency, the War Department was seriously hampered by Davis's strict control over it. No major decisions involving the selection and promotion of officers, military strategy, or supply occurred without the president's initiation or at least approval. This oversight gave an uncertain quality to the South's economic mobilization since Davis tended to take a narrow view of the war and was uncomfortable with the bureaucratic centralization pursued by his administration. Moreover, the president did not give overall direction to the war effort. Although he watched the War Department closely, he gave free rein to the two other mobilization agencies, the Navy and Treasury departments, about which he knew less.

In truth, Davis was not particularly well equipped generally to direct his administration because of his proclivity for becoming absorbed in details at the expense of larger issues. That sort of leadership denied the South the bold, innovative direction from the top necessary to maximize the Confederacy's limited economic strength.

THE QUARTERMASTER DEPARTMENT

In supply matters, the secretaries of war found themselves at a disadvantage because most of them held office for a short time, the bureau heads were selected or passed on by Davis, and no overall system emerged for coordinating the department's subdivisions or for calculating requirements. Consequently, the various bureaus operated more as separate units than as parts of a larger whole. In general, the Quartermaster Department did a reasonable job, the Office of the Commissary General of Subsistence performed adequately, and the Ordnance Department was outstanding. The other bureaus had only tangential involvement in supply efforts.

The Quartermaster Department was the principal Confederate supply bureau.[2] In March 1861 Davis selected Abraham C. Myers as acting, later permanent, quartermaster general. Myers was a Southerner and West Point graduate who, although fully qualified for the position, tended to be a stickler for regulations and was not especially aggressive. Myers reorganized the Quartermaster Department step by step in 1861 and 1862 so that it could handle constantly expanding duties. He also settled the chronic conflict between the line and the staff in favor of the latter. In spring 1863 a final restructuring brought the department to maturity, and it retained this form for the remainder of hostilities.

Myers divided the Confederacy into eleven purchasing districts, which generally were coterminous with the states. Each district was headed by a "principal purchasing officer" responsible for all contracting, purchasing, and manufacturing activity, and officers of one district could not raid the territory of another. Supplies were stored in twelve depots in nine states. Principal purchasing officers headed these depots, which were within reasonable reach of the various Confederate armies. The officers answered only to the quartermaster general, reporting to him monthly. Chief quartermasters for the armies made requisitions directly to the Quartermaster General's Office where they were reviewed and, if approved, sent to the appropriate purchasing officer for distribution from his depot. With few exceptions, field quartermasters could not purchase supplies. The district system was sufficiently flexible to allow special arrangements for procuring strategic items such as leather.

Although the district purchasing and depot system was basic to Quartermaster Department operations, the department supervised numerous other activities. Various manufacturing firms—owned, operated, or directed by the department—reported to the bureau's headquarters. Additionally, special organizations operated under the Quartermaster Department, including the post quartermasters, who collected the tax-in-kind, and the railroad superintendent. A host of quartermaster officials with particular specialties also reported directly to Richmond, such as those in charge of medical stores and wagon and ambulance construction. When these structures were combined with the network of paymasters and field quartermasters, the Confederacy was interlaced with an incredible number of often overlapping quartermaster representatives and bureaucracies.

Such a sprawling bureaucratic maze inevitably spawned inefficiency and corruption, particularly since the organization grew so rapidly and was staffed with so many inexperienced officers and enlisted men. Quartermaster officers ranged from excellent to execrable, with most falling somewhere in between. The officers who were ignorant, capricious, and corrupt got away with a great deal because accounting procedures tended to be lax, despite regular practices involving vouchers, reports, accounts, and bonds. Nevertheless, the Quartermaster Department was a competent organization on the whole. According to a leading scholar on the subject, "Inefficiency and corruption . . . were not crucial factors in Confederate supply failures."[3]

For most of the war, the Quartermaster Department did not supply the West. The trans-Mississippi West was largely on its own beginning in autumn of 1861. After the fall of New Orleans in April 1862, the region became increasingly isolated, a process that was completed with the loss of Vicksburg in July 1863. Until that time, Richmond took as much wool, leather, and beef on the hoof as it could from the area but sent few supplies in return. Military commanders in the trans-Mississippi West, therefore, set up their own supply systems, depending largely on the exchange of cotton for goods through the Mexican port of Matamoros on the Rio Grande. Western independence reached its most advanced stage after February 1863 under Gen. Edmund

Kirby Smith. He ran his department like a fiefdom free of Richmond's control, supplied an army of approximately 40,000 men reasonably well, repulsed the Union drive up the Red River in 1864, and surrendered his army intact after the collapse in the East in 1865.

In August 1863 over the heated objections of the Confederate Congress, Davis replaced Myers as quartermaster general with Alexander R. Lawton, a former brigade commander who had been wounded at Antietam. Although less experienced than Myers, Lawton was energetic and probably performed as well as his predecessor.

Throughout the war, the Quartermaster Department faced the momentous responsibility of providing troops with uniforms, footwear, bedding, shelter, camp and garrison equipment, and general supplies, in addition to managing transportation and pay. After the first year of war, the department appeared to handle the supplies without severe problems; paying the troops was often delayed due to the shortage of money. Although delays adversely affected soldiers' morale, the department considered the matter more an irritant than a major burden.

Events compelled the Quartermaster Department to move quickly in supplying the troops. The first volunteers were required to clothe and arm themselves, a responsibility assumed in part by many states. First Manassas showed that this system would not work. Troops were clothed in a bewildering array of outfits of generally poor quality. The textile-producing states of the Eastern seaboard were able to furnish their troops properly, but the other states did not do as well.

In efforts to clothe the troops, Myers by June 1861 began placing orders with all possible cotton and woolen factories and shoe shops throughout the Confederacy. Before the end of summer, the quartermaster general also had dispatched special agents to buy whatever clothing, blankets, and footwear were available in the Southern states. By that time it was clear that the Confederacy lacked the capacity to produce supplies at the rate needed; for example, Myers estimated annual shoe requirements at 1.6 million pairs, yet only 300,000 could be acquired domestically. The rest would have to be procured abroad. The situation was less drastic for wool cloth, blankets, and uniforms, but substantial imports were still essential. As early as May 1861 Myers warned Secretary of War Walker that foreign procurement was necessary, but the latter did nothing and the former did not move on his own. The quartermaster did receive foreign supplies in late 1861 and early 1862, but this was a result of other people's initiative.

To maximize the supply of clothing and footwear, the Quartermaster Department ultimately worked to expand and rationalize domestic and foreign sources. Domestically, activity involved increasing government production and growing compulsion applied to private establishments. Since ready-made clothing was not yet a staple item in the South, beginning in the latter half of 1861 and continuing throughout the war, the Quartermaster Department set up its own production facilities at various depots in the region. Two manufacturing processes seem to have been used: in some cases, cloth was cut and put out to homes for women to sew into uniforms; in others, all cutting and sewing took place under the same roof. Using one method or the other, Quartermaster facilities manufactured all Confederate uniforms except those imported, captured, or made by the states. Clothing factories at Richmond, Augusta, Atlanta, and Columbus were particularly efficient, but they struggled against the enormous odds that plagued most manufacturing in the Confederacy. Most of the work force was female. Women and girls, many of whom were soldiers' dependents, did piecework to protect their families against the ravages of inflation.

The Quartermaster Department never manufactured textiles; instead, it contracted with textile mills to fulfill its requirements. Almost from the outset, mills preferred to sell in the more lucrative civilian market than to the army. Compulsion, therefore, became necessary. Although the quartermaster general and commissary general had the power to impress goods as early as November 1861, the former avoided using such a harsh approach. He preferred relying on the less drastic, and probably more effective, controls over labor, transportation, and raw materials to bend mill owners to his will.

Manpower controls became available with the second draft and exemption acts in September–October 1862. These laws allowed the secretary of war to exempt, among others, superintendents and operators in wool and cotton factories that limited their profits to 75 percent of costs. From late 1862 to early 1864, threats by the Quartermaster Department to revoke the exemptions of textile mills usually brought recalcitrant firms into line.

Controls became more stringent as the war stretched on. The Conscription Act of February 1864 scrapped factory exemptions in favor of detailing men to textile mills for short periods. Quartermaster General Lawton and draft officials used the law to cut profit rates to 33.3 percent or lower, extend military pricing to civilian markets, and subject mill owners' account books to close scrutiny. Mills also had to agree to sell at least two-thirds of their output to the military. This system remained in effect until the Conscription Bureau was disestablished in March 1865. No new system arose to replace it since the Confederacy was in its death throes.

In addition to relying on manpower legislation, the Quartermaster Department depended upon authority over transportation and raw materials to regulate textile mills. Through a priority system on railroad freight, the department could deny all but locally available cotton to any uncooperative firm. The controls on wool were even greater than those on cotton. By 1863 the Quartermaster Department, alone and in conjunction with other government agencies, had established a virtual monopoly on wool, which allowed it to regulate the wool output of all textile firms until the end of the hostilities.

The Quartermaster Department in 1864 also succeeded to a degree in consolidating textile purchasing under its authority and in making allotments to other bureaus and the navy. This measure was intended to control prices by halting competition among government agencies. Moreover, after October 1862, when Congress ended all commutation compensation, the Quartermaster Department attempted without success to contract with textile firms in North Carolina. In 1861 the state agreed to clothe its troops in exchange for commutation payments and a pledge that the Confederate government would take no textiles from the state. Governor Zebulon B. Vance refused to acknowledge that conditions had changed; to the war's end he withstood departmental pressure and threats to place contracts in his state. As a result, North Carolina had textiles stockpiled for up to a year while Confederate troops were insufficiently clothed.

Leather also presented serious problems. The Quartermaster Department was the principal government consumer of leather, supplying troops with boots and shoes and baggage trains with harnesses. As with clothing, the department set up its own shops throughout the Confederacy to manufacture footwear. Factories at Columbus, Richmond, Atlanta, and Montgomery were especially important. They often had tanneries attached, but the department relied heavily upon private tanners for leather. Private shops in the Carolinas and elsewhere supplemented government footwear output in the early war years.

A leather shortage developed in spring 1862 and worsened thereafter due to the declining supply of hides as the Confederacy shrank. The situation deteriorated because of inefficiency in collecting hides, the Commissary Department's reluctance to turn hides over to the Quartermaster Department, and scheming by speculators and corrupt army officers. To deal with the growing shortage of hides and leather, the Quartermaster Department used controls over manpower and materials to restrict footwear production to its own shops and acted as a monopoly buyer of tannery output at set prices. It then consolidated production among government shoe factories for purposes of efficiency and reduced, by as much as 90 percent in some places, the number of tanneries with which it contracted. The department later took over collecting and tanning hides for most of the South. Like almost all Confederate manufacturing, the output of leather and leather goods was constantly disrupted by the draft.

Even these drastic measures did not provide the Quartermaster Department with enough leather to meet the demand for shoes and boots. As a result, in 1862 the department began experimenting with canvas-topped and later wooden-soled footwear, substitutes that were never well received by the troops.

Without imports acquired through blockade running, the Quartermaster Department would never have been able to fulfill its responsibilities. Myers realized that such was the case, but other officials moved first to tap foreign markets. In May and June 1861, two purchasing agents from the army and one from the navy were sent to England to buy weapons, clothing, and supplies. The Quartermaster Department finally dispatched its own agent, Maj. J. B. Ferguson, in July 1862.

Quartermaster statistics are too fragmentary to establish with certainty the portion of its supplies that came from abroad, but 50 percent seems a reasonable figure. Purchases from private blockade runners as early as September 1861 and supplies from ships arriving with government stores in fall 1861 and spring 1862 allowed the department to meet a considerable portion of its initial demand for uniforms, clothes, footwear, leather, and woolen cloth. By 1863, as the Union advanced against the South, the department had become heavily dependent upon foreign sources. Beyond the second half of 1864, dependence became nearly total. Near the end of 1864, the Union shut down Wilmington and Charleston, the last two ports servicing substantial numbers of blockade runners. The Confederacy's lifeline was cut.

Overall, the Quartermaster Department performed reasonably well. In 1861 and 1862, while it went through an organizational shakedown, the troops were indifferently supplied. By 1863 the quality and quantity of stores were adequate given the conditions the Confederacy faced. Those circumstances, however, were becoming dire by late 1863. The loss of most of the Upper South, the Mississippi River, and key ports and bases such as Norfolk and New Orleans entailed huge short-term losses of supplies through surrender and retreat and a drastic long-term reduction in the South's economic base. Increasingly stringent economic controls and steady improvement in blockade-running practices enabled the Quartermaster Department to supply most armies until the end, however, even though federal troops destroyed or occupied a large part of Confederate territory. Yet the department seldom had reserves, and the margins for error were always much too narrow. For example, a few ships slipping through the blockade in 1863 saved the department from a debacle. Field commanders were aware of the precarious nature of supply; that knowledge acted to sap their confidence. The North's ever-tightening economic noose restricted severely the Confederacy's fighting capacity.

Transportation was a major responsibility of the Quartermaster Department and involved its most significant failures. The department handled river, wagon, and railroad transport. To move men and supplies on rivers and inland waterways, the department hired steamboats with few apparent problems, but this was not a principal mode of transportation.

Wagon transportation was of the greatest significance for the Confederate armies. It was directed by Maj. A. H. Cole, the inspector general of Field Transportation. The department also appointed special officers to oversee the construction of wagons and ambulances and the output of horseshoes and nails. As wagon shortages grew, additional agencies were created to locate new ones and to repair old ones. Wagons, caissons, and other wheeled vehicles, like most Southern facilities, had become worn and fragile through overuse and underrepair by the end of the war.

The breakdown in Confederate supply operations was due less to problems with wheeled vehicles than to shortages and inadequate care of horses and mules, particularly to shortages, conditions that drastically weakened the fighting units in various ways.[4] The shortage of horses sapped the strength of the cavalry in 1862, significantly curtailed the South's offensive capabilities in 1863, and by 1864 left the Confederacy incapable of adequately handling supply and of protecting its supply lines.

The Confederacy's crisis over horses involved both supply and demand. The South had an adequate supply of horses and mules in 1860. Shortages arose by mid-1862 because of the loss to the Union of the prime horse-breeding areas of Missouri, Kentucky, western and middle Tennessee, and trans-Allegheny Virginia. Most mules came from the same regions. As supply fell, the demand for draft and riding animals skyrocketed. The army used horses for post and field transportation, artillery, and cavalry. Mules could be used for the first function, were not favored for the second, and were an unacceptable substitute for the third. Civilian use of draft animals also grew to transport military supplies to railroads and to collect the tax-in-kind.

Increased demand and decreased supply, combined with intense inflationary pressures, drove the price of horses to exorbitant heights. The cost made conditions especially difficult for cavalrymen, who had to purchase their own mounts, as well as for the Quartermaster Department, which was always short of funds. Beginning in mid-1862 horses became increasingly difficult to purchase at any price. The Quartermaster Department had growing difficulty impressing horses because it feared harming agricultural output; available draft animals were often unfit for military services; and healthy ones were hidden.

Efforts to acquire horses in Texas and Mexico from 1862 on failed because of the lack of specie, bureaucratic inertia, and the nearly impossible task of getting horses across the Mississippi River. A February 1865 bill requiring the department to supply horses to the cavalry had little effect since the Confederacy by then was so close to defeat.

The enormous effort required to feed the mounted and draft animals presented further problems. In 1862 the animals in the Army of Northern Virginia and the Army of Tennessee alone consumed 5,300 bushels of corn daily, requiring twenty-one railroads cars for transport. The railroads resisted tying up their scarce cars transporting bulky provender and often had to be forced to do so. They could never keep pace because the demand for fodder increased as armies exhausted forage in the countryside around them, a situation that occurred in Virginia as early as 1862–1863. Overworked and underfed animals inevitably became weak and susceptible to disease. The consequent reduction in the stock of draft animals forced decreases in the size of military baggage trains, restricted the operations of field artillery units, and cut the numbers and lightened the load of transportation wagons. Cavalry units shrank in size as fallen horses went unreplaced, and the units became increasingly ineffective as debilitated mounts were dispersed so that they could be properly pastured. All military units—the cavalry, supply and medical bureaus, artillery, and infantry—depended on horses and mules in one way or another, and all were adversely affected.

Unable to replace dead or disabled animals in adequate numbers, the Quartermaster Department tried to extend the longevity of those it had. Early in 1863 Major Cole informed the secretary of war that the Confederacy was losing 20,000 draft and artillery horses a year. Of that number, 5,000 had been lost in action; the rest had starved, suffered from disease, or been abandoned or sold. To ameliorate the situation, the department late in 1863 divided the Confederacy into four inspection districts. "Infirmaries" were set up in each to examine animals, segregate those that were diseased, and place those that were ill and emaciated under the care of trained personnel behind the lines. Animals that recovered returned to duty. The system had mixed results in the district that included Virginia and North Carolina; only 15 percent of horses returned to service, although 57 percent of stricken mules were rehabilitated.

The situation continued to deteriorate despite the efforts of the Quartermaster Department and the field commanders. Union armies advancing on Southern soil killed, drove off, or confiscated horses and mules. The falling number of animals reduced even further the performance of the supply and fighting forces. Robert E. Lee's once deadly cavalry units, which Frank Vandiver characterizes as "the forerunner of the blitzkrieg," were so disabled by weak, worn, and scattered horses that by 1864 they could not respond aggressively to the onslaught of the now-fleet Union cavalry.[5] Unable to protect his lines of supply and communication against Ulysses S. Grant's advancing army in 1864–1865, Lee's shrinking number of men and animals at times approached starvation and freezing while available supplies remained out of reach because of the breakdown in logistics.

There was not much the Quartermaster Department could have done to increase the supply of horses and mules. Earlier efforts might have been made to preserve existing stock, buy additional horses in Texas and Mexico, and trade more aggressively through the lines, but those expedients would never have been sufficient. The capture of 1,200–1,500 horses in a raid on the upper Potomac in May 1863 solved no long-term problems. One major improvement would have involved keeping horses and mules healthy through an adequate diet. Proper use of the railroads might have served that end, but the South failed to maximize railroad potential.

RAILROAD AND TELEGRAPH SYSTEMS

Why the Confederacy did not make optimal use of its railroads still remains somewhat of a mystery.[6] What is clear is that the numerous Southern railroad lines were unable to regulate themselves, and Richmond did not step in to do so. This lack of supervision contrasts to the situation with iron production and other vital areas in which the Confederate government intervened to impose order.

Facing an economically superior enemy, the South needed an equalizer that the railroads could have provided. Properly managed, the iron horse would have allowed the Confederacy to use interior lines to concentrate its strength rapidly. The railroads served that purpose to some degree but never in a systematic and reliable way. As early as 1862, the railroads began to show signs of dysfunction.

The difficulties stemmed in part from the nature of the prewar Southern railway system. It was a disparate collection of relatively small parts. Fewer than 10,000 miles of rails were divided among 113 companies. Most lines were short and local, seldom extending more than 200 miles, usually running from the back country to cities or ports and intended to facilitate the marketing of cotton and other agricultural products. There were no trunk lines, and through traffic was inhibited by the predominance of two different rail gauges. Roads using the same gauge were often not connected for various reasons, and even on some connecting lines transfer and transshipment were necessary since competing companies resisted lending one another cars.

Southern railroads usually had single tracks with few sidings. Roadbeds, ties, rails, and bridges were generally lightweight and carelessly built, requiring constant "renewal" for the roads to remain "viable."[7] The renewal process was not a problem before the war but that changed with hostilities. Most rails, locomotives, and cars came from the North or from Europe, and the South lacked enough capacity to supply itself.

Although the railroads used the corporate form and introduced at least the outlines of modern management, they were still run in a fairly primitive way. Schedules and rates were casual, standard time nonexistent, the telegraph hardly evident, and safety measures often ignored and accidents frequent. Railroad owners and managers were a mixed lot and did not include giants such as J. Edgar Thomson and Herman Haupt.

Extensive state involvement in railroads presented another complication to Richmond's prospects for coordinating them. States, along with towns, cities, and counties, played a major role in directly and indirectly financing railroad growth. Georgia owned and operated a road in the Western and Atlantic, and the Tarheel State controlled seven of the eleven seats on the board of directors of the North Carolina Railroad. Regulation within the states varied from the casual to the strict. Thus the Confederate government had to consider the response of the states to any plans it had for the railroads.

Although the Southern railways had not reached physical, financial, or managerial maturity by 1861, they constituted a system of considerable potential if properly mobilized. Two railroad routes (one completed, one with gaps) traversed the Confederacy from the East Coast to the Mississippi, two lateral lines connected the East-West routes with each other, and combinations of other lines made alternate paths possible. Moreover, some civilian and military leaders appreciated that careful, early planning and regulation of the railroads was essential for military victory. Indeed, at a critical point, the iron horse helped turn defeat into victory at First Manassas. Thereafter, the South had the distinction of building the first truly military railroad with the Manassas-Centreville line and of developing the first ambulance cars and rail-mounted guns.

Furthermore, the Confederacy executed some remarkable large-scale troop movements by rail. The outstanding example took place in July 1862 when Gen. Braxton Bragg directed the deployment of about 25,000 men and their equipment 776 miles from Tupelo, Mississippi, to Chattanooga in ten days. Rails continued to transport men and equipment in 1864 and 1865, but the miraculous accomplishments were over. Near the end of the war, trains could hardly move.

Richmond attempted to regulate the Southern railroads throughout the war years without much success. Despite informal agreements reached at state and national conventions held between April and July 1861 to apply common policies to the railroads, the Quartermaster Department could not impose its will on the carriers. Consequently, in July 1861, President Davis appointed William S. Ashe as assistant quartermaster in charge of rail transportation for Confederate armies in Virginia. Ashe was a talented Southern attorney, politician, and railroad executive who created an unofficial staff and introduced regulations for orderly railroad operations. All was for naught. Government and military officials bypassed Ashe to deal directly with the railroads; business struggled with the army for priority in shipment; cars were used for offices and warehouses; lines would not share rolling stock; Gov. Joseph E. Brown of Georgia threatened to use the military if Ashe tried seizing engines and cars in his state; and secretaries of war Walker and Benjamin would not support the assistant quartermaster in the face of unending challenges. Ashe simply gave up trying to fulfill his responsibilities before the year was out and resigned his position in April 1862.

The railroad situation became critical by the end of 1862. With Ashe inactive and then off the scene, Quartermaster General Myers was left to handle rail transport without time, experience, or expert advice. He opposed centralized control of the system, preferring to work with the railroads individually, an approach that led to crazy-quilt results. Some areas of the Confederacy had elaborate rules and regulations, others had none, and too often matters were left to the discretion of local quartermasters and railroad agents.

The Davis administration moved to resolve the crisis in December 1862. It removed the railroads from Quartermaster direction, placing them under an agency that eventually became the Railroad Bureau, reporting to the secretary of war. William M. Wadley, a transplanted New Englander and the ablest railroad executive in the South, headed the agency. Although Wadley supervised all railroads in the South, he had no more authority than Ashe had had. Despite long and patient efforts, he could not get the railroads or the army to follow his advice on any consistent basis.

Congress complicated matters with a law in May 1863 giving the president nearly unlimited authority over the railroads but specifying the Quartermaster Department as the supervising agency. Almost simultaneously, the Confederate legislators rejected Wadley's appointment to direct the Railroad Bureau, perhaps because of old rivalries, more likely because of his Northern origins. Davis matched Congress' capriciousness: in June 1863 he appointed Wadley's assistant, the Southerner Frederick W. Sims, as head of the Railroad Bureau without benefit of the authority in the May legislation. When Lawton replaced Myers as quartermaster general in August 1863, Davis transferred the Railroad Bureau to the Quartermaster Department. This change augured well since Sims and Lawton were friends, and the latter had a railroad background. Nonetheless, Sims enjoyed no greater authority than had Wadley.

The task of keeping the railroads running became increasingly difficult and near the war's end virtually impossible. Lawton was no more anxious to exercise extensive control over the railroads than Myers had been. Brandishing the May 1863 law, Sims persuaded various railroads to cooperate at critical points. A War Department effort to use the legislation for seizing the Piedmont Railroad in January 1865 miscarried, however. Most of the time, the military, railway companies, and shippers continued struggling to secure the iron horse for their own advantage. Even in the face of Confederate collapse, Davis did not move to end the unseemly and irresponsible squabbling. In February 1865 Congress strengthened Davis's hand even more over the railroads, but by then it was too late.

Robert C. Black III observes that the leaders of the Confederacy were plagued by a "fatal hesitation" when it came to the railroads.[8] This characteristic was true of both quartermaster generals, most secretaries of war, and particularly President Davis. Why this was the case remains unclear. An essentially local system, run by parochial managers who used states' rights to ward off Confederate control, presented major challenges. Yet the obstacles were no greater than those involved with national conscription and centralized direction over blockade running. Davis understood the importance of the railroads. Nonetheless, he, like many Southerners, appeared to have difficulty in conceiving of a Confederate-wide business operation. Perhaps for Davis and many Southerners, the railroads reflected too closely the values and ways of the hated Yankees they were rebelling against.

Although the Davis administration never established centralized control over the railroads, it assisted them in various ways. A $1-million subsidy was authorized in February 1861 to eliminate a forty-mile gap between Danville, Virginia, and Greensboro, North Carolina, and thereby open a critically important rail route. Quarrels over routing, shortages of labor and supplies, and the obstruction of Governor Vance of North Carolina delayed completion of the project until May 1864. Also in February 1861 Congress appropriated $150,000 to complete a connection from Selma, Alabama, to Meridian, Mississippi, to give the South a through line between Virginia and the West. Desperate military need forced Richmond to increase its investment and involvement in the endeavor, which was finished by December 1862. Two other projects never reached completion.

The South had enormous difficulty maintaining existing railroads, let alone adding new mileage. Cut off from suppliers in the North and Europe, the railroads had to improvise. A limited amount of rolling stock and rails were captured from the North or traded through the lines. Various railroad companies tried to purchase equipment in Europe, but they needed War Department assistance, and the latter usually refused to help, arguing that it was not the government's responsibility to assist private business. Overall, insignificant amounts of railroad supplies came from outside the Confederacy.

As a result, the railroads relied on sources of supply inside the Confederacy, a wholly inadequate solution. The Tredegar Iron Works at Richmond and the Atlanta Rolling Mill and Etowah Iron Works in Georgia could manufacture locomotives and their parts and roll rails, but these firms were few in number, had limited capacity, and always lacked an adequate supply of iron. Moreover, with rare exception, they were unavailable to the railroads because the Confederate government monopolized their output for munitions. No new rails were rolled in the Confederacy during the war years, and relatively few were rerolled. The railroad companies were thus forced to run their overloaded systems as best they could, repair rolling stock when possible, and replace worn-out track with rails taken up from less-used parts of their line or spurs. These conditions reduced Confederate railroads to a deplorable condition by 1862. Rails were worn thin, rolling stock worn out, and numerous engines and cars disabled by the unavailability of wheels, axles, and other parts. When they ran, trains moved more slowly, less frequently, and with reduced efficiency and safety.

Richmond had to step in to help. Late in 1862, the Railroad Bureau set up a facility that became a repair shop and equipment pool in Raleigh, North Carolina, to refurbish locomotives, cars, and parts and to distribute them to railroad lines based on priority. The army also began seizing and impressing railroad equipment. Engines, cars, and whole trains were taken over, and rails of one line removed to rehabilitate another. At first local commanders, quartermasters, and engineers supervised this action, but ultimately the highest levels of the armed services and Confederate government became involved because lines fought impressment or seizure, often ferociously. Among other complaints, railroads protested against nonexistent or inadequate compensation and the unlikelihood of reclaiming rolling stock because the army kept few reliable records. The situation grew so bad that armed troops moved against railroads receiving injunctions against impressment from state courts.

Transferring track from one part of a line to a different section or impressing it from one railroad to repair another, build new lines, or connect existing ones was a form of cannibalism by which the Confederacy consumed its most vital transportation system. Nonetheless, the practice grew more common. By late 1862 agents impressing rails for different departments, offices, and commands inundated the South. The Davis administration stepped in only when the practice was getting out of control. In January 1863 the administration created an Iron Commission to survey railroad lines throughout the Confederacy, recommend which ones could best be sacrificed for the benefit of others, and buy or seize railroads as needed. The Army Engineers dominated the commission even though various other agencies were represented on it.

In time, the Iron Commission became the primary source of rails in the South, and it also acquired locomotives, cars, and parts through impressment to distribute to selected railroads. Thus it competed with the Railroad Bureau's facility in Raleigh, and an intense, bitter, and needless rivalry emerged between the two agencies. The Railroad Bureau and the Iron Commission forced a partial and not particularly effective pooling arrangement on the railroads, which they had refused to institute among themselves.

The South never had a counterpart to the North's U.S. Military Railroad to repair and maintain lines critical for military use. At first, railroad companies, with or without government help, repaired their lines as best they could. As supplies became increasingly short and Union penetration more extensive, the army took a greater role, yet no set system ever developed. The Railroad or Engineer Bureau often supervised repair work, but depending on the circumstances, the railroad company itself and field commanders could also be involved. To carry out the repairs, equipment, supplies, and slaves were usually impressed and military details employed. Rebuilding was usually accomplished imaginatively and expeditiously. Despite extreme shortages in 1864 and 1865, damaged lines were often put back in service with remarkable rapidity, even during William T. Sherman's march through Georgia and South Carolina, when railroads were a primary object of destruction.

Extreme shortages of labor, ranging from skilled mechanics to woodcutters, exacerbated problems. Some workers left for better jobs and pay, others joined the service, and the draft took increasing numbers in the last years of the war. Replacements were hard to find, and even slaves could not be acquired in sufficient numbers to cut cordwood and crossties. To get workers, among other actions, railroads raided each others' work forces and engaged in fraud. Richmond made only begrudging efforts to relieve the mounting labor problems.

No matter how bad the railroads became, the Davis administration never moved decisively to regulate them, which seemingly encouraged the lines to place their own interests ahead of those of the Confederacy. It was not uncommon to see civilian freight on trains during the most extreme combat crises while military supplies remained piled up at depots. The disorder increased as a sense of unavoidable defeat grew.

Despite widespread shortcomings in the public and private sectors, the railroads still provided the Confederacy with an indispensable modern transportation system. Without it, the Confederacy would have succumbed much more quickly than it did. Wartime exigencies aside, Southern railroads were still running at the time of surrender, albeit barely in some cases. That capability speaks volumes about the resiliency of the iron horse. Nonetheless, the outcome of the war was partly determined by the increasing strength of the Northern railroads as the Southern system deteriorated.

Southern use of the telegraph system, as with the railroads, was far less advanced than in the North.[9] Two major systems operated in the region: the Southern Telegraph Company and the Southwestern Telegraph Company. The first was the Southern portion of the American Telegraph Company, which had split off from the Northern branch in May 1861; the second was centered in Louisville and owned lines extending from there to New Orleans. Since most of Southwestern's lines were in the border states and combat areas, the company became a victim of the war. Its property and equipment were usually under the military control of the Confederacy or the Union, and Southern Telegraph used its favored position to try to eliminate its competitor.

Congress authorized President Davis in July 1861 to seize all telegraph lines and operate them so as to maximize the security of the Confederacy. Davis delegated the responsibility to Postmaster General John H. Reagan, who in turn appointed Dr. William S. Morris, president of Southern Telegraph, as chief of military telegraphs. Few lines were ever actually seized. Reagan and Morris worked well together, and the former generally left the latter to direct events as he desired. Morris never established a formal organization. Outside combat areas, a few commanding officers, such as Gen. P. G. T. Beauregard at Charleston, created full-blown telegraph offices, but that was the exception. Military commanders usually took control of the wires in the vicinity of hostilities, erratically coordinated their efforts with Morris, and used the wires with varying degrees of effectiveness. Combat situations aside, private companies generally provided the military with the telegraphic capacity it needed.

Telegraph operators serving the army had a mixed status. Some were officers, noncommissioned officers, or enlisted men, others were civilians, and many had an undefined quasi-military standing. Shortages of telegraphers emerged during hostilities, and details from the ranks were often necessary to make up the shortfall. The newly created Signal Corps also had a part in military telegraph operations.

The poorly organized military telegraphs prevented the Confederacy from fully exploiting this new tool of war. The North built over 15,000 miles of military telegraph lines, but the South managed to put up only 500 miles. During the Gettysburg campaign, the Confederate military telegraph system strung some fifty-seven miles of lines in eleven days, but that was an exception. Generally speaking, military lines did not extend to the battlefront. Thus Richmond, in contrast to Washington, did not know the outcome of battles until the news reached a telegraph office. Certainly the South was limited to some degree by the lack of supplies and equipment, particularly the shortage of wire. Yet aggressive leadership could have overcome those obstacles.

Despite the drawbacks, the Confederacy's use of the telegraph has a bearing on its unhappy experience with the railroads. Had one or several corporations dominated the railroad system in the South, as with the telegraphs, or had the various railroad companies been united instead of divided and exceptionally competitive, they could have run the railroads for the Confederacy efficiently with little official interference, as occurred in the North. The railroads thus would have made up for the ideological and managerial limitations of the Confederate government.

Ultimately, the Quartermaster Department's handling of transportation was not especially effective. Although it performed as well as could be expected in terms of wagons and draft animals, it was not equipped to deal with the railroads and should not have had responsibility for them.

THE SUBSISTENCE DEPARTMENT

No supply bureau suffered more from the inadequacies of Confederate transportation than the Department of Subsistence, headed by Commissary General Lucius B. Northrop.[10] Northrop was a South Carolinian, a friend of Davis, and a West Point graduate with some commissary experience. Scholars have generally judged him harshly, an assessment in part related to his numerous eccentricities, which made him an easy target for the anger surrounding a lost cause. The troops did suffer food shortages for a large part of the war, especially in Virginia. Nevertheless, Northrop created and ran a good organization that was bedeviled by larger Confederate mobilization failures. Although not an inspiring leader, he understood the hard realities facing the Confederacy and what had to be done to overcome them. His chief assistant, Francis G. Ruffin, a talented, well-connected, and genial agricultural technocrat from Virginia, generally shared his views.

The Subsistence Department's organization resembled that of the Quartermaster Department, but it was simpler because of fewer duties. By April

1863 Northrop had structured his bureau along state lines. A chief commissary in each state supervised a group of subcommissaries and agents who did all purchasing in the state, set up depots and subdepots, and reported regularly to the commissary general in Richmond. The chief commissaries of field armies placed their orders with the states in which they operated or passed through, and one state or military district could draw upon the supplies of another state if necessary.

Like all supply bureaus, the Commissary Department had a slow start. Nonetheless, through diligent effort Northrop reported in January 1862 that all troops could be fed. By then, the commissary general had maximized the slaughter and packing of hogs and beef and had sufficient amounts of flour and cornmeal. The Confederate armies thus had provisions, but nothing else was ensured, and coffee, vinegar, and soap were already growing scarce. Future food supplies looked promising because cotton was being cut back in favor of staple crops, sweet potatoes, and other agricultural products. In 1861 the South produced 4.5 million bales of cotton; in 1864 only 300,000. For the South to feed itself adequately, however, it had to hold on to the principal staple- and meat-producing state of Tennessee, try to maintain access to Kentucky, protect the Mississippi Valley and the trans-Mississippi region, and at the same time work out viable financial and transportation policies.

None of these prerequisites was met; consequently, as early as 1862 the food supply was threatened and the offensive capabilities of the Confederate armies adversely affected. The fall of Forts Henry and Donelson in February 1862 was a major disaster for the Commissary Department because it led to the loss of Tennessee and opened up the entire Mississippi Valley to the Union. The consequences for the meat supply were especially grave. In November 1862 Northrop reported a 43 percent deficit in meat and pointed out that only one-third of the South's normal hog supply was within its military lines. Realizing the magnitude of the crisis, Northrop ordered a precautionary but substantial cut in the meat ration for all armies in spring 1862, an order ignored by most field commanders. A severe drought in the Upper South in 1862 further reduced the output of crops and livestock. Shortages of salt and the use of low-quality salt also decreased the availability of preserved meat.

No army suffered more from food shortages than Lee's. Huge commissary losses occurred during the pullback from Manassas, Williamsburg, and Norfolk early in 1862. Still, until the late autumn, the army secured provisions within the state and suffered no great privation. By December 1862, however, Lee's army had nearly stripped the state bare; provisions could no longer be bought or impressed. Nearly all food then had to be shipped into the state, which threatened starvation more than once and reduced the Army of Northern Virginia in spring 1863 and after to begging local citizens for food donations.

Once the border states and other areas were denied to the Confederacy as reliable sources of food, the Subsistence Department increasingly turned to the Lower South. This alternative stretched supply lines enormously and made long-range planning by the department imperative. Yet weaknesses in Confederate finances and transportation undermined planning and forced the Commissary Department to operate on a day-to-day basis.

Like the other supply bureaus, the Commissary Department was usually short of funds. Specie would have allowed the department to buy advantageously almost anywhere, but it did not even have adequate Confederate money, and suppliers and contractors resisted taking bonds. Inflationary forces, compounded by price gouging, profiteering, and hoarding, quickly emptied Commissary coffers and frequently priced products out of the army's reach. After the Subsistence Department endured an especially stressful winter in 1862–1863, the Davis administration won congressional approval in April 1863 for an ingenious tax-in-kind, or tithe, to provide food for the armies without expending limited Commissary funds. Under closely regulated procedures, each farmer delivered to nearby depots one-tenth of his taxable field crops and hogs, the latter in the form of bacon. The tithe had mixed results: the army ended up with mostly grain and little meat; collections were substantial in the Lower South but abysmal in Virginia where they were most needed; transportation failures often crippled the program and left food to rot or to be disposed of in other ways; fraud and corruption were commonplace; and Congress enacted numerous exemptions in 1863 and 1864. Nonetheless, by spring 1864 the tax-in-kind provided enough flour and cornmeal to feed an army of 200,000 for one year, and War Department officials projected collections of half that amount during the rest of the year.

Although the tithe provided food and fodder, it was much too limited and unreliable to do more than supplement other Commissary procurement programs. Before the tax-in-kind was even adopted, the Subsistence Department turned to impressment as a broader, more flexible means of forcing the public to support the army or sell to it at reasonable prices. Impressment took place on an infrequent local basis in 1861, became widespread among all supply bureaus by 1862, and was used most frequently by the Commissary Department. Public protests against impressment, particularly of food, were intense, and the War Department attempted to quell discontent by carefully overseeing seizures and taking various steps to guard against abuse. Northrop and Ruffin also persuaded Secretary of War Seddon in December 1862 to publish a schedule of prices for provisions, forage, labor, and transportation that applied to government purchases throughout the Confederacy. Persons, businesses, and contractors who refused the set prices for goods and services faced impressment. In instituting the program, the War Department provided for various exemptions and required impressing agents to pay immediately if possible, leave enough for subsistence, and maintain proper documents.

Broadened impressment at set prices generated a public furor and forced Congress to act. Opponents argued that the prices were too low, did not account for often drastic local variations, and were implemented without congressional sanction. Moreover, impressment exacerbated the shortages it was intended to alleviate. Farmers refused to bring crops to market out of fear of impressment, which hurt civilians as well as the military. In March 1863 Virginia courts granted an injunction against the massive impressment of flour for Lee's desperate army. After extended debate, Congress passed in March and amended in April a bill to regulate impressment. The law established elaborate procedures for determining who could impress what amounts of which goods at what times and made provisions for setting equitable prices and challenging seizures. Despite its drawbacks, impressment worked reasonably well in 1863. By necessity, almost all Commissary Department procurement in 1863 took place through impressment, with the tax-in-kind providing the rest. The army and navy fairly well regulated the price and availability of manufactured goods through controls over raw materials, transportation, and labor. Those restraints were largely unavailable for regulating often-greedy and wily farmers and middlemen, however, making impressment essential.

Impressment broke down in 1864–1865 as the Confederate economy started to collapse. Even before that occurred, military abuses had provoked widespread public resentment toward the practice. The armed forces ignored regulations to impress at will and beyond need; cavalry units acting like bandits often swept down on the population to plunder as they pleased; and unscrupulous elements masquerading as impressment agents stole from the people. An outraged public, backed by local and state officials and the courts, hid supplies and refused to cooperate with commissary agents. Military force was at times used to take stores, but that was no long-term solution. Once the public collectively said no to impressing agents, there was little to be done because the legislation authorizing impressment provided for no penalties. Secretary of War Seddon requested that Congress rectify this omission; instead, Confederate legislators limited the military's impressment authority drastically in February 1864. Virtually unable to impress goods and faced with disintegrating finances, Commissary's procurement in effect shut down by the end of 1864.

Transportation plagued the Commissary Department almost as much as finances did. A shortage of wagons and draft animals reduced the flexibility of supply operations and limited the effectiveness of the tithe and even impressment. Northrop's most significant problem involved the railroads, and the difficulties increased as the Subsistence Department had to go farther south to gather supplies for the armies of Northern Virginia and Tennessee and other troops. From the outset, the railroads had resisted carrying provisions because of the heavy demands their bulk and weight placed on the system. Those conditions worsened significantly as the railroads deteriorated and the Union disrupted services and severed lines. With Grant and Sherman waging full-scale war on the South's rail lines in 1864–1865, the Commissary Department was finally unable to deliver provisions to Lee's army as it made a last stand around Richmond.

In late 1862, mounting procurement problems had led Northrop to become a principal advocate of using cotton to trade through the lines. Secretary of War Randolph, Quartermaster General Myers, in time General Lee, and others backed this initiative. The commissary general argued that Confederate needs were so great that laws and policies against trading with the enemy must be ignored. In any case, private citizens were already engaging in such exchange. Davis testily resisted the proposal, insisting that it would help rescue failing Union finances, facilitate enemy spying, demoralize citizens and soldiers, and cost the Confederacy credibility in Europe. Desperate need and constant pressure from the supply bureaus wore down the president and Secretary of War Seddon. Beginning slowly in late 1862, increasing in 1863, and hitting stride in 1864–1865, the South exchanged cotton and tobacco through the lines for food, clothing, arms, and medicine. The government regulated the trade to the degree possible through permits and contracts and squelched private, wildcat operations. A substantial part of the meat the Subsistence Department supplied to the Army of Northern Virginia came through the lines; nearly all of it did so after Wilmington fell in February 1865. In the last months of the war, the Commissary Department and other supply bureaus scrambled madly to sell cotton to the North for greenbacks or gold so that they could buy supplies from the enemy.

According to the leading authority on the subject, "Trading with the enemy was a striking instance of the Confederate government's fatal penchant for too little and too late."[11] Davis and Seddon were so ambivalent about the practice that they never pursued it vigorously, shifting the responsibility to the supply bureaus and the field commanders. Since the views of the latter varied, as did the opinions of Union commanders, the exchange always had an unpredictable quality. Many supplies came through the lines, but a more coherent policy would have secured much greater deliveries to the needy Confederate armies.

The Subsistence Department also suffered from the failure to run the blockade early and in a comprehensive manner. As with trading through the line, blockade running often provided Northrop's bureau with badly needed provisions, particularly meat, at critical times. The practice was largely left to private parties until 1863, however, when the government began taking it over. Neither system worked particularly well for the Commissary Department. Private operators were reluctant to carry bulky meat and foodstuffs, and there were not enough public vessels to bring in Commissary provisions. Late in 1864, over the strong objections of Northrop and Ruffin, Confederate agencies cut back on contracts with private shipping lines without being able to take up the slack themselves, leaving the department without vessels to bring in desperately needed meat.

Another chronic complaint of the Subsistence Department centered on the lack of support from Secretary of War Seddon. More often than not, the secretary deferred to commanding officers in the field. Hence, when Northrop ordered a cut in rations in 1862 to build up reserves, commanders ignored his order with impunity. Such practices occurred regularly.

By early 1865 Northrop and Ruffin had become so distraught over administration policies obstructing their performance that they openly criticized Davis and Seddon before Congress, and their subordinates publicly joined the rebellion. The Confederate legislators had been seeking Northrop's head for a long time. In February 1865 both the commissary general and his assistant were forced out, Isaac M. St. John replacing the former. With spirit and style, St. John brought temporary relief to Lee's hungry troops, but he could not begin to solve the department's problems at that late date.

In one sense, the Commissary Department was the most fortunate supply bureau. It dealt in food, which the South produced in ample amounts. Indeed, output increased as cotton and tobacco fields were converted. Severe food shortages arose because territorial losses and Union military advances reduced the Confederate agricultural base, especially in livestock. Nonetheless, the agrarian South proved exceptionally resilient. Despite the scorched-earth policy, Georgia resumed sending food to Virginia once Sherman's army left. Clearly the Confederacy was not flush with provisions, for in fact soldiers and some civilians nearly starved. Nevertheless, the most reliable sources indicate that throughout hostilities there was always enough food, even within reduced Confederate borders, to feed armies and the civilian population with staple crops, although not with meat. Shortages, though severe, stemmed from problems of distribution, not production. Overall, then, the major shortcomings of the Commissary Department grew from the larger failings of civilian economic mobilization. Superficially, another officer could have performed better than Northrop; fundamentally, no one could have overcome the obstacles that finally blocked the Subsistence Department.

THE ORDNANCE DEPARTMENT

The Ordnance Department, in contrast to Subsistence, surmounted enormous barriers to provide the Confederacy with a steady supply of munitions.[12] During the last half of the war, no battle was lost or offensive delayed because of a shortage of arms, ammunition, or artillery. For an industrially underdeveloped region, this was a remarkable achievement.

At the center of the department's accomplishments was the Chief of Ordnance, Josiah Gorgas. A Northern-born West Point graduate who had served in the Ordnance Bureau of the U.S. Army for twenty years, Gorgas joined the Confederacy because, among other reasons, his wife was Southern and his ambitions were unrealized. He gave little indication before 1861 of his genius for organization and production under nearly impossible circumstances, but after the war began several talents in particular surfaced. He possessed the "gift of prescience," which allowed him to anticipate the movement of the various Confederate armies and prepare in advance for their munitions requirements.[13] Moreover, he selected and directed subordinates with uncanny skill. Many of these individuals, like Gorgas himself, were atypical members of the Southern elite in that they came from the North or abroad and had business or scientific backgrounds. For example, George W. Rains, the North Carolina native who built, equipped, and supervised the famous Augusta Powder Works, was a West Point graduate who later became president of an iron works in New York. John W. Mallet, who headed the Central Ordnance Laboratory at Macon, Georgia, was born in Ireland, moved to the United States in 1853, and later became a geologist for the state of Alabama and a professor of chemistry. Caleb Huse, whom Gorgas sent to England to purchase munitions and other army supplies, was a Massachusetts-born West Point graduate and belonged to the faculty of the University of Alabama. Others of similar background, some inside the department, others outside, upon whom Ordnance depended heavily, included Isaac M. St. John, James H. Burton, Colin J. McRae, Thomas L. Bayne, and Joseph R. Anderson. To staff his department in general and to determine promotions, Gorgas relied on a system of demanding written examinations.

The Ordnance Department did not have the pyramid structure used in whole or in part by the Subsistence and Quartermaster departments. Instead, over twenty arsenals, armories, powder mills, laboratories, and other centers reported directly to the chief of ordnance and his substantial staff in Richmond. At first, Gorgas personally oversaw most of the department's affairs, but in time he appointed subordinates and created subdivisions to help with the overwhelming workload. By August 1864 the chief of ordnance went one step further by dividing departmental functions among a relatively few deputies with himself acting as general supervisor. Gorgas had the ability to treat with the most mundane details while not losing sight of the larger issues. No ideas, proposals, or plans coming from below were ever ignored. Thus he ran a well-managed department that was also viable, flexible, and imaginative.

Beginning in mid-1863 Gorgas began decentralizing his organization after the major defeats at Gettysburg, Vicksburg, and elsewhere, the continued Union advances, and the increasing breakdown of the railroads and other transportation. He made the trans-Mississippi area independent and granted increasing latitude to the arsenals, depots, and laboratories, so that by the war's end most Ordnance facilities were operating on their own. Furthermore, almost from the beginning of the war until the end, the department constantly moved or tried to move facilities and the limited supply of munitions machinery to avoid Union advances. Despite extreme circumstances, Ordnance functioned well until surrender, a genuine tribute to its chief.

The Ordnance Department faced greater challenges than any other supply bureau. The South lacked sufficient facilities, raw materials, and trained personnel to mass-produce munitions. To supply the Confederate armies with the tools of war, Gorgas and his lieutenants had to built an extensive industrial plant from scratch and acquire many weapons and great quantities of raw materials from the enemy and abroad.

Gorgas wisely left to the secretary of war and others the task of persuading the states to give up their supply of arms while he concentrated on distributing armaments and expanding supply. Ultimately, Ordnance had three centers for the public production of muskets and rifles: the Richmond Armory, Arsenal, and Laboratory (the old Virginia Manufactory of Arms), the Fayetteville Arsenal and Armory, and the Asheville Armory, the last never producing in great quantity. Using machinery from the Harpers Ferry Arsenal, Richmond and Fayetteville became the major sources of shoulder arms manufactured in the Confederacy. A new arsenal in Macon, Georgia, did not commence production before hostilities ceased. The Ordnance Department also contracted with private arms makers, such as Cook and Brother of New Orleans and Athens, Georgia. As a rule, established firms performed better than new ones. It is difficult to determine exactly how many small arms the South produced since statistics are scanty and contradictory. Gorgas reported a rate of production of 35,000 weapons annually in 1863 and 20,000 in 1864, with the arsenals accounting for three-quarters of the total. If these numbers are correct, domestic output could not have exceeded 100,000 during the course of the war.

Battlefield captures were very high. Ordnance strove to retrieve all Northern weapons after each battle in 1861 and 1862. Between July 1861 and January 1863, the Confederacy claimed over 160,000 captured weapons, and the total probably reached 200,000 before hostilities ceased. Armories, arsenals, and depots throughout the South repaired, modified, and serviced small arms, which maximized the utility of battlefield captures.

Most of the South's shoulder arms were coveted Enfield rifles run through the blockade. The Ordnance Department imported about 330,000, and state and private parties brought in an additional 270,000, totaling about 600,000, approximately two-thirds of the Confederacy's small arms. Imports saved the South in winter 1861–1862, after the initial stock of weapons was exhausted and domestic production had not yet taken hold. Thereafter, blockade running delivered small arms to Ordnance on a fairly regular basis until the very last phases of the war. By fall 1862 Gorgas was regularly meeting all requisitions for shoulder arms. Although denied the luxury of ample reserves, the chief of ordnance managed to replace within months the 75,000 small arms lost at Gettysburg, Vicksburg, and elsewhere in 1863.

Small arms other than rifles presented the Ordnance Department with fewer problems. Pistols and revolvers were manufactured by public arsenals and private firms and imported as well; the same was true for swords, sabers, and bayonets. Ordnance often had to take over faltering private firms when their output of weapons was deemed essential.

Procuring artillery did not present extraordinary problems for the Confederacy either. Even after heavy losses of ordnance in 1863, Gorgas reported at the end of the year that the armies east of the Mississippi had artillery equal to that of the Union. Although some cannons were imported, the supply was principally domestic. The South took possession of a treasure trove of heavy ordnance at the numerous evacuated federal forts and armories, including at least 1,700 pieces of artillery along with ammunition, gun carriages, implements, and the like. Home production expanded this inventory. The Tredegar Iron Works in Richmond remained the Confederacy's basic source for big guns throughout the war. It was the only firm able to cast heavy siege and seacoast weapons reliably until the Bellona Foundry came back into production in 1862 and the Selma Arsenal and Naval Foundry began operating in Alabama in 1863. The Etowah Iron Works in Georgia and several firms in New Orleans had limited success in fulfilling contracts for heavy ordnance awarded in 1861. Field artillery was easier to manufacture. The Ordnance Department produced field guns at arsenals in Augusta and Macon, Georgia, and also successfully contracted for them with small foundries in Georgia, Alabama, Mississippi, Tennessee, Louisiana, South Carolina, and Virginia. Tredegar nonetheless produced many times more than the combined output of these facilities and led in modernizing ordnance. The combination of private and public establishments also met the Confederacy's needs for mortars, gun carriages, caissons, and battery wagons.

Once Ordnance was able to provide adequate small arms and artillery, it had ample facilities for producing ammunition as long as powder and other necessary ingredients were available. By 1863 the Ordnance Department had twelve arsenals making cartridges and a large number of facilities manufacturing shot, shells, artillery projectiles, time fuses, rockets, and the like. Ammunition was also imported and private companies did some manufacturing, but most of the supply came from Ordnance. Issues of ammunition were at times rationed to conserve stock, but that did not materially affect the outcome of any battle.

The Confederacy began hostilities with almost no facilities for producing gunpowder but developed ample capacity, a spectacular accomplishment that took place under the direction of Colonel Rains. He relied on the limited output of small powder mills scattered throughout the South while he designed, built, and equipped in Augusta, Georgia, between September 1861 and April 1862 the largest and most modern gunpowder plant in North America. Rains drew upon all his ingenuity and the Confederacy's industrial capacity to acquire and manufacture the machinery for this extraordinary plant, which had an assembly line two miles long. In three years, the plant manufactured 2.75 million pounds of gunpowder, costing about $1.08 a pound; another 2.7 million pounds were imported at $3.00 a pound. Output at Augusta was supplemented by the navy's gunpowder factory at Columbia, South Carolina, and by private plants at Raleigh, North Carolina, and elsewhere. Once in full operation, the Augusta Powder Works met all demand as long as the inputs of production were available.

Acquisition of niter, or saltpeter, posed the major problem for making gunpowder. Ultimately, 2.25 million pounds were imported, equaling two-thirds of Confederate wartime consumption. The remainder had to be acquired in the South. To secure domestic output, Congress in April 1862 created a Niter Corps within the Ordnance Department, which Major St. John headed. The corps began by surveying and exploiting niter caves in the Upper South. When Union troops advanced into those areas, the corps turned to known caves in the Lower South, hunted out new ones, arranged imports from Mexico, and created artificial niter beds throughout the South. St. John's agency at first depended on private contractors; when they proved inefficient, it took over the operations and used army details to good effect. Through diligent efforts, the corps kept the Augusta Powder Works and other facilities supplied with saltpeter throughout the war.

The Niter Corps performed so well that Congress in April 1863 made it a separate War Department entity called the Niter and Mining Bureau and gave it responsibility for lead, copper, coal, and iron ore in addition to niter. The new bureau also oversaw all War Department contracts for iron and determined priorities for its use. These materials were critically important for munitions output and in short supply. Lead shortages constantly menaced the Confederacy. Supplies came principally from mines in Wytheville, Virginia, which could produce in excess of 60,000 pounds a month, but bad weather and shortages of experienced foremen and workers often interrupted output. Early in the war, the trans-Mississippi area and a mine in North Carolina also contributed to supply. To increase lead stocks, the Niter and Mining Bureau gleaned battlefields, tore up storm drains, and collected window weights and the like, producing another 5.3 million pounds. An additional 2 million pounds came in through the blockade despite some difficulties beginning in 1862. Despite intense efforts, lead supplies remained low, periodically forcing arsenals onto quotas and restricting the amount of ammunition issued to the troops.

The Confederacy initially appeared well supplied with copper. Mines at Ducktown, Tennessee, produced ample amounts, accounting for 90 percent of Southern output. Gorgas uncharacteristically took this production for granted, and when the mines came under federal control in November 1863 the South faced a crisis. Very little copper could be imported. As a result, metal came primarily from the Niter and Mining Bureau's impressing turpentine and apple-brandy stills in North Carolina and sugar-boiling kettles in Louisiana. To conserve copper, Ordnance restricted the use of percussion caps and stopped producing the favored bronze Napoleon cannon.

A shortage of iron constituted the most serious weakness in the Confederacy's entire economic mobilization program. The greatest problem was the lack of capacity for making pig and gun iron rather than a lack of iron-processing facilities. Throughout the war, the Tredegar Iron Works never had one-third of the iron needed to operate at full capacity. In that facility and elsewhere, shortages of iron forced repeated halts and cutbacks in the production of cannons, armor, and small arms. Iron was also denied to the Southern railroads.

The Niter and Mining Bureau attempted to increase the output of pig and gun iron by taking over and running facilities such as the Brierfield Furnace in

Alabama and by purchasing failing iron firms in order to acquire their machinery and equipment. Nonetheless, raising iron output was an uphill struggle. In 1860 most Southern iron production took place in the border states and the Upper South, particularly in Kentucky, Tennessee, Maryland, Missouri, and the area that became West Virginia. To compensate for the lost output of these areas, the Confederacy shifted production to the Lower South, especially to Georgia and Alabama. In 1860 both states were just starting to make and process iron, Georgia with the Etowah Iron Works and Alabama with the Shelby Iron Works. The capacity at these facilities grew substantially during the war so that Alabama in time produced four times as much iron as Virginia. Yet transportation difficulties and the demand for iron from arsenals, armories, laboratories, and the like in the Lower South prevented any of this metal from reaching the Tredegar Iron Works. At the same time, precious little iron came from Georgia, the Carolinas, or the Confederate-occupied border and Upper South states. Desperately seeking to increase the supply of iron, Tredegar bought and attempted to revive production in many of the defunct charcoal iron furnaces in the area surrounding it, but the venture was unsuccessful.

Though on paper the South had many iron foundries and forges, most were primitive. Even in the advanced iron areas, technology tended to be a full generation behind the North with overall production declining, not increasing, when war broke out. With an adequate supply of iron, a major sinew of an industrial economy, the South would have had a better chance of winning independence. Greater iron output and an efficient system for distributing it could have enabled the Confederacy to maintain its economic infrastructure, especially the railroads, and thereby keep up a level of logistical support sufficient to hold off the Union. Rather typically, however, the Davis administration set up the wrong system for handling iron.

The administration turned to a bureau of the War Department—a claimant agency—for increasing iron output and prioritizing distribution when a superior and neutral department was essential. St. John and his Niter and Mining Bureau naturally operated for the benefit of the army while slighting the interests of the navy, according to that service, and certainly cutting out the railroads and other civilian users. This bias thwarted balanced economic mobilization policies.

The War Department also contributed to the iron shortfall by resisting exemptions for iron workers and opposing detailing soldiers to take their place. Similarly, it obstructed measures to maintain a qualified labor force in the iron-fabricating industries. Indeed, next to the shortage of pig and gun iron, the shortage of trained managers, mechanics, and workers most retarded the manufacture of iron products, including munitions. Because of the technical nature of its products, Ordnance suffered more than other bureaus from the lack of trained labor.

To encourage private production of niter, small arms, coal, iron, and other war materials, Congress in April 1862 and after began a program of subsidies and regulations. Richmond could advance to contractors 50 percent of start-up costs and one-third the value of anticipated output. In exchange, contractors guaranteed delivery of all munitions and two-thirds of any other production to the military. The Confederacy limited profits on such contracts to 75 percent (later 33.3 percent) and introduced measures to avoid the pitfalls of cost-plus contracting. Policies were enforced through controls over raw materials, manpower, and transportation. The amount of additional capacity these programs produced is difficult to establish.

Overall, the Ordnance Department and the affiliated Niter and Mining Bureau achieved an excellent record during the Civil War. The department was slow to get under way because of the long lead time essential to produce weapons. The delay induced Gen. Daniel H. Hill in April 1862 to charge Ordnance with treachery because it was staffed with so many Northerners. By the beginning of 1863, however, the Ordnance Department had clearly become the outstanding supply bureau.

Undoubtedly this excellent record resulted largely from the leadership of Gorgas and the assistants he recruited and directed, but another factor must be considered. Ordnance, compared with the Subsistence and Quartermaster departments, became the favored supply bureau and had first priority on budgets, transportation, supplies, and manpower. Richard D. Goff proposes that the more direct control a supply agency had over its operations, without interference from other bureaus and civilian administrations, the better it met its responsibilities. No War Department bureau had more independence than Ordnance; next in line was the Quartermaster Department, and the Subsistence Department came last. The quality of performance of the three supply bureaus followed exactly that order. In any case, there is a special irony in the fact that Lee's troops, who were fighting to preserve the prerogatives of an agrarian society, ended up with guns and ammunition but not always with enough food.

THE MEDICAL DEPARTMENT

Among the other War Department bureaus, only the Corps of Engineers and the Medical Department played a substantial role in supply. The Corps of Engineers was a small bureau that acquired limited quantities of fairly standard supplies and equipment to carry out its duties in construction and maintenance.

The Medical Department's operations were diminutive compared to the three principal supply bureaus, but it had quite specialized needs.[14] General Samuel P. Moore served as surgeon general for almost the entire war and directed over 3,200 medical officers. Moore and his core of officers had served for years in the U.S. Army Medical Department. He was a well-qualified physician and an excellent, innovative administrator, although autocratic and rather rigid. The department proved as ingenious in supply as Ordnance, acquiring drugs, medication, and supplies in the South, through the lines, and from abroad. It created many laboratories to make and test drugs and distilled and bought vast amounts of whiskey for medicinal purposes.

The department advanced from housing the sick and wounded in homes and vacant buildings in 1861 to caring for them by 1864 in 154 permanent hospitals. The outstanding facility was the Chimborazo complex in Richmond, consisting of 150 buildings organized on the one-story hut or pavilion principle and handling over 8,000 patients, making it one of the largest hospitals in the world. The Medical Department realized these accomplishments without the prodding of a private group like the Sanitary Commission in the North and with an organization designed to accommodate and encourage the participation of the states. Until 1864–1865, when the transportation system began to break down, the Medical Department seems to have had reasonably adequate supplies of medicine and other stores and to have suffered chronic shortages only in surgical instruments and equipment.

Although perhaps three-quarters of Confederate deaths resulted from diseases rather than from battlefield wounds, overall the South had a better mortality rate than other nineteenth-century armies except the Union. In cases where commanding officers enforced proper sanitation and preventative health measures, as occurred in the Army of Northern Virginia, the loss of men to disease was minimized. In general, Moore and his assistants compiled an enviable wartime record under exceptionally demanding circumstances.

BLOCKADE RUNNING

Since nearly all supply bureaus were heavily dependent on imports, blockade running took on ever-greater significance as the war progressed. The operation required agents in Great Britain, on the Continent, and in the West Indies to handle procurement, financing, shipping, and Southern exports.[15] Despite the critical importance of this exchange, the Confederacy allowed it to grow without centralized direction, remain largely in private hands, and become increasingly inefficient until nearly the last year of hostilities.

The South carried out most foreign purchasing in Great Britain. The earliest and most active buyer was Captain Huse, whom Chief of Ordnance Gorgas sent to London in May 1861. Although he concentrated on ordnance supplies, Huse procured for the entire War Department, operating basically through the English purchasing house of S. Isaac, Campbell and Company. Following Huse by a few weeks was the navy captain (later commander) James D. Bulloch, who was after ships of war. In December 1862 the Quartermaster Department sent Maj. J. B. Ferguson, a former merchant, as its representative. About the same time, Capt. William G. Crenshaw, a well-known Richmond merchant, parlayed an informal agreement with Secretary of War Seddon into a partnership with the London shipowner Alexander Collie and his company in which the firm would buy and ship goods for the South, with Richmond assuming most of the cost and risk.

Crenshaw's attempts to force out Huse led Seddon to divide the purchasing duties so that Crenshaw handled quartermaster and subsistence supplies while Huse focused on ordnance and medical goods. Numerous other temporary and permanent government agents purchased for the Confederacy; in addition, a host of state and private firms from the Confederacy and Britain and some free-lancing speculators contracted to buy and deliver goods to the South. All the buyers tended to compete with one another for supplies, facilities, ships, and manpower.

Finances in Great Britain were handled principally by John Fraser and Company of Charleston, the South's largest trading company, and the related firms of Trenholm Brothers in New York and Fraser, Trenholm and Company in Liverpool. George A. Trenholm, among the South's most wealthy and influential individuals, directed the three companies. Richmond deposited specie or bonds with the Charleston firm, and the Liverpool office issued letters of credit to the South's purchasing agents. The South also sent its agents bills of exchange.

The Confederacy's undeveloped financial system and low level of specie reserves sharply limited the efficacy of this approach. Yet it allowed the South to buy abroad while continuing to embargo cotton exports to Great Britain and the Continent, a policy designed to force Europe to join the Confederacy in the war. By late 1862, however, King Cotton diplomacy and Confederate international finances had failed. Foreign intervention was highly unlikely, and purchasing in Great Britain came to a standstill because the South ran out of specie and paper was no longer viable. Late in 1862, Huse had spent $5 million and received only $3 million from Richmond, with Isaac, Campbell and Company covering the rest but balking at further credit. Fraser, Trenholm and Company was also unable to help. All other agents faced similar circumstances. Continued buying abroad required that the Confederacy sell cotton.

Prominent Southerners advocated using cotton for financial rather than for diplomatic purposes before war broke out. Policies for hypothecating cotton—marketing certificates or bonds with cotton as collateral—were gradually and rather casually worked out between mid-1862 and early 1863 by the Navy, State, and Treasury departments in conjunction with Fraser, Trenholm and Company and other British financial houses. With a growing cotton shortage in Europe and the price of the commodity rising, this action was well received. It led in March 1863 to a $15-million loan based on cotton from the German and French banking house of Emile Erlanger, which netted the Confederacy about $8.5 million.

The general practice of hypothecating cotton and the Erlanger loan regenerated Confederate buying power. Yet the South's international finances, like its foreign buying practices, proceeded in a disorderly manner. A number of Confederate executive departments, various procurement agents, Fraser, Trenholm and Company, Erlanger, and several British banking houses played a role in the business and at times competed with each other.

The actual blockade running was also disorganized. The South had neither a navy to transport goods nor an established merchant marine to use or to take over. Consequently, the Davis administration turned to private firms, many of which were foreign. Trenholm-controlled firms proved to be the principal shippers for the Confederacy in addition to their role in financing the trade. With the outbreak of hostilities, the three Trenholm companies shut down peacetime operations to prepare for possible blockade running. Hence, in July 1861 when Huse and others had difficulty finding ships to transport supplies to the South, Fraser, Trenholm and Company stepped in, providing the first steamer to run the Union blockade in August–September 1861.

Thereafter, cargoes seldom moved directly between Britain or the Continent and the South. Instead, large steamers or sailing ships carried freight to the West Indies ports of Nassau, Bermuda, and Havana, and even Halifax, Nova Scotia. From there, light-draft steamers of increasingly specialized design carried goods to accessible Southern ports. British, Canadian, Cuban, Confederate, and even Union nationals entered this trade with operations ranging from single ships to fleets directed by stock companies. Not all blockade runners or even most succeeded, but substantial profits rewarded those who did. And no company outshone the Trenholm firms. Between 1861 and 1863 their ships carried more munitions and supplies to the West Indies and on to the Confederacy than any other single company. Indeed, at Nassau, their preferred port for transshipments, Trenholm and associates had their own agent. He and a representative of the brokerage firm of Henry Adderley and Company worked so closely with the War Department's special agent in handling blockade running that private and public interests became inextricably combined.

Shipping and blockade running by private firms involved many disadvantages. First, a combination of risk, desperate need, and business realities led carriers to charge exorbitant rates. Second, shipowners rejected military cargoes for luxury items in high demand and often refused to carry explosives and bulky or heavy items such as food and iron. Third, captains chose ports of entry, disregarding Southern priorities. Hence, centers such as Charleston became swamped while ports such as Mobile languished. Fourth, no inducements were enough to acquire adequate stowage for carrying in requisite supplies and carrying out sufficient cotton. Finally, quality of service, including reliability, the nature of the vessels, and the competence of captain and crew, was unpredictable and varied from first-rate to abysmal. Confederate firms were more dependable and patriotic than foreign ones, if only because their future was tied to that of the South. In short, blockade running through private enterprise left the South intolerably vulnerable, a condition that was fully evident at the end of 1862. In Nassau, the center of blockade running in the West Indies, the War Department agent was able to move only half the munitions and stores piled up in warehouses.

By early 1863 the entire Confederate supply program abroad reached the point of collapse. Despite repeated pleas for change, the Davis administration held back until it faced a genuine threat of foreign supplies being cut off in mid-to-late 1863. With the disasters of Gettysburg and Vicksburg escalating demand and the Union tightening its deadly economic grip, the administration had to devise more effective policies.

The first step came in September 1863 when Richmond appointed Colin J. McRae to direct finances and procurement centrally in Great Britain. McRae had traveled to Europe in April 1863 to manage the Erlanger loan and to investigate buying practices. Learning how basically chaotic Southern operations were, he took control of most Confederate finances from Fraser, Trenholm and Company and distributed funds by priority among the purchasing agents. Moreover, he clarified lines of authority among the various Confederate departments and bureaus, essentially limiting them to negotiating contracts and purchasing supplies subject to his review. McRae quickly brought efficiency to the South's overseas financing, buying, and shipping.

Even before McRae instituted reforms in Britain, Richmond began taking over blockade running. In August 1863 the secretary of war ordered private shippers to reserve half their outgoing cargo space and a like amount of incoming stowage for the government or face impressment. Richmond's involvement in blockade running actually predated the shift in policy, the Ordnance Department proving characteristically innovative in this regard. Gorgas never favored a role for private contractors in blockade running. In late 1862 and early 1863, he purchased five British-built steamers to run supplies from the Bermuda port of St. George to Wilmington. On the return trip, the vessels carried cotton to strengthen the bureau's purchasing power in Europe. Huse continued to handle Ordnance purchases in Great Britain; a military-business team was assembled in St. George; and Maj. Thomas L. Bayne, Gorgas's brother-in-law and a New Orleans attorney, headed operations in Wilmington, which included the purchase and shipment of cotton. The Ordnance steamers were among the best blockade runners, carrying in nearly 100,000 weapons, vast amounts of ammunition, and tons of other goods for the department. In the last months of 1863, though, all fell victim to the Union blockade.

Following the pattern that Gorgas had created for the Ordnance Department in 1862–1863, the Davis administration began setting up a system for the entire Confederacy in 1864–1865. Since Seddon's order of August 1863 lacked clear legal force and the need for foreign supplies continued to mount, Congress passed two laws in February and March 1864 that increased the administration's authority in foreign trade. The president was given unlimited control over the export of cotton and other products; importing nonessentials was severely limited; and all ships were brought under Confederate regulation, with most required to offer half or more of their stowage to Richmond at a set rate. Bayne took charge of a newly created Bureau of Foreign Supplies in the War Department for administering the program. The bureau ultimately placed agents at every major port to enforce regulations. Moreover, all government purchasing of cotton was centered in Bayne's office to halt the conflicting efforts of military and other agencies that had proliferated since 1861. Working with McRae abroad, Bayne rationalized foreign trade in short order. He increased the volume and lowered the cost of imports and exported more cotton under a system in which Richmond received up to four times the income it had collected when working with private parties.

With increased buying power and strengthened credit, the Confederacy took the next logical step of acquiring a fleet of blockade runners. McRae opened negotiations in April 1864 and over several months worked out agreements with Fraser, Trenholm and Company and the banking house of John K. Gilliat and Company for the purchase or construction of fourteen of the most advanced blockade runners. The deals stipulated that the South would use cotton exports to pay for the vessels and eventually take full control of them. In the interim, the Confederacy offered long- and short-term contracts to domestic and foreign firms under the new regulations. For a time, it was able to hire the services of more ships than ever before. Six of the ships McRae ordered were in service at the time of surrender, three more were en route, and the others were still under construction.

Centralized control of foreign trade and blockade running was strengthened in July 1864 when Trenholm took over from Christopher G. Memminger as secretary of the treasury. Trenholm's firms had been involved in all aspects of foreign trade from the outset, and he was probably more knowledgeable about shipping and financing than anyone else in the Confederacy. The Trenholm-dominated companies in Charleston and Liverpool profited handsomely from hostilities. Nonetheless, Trenholm and his associates always aided the South when possible and sacrificed profits at times to advance the cause.

The new secretary of the treasury probably helped Richmond face down opposition to the revamped export-import policies from private shippers and, more important, from the states, particularly North Carolina and Georgia. As long as a blockade runner was owned and operated by a state, as was the case with North Carolina between 1863 and 1864, the Confederate government exempted it from regulation; but once the Tarheel State and other states sold to or bought from private parties an interest in a blockade runner, that vessel was subject to Confederate regulation. Despite threats, appeals to other states, and even military confrontations, Richmond refused to yield to the North Carolina- and Georgia-led campaign to allow states freely to conduct export and import activities such as sovereign entities.

Despite numerous remaining weaknesses, the new system of foreign trade and finances served the South well. Between March and December 1864, Bayne shipped abroad 27,299 bales of cotton, which netted the Confederacy $5.3 million in gold. Purchases abroad and imports also reached an all-time high by the end of 1864 despite the increasing effectiveness of the Union blockade.

Nevertheless, the reforms delivered much too little, much too late. Cotton exports and blockade running never came close to meeting Confederate needs. Neither McRae nor Fraser, Trenholm and Company ever had enough funds to finance Confederate purchases; they depended upon credit, much of which was never paid off. From March to December 1864, cotton exports generated at most one-third of the foreign purchasing power anticipated by the military, and imports reached only around one-quarter of the armed services' projected requirements from abroad. Over the course of the war, Richmond realized meager returns from cotton sales. About 500,000 bales were exported during the war, but the Confederate government received the earnings on approximately 50,000 bales, 10 percent of the total. Regardless of statistics, Union advances on land and sea ultimately cut the Confederacy off from foreign suppliers. The fall of Wilmington and Charleston in January–February 1865 severed the lifeline of the South. Attempts to use the remaining Gulf ports offered no hope of genuinely aiding the foundering Confederacy.

Despite its failures, blockade running in all its phases kept the South fighting for four years. Although reliable figures are not available, imports accounted for at least half of all Southern war supplies and much more in many vital areas. A more effective program of blockade running and cotton sales should have been implemented much earlier. In 1861 the South had at least thirty steamers that could have served as the nucleus of a government-directed blockade-running fleet. The Ordnance Department's operation in 1862–1863 demonstrated what could be done. Besides the general limitations of the Davis administration, several obstacles blocked reform. King Cotton diplomacy was of major importance. Initially intended to embargo cotton, the policy was later modified to permit private firms to carry supplies into the Confederacy and cotton out to prove that the Union blockade was ineffective and hence illegal. Once that practice was under way, Benjamin, Seddon, Davis, and other Confederate leaders opposed replacing private firms with public ones. Moreover, the Navy Department, and particularly Secretary Stephen R. Mallory, was uninterested in blockade running but resisted other agencies intervening in an area the department considered to be its domain. As a result, many departments and their subdivisions became involved in blockade running instead of one agency's being in charge, producing inefficiency and confusion. Had the reforms of 1863–1864 been implemented in 1861–1862, all aspects of Confederate economic mobilization would have benefited greatly, a circumstance that might have tipped the scales in favor of Confederate independence.

SUPPLY BUREAUS, LOGISTICAL PLANNING, AND SYSTEM OF COMMAND

The army supply bureaus functioned reasonably well as individual units. Most logistical innovations during the war—such as blockade running, trading with the enemy, and reorganizing the supply agencies for greater efficiency and control—originated with the bureaus themselves rather than with the secretary of war. Toward the end of the hostilities, competition among the supply departments tended to give way to cooperation.

Several prominent Southern historians assert that the Confederacy avoided the widespread corruption that plagued mobilization in the Union.[16] Evidence does not support this judgment. Abuses may have been fewer because the South's level of economic activity was less than in the North. Otherwise, Southerners were just as prone to flout procurement regulations, maneuver for private gain, and act with raw greed.

Economic mobilization failures contributed significantly, even fundamentally, to the collapse of the Confederacy. Yet they were less the fault of the supply bureaus than of the secretaries of war and, to an even greater extent, the president. Davis and his secretaries of war failed to plan for and anticipate logistical requirements adequately. Instead, they reacted to emergencies as they arose, instituting half-measures, as with the railroads and trading with the enemy, or acting too late, as with blockade running. Moreover, they often did not keep the supply chiefs informed of military operations and troop movements.

By failing to plan for and coordinate operations of the supply bureaus effectively, Davis and Seddon put the South at a great disadvantage. It was the weaker adversary in a nearly unlimited war. Because of its constantly increasing strength, the Union could improvise and make repeated mistakes, a luxury the Confederacy did not have. Its continually diminishing economic resources had to be marshaled carefully and used with maximum effect from the outset. Since its leaders lacked such foresight, the South's drive for independence was badly weakened, if not doomed.

The failure of logistical planning grew out of inadequacies in the Confederacy's strategic planning and command system.[17] Basically, the South had no overall strategy. Davis and his generals allowed circumstances to force them into a defensive posture punctuated by three major offensive drives. Otherwise, the Confederacy responded to the Union's Anaconda Policy—enveloping the South and then strangling it by closing the military ring—as best it could. Victory for the South in these circumstances meant not losing. That feat required maximum flexibility and the ability to concentrate forces rapidly, capabilities the Confederacy never achieved in sufficient measure. Furthermore, Davis, without a formal decision, focused Confederate strength around Lee's Army of Northern Virginia in the East and neglected the West.

A sound command system would have facilitated strategic planning. Unlike the North's, the South's command structure never matured. Davis acted as his own general-in-chief, operating through the traditional American geographic departmental system with all commanders reporting directly to him. Though fundamentally sound, this approach became rigid without a structure for coordinating the geographic departments and transferring men and supplies among them with ease. No single person could oversee all Confederate ground forces, but Davis, with some modifications, tried to do so. The president had assistants, but they were ineffectively used. The secretaries of war fairly well restricted themselves to bureau management. Davis had intended the adjutant and inspector general to act as his chief of staff, but Gen. Samuel Cooper was capable of being little more than an office manager, and the president never replaced him. Instead, he selected Lee in 1862 and Braxton Bragg in 1864 to act as his principal military advisers.

Furthermore, at the urging of Seddon, Davis experimented in the West with a theater organization, appointing Joseph E. Johnston as commander in 1862 and P. G. T. Beauregard in 1864. Both men failed because they lacked initiative and perhaps authority. None of these expedients provided the overall system of command that the widely dispersed Confederate armies required, a weakness exaggerated manyfold by Davis's indecision, supersensitivity about prerogatives, and excessive involvement in detail.

Congress seldom asserted itself in military affairs, but it was interested in redressing the shortfall in command and planning by creating a general staff. Moreover, it passed legislation in 1862 and 1865 to create a commanding general for the Confederate armies. Davis opposed the congressional initiatives, vetoed legislation in 1862 and 1863 on the matter, and worked out a compromise with Congress in 1865 nominally to appoint Lee as general-in-chief. Lee could not have had much impact had he actually filled the office at that late date. Even if he had taken office earlier, he might not have been able to apply his strategic brilliance beyond the theater level. Nonetheless, if the Confederacy had achieved in the West the successes that Lee accomplished in Virginia, the South might have attained its independence. Such an accomplishment required planning and command of the highest caliber, goals that seemed beyond the reach of Davis and his military commanders.

MANPOWER MOBILIZATION

The Confederacy surpassed the Union in mobilizing manpower.[18] Before the conflict was over, it had tapped almost the entire population of white males between eighteen and forty-five for military or related service. This was a remarkable achievement, "never before matched in American history and seldom equaled in any nation."[19] Nonetheless, the South was unable to retain the manpower it mobilized. As early as 1863, at least half the enrolled troops were not present-for-duty, having left the service without authorization or deserted. This incredibly high absentee rate grew out of the collapsing war effort, class conflict, and Confederate-state tensions and left the Southern armies starved for troops. The weakness of general mobilization policies thus eroded manpower mobilization, which was efficient.

Between February 1861 and January 1862, Congress passed a crazy quilt of laws for raising a provisional or voluntary army of 400,000 troops. Men served anywhere from six months to the war's duration and could enter service as Confederate volunteers or as members of state militia. Not only was this approach unworkable, but it also threatened the South early in 1862 with losing veteran soldiers who had enlisted for twelve months.

By that time considerable support existed for conscripting troops. Davis called for legislation in March 1862, and Congress in April passed the first national conscription law in American history. It obligated all white males between eighteen and thirty-five to three years of service, less if the war ended sooner. Those already in the provisional army had to remain there to fulfill a compulsory term of service, and conscripts could provide a substitute from the ranks of those not obliged to serve. The conscription was a selective service system rather than a universal draft, since Congress quickly allowed exemptions based on health, profession, and occupation. In October 1862 the practice was extended and included exemptions for overseers on a plantation or a combination of plantations with twenty or more slaves. Controversy over this provision resulted in changes making it more stringent.

In September 1862 the age limit for conscription was raised from thirty-five to forty-five; and in February 1864 it was broadened to include all white men between seventeen and fifty, with those younger than eighteen and over forty-five designated as a reserve corps for detail duty and emergency military service within their states. The 1864 act also radically restricted exemptions, allowed the president to detail troops or conscripts for industrial or agricultural duty, and changed the military obligation from three years or less to the duration of the war, keeping in the army numerous troops who would otherwise have completed their service in early 1864. In December 1863 and January 1864, Congress also abolished the policy of substitutes and provided for conscripting those persons who had benefited from the practice. Late in 1864 Davis requested legislators to extend even further his authority over manpower. In no mood for accommodating the president, Congress in March 1865 reduced somewhat Davis's power in the area. The last act to expand the manpower pool came in March 1865 when, after long and agonizing deliberation, Congress voted to allow the president to arm and accept slaves into military service.

Conscription was initially carried out by the Adjutant and Inspector General's Office. Then in December 1862, the War Department created a separate Conscript Bureau, which reached down to the county level and was staffed by thousands of Confederate and state militia officials. In 1863 generals Bragg and Johnston set up their own conscription bureaus for the Army of Tennessee and the Department of the West, and in the trans-Mississippi area military commanders always handled the draft.

Conscription in the Confederacy has been vilified by contemporaries and historians as corrupt, lenient, abusive, run by incompetents, and resembling impressment gangs. Results indicate otherwise. The overall performance of selective service appears to have been quite good despite an expectable level of confusion and malfeasance. Two notable advantages of the system included bypassing states to centralize power under the Confederate government and assigning conscripts to fill up skeleton companies instead of creating new ones. The efficiency of the latter practice was hampered by the requirement that draftees serve in units from their home state. Despite its success, this approach was changed at the war's end. Quarreling with Davis over manpower policies, Congress in March 1865 abolished the Conscript Bureau and turned its duties over to the generals directing the state reserves.

Conscription was a troubled practice in the South. Substitution, exemption, physical requirements, and even detailing were subject to constant abuse. Although most states cooperated with Richmond in raising troops, they had reservations about enhancing Confederate power at the states' expense. Some governors, such as Brown of Georgia and Vance of North Carolina, actively opposed conscription and obstructed its enforcement, particularly by using the powers of exemption granted to public officials. Class tensions posed the greatest threat to the Confederate draft. The middle and upper classes primarily benefited from substitution and exemption, which created antagonism among the lower classes and especially among the people from the nonslave-holding, yeoman regions. They particularly resented the so-called twenty-slave law and the slow pace at which the planter elite yielded its privileges compared to the sacrifices that were demanded of the general population. The common man increasingly walked away from the war by deserting and by creating whole sections in the South that were beyond the reach of law and especially off-limits to those people seeking to return deserters or to enforce the draft. From early 1863, the Confederate armies had absentee rates that exceeded 50 percent. Conscription may have kept up with these unauthorized absences until the last months of the war, but it could not stay ahead of them.

Despite its weaknesses, conscription provided soldiers. The states could not or would not raise the necessary number of troops. The draft kept the Army of Northern Virginia intact for Lee's brilliant campaigns of 1862 and allowed the South to continue fighting thereafter. Scholars disagree over how many fought in Southern armies, with estimates ranging from 600,000 to 1.1 million, and on how many men the draft produced directly, with figures running from 82,000 to 300,000. Most authorities agree on two points: conscription acted as an indispensable spur to volunteering, and the South approached the limits in mobilizing its white, male, military-aged population. Thus, despite the problem of retention, Confederate troop mobilization was an extraordinary success.

Several reasons explain the Confederacy's effective mobilization of troops. Outnumbered nearly four to one by the North in manpower potential, the South had to be much more efficient than its adversary in order to survive. And since the South lacked the wealth to buy recruits with bounties, it had to be more coercive. Moreover, unlike in the North, the prewar militia system was alive and well in many Southern states, giving a certain familiarity, even legitimacy, to the idea of obligatory military service. Furthermore, as a West Pointer and former secretary of war, Davis knew the benefits of centralized, compulsory military service. Once convinced of its necessity, he supported the draft and worked to extend it. Ultimately, perhaps because of the slavery system and the manipulation of the lower-class whites that the institution entailed, the South was better able centrally to manage human beings than economic resources.

The importance of conscription extended beyond manpower: it touched on some of the most volatile issues in Southern society, including Confederate-state relations, habeas corpus, and slavery. Formidable powers of economic regulation were also involved, including exempting workers and detailing soldiers, limiting prices and profits, and forcing sales to Richmond.

The Confederacy's conscription experience is instructive. Thomas B. Alexander and Richard E. Beringer in studying Congress observe that "a man's position on conscription was one of the best indices of his support for the Confederate cause."[20] By that measure, the legislators stood strongly behind the war effort. From March 1862 through mid-1864, Congress never turned down Davis's requests for a progressively more rigorous draft. Only at the end did it hand the president a significant defeat in the area. This record strongly suggests that Congress would have supported proposals to strengthen other aspects of economic mobilization. The failure adequately to harness the Confederate economy stems more from the limitations of executive leadership than from obstruction by Congress.

Once the South assembled armies, officer selection and training did not differ much from the North. Davis selected all general officers, who were usually West Pointers. Below the general officer level, Confederate military efficiency was handicapped by state appointments of field-grade officers, election of company officers by enlisted men, and promotion by seniority, practices that were not fully excluded until the last months of fighting. In the meantime, without formal officer-training programs, the uninitiated learned their duties from experience and available literature. Enlisted men also were trained principally in the ranks and through combat experience. More revealing than any differences in training was the fact that at the war's end, the Confederacy had fewer than 150,000 troops present-for-duty compared to nearly 625,000 for the Union.

THE NAVY DEPARTMENT

Although not as important as the army, the navy was significant, both for what it did and did not do.[21] Stephen R. Mallory served as secretary of the navy throughout the war. A transplanted Northerner, Mallory was an attorney, businessman, and politician in Florida. He had been elected to the Senate in 1852 and ultimately chaired the Naval Affairs Committee. Davis chose him because of his experience and his Florida background, over the objection of those in and outside the state who doubted his commitment to secession.

The navy suffered a number of personnel problems. It had an excess of senior officers because over 100 officers had left the U.S. navy to join that of the Confederacy. Mallory and his aides struggled to assign them as best they could, keeping the talented and vigorous ones in the line and placing most of the older and less effective officers in administrative and logistical posts. The department also had a shortage of junior officers, which forced it to improvise. And there were never enough seamen. The service used whatever means possible to attract volunteers, but until 1864 it received little support from the president, secretary of war, or army commanders in transferring experienced men from the army to the navy. At its zenith in 1864, the navy had approximately 700 officers and 4,000 enlisted men.

Below Mallory and his two assistants were four bureaus and several semi-autonomous units. The Office of Orders and Detail handled personnel and placement and also outfitted, equipped, and supplied ships. Its chief was the principal adviser to the secretary of the navy and sat in for him during absences. Although competently run, the office was denied continuity. Seven officers served as its head, three of whom could have excelled in the position had they stayed longer. Such circulation required the secretary of the navy to devote more attention to the bureau than would otherwise have been the case.

The Office of Provisions and Clothing provided the navy with food, clothing, and miscellaneous supplies and acted as pay office and general fiscal agent. The Confederate navy followed U.S. navy practice of relying on civilian agents for most procurement. As in the army, food, clothing, and footwear were often scarce, although the navy tended to suffer less than the army because of its small size and more numerous sources of supply. At three major depots in North Carolina, Georgia, and Alabama and at various naval stations, yards, and establishments, the Office of Provisions and Clothing ground flour, baked bread, distilled whiskey, cut and sewed uniforms, manufactured rope and sail, sawed lumber, and made or processed other products. The Confederacy's perennially tight budgets and the navy's spot near the bottom of the priority list meant that sailors often went unpaid, resulting in hardship for their families. Overall, however, the bureau did a good job.

The Office of Medicine and Surgery also performed well. The bureau tended to the medical needs of the officers and men and manufactured a good part of the required medicines, in addition to paying proper attention to the diet, hygiene, and living conditions of the sailors.

The Office of Ordnance and Hydrography was the navy's outstanding bureau. Commander John M. Brooke dominated Ordnance from late 1861 until the end of hostilities. Serving first as assistant to the chief and then as chief, he was "one of the few men in the Confederate States Navy who showed genius during the Civil War."[22] Among the earliest graduates of Annapolis, Brooke quickly distinguished himself through work on the *Merrimack* and in the invention and production of the Brooke gun, rifled ordnance strengthened by banding the breech.

Although Brooke's accomplishments did not equal those of Gorgas, he did a remarkable job. Despite the South's loss of Norfolk and other valuable production centers, Ordnance still had an impressive number of facilities at Atlanta, Richmond, Selma, and elsewhere. Foundries, laboratories, and powder works produced virtually all navy munitions, including guns, gun carriages, ammunition, gunpowder, fuses, and sights. The bureau was especially resourceful in pursuing research and development, staying abreast of innovations, and converting obsolete weapons into workable ones. Navy Ordnance worked and shared information with army Ordnance and the Niter and Mining Bureau. It also dealt with private contractors, particularly the Tredegar Iron Works. Although initially dependent upon imports and the army to fulfill requirements, Ordnance largely met navy demands during the last years of the war.

The greatest difficulty the bureau faced at its various facilities was the lack of experienced artisans and the army's reluctance to help solve the problem. With serious results, the Office of Ordnance and Hydrography also neglected hydrographic duties dealing with navigational information and equipment.

Related to Ordnance was the navy's work with mines, known as torpedoes or submarine batteries during the Civil War. Introduced in 1861, these weapons were developed and manufactured under the agency that was ultimately called the Torpedo Bureau. A similar army bureau overlapped that of the navy's, but the two agencies appeared to cooperate. Commander Matthew F. Maury, founder and former chief of the U.S. Naval Observatory, was the Confederate navy's pioneer in torpedoes; however, the irascible, arrogant Maury and Secretary Mallory never worked well together. The former departed for Europe in October 1862, leaving the agency to his protégés, whom he assisted from abroad for a time before losing interest.

The Confederate arsenal included floating and submerged mines detonated by contact or electric charge and spar mines attached to rams and carried to the enemy's ships. Experiments with the latter led to the first successful use of the submarine as a ship of war. Mines proved to be the navy's most effective weapon. They destroyed as many as fifty-eight Union ships, forced the North to devote time, effort, and material defending against them, and, at times, made U.S. navy commanders overly cautious about attacking targets and patrolling Confederate shores.

Despite grossly inadequate private and public facilities and shortages of materials, experience, machinery, and skilled mechanics, the Confederate navy managed to build a remarkable number of vessels. Of the ten U.S navy yards, only Norfolk and Pensacola were located in the South, and the Confederacy made only limited use of them. Although the region also had several large, privately owned yards in New Orleans, Charleston, Savannah, and Mobile, most private yards were small, primitive operations. At the private and public yards, the navy converted, built, or contracted for a total of about 150 warships between 1861 and 1865, about 50 of which were steamers made over into gunboats. The rest were wooden gunboats or ironclads to be built from the keel up. Of the 100 such vessels started, 5 wooden and 22 armored ships were completed. The remainder were never finished due to time restraints, endless scarcities, or changed military circumstances. They were usually destroyed by retreating Confederates or advancing Union forces. Shortages were most acute in armor and steam propulsion machinery. Nonetheless, at the height of activity, the Confederate navy had almost 200 ships, including vessels that were purchased, donated by the states and other sources, or captured.

The numerous travails in shipbuilding were complicated enormously because the navy had no bureau to initiate and supervise the building of ships, thus leaving it ill-prepared to convert and construct vessels. All such activity was overseen by the secretary of the navy, who was unqualified for the job and had no talented assistant to aid him. The performance of John L. Porter, who took over as chief constructor in 1863, and of William P. Williamson, under whom the position of chief engineer evolved, illustrates the problems. At critical points, Porter provided the military with incorrect figures on the draft of the *Merrimack* and the James River squadron. Williamson's designs were often faulty, he set up no program to train officers in engineering, and he failed to inform crews about the requirements of operating and maintaining steam engines, which resulted in numerous preventable accidents and the neglect and abuse of ships' power plants. Moreover, vessels were often badly designed. The lack of coordination among the chief constructor, chief engineer, and Ordnance meant that steam propulsion and guns had to be fitted into craft after they were built. In general, Southern ironclads were grossly underpowered, nearly unmaneuverable hulks in which crews could remain for only short periods of time without threatening their health.

Mallory held off creating a construction bureau, intending to acquire most ships from abroad because of the difficulty of building them at home. Commander James D. Bulloch traveled to England in May 1861 to purchase and contract for vessels. An exceptionally capable officer, he had served in the U.S. Navy for twelve years and resigned to command mail steamers. He acquired three of the South's most famous commerce raiders, and Maury contributed one more of lesser quality. These and other Confederate vessels destroyed some 200 Union ships and prevented others from sailing or drove them to operate under a different registry. On his own and in cooperation with the army and private parties, Bulloch also had a hand in acquiring a number of blockade runners.

Captain James H. North followed Bulloch to Europe a few weeks later with the task of acquiring the latest ironclads from Britain and France. The Confederacy succeeded in having a number of these vessels built, but the Union's diligent detective work and hard-nosed diplomacy prevented the great powers from allowing such ships to leave their countries.

The Navy Department bought a wide range of munitions and supplies in Europe through a procurement apparatus that was ungainly and inefficient. Besides Bulloch, North, and Maury, most bureaus had purchasing representatives in Britain who competed with one another, the army, and private parties. Conflicts and resentments were rife among the supply agents, officers waiting for ships, diplomats, and so forth. Tensions were magnified many times because naval personnel were usually without adequate funds and the Navy Department had low priority in Confederate financing. Although Bulloch tended to direct affairs, he did so without formal authority. In August 1863 Mallory placed Flag Officer Samuel Barron in charge, but this rather easygoing officer commanded from Paris and concentrated on staffing Confederate ships. Only when McRae took over finances late in 1863 and the army centralized control in the hands of Huse did the Navy Department do likewise with Bulloch. Greater efficiency even as late as 1864–1865 had definite benefits, but the reforms came too late.

The acquisition of commerce raiders and ironclads from Europe lay at the heart of the navy's offensive strategy. By gravely disrupting Union commerce, swift ships would reduce significantly the North's ability to fight while at the same time weakening the blockade as vessels were diverted to chase the marauders. Meanwhile, ironclads would cross the ocean, destroy the remainder of the Union's blockading fleet, and then travel North to terrorize coastal cities.

These strategic aims were more fantasy than reality. Although commerce raiders wreaked havoc with Northern shipping, they in no way diminished Union trade because merchants changed registry and other countries picked up the slack. Raiding European vessels would have invited war with the very nations the South depended upon to win independence. Indeed, after decades of effort, Britain had almost succeeded in outlawing commerce raiding by 1860. As for ironclads, British firms gladly took Confederate money to build them, but Great Britain and France were not about to chance war with the North by releasing such vessels when the South's prospects for victory appeared slim. Had the ironclads managed to leave foreign ports, their chances of crossing the Atlantic were remote since they were not especially seaworthy. Had they accomplished that small miracle, the Union possessed or would have developed the capacity to handle the threat. In purchasing commerce raiders and contracting for ironclads, the navy wasted millions in dearly needed funds and misused the talents of diplomats, purchasing agents, and some of its best officers while failing to advance, and probably harming, the diplomatic ends it sought. The final legacy included little more than daring, romantic tales about commerce raiders and the intrigue of attempting to free ironclads from foreign restraints.

The Navy Department's strategic omissions were more significant than the actions it carried out. The navy never committed itself fully to blockade running. Had it done so, as advocated by Bulloch, many supply and financial problems could have been solved by bringing in goods and taking out cotton. Bulloch purchased the *Fingal*, loaded it with badly needed munitions and supplies, and sailed to Savannah in November 1861 to demonstrate the practicality of his proposal. His advocacy was initially ignored and then taken up in a desultory fashion in the last years of the conflict. Unlike the army, the navy never posted agents to the West Indies to facilitate transshipments. In 1862 Bulloch went further by pushing for an ingenious, radical, but proven method of prefabricating ships and ironclads. British-made engines, boilers, armor-plating, ordnance, and other parts would be delivered to the South by blockade runners and assembled with hulls and other wooden components constructed in the Confederacy, using identical designs on both sides of the Atlantic. This method would have allowed the Confederacy to obtain the

sought-after ships of war (and other vessels as well) without Europe technically violating principles of neutrality. Mallory did not bother to respond to
this initiative.

The Navy Department also failed to work out viable plans to protect the
Confederacy's harbors and inland waters, either alone or in conjunction with
the War Department. Indeed, throughout hostilities, the navy remained ignorant about the South's inland and coastal waters. It lacked adequate charts on
the subject and relied on former employees of the Light House and Revenue
Service and Coastal Survey and on the individuals who had experience with
river craft to act as pilots. Without their aid, navy vessels at times would have
been unable to sail safely. Mallory for a year appeared to resist using mines in
river and harbor defense and then failed to retain Maury's services because of
petty tensions. Lacking proper preparations, the Confederacy lost Forts Henry
and Donelson and ceded control of the Mississippi, New Orleans, Norfolk,
and other vital waterways and ports. In contrast, well-planned defenses allowed the Confederacy to beat back numerous Union attacks on the James
River and on Charleston Harbor. Yet because of the lack of comprehensive
naval defensive efforts, the Union was able to close one Confederate harbor
after another and gain access to the heart of the Confederacy via the South's
superb river system.

Of course, Mallory was not solely responsible for the navy's fundamentally
flawed strategy. Nonetheless, unlike the War Department, the Navy Department was virtually a free agent because Davis knew little about its functions
and placed a low priority on them. Mallory had talented advisers who stressed
blockade running and river and harbor defense, but the secretary of the navy
was a romantic dreamer drawn more to highly visible and daring proposals of
dubious merit than to the low-visibility, guerrilla operations that promised
genuine results. His instincts paid off in the case of the *Merrimack,* but that
was hardly the case with outlandish schemes for violating Canadian territory in
order to capture the Great Lakes and other numerous, silly, commandolike
raids on which Mallory wasted precious time, energy, resources, and his own
credibility. Less serious but still curious was the secretary's decision to create
a naval school similar to Annapolis to train midshipmen for a future independent Confederacy, when the South never had enough junior officers to carry
on its war for survival.

The secretary of the navy lacked sound command and administrative abilities. Mallory's assessment of officers was not especially good, and he did not
centralize operations, as the confused overseas purchasing operation illustrates.
His orders ranged from overspecific and preemptory to vague and indecisive.
The former quality was evident with the fall of New Orleans and the latter in

the operations of the *Merrimack*. The secretary allowed key officers, such as the numerous heads of the Office of Orders and Detail, to use their positions to secure coveted commands afloat, thus denying this critical agency continuity and himself a reliable assistant. Furthermore, Mallory permitted officers to transfer so rapidly that they were often unable to carry out their assignments competently, a situation that undermined the effectiveness of blockade running into the key port of Wilmington.

Mallory did not obstruct capable officers such as Brooke and Bulloch; indeed, he backed them when possible and often facilitated their work. But on the whole, the secretary did not run the department effectively. More important, by emphasizing offensive operations, he failed to exploit a supreme opportunity offered by blockade running and river and harbor defense to make the navy an indispensable participant in the Confederacy's fight for independence. Sadly but appropriately, army commanders in late 1864 came to view the navy as a nuisance: commerce raiders docked at Wilmington attracted Union blockade squadrons, thereby jeopardizing critically important blockade runners.

10
CONFEDERATE CIVILIAN ORGANIZATION

THE TREASURY DEPARTMENT

The Treasury Department was of critical importance to all facets of Confederate economic mobilization. Indeed, its inability to work out sound wartime finances contributed significantly to the South's defeat.

Jefferson Davis selected the German-born, South Carolina attorney and politician Christopher G. Memminger as secretary of the treasury.[1] Though not a financial expert, Memminger was competent in the area and consulted regularly with the South's leading bankers and merchants. He organized his department intelligently and benefited greatly from the experience of the numerous defectors from the U.S. Treasury Department. The president was not particularly informed about or interested in finances and learned to have confidence in the secretary, which gave Memminger a relatively free hand.

The secretary of the treasury's principal drawback was that he, like Davis, did not relate well to others; with his brusque, aloof manner he alienated many people whose political support he needed. Moreover, Memminger appeared uncertain in handling the South's precarious finances. When acting forcefully, he had his way with Congress fairly well in the first few years. Thereafter, the legislators began resisting his programs and from 1864 onward took an active role in shaping war finances. Not an outstanding financier in the best of circumstances, Memminger faced nearly intractable conditions. The Confederacy's limited liquid assets, aversion to taxation, and inability to sell bonds and other paper easily at home or abroad forced it to issue vast amounts of fiat money as the principal means for financing the war, which had devastating inflationary effects. Wrongheaded wartime financing may have been the single most important cause of the South's defeat.

At the outbreak of hostilities, the South had approximately $26 million in specie. Richmond managed to obtain much of it through loans, taxation, seizures, and the like; most of the rest was hoarded. Despite frequent talk of creating a Bank of the Confederate States, no such institution came into existence. Instead, Richmond handled its banking operations through a series of depositories for handling pay and funding.

State chartered banks were invaluable. On the eve of war, the South had a reasonably well-developed chartered banking system, ranging from New South banks that were mostly state-owned or closely regulated to Old South banks that were mainly private, subject to competition, and only loosely overseen. Virginia had an outstanding state banking system; Arkansas, in contrast, had none at all. The state-chartered banks provided the government with most of its specie, floated loans to Richmond, bought and sold bonds, helped legitimize Confederate paper by virtually treating it as legal tender, served as depositories, and provided numerous other services. Bank currency depreciated less than all other notes because it was usually carefully controlled. Most banks continued operating for the duration of hostilities and emerged from the war intact.

The Treasury Department never devised a coherent, overall program for financing the war. Instead, the Confederacy drifted into unsound policies during the first two years of hostilities and could not redirect policy effectively thereafter. Memminger began by borrowing for peacetime conditions and the prospects of a short war. In February 1861 Congress authorized the president to sell $15-million worth of 8 percent bonds payable in specie. The secretary of the treasury divided the loan, offering $5 million in March and the remainder in May 1861. The first issue oversold, but the second one dragged out until October 1861, despite a Confederate-wide system for promoting bonds that included public officials, appointed agents, and banks. Thereafter, no issue sold well. Banks could not absorb continued bond issues, and planters and farmers were unaccustomed to this form of paper and were reluctant to buy it in treacherous times. Obviously, borrowing would be an unreliable means for financing the war.

Consequently, Memminger experimented with unconventional forms of borrowing. Between May and August 1861, Congress passed and amended the Produce Loan Act, which provided for the sale of $100 million of 8 percent bonds that could be paid for in specie, military supplies, or proceeds from the sale of agricultural products or manufactured goods. By the end of the year, over 400,000 bales of cotton, along with other agricultural products and miscellaneous items, had been pledged in return for bonds. The pledged farm products were valued at approximately $34.5 million, although $11 million in pledges were never honored and collections went into 1864.

Even this experiment was less than successful. A variation on it was tried in April 1862 when Congress permitted individuals to buy bonds with any articles the government needed and allowed people who had pledged proceeds from cotton and other agricultural products under the Produce Loan to meet their obligation by turning over to the government the product itself at a determined price. As a result of this and other acts, Richmond ended up with at least 475,000 bales of cotton. It was used as collateral for loans, run through the blockade, traded through enemy lines, destroyed accidentally or purposefully, or seized by the Union. In addition, Richmond sold another $513 million or so in different forms of paper between February 1863 and 1865. By war's end, the total funded debt of the Confederacy stood at somewhat over $712 million.

The Confederacy did not tax heavily until 1863, although some levies occurred in 1861. In May 1861 Congress passed a comprehensive tariff law that provided for ad valorem rates ranging from 5 to 25 percent and other specific duties. Since the blockade interrupted all Southern trade, tariff income amounted to less than $3.5 million. Memminger favored stiff taxation from the outset but hesitated to advocate it because of the famed Southern opposition to taxes; hence, he called for taxes only to service the debt. Congress responded by including in the loan act of August 1861 a war tax of .5 percent on all real and personal property and most securities. The Treasury Department created special offices to facilitate taxation but collected taxes directly only in Mississippi and Texas. Those two states and South Carolina stood alone in taxing their population; the others paid their share of the tax by issuing state paper or by borrowing. Despite these expedients, efforts to collect the assessment extended into mid-1863 and produced under $17.5 million in revenue.

By late 1862 Memminger insisted on higher taxes and Congress began to listen. The Confederate legislators finally enacted the first broad-based taxation in April 1863. To get around the constitutional requirement that all direct taxes (interpreted as levies on land and slaves) had to be proportioned equally among the states based on a census, Congress taxed various goods from farms and forests, holdings of money, businesses, sales of goods, accommodations, and all income from salaries, profits, and other sources. It was this legislation that enacted a tithe or tax-in-kind. Under this system, one-tenth of enumerated farm products and three-fiftieths of all pork, in the form of bacon, had to be delivered to government depots within eight miles of farms or plantations. The tithe was collected by the War and Treasury departments. Various rules and regulations instituted then and later ensured that farmers and planters were not stripped of all their products, provided for the fair settlement of disputes, and made exemptions for low-income people and the needy families of servicemen. Other than for collections of the tax-in-kind, the 1863 law did not produce the desired results, raising about $82.3 million in the first year. This failure stemmed from the weakness of the collection service, widespread evasions and fraud, and the fact that large areas were off-limits to tax collectors because of Union occupation and internal opposition to authority and the war. The tithe, in the meantime, came in for scathing and persistent criticism because the intensity of collections varied between remote and accessible areas, instances of corruption and arbitrary and abusive practices were widespread, waste and inefficiency abounded, and planters and farmers ended up paying more than others. Nonetheless, the tithe yielded an estimated $62 million by March 1865. Food provided by the tax kept Southern troops from the brink of starvation.

In February 1864, with taxes producing small amounts of revenue and expenses mounting rapidly, Congress reenacted the 1863 law. It threw constitutional scruples to the wind and placed a 5 percent tax on all property and a 10 to 40 percent tax on luxury items and the profits of farms, factories, and businesses. Yet Confederate legislators then and in June 1864 vitiated the law by enacting generous rebates and exemptions that precluded the collection of substantial revenue. As a result, under the revised tax laws only $36.5 million was collected between April and October 1864, less than half of what was produced between April 1863 and April 1864 under the earlier statute. With the Confederacy failing fast and the Davis administration insisting on taxation to meet expenditures, a dispirited Congress in March and April 1865 raised the rates of existing taxes, cut out various exemptions and rebates, and provided for some new levies. Before new collections took place, the Confederacy collapsed. Taxation produced revenues of $207.5 million from 1861 to 1865, a very small percentage of total wartime spending.

The meager returns from loans and taxes forced the South to turn increasingly and almost thoughtlessly to paper currency. The first issue of March 1862 was modest in amount. After First Manassas, however, the Confederate presses began printing and hardly ever stopped. Richmond put into circulation over $311 million in Treasury notes by the end of 1861, $580 million by late 1862, and nearly $1.1 billion by April 1864. Some of these notes were redeemed, but in April 1864 almost $851.6 million were still in circulation. Treasury Department issues by the end of the war exceeded $1.5 billion. In addition, nearly all states printed their own notes, as did chartered banks. Moreover, various cities and businesses, including railroads, turnpikes, insurance companies, and savings banks, circulated small-denomination notes called shinplasters. No reliable figures exist on these non-Confederate issues, but they must have reached at least $50 million.

Early on, Memminger became alarmed about the amount of paper money in circulation. Estimating that the Confederacy needed a note circulation of around $200 million, he argued that amounts beyond that level would cause economic distortions. Hence, he consistently tried to reduce the amount of paper in circulation by persuading people to exchange their notes for bonds. But Southerners preferred depreciating paper to less liquid bonds because of its greater flexibility. Memminger then turned to compulsion. In October 1862, March 1863, and February 1864, Congress progressively increased the penalty for not converting notes to bonds, but Richmond undermined this approach by consistently issuing more paper than the amount redeemed. The February 1864 act, the most onerous, aimed at reducing the amount of currency by one-third through a form of repudiation. Over a ten-month period, paper money unconverted into bonds or new notes worth one-third less than the older issues would be phased out and become worthless. Currency in circulation declined and prices even dropped, but these effects were short-lived. Confusion and resentment grew over the complexity of the program and the tangle of paper money, and repudiation further eroded public confidence in Richmond.

Despite the hazards of financing the war primarily by paper money and borrowing, inflationary pressures were not totally out of control until after Gettysburg. At that point, military defeat, growing shortages of nearly all items, and weak financing proved a disastrous combination. Measured in gold, a Confederate dollar was worth a little under 91 cents in May 1861; somewhat less than 67 cents in May 1862; and slightly over 18 cents in May 1863. Then the dollar fell to less than 8 cents in August 1863; 5 cents in December 1863; 4 cents in September 1864; and around 1.7 cents in April 1865.

Inflation often exceeded the depreciation of the currency. Prices varied throughout the Confederacy but were highest in the largest cities. Rising prices set off a vicious cycle. Producers withheld goods to benefit from increased prices, hid livestock and nonperishable goods, refused to sell commodities, and engaged in barter whenever possible. Speculation and profiteering exaggerated these conditions. Such practices drove up government expenses and required more paper money, which only made the situation worse. Military procurement became nearly impossible, leading to widespread purchasing by certificates of indebtedness and then by impressment. Deep resentment against impressment among the general population had devastating consequences for civilian morale and the availability of goods. In mid-to-late 1863, with Confederate finances foundering, Southern war mobilization began to unravel at all levels.

In such circumstances, Memminger could not remain in office. Criticized from all sides, he resigned in June 1864. Davis all but drafted George A.

Trenholm to replace him. An unofficial adviser to Memminger, Trenholm had been at the center of Confederate economic mobilization since the beginning of hostilities and naturally supported Memminger's basic approach. Trenholm was an outgoing, politically astute individual of high prestige, and he improved the image of the Treasury Department, but he could not persuade Congress to adopt basic reforms. Legislators became convinced that finances were beyond repair; the nearly valueless currency would have to see the South through. In the last months of the conflict, the Treasury was asking for gifts of money, valuables, and food, and Trenholm desperately but unsuccessfully negotiated for a $75-million loan from abroad.

Confederate records are neither as reliable nor as available as those for the Union, making calculations of war costs and debt difficult at best. The war cost at least $2 billion, with some scholars putting the figure as high as $3.3 billion. Total recorded debt at the war's end was $1.61 billion, which does not include the $500 million in unpaid impressment receipts as of March 1865.

The massive use of paper money to finance the war resulted in forced loans and indirect taxes. The impact varied among different segments of the population. White-collar elements on fixed salaries were hardest hit, and wage earners also suffered greatly. Income of the latter increased about tenfold, but the cost of living based on representative price indices went up at least thirtyfold. Small farmers often experienced dire circumstances, and rural and urban families of servicemen frequently faced appalling living conditions. Yet certain manufacturers, merchants, shippers, bankers, planters, and enterprising sorts not only did well financially during hostilities, but they also managed to retain or acquire specie, greenbacks, and other tangible forms of wealth. Thus they were able to ride out the war successfully and to salvage their economic position in the postbellum period. In the last years of the war, for example, Joseph R. Anderson and his associates switched some of the resources of the Tredegar Iron Works to blockade running. By exporting cotton and importing luxury goods, they built up a sterling account in London to maintain control of the company after the war.

War financing was disastrous because Memminger and his advisers failed to break free from Southern rigidities. Denied the ability to borrow or tax effectively, they turned in frustration to paper money. Another feasible alternative existed in using cotton, the South's primary source of wealth, to the maximum: pursuing King Cotton finances, as it were, instead of King Cotton diplomacy. That meant, first, reducing the size of the cotton crop so that acreage could be converted for producing food; second, taking over services for marketing cotton, including networks in the West Indies and Europe to handle imports and exports; third, purchasing or building a fleet of ships to run cotton and imports through the blockade; fourth, extensive trading through the lines based on cotton; and, last, devising financial mechanisms for winning the cooperation of planters and farmers and compensating them for participating in such a broad-based system without undermining the economy.

These steps actually were followed but principally in a private and decentralized way. Millions of bales of cotton were sold or exchanged abroad and to the Union by private parties. In most cases, the Confederacy did not benefit even from the export tax due on sales. Around the beginning of 1864, the Davis administration began a successful effort to run cotton through the blockade and bring in goods, just as it reluctantly sanctioned trading with the enemy. Under a better mobilization program, these efforts would have started earlier, along with measures to control the railroads effectively.

The Confederacy had the talent to plan and administer such a program, as demonstrated by the accomplishments of Josiah Gorgas, Caleb Huse, James D. Bulloch, and Thomas L. Bayne, among others. The real barrier seemed to be the planter elite that dominated the South. According to Stanley Lebergott, the laissez-faire, profit-maximizing ethic of the planters accounts for the South's failure to maximize its economic potential. Davis certainly reflected key aspects of the planter mentality, particularly the dedication to preserving the prerogatives of private property. If financial policies were basic to the South's defeat and if Lebergott's analysis is accepted, the Confederacy was seriously, perhaps fatally, wounded by the irresponsible leadership of a narrow-minded elite driven by its own greed. This irresponsibility was manifest throughout hostilities in resistance to the use of slaves for war purposes, in cotton trading for private gain, in not honoring commitments for Produce Loans, in using states' rights to ward off Confederate control, and in conduct that generally failed to win the respect and loyalty of the masses.

Other cabinet posts did not play a particularly important role in economic mobilization. Although reports are somewhat conflicting, Davis apparently met with and polled the cabinet on many important issues. On critical military matters, however, the president tended to go his own way. Major policy decisions outside Davis's expertise or area of concentration were often made by key executives who worked with him and then consulted the cabinet. This approach appeared to be the case when James A. Seddon, Memminger, and Judah P. Benjamin joined Davis in centralizing blockade running and foreign economic operations in late 1863 and early 1864.[2]

A number of scholars claim that the Confederacy not only had the talent for effectively mobilizing the economy but also used it to institute a structure approximating wartime socialism,[3] a form of modern mercantilism,[4] or the most advanced effort at state-building on the American continent to that time.[5]

Such terms seem inappropriate for the Confederacy. Southern leaders prag-
matically groped for modern solutions to deal with a war that was taking on
total proportions. Their accomplishments were often innovative and daring,
but those qualities were never sufficiently widespread or sustained. As a result,
the South did not use to the maximum its human and material resources.

Davis's limitations as a leader are central to explaining the South's failure
to do so. Actively or passively, the president set the mode and tempo of economic mobilization by directing the operations of the War Department. Since
the army was the major claimant, this approach made some sense; nonetheless, it had major limitations. Without a human dynamo such as Edwin M.
Stanton, the Confederate War Department never became the vital center
required for harnessing the economy. Moreover, other executive departments
were not coordinated with the War Department, which adversely affected the
strategy and economics of war.

More important, Davis never fully and consistently focused on economic
mobilization. He appeared to recognize its importance early in 1861 and acted
accordingly, but once the fighting began in earnest with First Manassas, the
president lost perspective and was compulsively drawn to the battlefield. He
failed to appreciate that the economy demanded as much attention as the army
and that he needed institutional structures to fulfill his constitutional duties.
By creating a command system for the army, Davis would have taken the first
step toward centrally directing the war effort. Had that been followed by the
use of the cabinet, or more likely a subcabinet of the secretaries of war, navy,
treasury, and state or their representatives, to oversee economic mobilization,
the president would have had a balanced administrative structure for managing the war. The South would then have stood a greater chance of winning
independence. Instead, the Davis administration drifted, facing crises as they
arose. This makeshift approach worked after a fashion through mid-1863.
Thereafter, the crises mounted faster than Richmond could deal with them,
and the Confederacy began to fall apart before being overwhelmed.

CONGRESS

The Confederate Congresses on the whole were ineffective.[6] They usually followed the lead of the Davis administration on principal wartime legislation.
Although at times Congress refused to act on executive proposals, amended
others, and passed statutes Davis opposed, the legislators made no significant
contribution. Indeed, no outstanding leaders emerged, and Congress could
not claim authorship of any major bills.

Three Congresses sat during the Civil War. The first was the Montgomery Convention, which doubled as a unicameral Provisional Congress during and after the writing of the permanent constitution, serving from February 1861 to February 1862. This was the most august assembly of the Confederate years, made up of some of the South's most prominent leaders. It worked in close harmony with Davis in getting the Confederacy speedily under way. The two subsequent Congresses were popularly elected late in 1861 and 1863 and began sessions early in the following years. These bodies lacked the luster of the Provisional Congress since a number of leading citizens served in other official capacities; sought military glory; absented themselves from Richmond because of pique, illness, or both, as was the case with Vice-President Alexander H. Stephens; or failed at the ballot boxes, a humiliation suffered by Robert Barnwell Rhett.

Nonetheless, wartime leadership was continuous with that of the antebellum period. Of the 267 men who made up the various Congresses, fewer than 10 percent had no traceable political experience, slightly fewer than one-third had served in the U.S. Congress, and nearly two-thirds had experience as state legislators. For the most part, these were well-informed public men familiar with politics. Moreover, and again consistent with the prewar years, they were an economic, social, and political elite who were usually friendly or familiar with one another and often connected by intermarriage and kinship. A composite profile finds them to be middle-aged planters, farmers, and attorneys who owned substantial property, including slaves, and who were born on the Atlantic Seaboard or in the Deep South. The war years, like the antebellum ones, saw a high turnover rate among legislators. Only about 10 percent of the total congressional membership served continuously during the life of the Confederacy, although included were some of South's most prominent leaders, such as Sen. R. M. T. Hunter of Virginia.

The Southern Congresses were not nearly as aggressive as those of the Union in maintaining legislative prerogatives over the military. Congress regularly received reports on the armed services and nearly all combat situations, and it investigated reverses, especially major ones such as New Orleans. Through various statutes, legislators provided for the structure and operation of the army and navy, oversaw budgets, and set up and modified the conscription law. When Congress differed significantly from the president, however, it usually did not prevail, as was the case in terms of proposals for appointing a commanding general and general staff(s). Congress' role in controlling the military was weakened by cliques that favored and lobbied for various generals. Overall, it did not seriously affect the conduct of the war in a negative or a positive way.

In the First Congress, elected in November 1861 and serving for two years starting early in 1862, the Davis administration had a substantial working majority that it could rely upon to pass desired legislation. The Second Congress, elected late in 1863 and serving from May 1864 through March 1865, was much less reliable. With the military and economic situation bleak, morale low, and defeat almost certain, about 40 percent of the members of the new Congress opposed the president and his administration. Nonetheless, until the last months of the war, Davis could still manage the body, although the debates were more intense and hostile, the required compromises more significant, and the legislative process slower. The president also came under more severe attack in late 1863 and early 1864. Congress considered limiting his cabinet members to a two-year term, and legislators joined in hounding Memminger and Seddon from office. In the last months of the war, Congress finally became unmanageable, refusing to give the president his way on conscription, finances, and other matters and spitefully overriding a Davis veto for the first time.

Although the description risks oversimplification, Congresses divided into pro- and anti-Davis factions with identification growing more intense as the Confederacy waned. Those members supporting the president and his administration favored the centralization and nationalism that the war effort required; those opposing him stressed states' rights, localism, and individualism and manifested growing antagonism to conscription, impressment, and the suspension of habeas corpus. The strongest opposition to Richmond was increasingly centered in Georgia and North Carolina. These states had either a growing peace movement or a rebellion against wartime leadership, combined with elite dissent articulated by Joseph E. Brown and Zebulon B. Vance.

Davis controlled Congress throughout the war years but failed to work out a constructive relationship with it. His rigid notions about the separation of powers and his inability to reach out or respond to others for political expediency prevented him from selecting and cultivating leaders in Congress committed to his administration. Indeed, by refusing to participate in the give-and-take of politics, the president made bitter enemies of some who were once friends, such as Sen. Louis T. Wigfall (TX), and antagonized rather than placated political rivals such as William L. Yancey (AL). Davis and his administration had supporters in both houses of Congress, such as Benjamin H. Hill (GA) in the Senate and Ethelbert Barksdale (MS) in the House, and most of the time they could count on a majority of votes. Yet these realities appeared to develop in spite of, not because of, presidential effort. Davis preferred to believe that the members of Congress supporting his programs did so out of conviction, duty, and principle, not for political purposes. And, if Congress opposed him, the president had few compunctions about rejecting its work, as evidenced in his veto of thirty-nine bills. Clement Eaton wisely observes that in his relations with Congress, Davis "portrays some of the qualities needed in a successful general, but not suited to leading a democracy."[7]

Great fragmentation prevented Congress from ever mounting a significant challenge to the Davis administration. Unstable factions and cliques emerged, but they neither presented a coherent critique of the administration's conduct of the war nor offered a viable alternative to it. Too often, Congress appeared to be destructively attacking Davis and his cabinet, whose backs were to the wall, instead of offering constructive assistance. Hectoring by Wigfall, relentless opposition from Cong. Henry S. Foote (TN), and splenetic attacks from many others made the legislators appear disputatious, petty, and mean-spirited. High absenteeism, rumors of drunkenness and violence, continued seating of representatives from areas no longer under Confederate control, and frequent sessions behind closed doors made Congress seem irresponsible, even illegitimate. Davis's rigid probity and high purpose could seem attractive by comparison.

The lack of a two-party system badly weakened the Confederacy. Thomas B. Alexander and Richard E. Beringer conclude that without parties, the South's political structure "was not just faulty; it was fatally deficient."[8] Though parties would not have ensured victory, they would doubtless have checked the terrible fragmentation that occurred after mid-1863, by maintaining discipline within Congress and helping ameliorate the troubled relations between a temperamental president and the legislative branch. They would also have given the growing opposition the opportunity to advocate alternate wartime strategies and the leaders to implement them—whether dedicated to a more vigorous prosecution of the war or to a quicker and better peace. Political parties would furthermore have sanctioned and protected minority positions, including not only advocates of ending slavery, seeking peace, and other unpopular causes but also talented former Yankees such as Josiah Gorgas and Caleb Huse, who did so much for their adopted homeland and yet were viewed with suspicion by Southerners who often did much less. In short, political parties would have legitimized, and thereby probably tempered, criticism of the war effort and the administration conducting it, making critiques less destructive and channeling them into more productive paths. Such creative tension would have acted to maintain Southern unity and sustain morale and commitment to the war. It is sobering, yet uplifting, to remember that a few months before the presidential election of 1864, Abraham Lincoln was preparing for defeat by Democrat George B. McClellan. That reality stands as a rare tribute to the high but necessary costs of an open political system.

The absence of political parties was probably more a symptom of than a cause for the Confederacy's brittleness. Alexander and Beringer suggest such an interpretation:

> The workings of the Confederate Congress also help to document the extent of blunders of Southern leadership in the 1840s and 1850s, a leadership that had sought to make a mortal god of an institution and a holy terror of a race issue that together could not command adequate sacrifice from even the congressmen of the Confederacy.[9]

Social systems that create "mortal gods" and make critical issues "holy terrors" almost inevitably invite intolerance and threaten dissent in a way that can sound the death knell of democracy. If this line of analysis is correct, it is possible that the South collectively decided at some level that it could not have political parties without threatening its mortal gods and removing the holy terrors necessary to protect them. That in turn would mean that the Confederacy did not die from democracy, as David Donald proposes; rather, at some unconscious level, it may have died to regain democracy, because a point had been reached where only war could remove the "mortal god" of slavery.[10] The tragedy lies in the reality that not even war could remove the "holy terror" of race. Racial prejudice meant that any postwar democratic system would at best be exceptionally fragile and that the elite would not hesitate to use the monsters it had unleashed to maintain its privileged position.

Nevertheless, the South, without political parties, held together in war reasonably well when victory seemed possible, even probable. As hope gave way to despair, the Confederacy began to splinter and divide, resulting in an increasingly isolated yet dominant executive branch and a dysfunctional legislative one. As power at the Confederate level began to break down, people and leaders alike looked increasingly to their states for guidance because that was the level of government they were accustomed to dealing with. States' rights did not significantly weaken the Confederacy. Instead, Southerners rather naturally turned to the states for solace, support, and identity as it became obvious that the Confederate drive for independence was faltering and then failing.

THE CONFEDERACY

Why the Confederacy lost has been a source of often bitter controversy since 1865. The debate will continue, and no final answer is possible. Nonetheless, my analysis establishes that the inadequacies of the South's economic mobilization were a major, if not the major, cause for the Confederacy's downfall. My analysis and conclusion agree with the pioneering work of Charles W. Ramsdell, who argues that the primary failure of the Confederacy was finances, with transportation and especially the railroads following as a close second.[11] I go beyond Ramsdell in seeing a way out for the South through the early and constructive use of cotton and blockade running as a means of achieving both stable wartime financing and adequate sources of supply. For that approach to have worked, a reliable transportation system, in which the railroads were key, was essential.

Various authors emphasize the South's lack of commercial, financial, and managerial talent for handling the logistics of a long and relatively sophisticated war.[12] Yet once Richmond decided upon realistic programs, it usually found qualified persons to implement them. The performance of army and navy Ordnance and overseas procurement and finances in the last years of the war stand out in this regard. Moreover, the states conducted a remarkable range of activities, and private citizens and companies successfully ran the blockade, traded through the lines, and carried out manufacturing and commerce. Hence, native and returning Southerners and expatriate Northerners provided the South with adequate, although hardly ample, talent to meet the demands of a nearly modern war.

The shortcomings of Confederate leadership account for the failure to mobilize human and material resources to the maximum, and the failings started with Jefferson Davis, who shaped the mobilization program by his acts of commission and omission. Yet the president did not stand alone. He reflected the attitudes and limitations of the planter elite that dominated the South. Collectively, the ruling class seems to have gone through the looking glass. Its cotton, its slaves, and its privileges appeared more important than the survival of the society to which it was dedicated. The war had hardly started before the elite began dividing, dissenting, and withdrawing. As the pressures of total war mounted, the South's ruling class retreated under the banner of states' rights into the past rather than rising above it to salvage what was possible from a war it no longer wanted but the consequences of which it could not escape. In the process, much of the elite in effect abandoned Davis, with devastating consequences for his ability to lead. Without the approval and succor of the planters, he seemed to lose his way, his negative qualities became magnified, and he became indecisive and racked by anxiety. The failure of leadership, then, was that of an entire ruling class, not just of the president leading the region during its most critical ordeal.

Clement Eaton asks why the South's elite was found so wanting during the war. Was the democratization under Jacksonian Democracy to blame? Or was it the stagnation of an ingrown, homogenous, and conservative class that under attack grew defensive and intolerant? To ask the questions is virtually to answer them, for various studies demonstrate that the democratizing trends did not significantly change the structure of power in the South and that wartime and postwar leadership was continuous with that of the ante-bellum years.[13]

Two other explanations for the Confederate defeat should at least be briefly examined. The first stresses the North's overwhelming human and economic strength, which gradually but inexorably ground the South down.[14] With one reservation, I basically agree with this analysis. Certainly the odds facing the Confederacy prevented it from ever having a chance of defeating the Union. Yet better and more effective mobilization could have been the added measure the South needed to hold off the North and thus to win by not losing. The second interpretation stresses the failure of will, morale, and determination in the Confederacy.[15] This analysis I find unsatisfactory. Of course Southerners became demoralized, but better mobilization policies could have helped maintain esprit by limiting military reversals and by convincing the masses of their leaders' competence and of the elite's willingness to sacrifice along with the rest of the population. It is necessary, after all, to focus on the social illness, not on the fever that indicates it is there.

THE UNION AND THE CONFEDERACY

Examining the four factors shaping the political economy of warfare highlights the differences between the North and the South. Of paramount importance was the maturity of the economy. The North's rich and diversified market economy was relatively easy to convert for war purposes. Once the War and Navy departments perfected their operations and the Treasury Department worked out adequate (although hardly excellent) financing, the Union relied on competitive market forces for supplying its military without elaborate economic controls. Moreover, public and private, civilian and military organizations and personnel remained distinct. Only the railroads and the telegraph required specialized industry-military management teams, and war financing also eroded to some degree institutional barriers. By the war's end, Washington ran one of the largest, most accomplished logistical operations in history, which met all military requirements without economically squeezing the civilian population excessively.

Though not without exceptional achievements, the South's economic mobilization was piecemeal and wanting. Like the North, the South depended on established departments for harnessing the economy. Neither the War nor the Navy Department performed notably, and the supply bureaus outperformed their administrative parents. The War Department fell short most consequentially in its inability to regulate the railroads. By failing to devise effective means for financing the war, the Treasury Department undermined all facets of economic mobilization.

An underdeveloped economy forced the Confederacy to convert and to create industries and to regulate a large part of Southern economic life. Thus civilian and military, public and private institutions and personnel became combined in intricate ways. Overall, the economic controls were ineffectively used. The Davis administration failed systematically to assess the South's economic potential so as to gauge the feasibility of requirements, estimate goods that had to come from abroad and through the lines, and facilitate maximum production at home. Such rudimentary planning was not beyond Confederate capabilities; various mobilization agencies managed key materials such as iron. The North's economy of plenty made such planning unnecessary; the South's economy of want made it imperative.

The second factor shaping economic mobilization is the size, strength, and scope of the national government. The Civil War palpably demonstrated the difference between form and substance. The North and the South both worked with essentially the same governmental structure. Yet Washington consistently grew in effectiveness while Richmond never established its authority, began to wither in mid-1863, and died less than two years later. Critical to the North's success and the South's failure was the nature of their politically elitist systems. The North's was relatively open, representative, responsive, and flexible; the South's was closed, exclusive, unresponsive, and inflexible.

Washington initially had to rely heavily upon the states to initiate mobilization. Within a year, however, the Lincoln administration established its predominance over the wartime economy, and the states were reduced to a supportive but subordinate role. In his loose executive style, Lincoln set the general policies for conducting the war and left his cabinet members to devise the means for implementing them. With Congress, the president worked out a relationship of constructive tension that strengthened the federal government. Overall, Lincoln's leadership abilities were superb, and he met the numerous challenges to his authority adroitly. Active, intense party politics helped unify the North as it grappled with the multiple strains and demands of civil war.

The Confederacy never matched the Union. As in the North, the states stepped in at the outset to facilitate economic mobilization. Although Richmond generally had taken charge of the effort by mid-1862, the South's numerous weaknesses created greater challenges for Davis than those faced by Lincoln—challenges that were beyond the president's abilities. Though an intense and conscientious executive, Davis was not an outstanding leader. Unlike Lincoln, he failed to unite the branches and levels of government into a coherent whole, sharing a common goal. His administration was a collection of unrelated parts that never functioned well; the states always maintained a level of independence that grew as catastrophes mounted; and the president dominated Congress without ever winning the legislators' admiration or loyalty. A veneer of unity gave way to sharp divisions after mid-1863. By the time of Appomattox, the proud South was little more than a collection of broken pieces. A better leader might have made a difference, but that is a matter of conjecture. More certain was the Confederacy's need for political parties to control the centrifugal forces rending it as the pressures of war mounted.

The third factor shaping economic mobilization involves the character and structure of the military services and their relationship to civil society and authority. The North and the South were remarkably similar in this vital area because they shared the same experience and traditions. Both sections maintained unquestioned civilian control over the military despite the hazards of a civil war. The South relied on graduates from the military academies for economic mobilization to a greater degree than the North, but the blurring of lines between civilian and military spheres took place without adverse consequences. In both the Union and the Confederacy, most of the highest ranking officers had been trained at West Point and to a lesser degree at Annapolis. The regular armies of both regions remained marginal, and the burden of fighting was carried by provisional armies, recruited first through volunteering and state militia and then through conscription. The navies in both regions were viewed as secondary to the land forces.

The only major difference between the armed services of the two sections lay in their systems of command. In the North, Lincoln gradually devised the nation's most effective command structure, based upon himself as commander-in-chief, Stanton as secretary of war, Ulysses S. Grant as general-in-chief, and Henry W. Halleck acting as chief of staff. The president used that system to implement the North's Anaconda strategy for annihilating the South. The one flaw was the lack of formal coordination of the army and navy at the highest level.

Davis never created a command system, although he counseled with secretaries of war, military advisers, and field commanders. Congress' attempts to improve staff and command structures were rebuffed by the president. As commander-in-chief, Davis did not clearly define an overall strategy, interfered both too much and too little with department commanders, neglected the

West, and failed to devise joint army-navy policies for defending inland and coastal waterways. By default, the South fought a defensive war of attrition. Though at times brilliantly executed, the Confederate effort never halted the Union's relentless onslaught.

The state of military technology is the fourth factor shaping economic mobilization. The tools of war were in a transitional stage to modernity during the Civil War. That was the case even though a naval revolution was taking place, major advancements had been made in the mass production of small arms, ordnance and its uses were changing rapidly, conscript armies had become essential, and the telegraph and especially the railroads were transforming warfare. Nonetheless, armies and navies could still be armed and supplied with relatively little disruption to the economy because their demand was neither great enough nor so different from civilian usage as to require major economic alterations. Underdevelopment, not the sophistication of military hardware, forced the South to plan economically.

Whatever the stage in the political economy of warfare, economic power does not organize itself for war: that is the role of the political structure. The North maximized the use of its massive economic might to help achieve victory. Beginning with less, the Confederacy had to do much more; the results of its failure to do so were disastrous.

EPILOGUE

The American nation in 1865 included in its distinct regions warfare's past and future. The defeated Confederacy lay in literal and figurative ruins, a victim of its backward-looking society, which had failed to mobilize adequately the economic power needed to hold off the enemy in a brutal civil war. The mighty Union not only stood victorious, but it was also poised to begin a thirty-five-year rush to industrial maturity, freed of the fetters to economic growth imposed by the antebellum South.

The Union employed a new strategy of annihilation to overcome the Confederacy's war of attrition, which preindustrial America had successfully used during the Revolution and the War of 1812. Never again would the United States, or a part of it, fight a defensive war. Henceforth, offensive warfare designed to destroy the opposition became America's hallmark.

In 1865, therefore, the United States left the transitional stage of economic mobilization to enter the industrial stage. Its major wars of the future would be total ones, fought on foreign soil. Before America was prepared to undertake such conflicts, its economy had to reach industrial maturity; its political system had to be updated; and its armed services had to be fully professionalized. Moreover, military technology was entering a phase of rapid and constant change that would put strains on the economic, political, and military systems during peace and, along with the enormous demands of total war, would require planned economies during World Wars I and II. In the Cold War era and after, massive and ongoing military spending during years of relative peace would present the United States with new and threatening conditions.

In the preindustrial and transitional stages of the nation's political economy of warfare, military demobilization after hostilities was drastic and at times nearly total, which allowed Americans to virtually ignore the military between wars. Once it entered the industrial stage, the United States could no longer safely turn its back on the armed services, however. Wartime economics in the industrial stage brought home to America realities that the preindustrial and transitional stages had only suggested. Huge and prolonged spending for the armed forces in an advanced industrial system could fundamentally distort military and civilian institutions as well as the operations of domestic and foreign policies.

NOTES

The notes serve also as a bibliography. I use them not only to document my analysis but also to cite and comment upon the numerous primary and secondary sources and bibliographies relevant to it. Hence, some of the notes are quite lengthy and some read like a miniature bibliographic essay. I chose this approach because my analysis required me to synthesize a great deal of scholarship involving political, economic, military, and technological developments over a considerable period of time. By including in the notes the full range of sources consulted, I share with the reader the scholarly path I followed in formulating and presenting my version of the political economy of warfare in America. For the convenience of readers, I give the full citation of all primary and secondary materials the first time mentioned in each chapter (except for Chapter 5 for reasons that are explained there).

CHAPTER TWO. THE AMERICAN REVOLUTION

1. John J. McCusker and Russell R. Menard, *The Economy of British America, 1607–1789* (Chapel Hill: University of North Carolina Press, 1985), pp. 12–34, 52–60, 71–88, 267–70; James F. Shepherd and Gary M. Walton, *Shipping, Maritime Trade, and the Economic Development of Colonial North America* (Cambridge: Cambridge University Press, 1972), pp. 27–31—Walton and Shepherd have placed their earlier findings in a larger context in a subsequent publication, *The Economic Rise of Early America* (Cambridge: Cambridge University Press, 1979); and Edwin J. Perkins, *The Economy of Colonial America* (New York: Columbia University Press, 1980), pp. 1–13, 145–65—in chapters 2 and 8, Perkins analyzes the effects of wealth concentration upon the colonial political economy. Most of these books draw heavily upon the excellent work of Alice Hanson Jones, who has consolidated and refined her findings in *Wealth of a Nation to Be: The American Colonies on the Eve of the Revolution* (New York: Columbia University Press, 1980). See also Marc Egnal, "Economic Development of the Thirteen Continental Colonies, 1720–1775," *William and Mary Quarterly* 32 (April 1975): 191–222; Clarence L. Ver Steeg, *The Formative Years, 1607–1763* (New York: Hill and Wang, 1964), pp. 173–202, 301–6; and Edwin J.

Perkins, "The Entrepreneurial Spirit in Colonial America: The Foundations of Modern Business History," *Business History Review* 63 (Spring 1989): 160–86.

2. McCusker and Menard, *Economy of British America,* pp. 91–111, 321–24; Shepherd and Walton, *Shipping, Maritime Trade, and the Economic Development of Colonial North America,* include and analyze extensive information on trade that was so basic to the growth of New England; Walton and Shepherd, *Economic Rise of Early America,* pp. 46–50, 79–94, 96–111, 138–51; and Perkins, *Economy of Colonial America,* pp. 20–27, 40–50, 81–96, 150–59.

3. McCusker and Menard, *Economy of British America,* pp. 189–208; Shepherd and Walton, *Shipping, Maritime Trade, and the Economic Development of Colonial America,* present elaborate statistical information and analysis on the trade of the Middle States; Walton and Shepherd, *Economic Rise of Early America,* pp. 45–46, 49–50, 79–94, 96–111, 138–51; Perkins, *Economy of Colonial America,* 24–27, 48–49, 81–96, 150–59; Jones, *Wealth of a Nation to Be,* pp. 155–94; and Thomas M. Doerflinger, *A Vigorous Spirit of Enterprise: Merchants and Economic Development in Revolutionary Philadelphia* (Chapel Hill: University of North Carolina Press, 1986), pp. 3–196.

4. McCusker and Menard, *Economy of British America,* pp. 117–43; Shepherd and Walton, *Shipping, Maritime Trade, and the Economic Development of Colonial North America,* present extensive information and analysis regarding Southern trade patterns; Walton and Shepherd, *Economic Rise of Early America,* pp. 42–44, 79–94, 96–111, 134–36, 138–51; Perkins, *Economy of Colonial America,* pp. 27–33, 51–62, 67–78, 95, 150–59; Jones, *Wealth of a Nation to Be,* pp. 155–94; Edward C. Papenfuse, *In Pursuit of Profit: The Annapolis Merchants in the Era of the American Revolution, 1763–1805* (Baltimore: Johns Hopkins University Press, 1975), pp. 1–75; and John C. Rainbolt, *From Prescription to Persuasion: Manipulation of Eighteenth Century Virginia Economy* (Port Washington, NY: Kennikat Press, 1974).

5. McCusker and Menard, *Economy of British America,* pp. 169–88; Shepherd and Walton, *Shipping, Maritime Trade, and the Economic Development of Colonial North America,* give extensive information on trade patterns of the Lower South; Walton and Shepherd, *Economic Rise of Early America,* pp. 44–45, 58–61, 79–94, 96–111, 138–51; and Perkins, *Economy of Colonial America,* pp. 27–33, 51–62, 67–78, 150–59.

6. Controversy still surrounds the issue of whether the colonies benefited or suffered from their economic position in the British imperial system. The outline of the conflicting interpretations and the bibliography involving them are set forth in McCusker and Menard, *Economy of British America,* pp. 351–54; Perkins, *Economy of Colonial America,* pp. 17–38; Walton and Shepherd, *Economic Rise of Early America,* pp. 153–77; and Shepherd and Walton, *Shipping, Maritime Trade, and the Economic Development of Colonial North America,* who present the most elaborate and recent data relevant to the subject.

7. The best and most complete survey of the threats the colonists faced or created and the wars they fought is Douglas Edward Leach, *Arms for Empire: A Military History of the British Colonies in North America, 1607–1763* (New York: Macmillan, 1973). See also Leach, *Roots of Conflict: British Armed Forces and the Colonial Americans, 1677–1763* (Chapel Hill: University of North Carolina Press, 1986); John Ferling, *Struggle for a Continent: The Wars of Early America* (Arlington Heights, IL:

Harlan Davidson, 1993); John Shy, *Toward Lexington: The Role of the British Army in the Coming of the American Revolution* (Princeton: Princeton University Press, 1965); and David H. Overy, "The Colonial Wars and the American Revolution," in *The American Military Tradition: From Colonial Times to the Present,* ed. John M. Carroll and Colin F. Baxter, pp. 3–21 (Wilmington, DE: Scholarly Resources, 1993).

Leach (*Arms for Empire,* chapter 7, particularly p. 267) argues that on balance, the nearly constant warfare in the American colonies probably thwarted economic growth. Nonetheless, merchants could benefit handsomely acting as military suppliers. See Thomas C. Cochran, *Business in American Life: A History* (New York: McGraw-Hill, 1972), p. 21. Most authors who address the issue tend to agree with Cochran; for example, see McCusker and Menard, *Economy of British America,* pp. 365–67; Perkins, *Economy of Colonial America,* pp. 130–31; and Doerflinger, *Spirit of Enterprise,* p. 199. This very important subject is treated directly and indirectly by many authors; it is discussed further and documented later.

8. The brief discussion and analysis of the militia is based upon a rich literature on the subject, much of which has been published quite recently. For some of the more important works, see Walter Millis, *Arms and Men: A Study in American Military History* (New York: Putnam, 1956), pp. 13–53; Howard H. Peckham, *The War for Independence: A Military History* (Chicago: University of Chicago Press, 1958), pp. ix–x, 25–29, 199–209; Daniel J. Boorstin, *The Americans: The Colonial Experience* (New York: Random House, 1958), pp. 345–72; Louis Morton, "The Origins of American Military Policy," *Military Affairs* 22 (Summer 1958): 75–82; Russell F. Weigley, *Towards an American Army: Military Thought from Washington to Marshall* (New York: Columbia University Press, 1962), pp. 1–29, and Weigley, *History of the United States Army* (New York: Macmillan, 1967), pp. 3–28; John Shy, "A New Look at the Colonial Militia," *William and Mary Quarterly* 20 (April 1963): 175–83—this article is included in Shy's excellent collection of essays on the Revolution, *A People Numerous and Armed: Reflections on the Military Struggle for American Independence* (New York: Oxford University Press, 1976); Marcus Cunliffe, *Soldiers and Civilians: The Martial Spirit in America, 1775–1865* (Boston: Little, Brown, 1968), pp. 31–43; Robert A. Gross, *The Minutemen and Their World* (New York: Hill and Wang, 1976), pp. 10–67; John Kenneth Rowland, "Origins of the Second Amendment: The Creation of the Constitutional Rights of Militia and of Keeping and Bearing Arms" (Ph.D. diss., Ohio State University, 1978); John E. Ferling, *A Wilderness of Miseries: War and Warriors in Early America* (Westport, CT: Greenwood Press, 1980); Lawrence Delbert Cress, *Citizens in Arms: The Army and the Militia in American Society to the War of 1812* (Chapel Hill: University of North Carolina Press, 1982), pp. 1–52; James Kirby Martin and Mark Edward Lender, *A Respectable Army: The Military Origins of the Republic, 1763–1789* (Arlington Heights, IL: Harlan Davidson, 1982), pp. 1–29; Alan R. Millett and Peter Maslowski, *For the Common Defense: A Military History of the United States of America* (New York: Free Press, 1984), pp. 1–10; John K. Mahon, *History of the Militia and the National Guard* (New York: Macmillan, 1983); Steven Rosswurm, "The Philadelphia Militia, 1775–1783: Active Duty and Active Radicalism," in *Arms and Independence: The Military Character of the American Revolution,* ed. Ronald Hoffman and Peter J. Albert, pp. 75–118 (Charlottesville: University Press of Virginia, 1984); Rosswurm, *Arms, Country, and Class: The Philadelphia Militia and*

"Lower Sort" During the American Revolution, 1775–1783 (New Brunswick, NJ: Rutgers University Press, 1987); and Charles P. Neimeyer, *America Goes to War: A Social History of the Continental Army* (New York: New York University Press, 1996).

9. Don Higginbotham, *The War of American Independence: Military Attitudes, Policies, and Practice, 1763–1789* (New York: Macmillan, 1971), p. 10.

10. M. L. Brown, *Firearms in Colonial America: The Impact on History and Technology, 1492–1792* (Washington, DC: Smithsonian Institution Press, 1980); Leach, *Arms for Empire*, pp. 4–7; Peckham, *War for Independence*, pp. 12–15; James C. Bradford, "The Navies of the American Revolution," in *In Peace and War: Interpretations of American Naval History, 1775–1984*, ed. Kenneth J. Hagan, pp. 3–26, 2d ed. (Westport, CT: Greenwood Press, 1984); and Daniel R. Beaver, "Cultural Change, Technological Development, and the Conduct of War in the Seventeenth Century," in *New Dimensions in Military History: An Anthology*, ed. Russell F. Weigley, pp. 75–89 (San Rafael, CA: Presidio Press, 1975).

11. Michael Kammen, *Empire and Interest: The American Colonies and the Politics of Mercantilism* (Philadelphia: J. B. Lippincott, 1970), with brevity and insight traces the deterioration of British mercantilist policies from those imperfectly oriented toward balanced national or imperial concerns to those dictated by various interest groups for their own narrow benefit. The consequences of that deterioration, according to Kammen and other scholars, go far to explain the imperial crisis that precipitated the American Revolution. A similar analysis and a provocative essay on the mercantilist thought of American statesmen into the nineteenth century is found in William Appleman Williams, *The Contours of American History* (Cleveland, OH: World Publishing Company, 1961), and John E. Crowley, *The Privileges of Independence: Neomercantilism and the American Revolution* (Baltimore: Johns Hopkins University Press, 1993). Marc Egnal and Joseph A. Ernst, in "An Economic Interpretation of the American Revolution," *William and Mary Quarterly* 29 (January 1972): 3–32, place the Revolution within the context of long-term British-colonial antagonism (see note 6 for additional sources on this subject). See also Curtis P. Nettels, *The Roots of American Civilization: A History of American Colonial Life* (New York: Appleton-Century-Crofts, 1963), pp. 90–96; Richard B. Morris, *Government and Labor in Early America* (New York: Columbia University Press, 1946), pp. 1–3, 18–21, 55–91; Victor S. Clark, *History of Manufactures in the United States, 1607–1860* (Washington DC: Carnegie Institution, 1929), 1: 31–72; Emory R. Johnson et al., *History of Domestic and Foreign Commerce of the United States* (1915; reprint, Washington, DC: Carnegie Institution, 1922), 1: 54–65; Albert Anthony Giesecke, *American Commercial Legislation Before 1789* (1910; reprint, New York: Burt Franklin, 1970), pp. 17–22; and E. James Ferguson, *The American Revolution: A General History, 1763–1790*, rev. ed. (Homewood, IL: Dorsey Press, 1979), pp. 3–20. Economic regulations in the colonies resulted from the population's concept of "the public good" in a republican society. For a further explication of this point, see Gordon S. Wood, *The Creation of the American Republic, 1776–1787* (Chapel Hill: University of North Carolina Press, 1969), pp. 53–65. J. R. T. Hughes, *Social Control in the Colonial Economy* (Charlottesville: University Press of Virginia, 1976), presents a provocative analysis of elaborate social controls over the economy as a basic and necessary condition for the evolution of a vigorous capitalist economy.

12. Curtis P. Nettels, *The Emergence of a National Economy, 1775–1815* (New York: Holt, Rinehart and Winston, 1962), pp. 1–8; Vernon G. Setser, *The Commercial Reci-*

procity Policy of the United States, 1774–1829 (Philadelphia: University of Pennsylvania Press, 1937), pp. 6–51; John C. Miller, *Triumph of Freedom, 1775–1783* (Boston: Little, Brown, 1948), pp. 101–6.

13. The best and most complete study of the Secret Committee of Trade is Elizabeth Miles Nuxoll, *Congress and the Munitions Merchants: The Secret Committee of Trade During the American Revolution, 1775–1777* (New York: Garland Publishing, 1985). See also Clarence L. Ver Steeg, *Robert Morris, Revolutionary Financier* (Philadelphia: University of Pennsylvania Press, 1954), pp. 10–22; Jennings B. Sanders, *Evolution of Executive Departments of the Continental Congress, 1774–1789* (Chapel Hill: University of North Carolina Press, 1935), pp. 18–49, 75–92; Robert Greenhalgh Albion and Jennie Barnes Pope, *Sea Lanes in Wartime: The American Experience, 1775–1945*, 2d ed., rev. (Hamden, CT: Archon Books, 1968), pp. 43–64.

14. E. James Ferguson's *The Power of the Purse: A History of American Public Finance, 1776–1790* (Chapel Hill: University of North Carolina Press, 1961), pp. 31–32, remains the best single volume on the political economy of the Revolutionary War. See also Edwin J. Perkins, *American Public Finance and Financial Services, 1700–1815* (Columbus: Ohio State University Press, 1994), pp. 1–196, and Anne Bezanson, *Prices and Inflation During the American Revolution: Pennsylvania, 1770–1790* (Philadelphia: University of Pennsylvania Press, 1951).

15. Ferguson, *Power of Purse*, pp. 23–47; Nettels, *National Economy*, pp. 23–44; Miller, *Triumph of Freedom*, pp. 456–68. The most thorough examination of state taxation during the Revolutionary War is presented in Robert A. Becker, *Revolution, Reform, and the Politics of American Taxation, 1763–1783* (Baton Rouge: Louisiana State University Press, 1980).

16. Ferguson, *Power of the Purse*, pp. 26, 43–44.

17. John R. Alden, *A History of the American Revolution* (New York: Alfred A. Knopf, 1969), pp. 449–50, and Morris, *Government and Labor*, pp. 92–118.

18. Morris, *Government and Labor*, 92–118.

19. Ibid., pp. 118–35; Giesecke, *American Commercial Legislation*, pp. 123–52; Johnson, *History of Commerce*, 1: 132–33.

20. Kammen, *Empire*, pp. 15–17, 38–39, 40–41, 53, 91–92; Williams, *Contours*, pp. 12–117; Morris, *Government and Labor*, pp. 100–135; Ferguson, *Power of the Purse*, pp. 110–11; Joseph Dorfman, *The Economic Mind in American Civilization, 1606–1865* (New York: Viking Press, 1946), 1: 205–28; Wood, *American Republic*, pp. 322–24.

21. Robert A. East, *Business Enterprise in the American Revolutionary Era* (New York: Columbia University Press, 1938), pp. 44–47.

22. Albion and Pope, *Sea Lanes*, p. 35.

23. U.S. Bureau of the Census, *Historical Statistics of the United States, Colonial Times to 1970* (Washington, DC: U.S. Government Printing Office, 1975), pt. 2, p. 652, and Douglass C. North, *The Economic Growth of the United States, 1790–1860* (New York: W. W. Norton, 1966), pp. 24–25.

24. Nettels, *National Economy*, pp. 1–22.

25. Miller, *Triumph of Freedom*, pp. 105–7, and David Lewis Salay, "Arming for War: The Production of War Material in Pennsylvania for the American Armies During the Revolution" (Ph.D. diss., University of Delaware, 1977).

26. James A. Huston, *The Sinews of War: Army Logistics 1775–1953* (Washington, DC: Office of the Chief of Military History, 1966), pp. 18–26—the author develops

his themes more fully in his book-length study, *Logistics of Liberty: American Services of Supply in the Revolutionary War and After* (Newark, NJ: University of Delaware Press, 1991); Russell F. Weigley, *History of the United States Army*, 2d ed., rev. (Bloomington: Indiana University Press, 1984), pp. 60–61; Clark, *History of Manufactures*, 1: 31–72, 219–27; and Nettels, *National Economy*, pp. 40–42. A valuable work on logistics in general is Charles S. Sharader, *U.S. Military Logistics, 1607–1991: A Research Guide* (Westport, CT: Greenwood Press, 1992).

27. James A. Mulholland, *A History of Metals in Colonial America* (University: University of Alabama Press, 1981); Peter Temin, *Iron and Steel in Nineteenth Century America: An Economic Inquiry* (Cambridge: MIT Press, 1964), pp. 13–15; Neil Longley York, *Mechanical Metamorphosis: Technological Change in Revolutionary America* (Westport, CT: Greenwood Press, 1985), pp. 63–86; Nettels, *National Economy*, pp. 42–44; and Evart B. Greene, *The Revolutionary Generation, 1763–1790* (New York: Macmillan, 1943), pp. 58–66, 275–77.

28. Nettels, *National Economy*, pp. 34–40; Huston, *Sinews of War*, pp. 26–30; Erna Risch, *Quartermaster Support of the Army: A History of the Corps, 1775–1939* (Washington, DC: Office of the Quartermaster General, 1962), pp. 15–23.

29. John A. Fairlie, *The National Administration of the United States of America* (New York: Macmillan, 1905), pp. 133–34; Harry M. Ward, *The Department of War, 1781–1795* (Pittsburgh, PA: University of Pittsburgh Press, 1962), pp. 2–10; Sanders, *Executive Departments*, pp. 6–17; and E. Wayne Carp, *To Starve the Army at Pleasure: Continental Army Administration and American Political Culture, 1775–1783* (Chapel Hill: University of North Carolina Press, 1984), pp. 19–51.

30. Carp, *Starve the Army*, pp. 19–51; Sanders, *Executive Departments*, pp. 6–17; Miller, *Triumph of Freedom*, pp. 239–42; Ver Steeg, *Robert Morris*, pp. 10–11; Huston, *Sinews of War*, pp. 6–8; Marvin A. Kreidberg and Merton G. Henry, *History of Military Mobilization in the United States Army, 1775–1945* (Washington, DC: Department of the Army, 1955), pp. 17–19; Constance McLaughlin Green, Harry C. Thomson, and Peter C. Roots, *The Ordnance Department: Planning Munitions for War* (Washington, DC: Office of the Chief of Military History, 1955), p. 14.

31. Risch, *Quartermaster*, pp. 1–73, and Kreidberg and Henry, *Military Mobilization*, pp. 20–21 (the paragraph sets forth only a very general outline of the Quartermaster Corps and the Commissary General). For the most detailed and thorough study of the entire army's wartime supply structure and operations, see Erna Risch, *Supplying Washington's Army* (Washington, DC: Center of Military History, 1981).

32. Risch, *Supplying Washington's Army;* Risch, *Quartermaster*, pp. 1–73; Victor Leroy Johnson, *The Administration of the American Commissariat During the Revolutionary War* (Philadelphia: University of Pennsylvania Press, 1941); Louis Clinton Hatch, *The Administration of the American Revolutionary Army* (New York: Longmans Green, 1904), pp. 86–123.

33. Hatch, *American Revolutionary Army*, pp. 86–123; Huston, *Sinews of War*, pp. 6–17; Miller, *Triumph of Freedom*, p. 239; Risch, *Quartermaster*, pp. 3–5; and Risch, *Supplying Washington's Army*. See also Robert K. Wright, Jr., *The Continental Army* (Washington, DC: Center of Military History, 1983); Jonathan Gregory Rossie, *The Politics of Command in the American Revolution* (Syracuse, NY: Syracuse University Press, 1975); Ira D. Gruber, "The Anglo-American Military Tradition and the War for American Independence," in *Against All Enemies: Interpretations of American Mili-*

tary History from Colonial Times to the Present, ed. Kenneth J. Hagan and William R. Roberts, pp. 21–47 (Westport, CT: Greenwood Press, 1986); Theodore Thayer, *Nathanael Greene: Strategist of the American Revolution* (New York: Twayne, 1960); Gerald H. Clarfield, *Timothy Pickering and the American Republic* (Pittsburgh, PA: University of Pittsburgh Press, 1980); David McLean, *Timothy Pickering and the Age of the American Revolution* (New York: Arno Press, 1982); Martin H. Bush, *Revolutionary Enigma: A Re-appraisal of General Philip Schuyler of New York* (Port Washington, NY: Ira J. Friedman, 1969); Curtis P. Nettels, *George Washington and American Independence* (Boston: Little, Brown, 1951); Don Higginbotham, *George Washington and the American Military Tradition* (Athens: University of Georgia Press, 1985); and George F. Scheer, "Washington and His Lieutenants: Some Problems in Command," in *Military History of the American Revolution,* ed. Stanley J. Underdal, pp. 139–50 (Washington, DC: United States Air Force Academy, 1976).

34. Charles O. Paullin, *Paullin's History of Naval Administration, 1775–1911* (Annapolis, MD: U.S. Naval Institute, 1968), pp. 3–88; Nathan Miller, *Sea of Glory: The Continental Navy Fights for Independence, 1775–1783* (New York: David McKay, 1974); Fairlie, *National Administration,* pp. 152–53; Sanders, *Executive Departments,* pp. 18–37; E. B. Potter, ed., *The United States and World Sea Power* (Englewood Cliffs, NJ: Prentice-Hall, 1955), pp. 90–125; Harold and Margaret Sprout, *The Rise of American Naval Power, 1776–1918* (Princeton: Princeton University Press, 1946), pp. 7–15; George R. Clark et al., *A Short History of the United States Navy,* rev. ed. (Philadelphia: J. B. Lippincott, 1939), pp. 9–51; Stephen Tallichet Powers, "The Revolutionary War, 1775–1781," in *American Secretaries of the Navy, 1775–1913,* ed. Paolo E. Coletta, 1: 1–27 (Annapolis, MD: Naval Institute Press, 1980); Paolo E. Coletta, *The American Naval Heritage in Brief* (Washington, DC: University Press of America, 1978), pp. 1–73; and William Gary Anderson, "John Adams and the Creation of the American Navy" (Ph.D. diss., State University of New York, Stony Brook, 1975). The navy referred to was the Continental navy; thirteen other naval forces existed. Washington and Benedict Arnold organized temporary flotillas as adjuncts of their armies, and eleven states authorized squadrons of varying size and quality. These matters are covered fully in some of the preceding sources and in Bradford, "Navies of the American Revolution," pp. 3–26.

35. Johnson, *American Commissariat,* pp. 60–65, 74–76, 102–3; Huston, *Sinews of War,* pp. 18–30; Hatch, *American Revolutionary Army,* pp. 86–88; Risch, *Quartermaster,* pp. 7, 17, 39–42, 48, 54–59, 60–62; Risch, *Supplying Washington's Army;* Sanders, *Executive Departments,* pp. 89–90.

36. Huston, *Sinews of War,* pp. 31–34; Risch, *Quartermaster,* pp. 5–7, 49, 62; and Risch, *Supplying Washington's Army.*

37. Risch, *Supplying Washington's Army,* pp. 64–96; Risch, *Quartermaster,* pp. 19–23, 30, 33–37, 44–46, 63–64; Huston, *Sinews of War,* pp. 34–37, 58, 61–66; Miller, *Triumph of Freedom,* pp. 481–85; Nettels, *National Economy,* pp. 36–40; Johnson, *American Commissariat,* p. 99; and Carp, *Starve the Army,* pp. 55–64.

38. Recent publications by several scholars have placed the military experience of the Revolutionary War, including matters of supply, into the larger context of the American society as a whole and the values and attitudes therein, which helps to explain many of the contradictions and complexities of the wartime period. See Carp, *Starve the Army;* Charles Royster, *A Revolutionary People at War: The Continental Army and*

292   Notes to Pages 25–26

the American Character, 1775–1783 (Chapel Hill: University of North Carolina Press, 1979); Reginald C. Stuart, *War and American Thought from the Revolution to the Monroe Doctrine* (Kent, OH: Kent State University Press, 1982); and various essays in Ronald Hoffman and Peter J. Albert, eds., *Arms and Independence: The Military Character of the American Revolution* (Charlottesville: University Press of Virginia, 1984). The following books provide broad coverage of the Revolution as well as full bibliographies on the subject: Stephen Conway, *The War of American Independence, 1775–1783* (London: Edward Arnold, 1995), and Harry M. Ward, *The American Revolution: Nationhood Achieved, 1763–1788* (New York: St. Martin's Press, 1995).

Excellent work also has been done on British procurement, supply, and logistics for the American Revolution that enlightens not only the effort of Great Britain but also what the rebellious colonies did and how their record compared with England's. In this regard, see David Syrett, *Shipping and the American War, 1775–1783: A Study of British Transportation Organization* (London: Athlone Press, 1970); Norman Baker, *Government and Contractors: The British Treasury and War Supplies, 1775–1783* (London: Athlone Press, 1971); R. Arthur Bowler, *Logistics and the Failure of the British Army in America, 1775–1783* (Princeton: Princeton University Press, 1975), and Bowler, "Logistics and Operations in the American Revolution," in *Reconsiderations on the Revolutionary War: Selected Essays*, ed. Don Higginbotham, pp. 54–71 (Westport, CT: Greenwood Press, 1978). Lawrence H. Leder has written an insightful essay on prerevolutionary supply of British troops in America that lays bare the corruption and incompetence involving this crucial and lucrative area: "Military Victualing in Colonial New York," in *Business Enterprise in Early New York*, ed. Joseph R. Frese and Jacob Judd, pp. 16–54 (Tarrytown, NY: Sleepy Hollow Press, 1979). John Brewer, *The Sinews of Power: War, Money and the English State, 1688–1783* (New York: Alfred A. Knopf, 1989), perceptively analyzes Britain's formidable imperial reach under a "fiscal-military state," which became overextended during the American Revolution. See also Jonathan R. Dull, *The French Navy and American Independence: A Study of Arms and Diplomacy, 1774–1787* (Princeton: Princeton University Press, 1975).

39. The discussion of the nation's financial crisis, its consequences, and the attempted solutions is based principally upon Ferguson, *Power of the Purse*, pp. 46–69, 109–10; Johnson, *American Commissariat*, pp. 154–76; Ver Steeg, *Robert Morris*, pp. 42–57; Nettels, *National Economy*, pp. 25–31; Miller, *Triumph of Freedom*, pp. 459–563; Huston, *Sinews of War*, pp. 58–69; Broadus Mitchell, *The Price of Independence: A Realistic View of the American Revolution* (New York: Oxford University Press, 1974), pp. 86–112; Higginbotham, *War of American Independence*, pp. 288–96; Hatch, *American Revolutionary Army*, p. 18; and Wood, *American Republic*, pp. 360–63.

40. Recent scholarly publications on states and localities during the American Revolution have added substantially to information and understanding of the event. For a sampling of this literature, see Richard Buel, Jr., *Dear Liberty: Connecticut's Mobilization for the Revolutionary War* (Middletown, CT: Wesleyan University Press, 1980); Harold E. Selesky, *War and Society in Colonial Connecticut* (New Haven: Yale University Press, 1990); Chester McArthur Destler, *Connecticut: The Provisions State* (Chester, CT: Pequot Press, 1973); William C. Wright, ed., *New Jersey in the American Revolution*, vol. 2 (Trenton: New Jersey Historical Commission, 1973); Donald Wallace White, *A Village at War: Chatham, New Jersey, and the American Revolution* (Rutherford, NJ: Fairleigh Dickinson University Press, 1979); Ronald Hoffman, *A*

Spirit of Dissension: Economics, Politics, and the Revolution in Maryland (Baltimore: Johns Hopkins University Press, 1973); John E. Selby, *The Revolution in Virginia, 1775–1783* (Charlottesville: University Press of Virginia, 1988); Stephen E. Patterson, *Political Parties in Revolutionary Massachusetts* (Madison: University of Wisconsin Press, 1973); Edward Countryman, *A People in Revolution: The American Revolution and Political Society in New York, 1760–1790* (Baltimore: Johns Hopkins University Press, 1981); Roger J. Champagne, *Alexander McDougall and the American Revolution in New York* (Schenectady, NY: Union College Press, 1975); Ronald Hoffman and Peter J. Albert, eds., *Sovereign States in an Age of Uncertainty* (Charlottesville: University Press of Virginia, 1981); Lemuel David Molovinsky, "Pennsylvania's Legislative Efforts to Finance the War for Independence: A Study of the Continuity of Colonial Finance, 1775–83" (Ph.D. diss., Temple University, 1975); and John David McBride, "The Virginia War Effort, 1775–1783: Manpower Policies and Practices" (Ph.D. diss., University of Virginia, 1977).

41. Of course, a plethora of studies exists on the origins and evolution of the Federalist–Antifederalist factions. In terms of interpretation, I have found H. James Henderson, *Party Politics in the Continental Congress* (New York: McGraw-Hill, 1974) to be the most helpful and closest to my position, which I would characterize as modified Progressive in nature, in contrast to the neo-Whig interpretation of Robert E. Brown, Forrest McDonald, Bernard Bailyn, and others. For bibliographical and analytical discussions of revolutionary historiography, see Gordon S. Wood, "Rhetoric and Reality in the American Revolution," *William and Mary Quarterly* 23 (January 1966): 3–32; Jack P. Greene, ed., *The Reinterpretation of the American Revolution, 1763–1789* (New York: Harper and Row, 1968), pp. 2–74, and Greene, "Revolution, Confederation, and Constitution, 1763–1787," in *The Reinterpretation of American History and Culture*, ed. William H. Cartwright and Richard L. Watson, Jr., pp. 259–95 (Washington, DC: National Council for the Social Studies, 1973); Robert Middlekauff, *The Glorious Cause: The American Revolution, 1763–1783* (New York: Oxford University Press, 1982), pp. 669–74; and Linda K. Kerber, "The Revolutionary Generation: Ideology, Politics, and Culture in the Early Republic," in *The New American History*, ed. Eric Foner, pp. 25–49 (Philadelphia: Temple University Press, 1990).

Some of the volumes I have found insightful and helpful include Merrill Jensen, *The Articles of Confederation: An Interpretation of the Social-Constitutional History of the American Revolution, 1774–1781* (Madison: University of Wisconsin Press, 1940), Jensen, *The New Nation: A History of the United States During the Confederation, 1781–1789* (New York: Alfred A. Knopf, 1950), Jensen, *The Founding of a Nation: A History of the American Revolution, 1763–1776* (New York: Oxford University Press, 1968), and Jensen, *The American Revolution Within America* (New York: New York University Press, 1974); Jackson Turner Main, *The Anti-Federalist: Critics of the Constitution, 1781–1789* (Chapel Hill: University of North Carolina Press, 1961), Main, *The Upper House in Revolutionary America, 1763–1788* (Madison: University of Wisconsin Press, 1967), Main, *Political Parties Before the Constitution* (Chapel Hill: University of North Carolina Press, 1973), and Main, *The Sovereign States, 1775–1783* (New York: New Viewpoints, 1973); Gary B. Nash, *Red, White, and Black: The Peoples of Early America* (Englewood Cliffs, NJ: Prentice-Hall, 1974), and Nash, *The Urban Crucible: Social Change, Political Consciousness, and the Origins of the American Revolution* (Cambridge: Harvard University Press, 1979); Ferguson, *Power of the Purse,* and E. James Ferguson, "The Nationalists of 1781–1783 and the Economic Interpretation of the Constitution," *Journal of American History* 56 (July 1969): 241–61; Wood, *American Republic,* and Gordon S. Wood, *The Radicalism of the American Revolution* (New York: Alfred A. Knopf, 1992); Cathy D. Matson and Peter S. Onuf, *A Union of Interests: Political and Economic Thought in Revolutionary America* (Lawrence: University Press of Kansas, 1990); East, *Business Enterprise;* Roger H. Brown, *Redeeming the Republic: Federalists, Taxation, and the Origins of the Constitution* (Baltimore: Johns Hopkins University Press, 1993); James A. Henretta, *The Evolution of American Society, 1700–1815: An Interdisciplinary Analysis* (Lexington, MA: D. C. Heath, 1973); Esmond Wright, *Fabric of Freedom, 1763–1800,* rev. ed. (New York: Hill and Wang, 1978); W. W. Abbott, *The Colonial Origins of the United States: 1607–1763* (New York: John Wiley and Sons, 1975); Arthur M. Schlesinger, *The Colonial Merchants and the American Revolution* (new printing, New York: Frederick Ungar Publishing Company, 1957); Edmund S. Morgan and Helen M. Morgan, *The Stamp Act Crisis: Prologue to Revolution* (Chapel Hill: University of North Carolina Press, 1953); John A. Neuenschwander, *The Middle Colonies and the Coming of the American Revolution* (Port Washington, NY: Kennikat Press, 1973); Charles S. Olson, *Artisans for Independence: Philadelphia Mechanics and the American Revolution* (Syracuse, NY: Syracuse University Press, 1975); James Kirby Martin, *Men in Rebellion: Higher Governmental Leaders and the Coming of the American Revolution* (New Brunswick, NJ: Rutgers University Press, 1973); Eric Robson, *The American Revolution in Its Political and Military Aspects, 1763–1783* (Hamden, CT: Archon Books, 1965); Ralph Ketcham, *From Colony to Country: The Revolution in American Thought, 1750–1820* (New York: Macmillan, 1974); Marc Egnal, *A Mighty Empire: The Origins of the American Revolution* (Ithaca, NY: Cornell University Press, 1988); Joseph Albert Ernst, *Money and Politics in America, 1755–1775: A Study in the Currency Act of 1764 and the Political Economy of Revolution* (Chapel Hill: University of North Carolina Press, 1973); Morton White, *The Philosophy of the American Revolution* (New York: Oxford University Press, 1978); Richard D. Brown, *Modernization: The Transformation of American Life, 1600–1865* (New York: Hill and Wang, 1976); and James Henry Fowler II, "The Breakdown of Congressional Authority: A Study of the Relations Between the Continental Congress and the States, 1780–1783" (Ph.D. diss., Oklahoma State University, 1974).

Several anthologies also contain numerous essays of importance on the American Revolution and its divisions and consequences. See Stephen G. Kurtz and James H. Hutson, eds., *Essays on the American Revolution* (Chapel Hill: University of North Carolina Press, 1973); Alfred F. Young, ed., *The American Revolution: Explorations in the History of American Radicalism* (DeKalb: Northern Illinois University Press, 1976), and Young, ed., *Beyond the American Revolution: Explorations in the History of American Radicalism* (DeKalb: Northern Illinois University Press, 1993); Larry R. Gerlach, ed., *Legacies of the American Revolution* (Logan: Utah State University Press, 1978); William M. Fowler, Jr., and Wallace Coyle, eds., *The American Revolution: Changing Perspectives* (Boston: Northeastern University Press, 1979); and Jack P. Greene, ed., *The American Revolution: Its Character and Limits* (New York: New York University Press, 1987).

42. The commercial background and the military offices held by various individuals and groups during the Revolution are scattered throughout the extensive litera-

ture already cited. Risch, *Supplying Washington's Army,* pp. 426–38, addresses the issue directly and in the context of conflicts of interests and corruption.

43. The analysis of Morris is based principally upon the exceptionally detailed and thorough study by Nuxoll, *Congress and the Munitions Merchants;* other sources that I have used and that are crucial to the analysis are cited in notes 41 and 59.

44. Ferguson, *American Revolution,* pp. 210–13; see also the sources on British supply and logistics in note 38.

45. The most systematic survey of the various executive departments from 1781 to 1789 is found in Sanders, *Executive Departments,* pp. 95–192.

46. Ward, *Department of War,* pp. 11–19, and Weigley, *United States Army,* pp. 47–49.

47. Jensen, *New Nation,* pp. 56–57; Ferguson, *Power of the Purse,* pp. 117–22; Ver Steeg, *Robert Morris,* pp. 57–64; Nettels, *National Economy,* p. 31.

48. Carp, *Starve the Army,* pp. 210–16; Clarfield, *Timothy Pickering,* pp. 73–74; and Royster, *Revolutionary People,* pp. 308–11. Risch, *Supplying Washington's Army,* pp. 134–40, 246–51, 307–9, emphasizes Washington's importance in directing supply operations for Yorktown more than Morris's. The two approaches need not be seen as contradictory but as a difference in focus and emphasis. Huston, *Logistics of Liberty,* pp. 263–72, gives equal credit to Morris and Washington.

49. Ferguson, *Power of the Purse,* pp. 125–31.

50. Bray Hammond, *Banks and Politics in America, from the Revolution to the Civil War* (Princeton: Princeton University Press, 1957), pp. 42–53; Nettels, *National Economy,* pp. 31–33; Roy A. Foulke, *The Sinews of American Commerce* (New York: Dun and Bradstreet, 1941), pp. 131–33.

51. Ferguson, *Power of the Purse,* pp. 122, 131–35; Risch, *Quartermaster,* 70–73; Risch, *Supplying Washington's Army,* pp. 246–58; Paullin, *Naval Administration,* pp. 41–53; Hatch, *American Revolutionary Army,* pp. 113–23; and Ver Steeg, *Robert Morris,* pp. 72–84.

52. For a thorough treatment of the war's effects upon most aspects of pure and applied science, see Brooke Hindle, *The Pursuit of Science in Revolutionary America, 1735–1789* (Chapel Hill: University of North Carolina Press, 1956). York, *Mechanical Metamorphosis,* presents a detailed survey of technological change during the revolutionary era.

53. Jensen, *New Nation,* pp. 58–67; Ver Steeg, *Robert Morris,* pp. 98–103; Ferguson, *Power of the Purse,* pp. 116–17, 141–42; Miller, *Triumph of Freedom,* pp. 661–67.

54. Jensen, *New Nation,* pp. 63–66, 74–76, 375–82, 388–91, 399–400, 407–8; Ferguson, *Power of the Purse,* pp. 142–55; Ver Steeg, *Robert Morris,* pp. 89–96, 120–34, 166–78, 184–86.

55. Ver Steeg, *Robert Morris,* pp. 78–79, 156, 185–86, and Ferguson, *Power of the Purse,* pp. 114–15, 121–24.

56. Ferguson, *Power of the Purse,* pp. 114–15, 121–24.

57. Ibid., pp. 175–76; Jensen, *New Nation,* pp. 399–428; Ver Steeg, *Robert Morris,* pp. 193–99.

58. Ver Steeg, *Robert Morris,* pp. 170–76; Jensen, *New Nation,* pp. 76–84, 389–91; Ferguson, *Power of the Purse,* pp. 140–74; Weigley, *United States Army,* pp. 74–79; and Miller, *Triumph of Freedom,* pp. 669–80. One of the most thorough analyses of the Newburgh conspiracy within the larger issue of American military policy during

the revolutionary period and after is Richard H. Kohn, *Eagle and Sword: The Federalists and the Creation of the Military Establishment, 1783–1802* (New York: Free Press, 1975), pp. 17–39. See also Minor Meyers, Jr., *Liberty Without Anarchy: A History of the Society of Cincinnati* (Charlottesville: University Press of Virginia, 1983).

59. The best sources for tracing and analyzing the private-public commercial activities and extensive national and international connections of Robert Morris are Nuxoll, *Congress and the Munitions Merchants;* Ferguson, *Power of the Purse;* Ver Steeg, *Robert Morris;* and Robert F. Jones, *"The King of the Alley": William Duer, Politician, Entrepreneur, and Speculator, 1768–1799* (Philadelphia: American Philosophical Society, 1992). E. James Ferguson et al., eds., *The Papers of Robert Morris, 1781–1784* (Pittsburgh, PA: University of Pittsburgh Press, 1973–1988), offer the opportunity to trace Morris's methods and connections through primary documents. William Graham Sumner, *The Financier and the Finances of the American Revolution*, 2 vols. (1891; reprint, New York: Augustus M. Kelley, 1968), also presents helpful material in his "balanced" but confusing study of the superintendent of finance. Ellis Paxson Oberholtzer, *Robert Morris: Patriot and Financier* (New York: Macmillan, 1903), is much too defensive about his subject to be of much assistance. Stuart Bruchey, *The Roots of American Economic Growth, 1607–1861: An Essay in Social Causation* (New York: Harper and Row, 1965), presents a useful context for understanding the role of the businessperson in the nation's economic life. East's *Business Enterprise* is invaluable as a broad-gauged analysis of the emerging business community and its patterns and practices. Although less significant, the following books should be consulted about persons and institutions, both private and public, that helped shape the revolutionary record in the area of commerce and political economy: Robert Zemsky, *Merchants, Farmers, and River Gods: An Essay on Eighteenth-Century American Politics* (Boston, MA: Gambit, 1971), pp. 178–215; Peter Dobkin Hall, *The Organization of American Culture, 1700–1900: Private Institutions, Elites, and the Origins of American Nationality* (New York: New York University Press, 1982), pp. 55–75; E. A. J. Johnson, *The Foundations of American Economic Freedom: Government and Enterprise in the Age of Washington* (Minneapolis: University of Minnesota Press, 1973), pp. 3–39; Miller, *Triumph of Freedom;* Greene, *Revolutionary Generation;* Joseph S. Davis, *Essays in the Earlier History of American Corporations*, 2 vols. (1917; reprint, New York: Russell and Russell, 1965); Risch, *Quartermaster* and *Supplying Washington's Army;* Foulke, *Sinews of American Commerce;* Johnson, *American Commissariat;* Max M. Mintz, *Gouverneur Morris and the American Revolution* (Norman: University of Oklahoma Press, 1970); Daniel Walther, *Gouverneur Morris: Witness of Two Revolutions* (New York: Funk and Wagnalls, 1934); Kenneth R. Rossman, *Thomas Mifflin and the Politics of the American Revolution* (Chapel Hill: University of North Carolina Press, 1952); Huston, *Sinews of War* and *Logistics of Liberty;* Thayer, *Nathanael Greene;* Hatch, *American Revolutionary Army;* Sanders, *Executive Departments.*

Many of these authors discuss in varying degrees of length and depth the general attitude of Americans toward business. For some examples, see Jackson Turner Main, *The Social Structure of Revolutionary America* (Princeton: Princeton University Press, 1965), pp. 207–9; Wood, *American Republic*, pp. 418–25; and E. James Ferguson, "Business, Government, and Congressional Investigation in the Revolution," *William and Mary Quarterly* 16 (July 1959): 293–318.

60. Henderson, *Party Politics*, pp. 247, 239.

61. Main, *Sovereign States*, p. 250. J. E. Crowley, *This Sheba, Self: The Conceptualization of Economic Life in Eighteenth-Century America* (Baltimore: Johns Hopkins University Press, 1974), on a high level of conceptualization and with great subtlety analyzes the shift in economic mobilization from emphasis upon the state to stress upon the merchants and its consequences for American society then and in the future. Allan Kulikoff, *The Agrarian Origins of American Capitalism* (Charlottesville: University Press of Virginia, 1992), analyzes the periods before, after, and during the Revolution through an exceptionally clear rural prism.

62. We know a great deal about the politics of the revolutionary period, but monographs on many of the economic consequences of the war, let alone a general work of synthesis, are yet to be written. The preceding works on the colonial economy and those in notes 1 through 6 have made a good start along these lines. Moreover, in *The Sovereign States*, chapter 7, Main offers some substantial and suggestive information and analysis about the wartime economy. Also, various essays in Ronald Hoffman et al., eds., *The Economy of Early America: The Revolutionary Period, 1763–1790* (Charlottesville: University Press of Virginia, 1988), are useful. Edwin J. Perkins has written a fine article on colonial business: "The Entrepreneurial Spirit in Colonial America." Nonetheless, in "The American Revolution Considered as an Economic Movement," *Huntington Library Quarterly* 20 (August 1957); 361–72, Clarence L. Ver Steeg's call for filling the vacuum on the economics of the Revolution still remains largely unanswered.

63. Bowle offers this line of analysis in "Logistics and Operations in the American Revolution," pp. 70–71. Marshall Smelser, *The Winning of Independence* (Chicago: Quadrangle Books, 1972), pp. 370–76, sets forth an especially evenhanded and insightful conclusion about the "winning of independence."

CHAPTER THREE. THE POLITICAL ECONOMY OF WARFARE: 1790–1815

1. The Washington administration, Hamilton's place in it, and the rise and the consequences of the Federalist party in terms of both domestic and foreign policy are surveyed and analyzed in John C. Miller, *The Federalist Era, 1789–1801* (New York: Harper and Row, 1960), and see also Miller's *Toward a More Perfect Union: The American Republic, 1783–1815* and *The Emergence of the Nation, 1783–1815* (Glenview, IL: Scott, Foresman and Company, 1970, 1972); Marcus Cunliffe, *The Nation Takes Shape: 1789–1837* (Chicago: University of Chicago Press, 1959), pp. 11–121; Morton Borden, *Parties and Politics in the Early Republic, 1789–1815* (New York: Thomas Y. Crowell Company, 1967), pp. 1–56; Robert H. Wiebe, *The Opening of American Society: From the Adoption of the Constitution to the Eve of Disunion* (New York: Alfred A. Knopf, 1984), pp. 3–125; Richard Hofstadter, *The Idea of a Party System: The Rise of Legitimate Opposition in the United States, 1780–1840* (Berkeley: University of California Press, 1969), pp. 1–169; Joseph Charles, *The Origins of the American Party System* (New York: Harper and Row, 1956); William Nisbet Chambers, *Political Parties in a New Nation: The American Experience, 1776–1809* (New York: Oxford University Press, 1963), pp. 1–169; James M. Banner, Jr., *To The Hartford Convention: The Federalists and the Origins of Party Politics in Massachusetts, 1789–1815* (New York:

Alfred A. Knopf, 1970); Richard Buel, Jr., *Securing the Revolution: Ideology in American Politics, 1789–1815* (Ithaca, NY: Cornell University Press, 1972), pp. 1–240; Leonard D. White, *The Federalists: A Study in Administrative History, 1789–1801* (New York: Macmillan, 1948); Benjamin W. Labaree, *Patriots and Partisans: The Merchants of Newburyport, 1764–1815* (Cambridge: Harvard University Press, 1962), pp. 1–119; Lisle A. Rose, *Prologue to Democracy: The Federalist in the South, 1789–1800* (Lexington: University of Kentucky Press, 1968); E. A. J. Johnson, *The Foundations of American Economic Freedom: Government and Enterprise in the Age of Washington* (Minneapolis: University of Minnesota Press, 1973); Rudolph M. Bell, *Party and Faction in American Politics: The House of Representatives, 1789–1801* (Westport, CT: Greenwood Press, 1973); Forrest McDonald, *The Presidency of George Washington* (Lawrence: University Press of Kansas, 1974); McDonald, *Alexander Hamilton: A Biography* (New York: W. W. Norton, 1979); Paul A. Varg, *New England and Foreign Relations, 1789–1850* (Hanover, NH: University Press of New England, 1983), pp. 3–72; Ralph Ketcham, *Presidents Above Party: The First American Presidency, 1789–1829* (Chapel Hill: University of North Carolina Press, 1984); and Vernon G. Setser, *The Commercial Reciprocity Policy of the United States, 1774–1829* (Philadelphia: University of Pennsylvania Press, 1937), pp. 52–149. The most recent, thorough, and authoritative treatment of these years is that of Stanley Elkins and Eric McKitrick, *The Age of Federalism* (New York: Oxford University Press, 1993). See also James Roger Sharp, *American Politics in the Early Republic* (New Haven: Yale University Press, 1993). See also the latest biographies on Washington: Glenn A. Phelps, *George Washington and American Constitutionalism* (Lawrence: University Press of Kansas, 1993), and Richard N. Smith, *Patriarch: George Washington and the New American Nation* (Boston: Houghton Mifflin, 1993).

2. The discussion of Adams draws upon the sources in note 1 and on Manning J. Dauer, *The Adams Federalists* (Baltimore: Johns Hopkins University Press, 1953); Ralph Adams Brown, *The Presidency of John Adams* (Lawrence: University Press of Kansas, 1975); John Ferling, *John Adams: A Life* (Knoxville: University of Tennessee Press, 1992); Joseph J. Ellis, *Passionate Sage: The Character and Legacy of John Adams* (New York: W. W. Norton, 1993); Alexander DeConde, *The Quasi-War: The Politics and Diplomacy of the Undeclared War with France, 1797–1801* (New York: Charles Scribner's Sons, 1966); and Reginald Horsman, *The Diplomacy of the New Republic, 1776–1815* (Arlington Heights, IL: Harlan Davidson, 1985), pp. 42–78.

3. The analysis of the Republicans under the administrations of Jefferson and Madison is drawn partly on some of the surveys and monographs cited in the preceding notes and more importantly on John Mayfield, *The New Nation, 1800–1845* (New York: Hill and Wang, 1982)—Charles M. Wiltse's original version of this volume (Hill and Wang, 1961) is still worth consulting; Marshall Smelser, *The Democratic Republic, 1801–1815* (New York: Harper and Row, 1968); Noble E. Cunningham, Jr., *The Jeffersonian Republicans: The Formation of Party Organization, 1789–1801* (Chapel Hill: University of North Carolina Press, 1957); Cunningham, *Jeffersonian Republicans in Power;* Cunningham, *The Process of Government Under Jefferson* (Princeton: Princeton University Press, 1978); Leonard D. White, *The Jeffersonians: A Study in Administrative History, 1801–1829* (New York: Macmillan, 1951); Charles A. Beard, *Economic Origins of Jeffersonian Democracy* (New York: Macmillan, 1915); James Sterling Young, *The Washington Community, 1800–1818* (New York: Columbia Univer-

sity Press, 1966); Merrill D. Peterson, *Thomas Jefferson and the New Nation* (New York: Oxford University Press, 1970); James A. Henretta, *The Evolution of American Society, 1700–1815: An Interdisciplinary Analysis* (Lexington, MA: D. C. Heath, 1973); Daniel Sisson, *The American Revolution of 1800* (New York: Alfred A. Knopf, 1974); Forrest McDonald, *The Presidency of Thomas Jefferson* (Lawrence: University Press of Kansas, 1976); Norman K. Risjord, *Jefferson's America, 1760–1815* (Madison, WI: Madison House, 1991); Robert Doherty, *Society and Power: Five New England Towns, 1800–1860* (Amherst: University of Massachusetts Press, 1977); Lance Banning, *The Jeffersonian Persuasion: Evolution of a Party Ideology* (Ithaca, NY: Cornell University Press, 1978); Robert M. Johnstone, Jr., *Jefferson and the Presidency: Leadership in the Young Republic* (Ithaca, NY: Cornell University Press, 1978); Drew R. McCoy, *The Elusive Republic: Political Economy in Jeffersonian America* (New York: W. W. Norton, 1980); Joyce Appleby, *Capitalism and a New Social Order: The Republican Vision of the 1790s* (New York: New York University Press, 1984); Richard K. Matthews, *The Radical Politics of Thomas Jefferson: A Revisionist View* (Lawrence: University Press of Kansas, 1984); Lawrence S. Kaplan, *Entangling Alliances with None: American Foreign Policy in the Age of Jefferson* (Kent, OH: Kent State University Press, 1987); John R. Nelson, Jr., *Liberty and Property: Political Economy and Policymaking in the New Nation, 1789–1812* (Baltimore: Johns Hopkins University Press, 1987); Doron S. Ben-Altar, *The Origins of Jeffersonian Commercial Policy and Diplomacy* (New York: St. Martin's Press, 1993); Stephen Skowronek, *The Politics Presidents Make: Leadership from John Adams to George Bush* (Cambridge: Harvard University Press, 1993), pp. 61–127; Alvin Kass, *Politics in New York State, 1800–1830* (Syracuse, NY: Syracuse University Press, 1965); and G. S. Rowe, *Thomas McKean: The Shaping of an American Republicanism* (Boulder: Colorado Associated University Press, 1978).

4. Smelser, *Democratic Republic*, pp. 317–19, defends Madison against his many detractors. Madison's biographers are generally positive. See Irving Brant, *The Fourth President: A Life of James Madison* (Indianapolis: Bobbs-Merrill, 1970); Drew R. McCoy, *The Last of the Fathers: James Madison and the Republican Legacy* (New York: Cambridge University Press, 1989); Robert A. Rutland, *The Presidency of James Madison* (Lawrence: University Press of Kansas, 1990); and Jack N. Rakove, *James Madison and the Creation of the American Republic* (Glenview, IL: Scott, Foresman, 1990). The overall quality of Madison's leadership during the War of 1812, along with the nation's reasons for entering the war, will be analyzed later.

5. Lee Soltow, *Men and Wealth in the United States, 1850–1870* (New Haven: Yale University Press, 1975), pp. 24–25, 59–91, 123, 145, 179–80. Soltow's entire volume must be read and consulted to appreciate the full quality and extent of his analysis. Most of his figures are for the period 1850–1870, although he argues that there was no basic difference between those years and the period 1790–1800. He develops, refines, and broadens this theme in a later publication: *Distribution of Wealth and Income in the United States in 1798* (Pittsburgh, PA: Pittsburgh University Press, 1989).

Wealth distribution, of course, is a controversial study that has received considerable attention of late and resulted in some significant publications. For some important examples, see Edward Pessen, *Riches, Class, and Power Before the Civil War* (Lexington, MA: D. C. Heath, 1973), whose notes offer a fairly good summary of other relevant studies, how they differ from his, and their interpretative significance (Soltow is also helpful in this regard); Pessen, ed., *Three Centuries of Social Mobility in*

America (Lexington, MA: D. C. Heath, 1974); Soltow, ed., *Six Papers on the Size Distribution of Wealth and Income,* vol. 33, *Studies in Income and Wealth,* National Bureau of Economic Research (New York: Columbia University Press, 1969); Jackson Turner Main, *The Social Structure of Revolutionary America* (Princeton: Princeton University Press, 1965); Main, "Trends in Wealth Concentration Before 1860," *Journal of Economic History* 31 (June 1971): 445–47; Alice Hanson Jones, *Wealth of a Nation to Be: The American Colonies on the Eve of the Revolution* (New York: Columbia University Press, 1980)—the author's bibliography is one of the most complete on the subject and includes citations for all the important studies of Simon Kuznets and Robert E. Gallman; John J. McCusker and Russell R. Menard, *The Economy of British America, 1607–1789* (Chapel Hill: University of North Carolina Press, 1985), particularly chapter 12; various essays in Robert E. Gallman and John Joseph Wallis, eds., *American Economic Growth and Standards of Living Before the Civil War* (Chicago: University of Chicago Press, 1992); Carole Shammas, "A New Look at Long-Term Trends in Wealth Inequality in the United States," *American Historical Review* 98 (April 1993): 412–31; and James L. Huston, "The American Revolutionaries, the Political Economy of Aristocracy, and the American Concept of the Distribution of Wealth, 1765–1900," *American Historical Review* 98 (October 1993): 1079–1105.

6. Sidney H. Aronson, *Status and Kinship in the Higher Civil Service: Standards of Selection in the Administrations of John Adams, Thomas Jefferson, and Andrew Jackson* (Cambridge: Harvard University Press, 1964); Carl E. Prince, *The Federalists and the Origins of the U.S. Civil Service* (New York: New York University Press, 1977); and Noble E. Cunningham, Jr., *The Jeffersonian Republicans in Power: Party Operation, 1801–1809* (Chapel Hill: University of North Carolina Press, 1963), pp. 302–3. Leonard D. White presents a plethora of information on the status, background, and performance of federal officials from 1789 through 1829: see *Federalists and Jeffersonians.* The most systematic study of America's political leadership at the highest national levels between 1790 and 1815 and including background, wealth, status, and kinship is presented in Philip H. Burch, Jr., *Elites in American History: The Federalist Years to the Civil War* (New York: Holmes and Meier Publishers, 1981), pp. 45–100.

7. Alexander Hamilton, James Madison, and John Jay, *The Federalist or, the New Constitution* (New York: E. P. Dutton, 1911), nos. 4, 23, 24, 30, 31, and 34; Jacob E. Cooke, ed., *The Reports of Alexander Hamilton* (New York: Harper and Row, 1964), the reports on public credit, "Opinion on the Constitutionality of the Bank," and "Report on Manufactures"; Louis M. Hacker, *Alexander Hamilton in the American Tradition* (New York: McGraw-Hill, 1957), pp. 148, 151, 165–90, 249; John C. Miller, *Alexander Hamilton: Portrait in Paradox* (New York: Harper and Row, 1959), pp. 282–86; Curtis R. Nettles, *The Emergence of a National Economy, 1775–1815* (New York: Harper and Row, 1962), pp. 89–108. Washington and Hamilton's views on military and economic power are excerpted from documents in Walter Millis, ed., *American Military Thought* (Indianapolis: Bobbs-Merrill, 1966), pp. 16–28, 41–46, 70–73. See also R. Ernest Dupuy and Trevor N. Dupuy, *Military Heritage of America* (New York: McGraw-Hill, 1956), pp. 120–21; W. R. Brock, "Alexander Hamilton, Economic Nationalist," in *Essays on the Early Republic, 1789–1815,* ed. Leonard W. Levy and Carl Siracusa, pp. 35–52 (Hinsdale, IL: Dryden Press, 1974); and Richard H. Kohn, *Eagle and Sword: The Federalists and the Creation of the Military Establishment,*

1783–1802 (New York: Free Press, 1975), pp. 73–81. National security and national defense as prerequisites for genuine national independence are central to the entire analysis of Frederick W. Marks III, *Independence on Trial: Foreign Affairs and the Making of the Constitution,* 2d ed. (Wilmington, DE: Scholarly Resources, 1986).

8. Nettles, *National Economy,* pp. 122–26.

9. U.S. Bureau of the Census, *Historical Statistics of the United States, Colonial Times to 1970* (Washington, DC: U.S. Government Printing Office, 1975), pt. 2, pp. 750–51, 761, 866–68; and Emory R. Johnson et al., *History of Domestic and Foreign Commerce of the United States* (1915; reprint, Washington, DC: Carnegie Institution, 1922), 2: 14–30.

10. The standard and best source on this topic is Harold D. Woodman, *King Cotton and His Retainers: Financing and Marketing the Cotton Crop of the South, 1800–1925* (Lexington: University of Kentucky Press, 1968). See also Stuart Bruchey, ed., *Cotton and the Growth of the American Economy: 1790–1860* (New York: Harcourt, Brace, and World, 1967), pp. 14–21, 29–30, 221–32; Johnson, *Domestic and Foreign Commerce,* 2: 20; and Nettles, *National Economy,* pp. 183–204.

11. Interregional trade and American economic growth in the nineteenth century are the subject of great controversy among demand-oriented scholars such as Douglass North and their numerous supply-oriented detractors such as Albert Fishlow, Diane Lindstrom, and Robert Gallman. I have essentially taken the position of the supply-explanation school. The varying interpretations and their implications, including full citations of the publications involved, are competently summarized in Susan Previant Lee and Peter Passell, *A New Economic View of American History* (New York: W. W. Norton, 1979), pp. 146–53.

12. Johnson, *Domestic and Foreign Commerce,* 1: 206–12.

13. Douglass C. North, *The Economic Growth of the United States, 1790–1860* (New York: W. W. Norton, 1966), pp. 42–45, 47–51, and Nettles, *National Economy,* pp. 232–42.

14. George Rogers Taylor, *The Transportation Revolution, 1815–1860* (New York: Harper and Row, 1951), pp. 15–19; Carter Goodrich, *Government Promotion of American Canals and Railroads, 1800–1890* (New York: Columbia University Press, 1960), pp. 19–48; Johnson, *Domestic and Foreign Commerce,* 1: 202–10; Nettles, *National Economy,* pp. 251–62; and North, *Economic Growth,* pp. 32–35.

15. Johnson, *Domestic and Foreign Commerce,* 2: 20–30.

16. Victor S. Clark, *History of Manufactures in the United States, 1607–1860* (Washington, DC: Carnegie Institution, 1929), 1: 438–48.

17. North, *Economic Growth,* pp. 56–58, and Stanley Lebergott, *The Americans: An Economic Record* (New York: W. W. Norton, 1984), pp. 124–38. Both Nettles, *National Economy,* chapter 13, and Clark, *History of Manufactures,* 1, contain rich detail on manufacturing between 1807 and 1815. For a sophisticated analysis of the growth of manufacturing before and during the War of 1812, including a discussion and evaluation of what various scholars have said on the subject, see Barry Warren Poulson, *Value Added in Manufacturing, Mining, and Agriculture in the American Economy from 1809 to 1839* (New York: Arno Press, 1975).

18. William Hays Simpson, *Some Aspects of America's Textile Industry with Reference to Cotton* (Columbia: University of South Carolina Press, 1966), pp. 1–13; Walter Adams, ed., *The Structure of American Industry: Some Case Studies,* 3d ed. (New

York: Macmillan, 1961), pp. 42–45; Robert Brooke Zevin, *The Growth of Manufacturing in Early Nineteenth Century New England* (New York: Arno Press, 1975), pp. 1–16; and Clark, *History of Manufactures,* 1: 188–93, 260–62, 356–60, 422–31, 448–63, 529–77.

19. Alfred D. Chandler, Jr., *The Visible Hand: The Managerial Revolution in American Business* (Cambridge, MA: Belnap Press, 1977), pp. 50–78; Nettles, *National Economy,* pp. 263–88; and Clark, *History of Manufactures,* 1: 179–80, 408–9, 507, 509. Clark's first volume is a treasure trove of detailed and analytical information about the American industrial scene between 1790 and 1815. However, the information is scattered among most of the chapters and must be sought out.

20. Several works are especially helpful in tracing the organization and evolution of the corporation in the colonial and early national periods; see Joseph S. Davis, *Essays in the Earlier History of American Corporations,* 2 vols. (Cambridge: Harvard University Press, 1917), and Ronald E. Seavoy, *The Origins of the American Business Corporation, 1784–1855* (Westport, CT: Greenwood Press, 1982).

21. Stuart Bruchey, *The Roots of American Economic Growth, 1607–1861: An Essay in Social Causation* (New York: Harper and Row, 1965), pp. 128–33; Bray Hammond, *Banks and Politics in America from the Revolution to the Civil War* (Princeton: Princeton University Press, 1957), pp. 40–171; Paul Studenski and Herman E. Krooss, *Financial History of the United States: Fiscal, Monetary, Banking, and Tariff, Including Financial Administration and State and Local Finance* (New York: McGraw-Hill, 1952), pp. 25–81; Clark, *History of Manufactures,* 1: 455–63; and Nettles, *National Economy,* pp. 123–25, 289–301.

22. In *Economic Development in the Philadelphia Region, 1810–1850* (New York: Columbia University Press, 1978), Diane Lindstrom's analysis applies more to the years after 1815 than before, but much of her information and many of her key observations are still relevant. See Lee and Passell, *New Economic View,* pp. 146–53, for information on the controversy over economic growth about which Lindstrom is an important participant. See also in this regard Bruchey, *Roots of American Economic Growth,* pp. 74–91. Additionally, see David T. Gilchrist, ed., *The Growth of Seaport Cities, 1790–1825* (Charlottesville: University Press of Virginia, 1967); Johnson, *History of Domestic and Foreign Commerce,* 1: 202–16; and Nettles, *National Economy,* pp. 173–82, 209–16. A thorough and imaginative description/analysis of the founding, rise, and development of Pittsburgh, Cincinnati, Lexington, Louisville, and St. Louis is presented in Richard C. Wade, *The Urban Frontier: The Rise of Western Cities, 1790–1830* (Cambridge: Harvard University Press, 1959).

23. Studenski and Krooss, *Financial History of the U.S.,* pp. 12–74; Paul B. Trescott, *Financing American Enterprise: The Story of Commercial Banking* (New York: Harper and Row, 1963), pp. 1–40; Hammond, *Banks,* pp. 3–250; Herman E. Krooss and Martin R. Blyn, *A History of Financial Intermediaries* (New York: Random House, 1971), pp. 3–39; C. Joseph Pusateri, *A History of American Business* (Arlington Heights, IL: Harlan Davidson, 1984), pp. 81–97; Clark, *History of Manufactures,* 1: 335–63, 529–77.

24. For an analysis of growing specialization in economic functions, see Glenn Porter and Harold C. Livesay, *Merchants and Manufacturers: Studies in the Changing Structure of Nineteenth-Century Marketing* (Baltimore: Johns Hopkins University Press, 1971), pp. 1–78; Chandler, *Visible Hand,* pp. 1–49; Thomas C. Cochran, *Busi-*

ness in American Life: A History (New York: McGraw-Hill, 1972), pp. 1–142; Cochran, *200 Years of American Business* (New York: Basic Books, 1977), pp. 3–47; Elisha P. Douglass, *The Coming of Age of American Business: Three Centuries of Enterprise, 1600–1900* (Chapel Hill: University of North Carolina Press, 1971), pp. 1–208; Herman Krooss and Charles Gilbert, *American Business History* (Englewood Cliffs, NJ: Prentice-Hall, 1972), pp. 21–143; Lewis E. Atherton, *The Frontier Merchant in Mid-America* (Columbia: University of Missouri Press, 1971); and Taylor, *Transportation Revolution,* pp. 10–14.

25. The nation's political economy from 1789 to 1815 is covered extensively and with often widely varying interpretations in the numerous sources cited in notes 1–3.

26. The subject of American attitudes toward the military before and during the Revolution is covered in Chapter 2. For sources on the subject, many of which are relevant for the early national period, see notes 8 and 34 of that chapter.

27. Russell F. Weigley, *History of the United States Army* (New York: Macmillan, 1967), pp. 74–84; Allan R. Millett and Peter Maslowski, *For the Common Defense: A Military History of the United States of America* (New York: Free Press, 1984), pp. 83–87; and Marvin A. Kreidberg and Merton G. Henry, *History of Military Mobilization in the United States, 1775–1945* (Washington, DC: Department of the Army, 1955), pp. 23–24.

28. Almost all texts and monographs on the military during the Revolution and after handle this subject. Far and away the outstanding treatment is Russell F. Weigley, *Towards an American Army: Military Thought from Washington to Marshall* (New York: Columbia University Press, 1962), pp. 1–18. See also Elliot M. Bartky, "War and the American Founding: Volunteerism and the Origins of American Military Policy" (Ph.D. diss., Rutgers University, 1983).

29. The best source for this subject is the Constitution itself. I am taking my quotation from a copy reproduced in Alfred H. Kelly, Winfred A. Harbison, and Herman Belz, *The American Constitution: Its Origins and Development,* 6th ed., rev. (New York: W. W. Norton, 1983), pp. 748–67, quotation, p. 752. Of the numerous possible sources on this subject, Weigley, *Towards an American Army,* pp. 1–29, remains the best. See also Howard White, *Executive Influence in Determining Military Policy in the United States* (Urbana: University of Illinois Press, 1925), pp. 18–28; Samuel P. Huntington, *The Soldier and the State: The Theory and Policies of Civil-Military Relations* (Cambridge: Harvard University Press, 1957), pp. 163–221; and various essays in Richard H. Kohn, ed., *The United States Military Under the Constitution of the United States, 1789–1989* (New York: New York University Press, 1991).

30. James Ripley Jacobs, *The Beginning of the U.S. Army, 1783–1812* (Princeton: Princeton University Press, 1947); White, *Federalists,* pp. 145–47; Erna Risch, *Quartermaster Support of the Army: A History of the Corps, 1775–1939* (Washington, DC: Office of the Quartermaster General, 1962), pp. 76–84; Weigley, *U.S. Army,* pp. 79–90. The latest, most complete, and important study of army professional growth in the early national years is William B. Skelton, *An American Profession of Arms: The Army Officer Corps, 1784–1861* (Lawrence: University Press of Kansas, 1992).

31. Weigley, *U.S. Army,* pp. 89–93; Millett and Maslowski, *Common Defense,* pp. 90–94; and Kreidberg and Henry, *Military Mobilization,* pp. 26–30.

32. John K. Mahon, *History of the Militia and the National Guard* (New York: Macmillan, 1983), pp. 46–96; Lawrence Delbert Cress, *Citizens in Arms: The Army*

and the Militia in American Society to the War of 1812 (Chapel Hill: University of North Carolina Press, 1982), pp. 115–49; and Cress, "Reassessing American Military Requirements, 1783–1807," in *Against All Enemies: Interpretations of American Military History from Colonial Times to the Present,* ed. Kenneth J. Hagan and William R. Roberts, pp. 49–69 (New York: Greenwood Press, 1986).

33. The larger context for these military developments is analyzed and documented in notes 1–3. See also the sources in note 32 and Weigley, *U.S. Army,* pp. 97–104, and Millett and Maslowski, *Common Defense,* pp. 93–94.

34. These themes are explored in Harold and Margaret Sprout, *The Rise of American Naval Power: 1776–1918* (Princeton: Princeton University Press, 1946), pp. 7–32; G. Terry Sharrer, "The Search for a Naval Policy, 1783–1812," in *In Peace and War: Interpretations of American Naval Policy, 1775–1884,* ed. Kenneth J. Hagan, pp. 27–38, 2d ed. (Westport, CT: Greenwood Press, 1984); and Marshall Smelser and Stephen T. Powers, "The Fleetless Nation, 1781–1798," in *American Secretaries of the Navy,* 1, *1775–1913,* ed. Paolo E. Coletta, pp. 29–57 (Annapolis, MD: Naval Institute Press, 1980).

35. Charles Oscar Paullin, *Paullin's History of Naval Administration, 1775–1911* (Annapolis, MD: U.S. Naval Institute, 1968), pp. 50–53, 89–118; Marshall Smelser, *The Congress Founds the Navy, 1787–1798* (Notre Dame, IN: University of Notre Dame Press, 1959); Sprout, *American Naval Power,* pp. 16–49; Sharrer, "Search for a Naval Policy," in Hagan, ed., *Peace and War,* pp. 27–38; John J. Carrigg, "Benjamin Stoddert, 18 June 1798–31 March 1801," in Coletta, ed., *American Secretaries of the Navy,* 1: 59–75; A. T. Mahan, *Naval Administration and Warfare: Some General Principles* (London: Sampson Low, Marston, and Company, 1908), pp. 20–48; Weigley, *U.S. Army,* pp. 98–99; Millett and Maslowski, *Common Defense,* pp. 94–99; Spencer C. Tucker, *The Jeffersonian Gunboat Navy* (Columbia: University of South Carolina Press, 1993); and Raymond G. O'Connor, *Origins of the American Navy: Sea Power in the Colonies and the New Nation* (Lanham, MD: University Press of America, 1994). Christopher McKee's *A Gentlemanly and Honorable Profession: The Creation of the U.S. Naval Officer Corps, 1794–1815* (Annapolis, MD: Naval Institute Press, 1991) is a rich and encyclopedic study of the navy's early professional growth.

36. Weigley, *U.S. Army,* pp. 103–4.

37. Millett and Maslowski, *Common Defense,* pp. 98–99.

38. The discussion and analysis of the Republican policies toward the military under the administrations of Jefferson and Madison are based on Reginald C. Stuart, *The Half-way Pacifist: Thomas Jefferson's View of War* (Toronto: University of Toronto Press, 1978); Stuart, *War and American Thought: From the Revolution to the Monroe Doctrine* (Kent, OH: Kent State University Press, 1982), pp. 1–122; Russell F. Weigley, *The American Way of War: A History of United States Military Strategy and Policy* (New York: Macmillan, 1973), pp. 40–55; Weigley, *U.S. Army,* pp. 104–16; Walter Millis, *Arms and Men: A Study in Military History* (New York: Putnam, 1956), pp. 13–71; Steven Watts, *The Republic Reborn: War and the Making of Liberal America, 1790–1820* (Baltimore: Johns Hopkins University Press, 1987); Cress, *Citizens in Arms,* pp. 150–77; Mahon, *History of the Militia,* pp. 63–77; White, *Jeffersonians,* pp. 211–98; Cunningham, *Process of Government Under Jefferson;* Cress, "Reassessing American Military Requirements, 1783–1807," pp. 58–62, and Harry L. Coles, "From Peaceful Coercion to Balanced Forces, 1807–1815," pp. 71–87, in Hagan and

Roberts, eds., *Against All Enemies;* Paullin, *History of Naval Administration,* pp. 119–37; Sprout, *American Naval Power,* pp. 50–72; Frank L. Owsley, Jr., "Robert Smith, 27 July 1801–7 March 1809," 1: 77–90, and Owsley, "Paul Hamilton, 15 May 1809–31 December 1812," 1: 93–98, in Coletta, ed., *American Secretaries of the Navy;* Kreidberg and Henry, *Military Mobilization,* pp. 36–44; and Millett and Maslowski, *Common Defense,* 99–102.

The most recent study of Republican military policy maintains that Jefferson and his secretary of war, Henry Dearborn, gave a high priority to, devoted much time and effort to, and realized great success in both republicanizing and Republicanizing the army between 1801 and 1809. However, much of their effort was lost under Madison's lax approach to the military. Nonetheless, Jefferson and Dearborn had created conditions for making the army, in effect, nonpartisan. This analysis is suggestive, but the author strains excessively and unnecessarily in pressing his line of argument, and he allows the analysis to suffer from inadequately or casually articulated ideas and material. See Theodore J. Crackel, *Mr. Jefferson's Army: Political and Social Reform of the Military Establishment, 1801–1809* (New York: New York University Press, 1987).

39. Risch, *Quartermaster,* pp. 75–84.

40. Ibid., pp. 84–110; James A. Huston, *The Sinews of War: Army Logistics, 1775–1953* (Washington, DC: Office of the Chief of Military History, 1966), pp. 86–89; Lloyd Milton Short, *The Development of National Administrative Organization in the United States* (Baltimore: Johns Hopkins University Press, 1923), pp. 119–25; White, *Federalists,* pp. 145–55; Weigley, *United States Army,* pp. 88–93; Kreidberg and Henry, *Military Mobilization,* pp. 26–30; and Millett and Maslowski, *Common Defense,* pp. 90–94.

41. Risch, *Quartermaster,* pp. 110–33.

42. Ibid.

43. Constance McLaughlin Green, Harry C. Thomson, and Peter C. Roots, *The Ordnance Department: Planning Munitions for War* (Washington, DC: Office of the Chief of Military History, 1955), pp. 14–16, and Huston, *Sinews of War,* pp. 89–101. The subject of arms production will be developed much more fully and analyzed more completely in Chapter 4.

44. Risch, *Quartermaster,* pp. 115–33.

45. The discussion and analysis of the navy and Navy Department under the Federalists is based on Maury Baker, "Cost Overrun, an Early Naval Precedent: Building the First U.S. Warships, 1794–98," *Maryland Historical Magazine* 72 (Fall 1977): 361–72; Paullin, *Naval Administration,* pp. 89–118; John J. Carrigg, "Benjamin Stoddert," in Coletta, ed., *American Secretaries of the Navy,* 1: 59–75; Sharrer, "Search for a Naval Policy," in Hagan, ed., *Peace and War,* pp. 27–38; Sprout, *American Naval Power,* pp. 25–49; and White, *Federalists,* pp. 156–63.

46. The discussion and analysis of naval supply operations under the Republicans is based on Paullin, *Naval Administration,* pp. 119–43; Owsley, "Robert Smith," and "Paul Hamilton," in Coletta, ed., *American Secretaries of the Navy,* 1: 77–98; Sharrer, "Search for a Naval Policy," in Hagan, ed., *Peace and War,* pp. 38–45; Sprout, *American Naval Power,* pp. 50–72; and White, *Jeffersonians,* pp. 265–98.

47. As quoted in White, *Jeffersonians,* p. 229.

48. Ibid., pp. 83–84, 91, 108–9; Risch, *Quartermaster,* pp. 75–133; White, *Federalists,* pp. 147–50; White, *Jeffersonians,* pp. 224–32; and Huston, *Sinews of War,*

86–101. An invaluable source for the day-to-day operations of the peacetime army is Edward M. Coffman, *The Old Army: A Portrait of the American Army in Peacetime, 1784–1898* (New York: Oxford University Press, 1986), pp. 3–41. Also helpful along these lines but with much more emphasis upon war is Francis Paul Prucha, *The Sword of the Republic: The United States Army on the Frontier, 1783–1846* (New York: Macmillan, 1969), pp. 1–137.

49. Risch, *Quartermaster,* pp. 84–113; Huston, *Sinews of War,* pp. 86–92; Weigley, *U.S. Army,* pp. 90–93; and White, *Federalists,* pp. 146–50, 152–53.

50. For sources on the Navy Department's supply operations, see notes 45 and 46; see also Smelser, *Navy,* pp. 72–123.

51. Owsley, "Robert Smith," in Coletta, ed., *American Secretaries of the Navy,* 1: 80.

52. Risch, *Quartermaster,* pp. 98–99, 102–7, 127–29, 150, 162–64. See also the relevant portions of Coffman, *Old Army,* and Prucha, *Sword of the Republic,* on this topic.

53. Risch, *Quartermaster,* pp. 82–84, 120–27.

54. Ibid., pp. 94, 118–19, 159–64, and White, *Jeffersonians,* pp. 228–31.

55. Weigley, *U.S. Army,* pp. 113–14. See also Risch, *Quartermaster,* pp. 119, 159–64.

56. White, *Jeffersonians,* p. 215.

57. The figures are taken from information in U.S. Bureau of the Census, *Historical Statistics,* pt. 2, p. 1115.

58. White, *Federalists,* pp. 323–34, and White, *Jeffersonians,* pp. 108–16. White, *Executive Influence in Military Policy,* examines most issues involved in executive versus legislative control over the military, including appropriations, with considerable insight and much detail. Huntington, *Soldier and the State,* examines civil-military relations in their broadest possible context. The most subtle and supple treatment of this topic for the early years of the republic is found in Marcus Cunliffe, *Soldiers and Civilians: The Martial Spirit in America, 1775–1865* (Boston: Little, Brown, 1968). A narrower perspective but nonetheless valuable insights on war, the military, and constitutional authority are provided in Abraham D. Sofaer, *War, Foreign Affairs and Constitutional Power: The Origins* (Cambridge, MA: Ballinger Publishing Company, 1976), and Francis D. Wormuth and Edwin R. Firmage, *To Chain the Dog of War: The War Power of Congress in History and Law* (Dallas: Southern Methodist University Press, 1986).

Henry Adams, *History of the United States During the Second Administration of James Madison,* vol. 9, pt. 3 (New York: Charles Scribner's Sons, 1921), pp. 226–37, makes some interesting observations on the attitude and aptitude of Americans involving war and the military, a subject that never ceases to intrigue scholars.

The best discussion/analysis of economic forces as they affected the military from the colonial period through the War of 1812 remains the Millis' classical study, *Arms and Men,* pp. 13–80.

59. White, *Federalists,* pp. 471–78. For a more extended list of sources on the business community during this period of time and its nature and functions, see note 24.

60. See Chapter 2.

61. White, *Jeffersonians,* pp. 270–71.

62. This discussion of the merchant/financial community during the revolutionary years largely holds true for the early national period as well (see Chapter 2); note 59 of that chapter is particularly significant. See also note 24 in this chapter.

63. Carrigg, "Stoddert," in Coletta, ed., *American Secretaries of the Navy*, 1: 62, 65, 71; Sprout, *American Naval Power*, pp. 21–22, 34–37, 42; Paullin, *Naval Administration*, pp. 95, 117–18; Smelser, *Navy*, p. 73; Allan Westcott, ed., *American Seapower Since 1775*, rev. ed. (Philadelphia: J. B. Lippincott, 1952), p. 29; and Paolo E. Coletta, *The American Naval Heritage in Brief* (Washington, DC: University Press of America, 1978), p. 78.

64. Merritt Roe Smith, *Harpers Ferry and the New Technology* (Ithaca, NY: Cornell University Press, 1977), pp. 28–36.

65. Wade, *Urban Frontier*, pp. 26, 57–64, 66–68, 71, 161–63.

66. Coles, "From Peaceful Coercion to Balanced Forces," in Hagan and Roberts, eds., *Against All Enemies*, p. 81. See also John Allen Krout and Dixon Ryan Fox, *The Completion of Independence, 1790–1830* (New York: Macmillan, 1944), pp. 202–7, and Samuel E. Morison, Frederick Merk, and Frank Freidel, *Dissent in Three American Wars* (Cambridge: Harvard University Press, 1970), pp. 3–31.

67. An excellent source for dealing with the political intricacies at home preceding the War of 1812 that helped to push the nation toward conflict is J. C. A. Stagg, *Mr. Madison's War: Politics, Diplomacy, and Warfare in the Early American Republic, 1783–1830* (Princeton: Princeton University Press, 1983). See also the dissertation upon which Stagg's book is based: "Revolt Against Virginia: Republican Politics and the Commencement of the War of 1812" (Ph.D. diss., Princeton University, 1974).

68. Stagg, *Mr. Madison's War*, also presents a good analysis of the nation's final entry into the war. I attributed some influence to the so-called War Hawks and land hunger for American entry into war. These I consider to be secondary reasons, with maritime grievances, national honor, and Republican political survival to be the primary causes.

Historians have been increasingly emphasizing the Republican Synthesis, meaning a defense of republicanism growing out of the American Revolution and the national honor associated with that concept, as the primary cause for war. Some of the key works involved in this interpretation include Norman K. Risjord, "1812: Conservatives, War Hawks, and the Nation's Honor," *William and Mary Quarterly* 18 (April 1961): 196–210; Bradford Perkins, *Prologue to War: England and the United States, 1805–1812* (Berkeley: University of California Press, 1961); Roger H. Brown, *The Republic in Peril: 1812* (New York: Columbia University Press, 1964); J. G. A. Pocock, *The Machiavellian Moment: Florentine Political Thought and the Atlantic Republican Tradition* (Princeton: Princeton University Press, 1975); and Banning, *Jeffersonian Persuasion*. Other volumes already cited contribute to this analysis. A good bibliographic discussion is found in chapter 1, Ronald L. Hatzenbuehler and Robert L. Ivie, *Congress Declares War: Rhetoric, Leadership, and Partisanship in the Early Republic* (Kent, OH: Kent State University Press, 1983). See also Horsman's brief synthesis, *Diplomacy of the New Republic*, and his bibliographic essay, pp. 131–46. Victor A. Sapio, *Pennsylvania and the War of 1812* (Lexington: University Press of Kentucky, 1970), stresses more the "welfare and unity of the Republican party" (p. 4) and less the reputation of republican institutions in the move to support the war in Pennsylvania. Robert A. Rutland, *James Madison: The Founding Father* (New York: Macmillan, 1987), pp. 224–26, observes that in opting for war, Madison faced the need to surrender republican theories for the benefit of the republic's honor. In what he calls "a new interpretative synthesis," Watts, *Republic Reborn,* argues that the years before and after the War of 1812 "encompassed a massive, multifaceted transformation away from republican traditions and toward modern liberal capitalism in America" (p. xvii). Actually, this line of analysis has been put forth most recently by Appleby, *Capitalism and a New Social Order,* and by other scholars, and before them, among others, by Louis Hartz, *The Liberal Tradition in America: An Interpretation of American Political Thought Since the Revolution* (New York: Harcourt Brace Jovanovich, 1955). See also note 4. Reginald Horsman, "The War of 1812 Revisited," *Diplomatic History* 15 (Winter 1991): 115–24, perceptively reviews the scholarship on the war, including his numerous publications on the subject. For a useful bibliography on the war that deals primarily with military events but also devotes a section to other events, "The Internal Scene," see Dwight L. Smith, *The War of 1812: An Annotated Bibliography* (New York: Garland Publishing, 1985).

    69. U.S. Bureau of the Census, *Historical Statistics,* pt. 2, pp. 1106, 1118, 1140; Studenski and Krooss, *Financial History,* pp. 75–81; and Nettles, *National Economy,* p. 332.

    70. Studenski and Krooss, *Financial History,* pp. 75–76; Stagg, *Mr. Madison's War,* pp. 48–176; and Hatzenbuehler and Ivie, *Congress Declares War,* pp. 26–33.

    Several biographies of Gallatin provide information, insight, and analysis involving his economic and political leadership before and during the War of 1812. Raymond Walters, Jr., *Albert Gallatin: Jeffersonian Financier and Diplomat* (New York: Macmillan, 1957) is quite favorable to his subject. Alexander Balinky, *Albert Gallatin: Fiscal Theories and Policies* (New Brunswick, NJ: Rutgers University Press, 1958), is exceptionally critical of the secretary of the treasury. He is less so in "Gallatin's Theory of War Finance," *William and Mary Quarterly* 16 (January 1959): 73–82.

    71. Hammond, *Banks and Politics in America,* pp. 114–226; Nettles, *National Economy,* pp. 295–301; and Studenski and Krooss, *Financial History,* pp. 72–73.

    72. U.S. Bureau of the Census, *Historical Statistics,* pt. 1, pp. 201–2, pt. 2, pp. 1018, 1106; Nettles, *National Economy,* pp. 333–34; and Chester W. Wright, *Economic History of the United States* (New York: McGraw-Hill, 1949). For statistics on the cost of living and its increases during the war, see Paul A. David and Peter Solar, "A Bicentenary Contribution to the History of the Cost of Living in America," in *Research in Economic History: An Annual Compilation of Research,* ed. Paul Uselding, 2: 1–80 (Greenwich, CT: JAI Press, 1977).

    73. Hammond, *Banks and Politics in America,* pp. 227–33; Studenski and Krooss, *Financial History,* pp. 79–80; and Nettles, *National Economy,* pp. 333–35.

    74. U.S. Bureau of the Census, *Historical Statistics,* pt. 2, pp. 1106, 1115; Dall W. Forsythe, *Taxation and Political Change in the Young Nation, 1781–1833* (New York: Columbia University Press, 1977), pp. 57–68; Studenski and Krooss, *Financial History,* pp. 76–81; and Wright, *Economic History,* pp. 226–29.

    75. Nettles, *National Economy,* pp. 332–35; Edwin J. Perkins, *American Public Finance and Financial Services, 1700–1815* (Columbus: Ohio State University Press, 1994), pp. 324–48; Donald R. Adams, Jr., *Finance and Enterprise in Early America: A Study of Stephen Girard's Bank, 1812–1831* (Philadelphia: University of Pennsylvania Press, 1978), pp. 7–67; Robert A. Love, *Federal Financing: A Study of the Meth-*

ods Employed by the Treasury in Its Borrowing Operations (New York: Columbia University Press, 1931), pp. 36–56; and Studenski and Krooss, *Financial History,* pp. 76–81.

76. Hammond, *Banks and Politics in America,* pp. 227–33, and Studenski and Krooss, *Financial History,* p. 78.

77. Millett and Maslowski, *Common Defense,* p. 102.

78. Mahon, *History of Militia,* pp. 63–77. Samuel Smith's leadership of the Maryland militia during the Battle of Baltimore is instructive. Several biographies provide some information and insight concerning Smith's abilities and activities: Frank A. Cassell, *Merchant Congressman in the Young Republic* (Madison: University of Wisconsin Press, 1971), and John S. Pancake, *Samuel Smith and the Politics of Business: 1752–1839* (University: University of Alabama Press, 1972). Sapio, *Pennsylvania,* provides elaborate details about the states' efforts during the war, including the raising and fielding of troops.

79. Coles, "From Peaceful Coercion to Balanced Forces," in Hagan and Roberts, eds., *Against All Enemies,* p. 83; Mahon, *History of the Militia,* p. 67; and Weigley, *U.S. Army,* pp. 118–20.

80. Coles, "From Peaceful Coercion to Balanced Forces," in Hagan and Roberts, eds., *Against All Enemies,* pp. 83–84.

81. Ibid., pp. 84–85, and Kreidberg and Henry, *Military Mobilization,* pp. 47–56.

82. Weigley, *U.S. Army,* pp. 123–32; and Mahon, *History of Militia,* p. 75.

83. Risch, *Quartermaster,* pp. 135–42, 152–54; Green, Thomson, and Roots, *Ordnance Department,* p. 16; Kreidberg and Henry, *Military Mobilization,* p. 48; Huston, *Sinews of War,* pp. 102–4; and Weigley, *U.S. Army,* pp. 112–13.

84. Risch, *Quartermaster,* pp. 142–44, and Huston, *Sinews of War,* pp. 104–5.

85. White, *Jeffersonians,* pp. 218–19, and Weigley, *U.S. Army,* pp. 122–23.

86. White, *Jeffersonians,* pp. 217–23; Weigley, *U.S. Army,* pp. 119–21; and Huston, *Sinews of War,* p. 104.

87. Kreidberg and Henry, *Military Mobilization,* pp. 48–49; Weigley, *U.S. Army,* pp. 121–23; White, *Jeffersonians,* pp. 218–23; and C. Joseph Bernardo and Eugene H. Bacon, *American Military Policy: Its Development Since 1775* (Harrisburg, PA: Stackpole Company, 1955), pp. 124–27, 143–44.

88. Risch, *Quartermaster,* pp. 125–27, 130–31, 136–42, 144–54, 167–69, and Marguerite M. McKee, "Service of Supply in the War of 1812," *Quartermaster Review* 6 and 7 (January–February 1927): 6–19, (March–April 1927): 45–55, (May–June 1927): 27–39, (September–October 1927): 23–32 (the first and a portion of the second of this series of articles deal with the revolutionary and early national period Quartermaster Corps background to the War of 1812).

89. Peter Temin, *Iron and Steel In Nineteenth-Century America: An Economic Inquiry* (Cambridge, MA: MIT Press, 1964), pp. 14–19; Huston, *Sinews of War,* pp. 96–99, 105–7; Weigley, *U.S. Army,* p. 124; Nettles, *National Economy,* pp. 335–40; White, *Jeffersonians,* p. 226, n. 10; and Clark, *History of Manufactures,* 1: 412. See also Arthur P. Wade, "Artillerists and Engineers: The Beginnings of American Seacoast Fortifications, 1794–1815" (Ph.D. diss., Kansas State University, 1977).

90. John K. Winkler, *The Dupont Dynasty* (New York: Blue Ribbon Books, 1935), pp. 51–86; William S. Dutton, *Du Pont: One Hundred and Forty Years* (New York: Charles Scribner's Sons, 1942), pp. 38–55; William H. A. Carr, *The du Ponts of*

Delaware (New York: Dodd, Mead, 1964), pp. 67–92; Leonard Mosley, *Blood Relations: The Rise and Fall of the du Ponts of Delaware* (New York: Atheneum, 1980), pp. 21–29; and Gerard Colby, *Dupont Dynasty* (Secaucus, NJ: Lyle Stuart, 1984), pp. 43–55.

91. Risch, *Quartermaster,* pp. 144–49; Kreidberg and Henry, *Military Mobilization,* pp. 56–57; and Clark, *History of Manufactures,* 1: 529–77.

92. Risch, *Quartermaster,* pp. 157, 164–70.

93. Ibid., 149–52; Kreidberg and Henry, *Military Mobilization,* pp. 57–58; and Huston, *Sinews of War,* pp. 103–5.

94. Risch, *Quartermaster,* pp. 154–64, 170–74, and Huston, *Sinews of War,* pp. 108–9.

95. Risch, *Quartermaster,* pp. 159–64, 171–74, and Huston, *Sinews of War,* pp. 108–9.

96. Risch, *Quartermaster,* pp. 164–74, 176–77, and Huston, *Sinews of War,* pp. 109–11.

97. Risch, *Quartermaster,* pp. 175–76, and Huston, *Sinews of War,* pp. 111–12.

98. Harry L. Coles, *The War of 1812* (Chicago: University of Chicago Press, 1965), pp. 71–106; Linda Maloney, "The War of 1812: What Role for Sea Power," in Hagan, ed., *Peace and War,* pp. 46–55; Millett and Maslowski, *Common Defense,* pp. 106–7; Edward K. Eckert, *The Navy Department in the War of 1812* (Gainsville: University of Florida Press, 1973), pp. 1–77; Robert Greenhalgh Albion, *Makers of Naval Policy, 1798–1947* (Annapolis, MD: Naval Institute Press, 1980), pp. 178–87; and White, *Jeffersonians,* pp. 269–83.

99. U.S. Bureau of the Census, *Historical Statistics,* pt. 2, p. 1115; Paullin, *Naval Administration,* pp. 142–54; and Bernardo and Bacon, *American Military Policy,* pp. 116–17.

100. Paullin, *Naval Administration,* pp. 151–54, and Maloney, "War of 1812," in Hagan, ed., *Peace and War,* pp. 54–57. Jerome R. Garitee, *The Republic's Private Navy: The American Privateering Business as Practiced by Baltimore During the War of 1812* (Middletown, CT: Wesleyan University Press, 1977), covers his subject with meticulous detail and good insight.

101. The account of the navy's lake warfare is based on Paullin, *Naval Administration,* pp. 144–45, 153–54; Maloney, "War of 1812," in Hagan, ed., *Peace and War,* pp. 54–61; William M. Fowler, Jr., *Jack Tars and Commodores: The American Navy, 1783–1815* (Boston: Houghton Mifflin, 1984), pp. 211–43; John K. Mahon, *The War of 1812* (Gainesville: University of Florida Press, 1972), pp. 86–95, 135–58, 257–89, 317–28; Owsley, "William Jones," in Coletta, ed., *Secretaries of the Navy,* 1: 101–5; Sprout, *Naval Power,* pp. 73–76, 84–85; Millett and Maslowski, *Common Defense,* 103–10; T. C. Smith, *The War Between England and America* (1914; Port Washington, NY: Kennikat Press, 1969), pp. 215–36; William J. Welsh and David C. Skaggs, eds., *War on the Great Lakes: Essays Commemorating the 175th Anniversary of the Battle of Lake Erie* (Kent, OH: Kent State University Press, 1991); and Risch, *Quartermaster,* pp. 172–74. See also George F. G. Stanley, *The War of 1812: Land Operations* (Canada: Macmillan of Canada, 1983). Donald R. Hickey, *The War of 1812: A Forgotten Conflict* (Urbana: University of Illinois Press, 1989), touches briefly on the lake warfare (pp. 182–94) in his valuable general survey of the conflict.

102. Secretary of the Navy Jones referred to the contest on Lake Ontario as a "war-

fare of Dockyards and Arsenals" (quoted in Paullin, *Naval Administration,* p. 154). Fowler, *Jack Tars and Commodores,* p. 229, is less kind when he refers to Chauncey and Yeo as choosing to "wage a war of shipwrights" instead of one of naval engagements.

103. Maloney, "War 1812," in Hagan, ed., *Peace and War,* pp. 58–59.

104. Paullin, *Naval Administration,* p. 153.

105. This is essentially the conclusion of two careful scholars of the period, Coles, *War of 1812,* p. 257, and Stagg, *Mr. Madison's War,* pp. 435–36. The most recent and authoritative biographer of Madison, Rutland, *Presidency of James Madison,* elliptically agrees with this judgment (pp. 207–13). Ralph Ketcham, *James Madison: A Biography* (New York: Macmillan, 1971), pp. 585–86, argues that Madison's deep-seated commitment to republican virtues prevented him from being an effective wartime executive. Horsman, "War of 1812 Revisited," discusses how scholars have judged Madison's wartime leadership.

106. The Madison administrations and the Republicans have been criticized along traditional lines for not maintaining an adequate military in general and especially in the face of impending war. Good examples of the traditionally oriented critics include Kreidberg and Henry, *Military Mobilization,* pp. 23–60, and Bernardo and Bacon, *American Military Policy,* pp. 96–142. Coles, *War of 1812,* pp. 99–106, presents a good analysis of the interpretations of Theodore Roosevelt, Alfred Thayer Mahan, and Henry Adams along with his own assessments of the realistic naval options open to the United States in the early nineteenth century.

CHAPTER FOUR. THE POLITICAL ECONOMY OF WARFARE: 1815–1860

1. Several surveys cover these years reasonably well. See John Allen Krout and Dixon Ryan Fox, *The Completion of Independence, 1790–1830* (New York: Macmillan, 1944); Marcus Cunliffe, *The Nation Takes Shape, 1789–1837* (Chicago: University of Chicago Press, 1959); George Dangerfield, *The Awakening of American Nationalism, 1815–1828* (New York: Harper and Row, 1965); and John Mayfield, *The New Nation, 1800–1845* (New York: Hill and Wang, 1982). See also Ralph Ketcham, *Presidents Above Party: The First American Presidency, 1789–1829* (Chapel Hill: University of North Carolina Press, 1984), pp. 113–58. James Sterling Young's *The Washington Community, 1800–1828* (New York: Columbia University Press, 1966), among numerous other virtues, is particularly good in examining the effects of party and governmental deterioration in the last phases of the first party system.

2. Jacksonian Democracy continues to be a subject of ongoing research and debate. A good bibliographical guide to the varying interpretations up to 1972 is presented by Frank Otto Gatell, "The Jacksonian Era, 1824–1848," in *The Reinterpretation of American History and Culture,* ed. William H. Cartwright and Richard L. Watson, Jr., pp. 309–26 (Washington, DC: National Council for Social Studies, 1973). See also Sean Wilentz, "Society, Politics, and the Market Revolution, 1815–1848," in *The New American History,* ed. Eric Foner, pp. 51–71 (Philadelphia: Temple University Press, 1990). In his series of published essays, Richard L. McCormick, *The Party Period and Public Policy: American Politics from the Age of Jackson to the Progressive Period* (New York: Oxford University Press, 1986), covers well and critiques excel-

lently the trends since 1972. Joel H. Silbey, ed., *Political Ideology and Voting Behavior in the Age of Jackson* (Englewood Cliffs, NJ: Prentice-Hall, 1973), introduces examples of the so-called new political history and the ethnocultural approach to the study of the Jacksonian period. In his most recent publication, *The American Political Nation, 1838–1893* (Stanford, CA: Stanford University Press, 1991), Silbey adjusts while reaffirming "realignment theory" for understanding American politics, a theory challenged by various authors in Byron E. Shafer, ed., *The End of Realignment? Interpreting American Electoral Eras* (Madison: University of Wisconsin Press, 1991). See also John H. Aldrich, *Why Parties? The Origin and Transformation of Political Parties in America* (Chicago: University Press of Chicago, 1995). Charles Sellers has incorporated his penetrating insights about Jacksonian America into his fine synthesis of the era, *The Market Revolution: Jacksonian America, 1815–1846* (New York: Oxford University Press, 1991). See also Harry L. Watson, *Liberty and Power: The Politics of Jacksonian America* (New York: Hill and Wang, 1990), and Donald B. Cole, *The Presidency of Andrew Jackson* (Lawrence: University Press of Kansas, 1993). The various works of Edward Pessen must be added to any list of works on or about the Jacksonian period: *New Perspectives on Jacksonian Parties and Politics* (Boston: Allyn and Bacon, 1969); *Riches, Class, and Power Before the Civil War* (Lexington, MA: D. C. Heath, 1973); *Three Centuries of Social Mobility in America* (Lexington, MA: D. C. Heath, 1974); *The Many-Faceted Jacksonian Era: New Interpretations* (Westport, CT: Greenwood Press, 1977); and *Jacksonian America: Society, Personality, and Politics,* rev. ed. (Homewood, IL: Dorsey Press, 1978). In terms of Pessen's work, see also Donald M. Roper, "Beyond the Jacksonian Era: A Comment on the Pessen Thesis," *New York History* 61 (April 1975): 226–33, and Robert E. Gallman, "Professor Pessen on the 'Egalitarian Myth,'" *Social Science History* 2 (Winter 1978): 194–207. See also Lawrence F. Kohl, *The Politics of Individualism: Parties and the American Character in the Jacksonian Era* (New York: Oxford University Press, 1989).

The capricious nature of Jackson's leadership and its effects on the Democratic party and the presidency figure large in the analysis of James C. Curtis, *Andrew Jackson and the Search for Vindication* (Boston: Little, Brown, 1976). Richard E. Ellis, *The Union at Risk: Jacksonian Democracy, States' Rights, and the Nullification Crisis* (New York: Oxford University Press, 1987), argues that during the Nullification Controversy a critical and disastrous shift occurred in the states' rights doctrine from that supporting union to that justifying disunion. Such a development alone signaled a defeat for Jackson, and his handling of the dispute raised in many quarters the fear of Old Hickory abusing executive power and manifesting poor judgment. See also William W. Freehling, *Prelude to Civil War: The Nullification Controversy in South Carolina, 1816–1836* (New York: Harper and Row, 1965).

3. Of the numerous works on the bank war, I have found particularly useful Arthur M. Schlesinger, Jr., *The Age of Jackson* (Boston: Little, Brown, 1945); Bray Hammond, *Banks and Politics in America: From the Revolution to the Civil War* (Princeton: Princeton University Press, 1957); Robert V. Remini, *Andrew Jackson and the Bank War* (New York: W. W. Norton, 1967); Peter Temin, *The Jacksonian Economy* (New York: W. W. Norton, 1969); James Roger Sharp, *The Jacksonians versus the Banks: Politics in the States After the Panic of 1837* (New York: Columbia University Press, 1970); John M. McFaul, *The Politics of Jacksonian Finance* (Ithaca, NY: Cornell University Press, 1972); William Gerald Shade, *Banks or No Banks: The Money Issue in Western Politics, 1832–1865*

(Detroit: Wayne State University Press, 1972); Hugh Rockhoff, *The Free Banking Era: A Re-Examination* (New York: Arno Press, 1975); and Edwin J. Perkins, "Lost Opportunities for Compromise in the Bank War: A Reassessment of Jackson's Veto Message," *Business History Review* 61 (Winter 1987): 531–50. These studies of the bank war, of course, offer good insights into the debate over the nature of the Jacksonian era and are often intended to probe the larger issues involving Jacksonian Democracy. A recent bibliographic essay on banking in America provides an excellent context for the conflict of the Jacksonian era: Larry Schweikart, "U.S. Commerical Banking: A Historiographical Survey," *Business History Review* 65 (Autumn 1991): 606–61.

4. The Whig party and its successes and failures are covered reasonably well in Mayfield, *New Nation;* Robert H. Wiebe, *The Opening of American Society: From the Adoption of the Constitution to the Eve of Disunion* (New York: Alfred A. Knopf, 1984); and Merrill D. Peterson, *The Great Triumvirate: Webster, Clay, and Calhoun* (New York: Oxford University Press, 1987).

5. Pessen, *Jacksonian America,* pp. 90, 101–2, 149–260; McCormick, *Party Period,* pp. 89–140, 197–227; Wiebe, *American Society,* pp. 129–384; Lynn L. Marshall, "The Strange Stillbirth of the Whig Party," *American Historical Review* 72 (January 1967): 445–68; and Eric Foner, *Free Soil, Free Labor, Free Man: The Ideology of the Republican Party Before the Civil War* (New York: Oxford University Press, 1970), pp. 11–39.

6. The causes for and the drive to the Civil War have been the source of an incredibly rich, varied, and voluminous scholarship. Bibliographic essays are the only way even to begin introducing the works that are involved. The best available at this time, and one that reflects most closely my views on the coming of the Civil War, is that of Kenneth M. Stampp, "The Irrepressible Conflict," in *The Imperiled Union: Essays on the Background of the Civil War* (New York: Oxford University Press, 1980), pp. 191–245. See also Eric Foner, "The Causes of the American Civil War: Recent Interpretations and New Directions," in *Politics and Ideology in the Age of the Civil War* (New York: Oxford University Press, 1980), pp. 15–33. The other essays by both authors in the anthologies of their own work are also helpful on the subject of the Civil War. Additionally, see Eric Foner, "Slavery, the Civil War, and Reconstruction," in Foner, ed., *New American History,* pp. 73–92. James M. McPherson, *Ordeal by Fire: The Civil War and Reconstruction* (New York: Alfred A. Knopf, 1982), pp. 657–87, has the most complete bibliography on the Civil War and its background. McPherson's sources are updated where that is essential by his subsequent volume, *Battle Cry of Freedom: The Civil War Era* (New York: Oxford University Press, 1988), pp. 865–82, by Richard E. Sewell, *A House Divided: Sectionalism and Civil War, 1848–1865* (Baltimore: Johns Hopkins University Press, 1988), pp. 197–214, by Phillip S. Paludan, *"A People's Contest": The Union and the Civil War, 1861–1865* (New York: Harper and Row, 1988), pp. 441–70, and by John Niven, *The Coming of the Civil War, 1837–1861* (Arlington Heights, IL: Harlan Davidson, 1990), pp. 144–73. McCormick, *Party Period,* is also essential for understanding the so-called new political history, ethnocultural approaches, and social analysis as it relates to the coming of the Civil War. See also Don E. Fehrenbacher, "The New Political History and the Coming of the Civil War," *Pacific Historical Review* 54 (May 1985): 117–42.

The other various surveys that I have found most helpful include David M. Potter, *The Impending Crisis, 1848–1861* (New York: Harper and Row, 1976); Thomas H. O'Connor, *The Disunited States: The Era of Civil War and Reconstruction,* 2d ed. (New

York: Harper and Row, 1978); Roy F. Nichols and Eugene H. Berwanger, *The Stakes of Power, 1845–1877* (New York: Hill and Wang, 1982); and William W. Freehling, *The Road to Disunion,* vol. 1: *Secessionists at Bay, 1776–1854* (New York: Oxford University Press, 1990).

I have seriously attempted to give the new political history, as represented by Joel H. Silbey, *The Shrine of Party: Congressional Voting Behavior, 1841–1852* (Pittsburgh, PA: University of Pittsburgh Press, 1967), and *The Partisan Imperative: The Dynamics of American Politics Before the Civil War* (New York: Oxford University Press, 1985), a fair hearing, but, alas, along with Stampp and Foner, I find it to be wanting in the extreme. A recent example of revisionism I find to be even less compelling is Mark W. Summers, *The Plundering Generation: Corruption and the Crisis of the Union, 1849–1861* (New York: Oxford University Press, 1987).

The rise of the Republican party is, of course, central to the coming of the Civil War. Consequently, the scholarship concerning it is covered in the bibliography just discussed. Several volumes, however, deserve special mention. Foner, *Free Soil, Free Labor, Free Man,* is a cogent, powerful, and convincing analysis in the irrepressible-conflict tradition. Michael F. Holt, "Forging A Majority: The Formation of the Republican Party in Pittsburgh, Pennsylvania, 1848–1860" (Ph.D. diss., Johns Hopkins University, 1967), and William E. Gienapp, *The Origins of the Republican Party, 1852–1856* (New York: Oxford University Press, 1987), are fine examples of the ethnocultural emphasis. Although I find their analysis to be interesting and their scholarship impressive, their interpretations remain less than convincing.

7. McCormick, *Party Period,* p. 3 (quotation), pp. 200–201; Richard L. McCormick, *The Second American Party System: Party Formation in the Jacksonian Era* (Chapel Hill: University of North Carolina Press, 1966); Marshall, "Whig Party," pp. 445–68; and Pessen, *Jacksonian America,* pp. 149–70, 222.

8. Robert E. Gallman, "Trends in the Size Distribution of Wealth in the Nineteenth Century: Some Speculations," in *Six Papers on the Size Distribution of Wealth and Income,* vol. 33, *Studies in Income and Wealth,* National Bureau of Economic Research, ed. Lee Soltow, p. 6 (New York: Columbia University Press, 1969). Soltow's *Men and Wealth in the United States, 1850–1870* (New Haven: Yale University Press, 1975) is the best study on this vital subject. Stuart Blumin, "Residential and Occupational Mobility in Antebellum Philadelphia," in Pessen, ed., *Three Centuries of Social Mobility,* pp. 59–92, presents figures on the distribution of wealth for Philadelphia that show a much more skewed pattern than those given by Gallman for the entire society. Pessen's book contains other essays of significance on the subject of wealth distribution, social mobility, and the like. See also Pessen, *Jacksonian America,* pp. 104–13, and various essays in Robert E. Gallman and John Joseph Wallis, eds., *American Economic Growth and Standards of Living Before the Civil War* (Chicago: University of Chicago Press, 1992). For agrarian regions in general, see Jeremy Atack and Fred Bateman, *To Their Own Soil: Agriculture in the Antebellum North* (Ames: Iowa State University Press, 1987), pp. 86–101. For the South, see Gavin Wright: "'Economic Democracy' and the Concentration of Agricultural Wealth in the Cotton South, 1850–1860," *Agriculture History* 64 (January 1970): 63–93, and Wright, *The Political Economy of the Cotton South: Households, Markets, and Wealth in the Nineteenth Century* (New York: W. W. Norton, 1978), pp. 10–42. Wiebe, *American Society,* treats the subject both directly and indirectly in a sophisticated way.

9. Pessen, *Jacksonian Democracy*, pp. 149–70. For an introduction to movements of dissent and reform before the Civil War, see C. S. Griffin, *The Ferment of Reform, 1830–1860* (New York: Thomas Y. Crowell Company, 1967); Russell Blain Nye, *Society and Culture in America, 1830–1860* (New York: Harper and Row, 1974); and Pessen, ed., *Many-Faceted Jacksonian Era,* "Section Four: Reform," pp. 261–326.

10. Sidney H. Aronson, *Status and Kinship in the Higher Civil Service: Standards of Selection in the Administrations of John Adams, Thomas Jefferson, and Andrew Jackson* (Cambridge: Harvard University Press, 1964); Pessen, *Jacksonian America,* pp. 97–99; and Philip H. Burch, Jr., *Elites in American History: The Federalist Years to the Civil War* (New York: Holmes and Meier Publishers, 1981), pp. 129–250. See also Clinton Williamson, *American Suffrage: From Prosperity to Democracy, 1760–1860* (Princeton: Princeton University Press, 1960); William H. Pease and Jane H. Pease, *The Web of Progress: Private Values and Public Styles in Boston and Charleston, 1828–1843* (New York: Oxford University Press, 1985); Peter Dobkin Hall, *The Organization of American Culture, 1700–1900: Private Institutions, Elites, and the Origins of American Nationality* (New York: New York University Press, 1982); Douglas T. Miller, *Jacksonian Aristocracy: Class and Democracy in New York, 1830–1860* (New York: Oxford University Press, 1967); and Herbert G. Gutman, *Work, Culture, and Society in Industrializing America* (New York: Alfred A. Knopf, 1976).

11. Burch, *Elites,* pp. 129–250.

12. Marshall, "Whig Party," pp. 445–68; Matthew A. Crenson, *The Federal Machine: Beginnings of Bureaucracy in Jacksonian America* (Baltimore: Johns Hopkins University Press, 1975); and William E. Nelson, *The Roots of American Bureaucracy, 1830–1900* (Cambridge: Harvard University Press, 1982), pp. 1–61. Leonard D. White's earlier study and analysis, *The Jacksonians: A Study in Administrative History, 1829–1861* (New York: Macmillan, 1954), both supports and contradicts this later interpretation. Nonetheless, his survey/analysis provides much information on government during the three decades before the Civil War.

13. Several secondary sources ably summarize the scholarly debate over nineteenth-century economic growth and cite the contributions of Victor Clark, Paul David, Richard Easterlin, Robert Gallman, Simon Kuznets, Stanley Libergott, Robert Martin, Douglass North, Walter Rostow, George Taylor, Frank Taussig, and others. See Stuart Bruchey, *The Roots of American Economic Growth, 1607–1861: An Essay in Social Causation* (New York: Harper and Row, 1965), pp. 74–91; Barry Warren Poulson, *Value Added in Manufacturing, Mining, and Agriculture in the American Economy from 1809 to 1839* (New York: Arno Press, 1975), pp. 1–31; and Susan Previant Lee and Peter Passell, *A New Economic View of American History* (New York: W. W. Norton, 1979), pp. 55–62. See also Sidney Ratner, James H. Soltow, and Richard Sylla, *The Evolution of the American Economy: Growth, Welfare, and Decision Making* (New York: Basic Books, 1979), pp. 233–41, and Barry W. Poulson, *Economic History of the United States* (New York: Macmillan, 1981), pp. 185–208.

Diane Lindstrom, *Economic Development in the Philadelphia Region, 1810–1850* (New York: Columbia University Press, 1978), is critically important for understanding early nineteenth-century trade and growth. See also Richard C. Wade, *The Urban Frontier: The Rise of Western Cities, 1790–1830* (Cambridge: Harvard University Press, 1959).

The most prominent advocate of interregional, as opposed to intraregional, trade as the principal stimulus for American economic growth in the early nineteenth century is Douglass C. North, *The Economic Growth of the United States, 1790–1860* (Englewood Cliffs, NJ: Prentice-Hall, 1961), and *Growth and Welfare in the American Past: A New Economic History,* 2d ed. (Englewood Cliffs, NJ: Prentice-Hall, 1974), chapter 6. Albert Fishlow, *American Railroads and the Transformation of the Ante-Bellum Economy* (Cambridge: Harvard University Press, 1965), Lindstrom, in *Economic Development* and in other publications, Robert Gallman, and others have challenged and effectively refuted North's thesis. This scholarly debate and its participants are summarized in Lee and Passell, *Economic View,* pp. 146–53. See also Ratner, Soltow, and Sylla, *American Economy,* pp. 222–31.

14. Poulson, *Economic History,* pp. 301–32.

15. George Rogers Taylor, *The Transportation Revolution, 1815–1860* (New York: Holt, Rinehart and Winston, 1951), pp. 15–31; Edward Chase Kirkland, *Men, Cities, and Transportation: A Study in New England History, 1820–1900,* 2 vols. (Cambridge: Harvard University Press, 1948), 1: 32–59; Carter Goodrich, *Government Promotion of American Canals and Railroads, 1800–1890* (New York: Columbia University Press, 1960), pp. 3–48; and Forest G. Hill, *Roads, Rails, and Waterways: The Army Engineers and Early Transportation* (Norman: University of Oklahoma Press, 1957), pp. 3–95. See also Harry N. Scheiber, Harold G. Vatter, and Harold Underwood Faulkner, *American Economic History* (New York: Harper and Row, 1976), pp. 145–47, and Ratner, Soltow, and Sylla, *American Economy,* pp. 105–11.

16. Eric F. Haites, James Mak, and Gary M. Walton, *Western River Transportation: The Era of Early Internal Development, 1810–1860* (Baltimore: Johns Hopkins University Press, 1975); Taylor, *Transportation Revolution,* pp. 56–73; and Louis C. Hunter, *Steamboats on the Western Rivers: An Economic and Technological History* (Cambridge: Harvard University Press, 1949).

17. For the Canal era, see Carter Goodrich, ed., *Canals and American Economic Development* (New York: Columbia University Press, 1961); Goodrich, *Government Promotion,* pp. 51–165; Taylor, *Transportation Revolution,* pp. 32–55; Kirkland, *Men, Cities, and Transportation,* 1: 60–91; H. Jerome Cranmer, "Canal Investment, 1815–1860," with Harvey H. Segal, "Comment," in *Trends in the American Economy in the Nineteenth Century, Studies in Income and Wealth,* vol. 24, Conference on Research in Income and Wealth (Princeton: Princeton University Press, 1960), pp. 547–70; Roger L. Ransom, "Public Canal Investment and the Opening of the Old North-West," in *Essays in Nineteenth Century Economic History: The Old Northwest,* ed. David G. Klingaman and Richard K. Vedder, pp. 246–68 (Athens: Ohio University Press, 1975); John F. Stover, "Canals and Turnpikes: America's Early-Nineteenth-Century Transportation Network," in *An Emerging Independent American Economy, 1815–1875,* ed. Joseph R. Frese and Jacob Judd, pp. 60–98 (Tarrytown, NY: Sleepy Hollow Press, 1980); Harry N. Scheiber, *Ohio Canal Era: A Case Study of Government and the Economy, 1820–1861* (Athens: Ohio University Press, 1969); and Robert E. Shaw, *Canals for a Nation: The Canal Era in the United States, 1790–1860* (Lexington: University Press of Kentucky, 1990).

18. For some of the better sources on railroads, see Taylor, *Transportation Revolution,* pp. 74–103, 132–52; Goodrich, *Canals and Railroads,* pp. 121–297; Fishlow, *American Railroads;* Alfred D. Chandler, Jr., ed., *The Railroads: The Nation's First Big Business* (New York: Harcourt, Brace and World, 1965), and Chandler, *The Visible Hand: The Managerial Revolution in American Business* (Cambridge, MA: Belknap

Press, 1977), pp. 79–205; Robert William Fogel, *Railroads and American Economic Growth: Essays in Econometric History* (Baltimore: Johns Hopkins University Press, 1964); Robert J. Parks, *Democracy's Railroads: Public Enterprise in Jacksonian Michigan* (Port Washington, NY: Kennikat Press, 1972); Kirkland, *Men, Cities, and Transportation,* 1: 92–432; North, *Growth and Welfare in the American Past,* pp. 105–17; and Hill, *Roads, Rails, and Waterways,* pp. 96–152. Albert Fishlow's chapter, "Internal Transportation," in Lance E. Davis et al., *American Economic Growth: An Economist's History of the United States* (New York: Harper and Row, 1972), pp. 468–547, covers most forms of transportation and is an excellent summary of the major developments for the entire nineteenth century and beyond. Poulson, *Economic History,* pp. 287–91, surveys the debate over the social rate of return and the social savings involving the railroads, including the contributions of Robert Fogel, Lloyd Mercer, Roger Ransom, Albert Fishlow, J. Hayden Boyd and Gary Walton, and Jeffrey Williamson.

19. Robert L. Thompson, *Wiring a Continent: The History of the Telegraph Industry in the United States, 1832–1866* (Princeton: Princeton University Press, 1947).

20. For antebellum agriculture, see Paul W. Gates, *The Farmer's Age: Agriculture, 1815–1860* (New York: Holt, Rinehart and Winston, 1960); Clarence H. Danhof, *Change in Agriculture: The Northern United States, 1820–1870* (Cambridge: Harvard University Press, 1969); James W. Whitaker, ed., *Farming in the Midwest, 1840–1900* (Washington, DC: Agricultural History Society, 1974); Robert E. Gallman, "The Agricultural Sector and the Pace of Economic Growth: U.S. Experience in the Nineteenth Century," and Richard E. Easterlin, "Farm Production and Income in Old and New Areas at Mid-Century," in Klingaman and Vedder, eds., *Essays,* pp. 35–117; Poulson, *Value Added,* pp. 115–37; Atack and Bateman, *To Their Own Soil;* C. Joseph Pusateri, *A History of American Business* (Arlington Heights, IL: Harlan Davidson, 1984), pp. 111–16. See also William Parker, "Agriculture," in Davis et al., *American Economic Growth,* pp. 369–417; Scheiber, Vatter, and Faulkner, *American Economic History,* pp. 127–43; and Ratner, Soltow, and Sylla, *American Economy,* pp. 142–55. The rich and controversial literature on slavery and the Southern economy is noted, summarized, and analyzed in Lee and Passell, *Economic View,* pp. 154–207.

21. Industrial development in the antebellum period is covered in Bruchey, *American Economic Growth,* pp. 74–91; Chandler, *Visible Hand,* pp. 50–80; Victor S. Clark, *History of Manufactures in the United States, 1607–1860* (Washington, DC: Carnegie Institution, 1929), 1: 233–582; Robert E. Gallman, "Commodity Output, 1839–1899," in *American Economy,* vol. 24, Conference on Research in Income and Wealth, pp. 13–71, and other essays; Robert E. Gallman, "Gross National Product in the United States, 1834–1909," in *Output, Employment, and Productivity in the United States After 1800,* vol. 30, Conference on Research in Income and Wealth (New York: National Bureau of Economic Research, 1966), pp. 3–90, and other essays; Thomas R. Navin, *The Whitin Machine Works Since 1831: A Textile Machinery Company in an Industrial Village* (Cambridge: Harvard University Press, 1950); Louis C. Hunter, *A History of Industrial Power in the United States, 1780–1930,* 2 vols. (Charlottesville: University Press of Virginia, 1979–1985); Paul F. Paskoff, *Industrial Evolution: Organization, Structure, and Growth of the Pennsylvania Iron Industry, 1750–1860* (Baltimore: Johns Hopkins University Press, 1983); Poulson, *Value Added,* pp. 35–114; W. J. Rorabaugh, *The Craft Apprentice: From Franklin to the Machine Age in Amer-*

ica (New York: Oxford University Press, 1986); Philip Scranton, *Proprietary Capitalism: The Textile Manufacture at Philadelphia, 1800–1885* (Cambridge: Cambridge University Press, 1983); Robert William Fogel and Stanley L. Engerman, "A Model for the Explanation of Industrial Expansion During the Nineteenth Century: With an Application to the American Iron Industry," and other relevant essays in *The Reinterpretation of American Economic History,* ed. Fogel and Engerman, pp. 148–74 (New York: Harper and Row, 1971); Kenneth L. Sokoloff, "Productivity Growth in Manufacturing During Early Industrialization: Evidence from the American Northeast, 1820–1860," in *Long-Term Factors in American Economic Growth,* ed. Stanley Engerman and Robert E. Gallman, pp. 679–736 (Chicago: University of Chicago Press, 1986); Taylor, *Transportation Revolution,* pp. 207–300; Peter Temin, *Iron and Steel in Nineteenth-Century America: An Economic Inquiry* (Cambridge, MA: MIT Press, 1964), pp. 13–121, 264–65; Temin, "Manufacturing," in Davis et al., *American Economic Growth,* pp. 418–67; Barbara M. Tucker, *Samuel Slater and the Origins of the American Textile Industry, 1790–1860* (Ithaca, NY: Cornell University Press, 1984); Paul John Uselding, *Studies in the Technological Development of the American Economy During the First Half of the Nineteenth Century* (New York: Arno Press, 1975); and Robert Brooke Zevin, *The Growth of Manufacturing in Early Nineteenth Century New England* (New York: Arno Press, 1975). See also Poulson, *Economic History,* pp. 260–71; Ratner, Soltow, and Sylla, *American Economy,* pp. 182–207; Scheiber, Vatter, and Faulkner, *American Economic History,* pp. 159–74; and W. Elliot Brownlee, *Dynamics of Ascent: A History of the American Economy,* 2d ed. (New York: Alfred A. Knopf, 1979), pp. 121–72.

22. For commercial banking, see note 3. Of particular importance is Temin, *Jacksonian Economy.* For a good survey, see Paul Studenski and Herman E. Krooss, *Financial History of the United States: Fiscal, Monetary, Banking, and Tariff, Including Financial Administration and State and Local Finance* (New York: McGraw-Hill, 1952), pp. 82–127. See also Paul B. Trescott, *Financing American Enterprise: The Story of Commercial Banking* (New York: Harper and Row, 1963), pp. 1–40; Howard Bodenhorn and Hugh Rockoff, "Regional Interest Rates in Antebellum America," in *Strategic Factors in Nineteenth Century American Economic History: A Volume to Honor Robert W. Fogel,* ed. Claudia Goldin and Hugh Rockoff, pp. 159–87 (Chicago: University of Chicago Press, 1992); Ratner, Soltow, and Sylla, *American Economy,* pp. 161–74; and Lance E. Davis, "Banks and Their Economic Effects," in Davis et al., *American Economic Growth,* pp. 340–65. Lee and Passell, *Economic View,* pp. 108–29, survey and assess the substance and bibliography surrounding the controversies over money and banking.

23. Herman E. Krooss and Martin R. Blyn, *A History of Financial Intermediaries* (New York: Random House, 1971), pp. 41–90, and Walter Werner and Steven T. Smith, *Wall Street* (New York: Columbia University Press, 1991).

24. The outstanding work on the role of the distributor in the nineteenth-century economy is Glenn Porter and Harold C. Livesay, *Merchants and Manufacturers: Studies in the Changing Structure of Nineteenth Century Marketing* (Baltimore: Johns Hopkins University Press, 1971). See also Chandler, *Visible Hand,* pp. 15–49; Thomas C. Cochran, *Business in American Life: A History* (New York: McGraw-Hill, 1972), pp. 61–142, and Cochran, *200 Years of American Business* (New York: Dell Publish-

ing Company, 1977), pp. 3–109; Elisha P. Douglas, *The Coming of Age of American Business, 1600–1900* (Chapel Hill: University of North Carolina Press, 1971), pp. 112–30; Pusateri, *American Business,* pp. 79–172; Herman E. Krooss and Charles Gilbert, *American Business History* (Englewood Cliffs, NJ: Prentice-Hall, 1972), pp. 77–161; Keith L. Bryant, Jr., and Henry C. Dethloff, *A History of American Business* (Englewood Cliffs, NJ: Prentice-Hall, 1983), pp. 55–130; and Mansel G. Blackford and K. Austin Kerr, *Business Enterprise in American History* (Boston: Houghton Mifflin, 1986), pp. 82–195.

25. The most thorough and original scholarship on this topic is Chandler, *Visible Hand,* pp. 50–208, but see also note 24.

26. U.S. Bureau of the Census, *Historical Statistics of the United States* (Washington, DC: U.S. Government Printing Office, 1975), pt. 2, pp. 1100–1106, 1114–15, 1118; Studenski and Krooss, *Financial History,* pp. 82–127; Lance E. Davis and John Legler, "The Government in the American Economy, 1815–1902: A Quantitative Study," *Journal of Economic History* 26 (December 1966): 514–55; and Scheiber, Vatter, and Faulkner, *American Economic History,* p. 99.

27. Studenski and Krooss, *Financial History,* pp. 128–36. See also Daniel J. Elazar, *The American Partnership: Intergovernmental Co-operation in the Nineteenth-Century United States* (Chicago: University of Chicago Press, 1962).

28. The analysis of the American System of Manufactures is based on Felicia Johnson Deyrup, *Arms Makers of the Connecticut Valley: A Regional Study of the Economic Development of the Small Arms Industry, 1798–1870* (Northampton, MA: Smith College, 1948); Gene Silvero Cesari, "American Arms-Making Machine Tool Development, 1788–1855" (Ph.D diss., University of Pennsylvania, 1970); Nathan Rosenberg, "Technological Change in the Machine Tool Industry, 1840–1910," *Journal of Economic History* 23 (December 1963): 414–43; Rosenberg, *Technology and American Economic Growth* (New York: Harper and Row, 1972), pp. 1–116; Chandler, *Visible Hand,* pp. 72–75; Merritt Roe Smith, *Harpers Ferry Armory and the New Technology: The Challenge of Change* (Ithaca, NY: Cornell University Press, 1977); Smith, "Army Ordnance and the 'American System' of Manufacturing, 1815–1861," in *Military Enterprise and Technological Change,* ed. Smith, pp. 39–86 (Cambridge, MA: MIT Press, 1985); Smith, "Two Cultures in Conflict: Soldiers and Civilians at Harpers Ferry, VA," in *Soldiers and Civilians: The U.S. Army and the American People,* ed. Garry D. Ryan and Timothy K. Nenninger, pp. 81–90 (Washington, DC: National Archives and Records Administration, 1987); David A. Hounshell, *From the American System to Mass Production, 1800–1932: The Development of Manufacturing Technology in the United States* (Baltimore: Johns Hopkins University Press, 1984), pp. 1–65; Ross Thomson, *The Path to Mechanized Shoe Production in the United States* (Chapel Hill: University of North Carolina Press, 1989); and Carolyn C. Cooper, *Shaping Invention: Thomas Blanchard's Machinery and Patent Management in Nineteenth-Century America* (New York: Columbia University Press, 1991). See also Giles Cromwell, *The Virginia Manufactory of Arms* (Charlottesville: University Press of Virginia, 1975), and Brooke Hindle and Steven Lubar, *Engines of Change: The American Industrial Revolution, 1790–1860* (Washington, DC: Smithsonian Institution Press, 1986). For the reports growing out of British studies of the American System, see Nathan Rosenberg, ed., *The American System of Manufactures: The Report of the Committee on the*

Machinery of the United States 1855 and the Special Reports of George Wallis and Joseph Whitworth 1854 (Edinburgh: Edinburgh University Press, 1969). Rosenberg's 86-page introduction is very helpful.

In a recently published monograph, Donald R. Hoke, *Ingenious Yankees: The Rise of the American System of Manufactures in the Private Sector* (New York: Columbia University Press, 1990), argues that the American System originated in both the public and private sectors, but the contributions of the latter were much more significant. He concludes that Hounshell and Smith are wrong in crediting the federal armories with originating and advancing the American System that was later picked up by private firms. Hoke's work is impressively researched and forcefully argued. However, much of what he says is at least implied by Hounshell, Smith, and other authors; thus, he complements as much as he contradicts these scholars. James J. Farley, *Making Arms in the Machine Age: Philadelphia's Frankford Arsenal, 1816–1870* (University Park: Pennsylvania University Press, 1994), sides with Hounshell and Smith over the claims of Hoke. See also Keir B. Sterling, *Serving the Line with Excellence: The Development of the U.S. Army Ordnance Corps* (Washington, DC: U.S. Government Printing Office, 1987).

29. Werner Sombart, *Krieg und Kapitalismus,* vol. 2, *Studien zur Entwicklungs-geschichte des modernen Kapitalismus* (Munich: Dunker and Humblot, 1913); Lewis Mumford, *Technics and Civilization* (New York: Harcourt, Brace, 1934); Quincy Wright, *A Study of War* (Chicago: University of Chicago Press, 1942); John U. Nef, *War and Human Progress: An Essay on the Rise of Industrial Civilization* (Cambridge: Harvard University Press, 1950); William H. McNeill, *The Pursuit of Power: Technology, Armed Force, and Society Since A.D. 1000* (Chicago: University of Chicago Press, 1982); Maurice Pearton, *Diplomacy, War and Technology Since 1830* (Lawrence: University Press of Kansas, 1984); and Martin van Creveld, *Technology and War: From 2000 B. C. to the Present* (New York: Free Press, 1989). The literature on this subject is surveyed and analyzed in a perceptive way in Alex Roland, "Technology and War: A Bibliographic Essay," in Smith, ed., *Military Enterprise,* pp. 347–79.

30. For the dated interpretation of Whitney, see Jeannette Mirsky and Allan Nevins, *The World of Eli Whitney* (New York: Macmillan, 1952), and Constance McL. Green, *Eli Whitney and the Birth of American Technology* (Boston: Little, Brown, 1956). Merritt Roe Smith—"Eli Whitney and the American System of Manufacturing," in *Technology in America: A History of Individuals and Ideas,* ed. Carroll W. Pursell, Jr., 2d ed., rev., pp. 45–61, 293 (Cambridge: MIT Press, 1990)—analyzes the older approach.

31. Rosenberg, "Technological Change."

32. Hounshell, *American System,* p. 46.

33. Smith, "Army Ordnance," in *Military Enterprise,* pp. 64–75.

34. Ibid., pp. 57–61, 64–75, and "Introduction," pp. 10–14; Charles F. O'Connell, Jr., "The Corps of Engineers and the Rise of Modern Management, 1827–1856," in Smith, ed., *Military Enterprise,* pp. 87–116; and Paul Uselding, "An Early Chapter in the Evolution of American Industrial Management," in *Business Enterprise and Economic Change: Essays in Honor of Harold F. Williamson* (Kent, OH: Kent State University Press, 1973), pp. 51–84. See also Glenn Porter, "Technology and Business in the American Economy," in Frese and Judd, eds., *An Emerging Independent American Economy 1815–1875,* pp. 1–28.

Smith and O'Connell maintain that their interpretations differ fundamentally from Chandler's. Actually, Chandler appears to be more flexible on the subject than they claim. Moreover, and more important, extended disputes over the origins of ideas and practices can become tedious without being particularly enlightening.

35. The account of Calhoun's reforms and their consequences for the War Department and the army is based on John C. Calhoun, *The Works of John C. Calhoun*, ed. Richard K. Cralle, 6 vols. (New York: Russell and Russell, 1968, reproduced from the edition of 1851–1856); John C. Calhoun, *The Papers of John C. Calhoun*, ed. Robert L. Meriwether, W. Edwin Hemphill, and Clyde N. Nelson, 28 vols. (Columbia: University of South Carolina Press, 1959–1989), 2–9; *American State Papers*, Class 5: *Military Affairs*, 7 vols. (Washington, DC: Gales and Seaton, 1832–1861); U.S. Bureau of the Census, *Historical Statistics*, pt. 2, pp. 1114–15, 1142; Charles M. Wiltse, *John C. Calhoun: Nationalist, 1782–1828* (Indianapolis: Bobbs-Merrill, 1944), pp. 138–263; White, *Jeffersonians*, pp. 231–64; Russell F. Weigley, *Towards an American Army: Military Thought from Washington to Marshall* (New York: Columbia University Press, 1962), pp. 30–78; Weigley, *History of the United States Army* (New York: Macmillan, 1967), pp. 133–72; Weigley, *The American Way of War: A History of United States Military Strategy and Policy* (New York: Macmillan, 1973), pp. 59–91; Samuel P. Huntington, *The Soldier and the State: The Theory and Politics of Civil-Military Relations* (Cambridge: Harvard University Press, 1957), pp. 193–221; William H. Carter, *The American Army* (Indianapolis: Bobbs-Merrill, 1915), pp. 163–92; R. Ernest Dupuy and Trevor N. Dupuy, *Military Heritage of America* (New York: McGraw-Hill, 1956), pp. 172–98; Allan R. Millett and Peter Maslowski, *For the Common Defense: A Military History of the United States of America* (New York: Free Press, 1984), pp. 117–37; C. Joseph Bernardo and Eugene H. Bacon, *American Military Policy: Its Development Since 1775* (Harrisburg, PA: Stackpole Company, 1961), pp. 143–65; Erna Risch, *Quartermaster Support of the Army: A History of the Corps, 1775–1939* (Washington, DC: Office of the Quartermaster General, 1962), pp. 181–235; Mary C. Gillett, *The Army Medical Department, 1818–1865* (Washington DC: Center of Military History, 1987), pp. 3–149—see also her companion volume, *The Army Medical Department, 1775–1818* (Washington, DC: Center of Military History, 1990); Sidney Forman, *West Point: A History of the United States Military Academy* (New York: Columbia University Press, 1950), pp. 3–133; Stephen E. Ambrose, *Duty, Honor, Country: A History of West Point* (Baltimore: Johns Hopkins University Press, 1966), pp. 1–166; James L. Morrison, Jr., *"The Best School in the World": West Point, the Pre-Civil War Years, 1833–1866* (Kent, OH: Kent State University Press, 1986); William B. Skelton, "The Commanding General and the Problem of Command in the United States Army, 1821–1841," *Military Affairs* 34 (December 1970): 117–22; Skelton, "Professionalization in the U.S. Army Corps During the Age of Jackson, *Armed Forces and Society* 1 (Summer 1975): 443–71; Skelton, "The Army in the Age of the Common Man, 1815–1845," in *Against All Enemies: Interpretations of American Military History from Colonial Times to the Present*, ed. Kenneth L. Hagan and William R. Rogers (Westport, CT: Greenwood Press, 1986), pp. 91–112; Roger J. Spiller, "Calhoun's Expansible Army: The History of a Military Idea," *South Atlantic Quarterly* 79 (Spring 1980): 189–203. See also relevant essays in Peter Karsten, *The Military in America: From the Colonial Era to the Present*, rev. ed. (New York: Free Press, 1986); Edward Mead Earle, ed., *Makers of Modern Strategy: Military Thought from Machiavelli to Hitler* (Princeton: Princeton University Press, 1943); and Peter Paret, ed., *Makers of Modern Strategy from Machiavelli to the Nuclear Age* (Princeton:

Princeton University Press, 1986). See also Francis P. Prucha, *Broadax and Bayonet: The Role of the United States Army in the Development of the Northwest, 1815–1860* (Lincoln: University of Nebraska Press, 1953), and Prucha, *The Sword of the Republic: The United States Army on the Frontier, 1783–1846* (New York: Macmillan, 1969); William H. Goetzmann, *Army Exploration in the American West, 1803–1863* (New Haven: Yale University Press, 1959); Robert M. Utley, *Frontiersmen in Blue: The United States Army and the Indians, 1848–1865* (New York: Macmillan, 1967); Robert W. Frazer, *Forts and Supplies: The Role of the Army in the Economy of the Southwest, 1846–1861* (Albuquerque: University of New Mexico Press, 1983); Todd Shallat, *Structures in the Stream: Water, Science, and the Rise of the U.S. Corps of Engineers* (Austin: University of Texas Press, 1994); Roger Joseph Spiller, "John C. Calhoun as Secretary of War, 1817–1825" (Ph.D. diss., Louisiana State University, 1978); J. Patrick Hughes, "The Adjutant General's Office 1821–1861: A Study in Administrative History" (Ph.D. diss., Ohio State University, 1978); and Charles Francis O'Connell, Jr., "The United States Army and the Origins of Modern Management, 1818–1860" (Ph.D. diss., Ohio State University, 1982).

No bibliography of the antebellum army is complete without the brilliant volume of Marcus Cunliffe, *Soldiers and Civilians: The Martial Spirit in America, 1775–1865* (Boston: Little, Brown, 1968). The latest and best work on army reform and professional growth is William B. Skelton, *An American Profession of Arms: The Army Officer Corps, 1784–1861* (Lawrence: University Press of Kansas, 1992).

36. These reports are conveniently available in *American State Papers: Military Affairs*, 1: 773, 779–810, 834–48, and 2: 33–34, 75–98, 188–98, 199–274, 345, 698–727. Almost all are also included in Calhoun, *Papers*, 3: 335–36, 374–86, 495–97; 4: 519–24, 679; 5: 480–91; 6: 686–88; and 9: 421–29. Additionally, nearly all the reports and others not usually considered a part of Calhoun's collection are included in Calhoun, *Works*, 5: 8–147.

37. Chase C. Mooney, *William H. Crawford, 1772–1834* (Lexington: University Press of Kentucky, 1974), pp. 78–92.

38. O'Connell, "Army and Origins of Modern Management," p. 57.

39. Several scandals, charges of gross irregularities, or both, concerning supply operations and army construction programs, plagued Calhoun during his years in office. These were no petty matters, involving chairman of the House Military Affairs Committee Richard M. Johnson, Calhoun's chief clerk Maj. Christopher Vandeventer, various relatives of principals implicated, and other military personnel. In these and related matters the judgment, if not the ethicality, of Calhoun, President Monroe, chief of engineers Gen. Joseph G. Swift, and other public officials at best appears to have been open to question. Moreover, even at this early date there is evidence of military officers, such as Chief of Engineers Swift and former quartermaster general Robert Swartout, returning to civilian life and drawing upon their military experience and connections to advance their own interests, including that of military contracting. Highly placed public officials maintained relations with them that can only be labeled as compromising. For details, see Risch, *Quartermaster*, pp. 188–94; Wiltse, *Calhoun*, pp. 167–68, 182–85, 203–5, 214–16, 225, 253, 276, 344–46; and Spiller, "Calhoun," pp. 132–42.

Spiller notes that in Calhoun's generation, "public men of apparent means and influence" were habitually nearly bankrupt, including the secretary of war and the president, both of whom constantly had to scramble to keep themselves financially afloat. Although the author speculates that neither Calhoun nor Monroe would abuse their public trust, lower-level military officers were tempted by the large amounts of money involved in army operations, the service's casual relations with civilian contractors, and the difficulty at that time of uncovering corruption and graft. The temptation was strong because officers' salaries were so low and monetary demands on them often so great.

40. Millett and Maslowski, *Common Defense,* p. 121.

41. Calhoun, *Papers,* 5: 480–91.

42. See the sections "The Political Structure" and "The Economic Structure" in Chapter 4.

43. The analysis of the navy and Navy Department between 1815 and 1845 is based on U.S. Bureau of the Census, *Historical Statistics,* pt. 2, pp. 1114–15, 1142; Charles Oscar Paullin, *Paullin's History of Naval Administration, 1775–1911* (Annapolis, MD: U.S. Naval Institute, 1968), pp. 159–247; Harold and Margaret Sprout, *The Rise of American Naval Power, 1776–1918* (Princeton: Princeton University Press, 1946), pp. 86–126; David F. Long, "The Navy Under the Board of Navy Commissioners, 1815–1842," in *In Peace and War: Interpretations of American Naval History, 1775–1984,* ed. Kenneth J. Hagan, pp. 63–78, 2d ed. (Westport, CT: Greenwood Press, 1984); White, *Jeffersonians,* pp. 265–98; White, *Jacksonians,* pp. 213–50; Robert Greenhalgh Albion, *Makers of Naval Policy, 1798–1947* (Annapolis, MD: Naval Institute Press, 1980), pp. 6–9, 49–53, 187–94; Albion, "The Administration of the Navy, 1798–1945," *Public Administration Review* 5 (Autumn 1945): 293–302; Paolo E. Coletta, ed., *American Secretaries of the Navy,* 1, *1775–1913* (Annapolis, MD: Naval Institute Press, 1980), pp. 101–229; Coletta, *The American Naval Heritage in Brief* (Washington, DC: University Press of America, 1978), pp. 94–109; Charles Todorich, *The Spirited Years: A History of the Antebellum Naval Academy* (Annapolis, MD: Naval Institute Press, 1984); Peter Karsten, *The Naval Aristocracy: The Golden Age of Annapolis and the Emergence of Modern American Navalism* (New York: Free Press, 1972); Christopher McKee, *A Gentlemanly and Honorable Profession: The Creation of the U.S. Naval Officer Corps, 1794–1815* (Annapolis, MD: Naval Institute Press, 1991); A. T. Mahan, *Naval Administration and Warfare: Some General Principles* (London: Sampson, Low, Marston and Company, 1908), pp. 7–85, 177–213; Herman F. Krafft and Walter B. Norris, *Sea Power in American History: The Influence of the Navy and the Merchant Marine Upon American Development* (New York: Century Company, 1920), pp. 172–210; Dudley W. Knox, *A History of the United States Navy* (New York: G. P. Putnam's Sons, 1936), pp. 136–90; Bernard Brodie, *Sea Power in the Machine Age* (Princeton: Princeton University Press, 1941), pp. 3–77; Allan Westcott, ed., *American Seapower Since 1775* (Philadelphia: J. B. Lippincott, 1947), pp. 88–106; Fletcher Pratt, *The Compact History of the United States Navy* (New York: Hawthorne Books, 1962), pp. 103–17; Millett and Maslowski, *Common Defense,* pp. 124–26; Bernardo and Bacon, *Military Policy,* pp. 144–46, 165–71; Vincent Ponko, Jr., *Ships, Seas, and Scientists: U.S. Naval Exploration and Discovery in the Nineteenth Century* (Annapolis, MD: Naval Institute Press, 1974); A. Hunter Dupree, *Science in the Federal Government: A History of Policies and Activities to 1940* (Cambridge, MA: Belknap Press, 1957), pp. 1–119; John H. Schroeder, *Shaping a Maritime Empire: The Commercial and Diplomatic Role of the American Navy, 1829–1861* (Westport, CT: Greenwood Press, 1985); John M. Belohlavek, *"Let the Eagle Soar!" The Foreign Pol-*

icy of Andrew Jackson (Lincoln: University of Nebraska Press, 1985); David F. Long, *Gold Braid and Foreign Relations: Diplomatic Activities of U.S. Naval Officers, 1798–1883* (Annapolis, MD: Naval Institute Press, 1988); Thomas R. Hietala, *Manifest Design: Anxious Aggrandizement in Late Jacksonian America* (Ithaca, NY: Cornell University Press, 1985); and Paul A. Varg, *New England and Foreign Relations, 1789–1850* (Hanover, NH: University Press of New England, 1983).

A number of surveys of the navy have been published in the last decade: Edward L. Beach, *The United States Navy: 200 Years* (New York: Henry Holt, 1986); Kenneth J. Hagan, *This People's Navy: The Making of American Sea Power* (New York: Free Press, 1991); Stephen Howarth, *To Shining Sea: A History of the United States Navy, 1775–1991* (New York: Random House, 1991); Robert W. Love, Jr., *History of the U.S. Navy, 1775–1941* (Harrisburg, PA: Stackpole Books, 1992); and Frank Uhlig, Jr., *How Navies Fight: The U.S. Navy and Its Allies* (Annapolis, MD: Naval Institute Press, 1993).

44. The account and analysis of the Mexican War is based on James K. Polk, *The Diary of James K. Polk During His Presidency, 1845–1849,* ed. Milo Milton Quaife, 4 vols. (Chicago: A. C. McClurg and Company, 1910), and an abbreviated version is provided in James K. Polk, *Polk: The Diary of a President, 1845–1849; Covering the Mexican War, the Acquisition of Oregon, and the Conquest of California and the Southwest,* ed. Allan Nevins (New York: Longmans, Green and Company, 1929); U.S. Bureau of the Census, *Historical Statistics,* pt. 2, pp. 1106, 1114–15, 1118, 1140, 1142; U. S. Grant, *Personal Memoirs of U. S. Grant,* ed. E. B. Long (Cleveland, OH: World Publishing Company, 1952), pp. 11–95; Charles Sellers, *James K. Polk: Continentalist, 1843–1846* (Princeton: Princeton University Press, 1966); Paul H. Bergeron, *The Presidency of James K. Polk* (Lawrence: University Press of Kansas, 1987); Justin H. Smith, *The War with Mexico,* 2 vols. (New York: Macmillan, 1919); Otis Singletary, *The Mexican War* (Chicago: University of Chicago Press, 1960); Charles L. Dufour, *The Mexican War: A Compact History, 1846–1848* (New York: Hawthorn Books, 1968); David M. Pletcher, *The Diplomacy of Annexation: Texas, Oregon, and the Mexican War* (Columbia: University of Missouri Press, 1973); K. Jack Bauer, *The Mexican War, 1846–1848* (New York: Macmillan, 1974); Seymour V. Connor and Odie B. Faulk, *North America Divided: The Mexican War, 1846–1848* (New York: Oxford University Press, 1971); Douglas W. Richmond, ed., *Essays on the Mexican War* (College Station: Texas A & M University Press, 1986); John S. D. Eisenhower, *So Far from God: The U.S. War with Mexico, 1846–1848* (New York: Random House, 1989); Studenski and Krooss, *Financial History,* pp. 122–26; Henry Cohen, *Business and Politics in America from the Age of Jackson to the Civil War: The Career Biography of W. W. Corcoran* (Westport, CT: Greenwood Publishing Corporation, 1971); Weigley, *U.S. Army,* pp. 173–89; Weigley, *American Way of War,* pp. 70–76; Marvin A. Kreidberg and Merton G. Henry, *History of Military Mobilization in the United States Army, 1775–1945* (Washington, DC: Department of the Army, 1955), pp. 61–82; Dupuy and Dupuy, *Military Heritage,* pp. 144–71; Risch, *Quartermaster Support,* pp. 237–99; James A. Huston, *The Sinews of War: Army Logistics, 1775–1953* (Washington, DC: Office of the Chief of Military History, 1966), pp. 125–58; James L. Morrison, Jr., "Military Education and Strategic Thought, 1846–1861," in Hagan and Roberts, eds., *Against All Enemies,* pp. 113–31; Harry L. Coles, "The War of 1812 and the Mexican War," in *New Dimensions in Military History: An Anthology,* ed. Rus-

sell F. Weigley, pp. 313–25 (San Rafael, CA: Presidio Press, 1975); John K. Mahon, *History of the Militia and the National Guard* (New York: Macmillan, 1983), pp. 90–96; Bernardo and Bacon, *American Military Policy,* pp. 172–79; Millett and Maslowski, *Common Defense,* pp. 137–50; Walter Millis, *Arms and Men: America's Military History and Military Policy from the Revolution to the Present* (New York: Putnam, 1956), pp. 103–8; Arthur A. Ekirch, Jr., *The Civilian and the Military* (New York: Oxford University Press, 1956), pp. 60–89; White, *Jacksonians,* pp. 50–103; Sprout, *Naval Power,* 128–36; Paullin, *Naval Administration,* pp. 205–47; Geoffrey S. Smith, "An Uncertain Passage: The Bureaus Run the Navy, 1842–1861," in Hagan, ed., *Peace and War,* pp. 79–106; Coletta, ed., *Secretaries of Navy,* 1: 217–40; Coletta, *Naval Heritage,* pp. 108–11.

See also Albert K. Weinberg, *Manifest Destiny: A Study of Nationalist Expansionism in American History* (Baltimore: Johns Hopkins University Press, 1935), pp. 160–89; Norman A. Graebner, *Empire on the Pacific: A Study in American Continental Expansion* (New York: Ronald Press Company, 1955); Graebner, "Lessons of the Mexican War," *Pacific Historical Review* 67 (August 1978): 325–42; Frederick Merk, *Manifest Destiny and Mission in American History: A Reinterpretation* (New York: Alfred A. Knopf, 1963); Samuel Eliot Morison, Frederick Merk, and Frank Freidel, *Dissent in Three American Wars* (Cambridge: Harvard University Press, 1970), pp. 33–63; Glenn W. Price, *Origins of the War with Mexico: The Polk-Stockton Intrigue* (Austin: University of Texas Press, 1967); John H. Schroeder, *Mr. Polk's War: American Opposition and Dissent, 1846–1848* (Madison: University of Wisconsin Press, 1973); David Clifton Lawson, "Swords into Plowshares, Spears into Pruninghooks: The Intellectual Foundations of the First American Peace Movement, 1815–1865" (Ph.D. diss., University of New Mexico, 1975); Robert W. Johannsen, *To the Halls of the Montezuma: The Mexican War in the American Imagination* (New York: Oxford University Press, 1985); and Anna Kasten Nelson, *Secret Agents: President Polk and the Search for Peace with Mexico* (New York: Garland Publishing, 1988).

45. Weigley, *U.S. Army,* p. 179.

46. Grant, *Personal Memoirs,* p. 84.

47. See the section "The Economic Structure" in Chapter 4.

48. The analysis of the army between 1848 and 1860 is based on the sources in note 35.

49. The analysis of the navy between 1848 and 1860 is based on the sources cited in note 43.

50. See the discussion of the navy in the section "The Military Structure, 1815–1846" in Chapter 4.

CHAPTER FIVE. ECONOMIC MOBILIZATION IN THE NORTH

1. The secondary sources on the Northern states are voluminous. My *Bibliography on Northern States and Regions During the Civil War,* which also covers the border states, is current and nearly exhaustive. Many of the volumes written or compiled in the late nineteenth and early twentieth centuries are closer to primary than secondary sources because they either quote extensively from or include numerous documents in their text.

Including the entire bibliography in this volume or incorporating extensive citations from it in the notes would be cumbersome and probably not that helpful to most readers. Consequently, the Oviatt Library at California State University, Northridge, has included a copy of the bibliography in its holdings and will make it available to any interested party through interlibrary loan. In the following analysis of the states, I provide notes only when necessary; otherwise, I am drawing upon the sources included in *Bibliography on Northern States.*

2. This subject is treated in many of the sources cited on the states in *Bibliography on Northern States.* The best source is William B. Hazeltine, *Lincoln and War Governors* (New York: Alfred A. Knopf, 1948).

3. The best source of information on the UDC is John Austin Stevens, ed., *The Union Defence Committee of the City of New York: Minutes, Reports, and Correspondence with an Historical Introduction* (New York: Union Defence Committee, 1885). *The War of the Rebellion: A Compilation of the Official Records of the Union and Confederate Armies* (Washington, DC: U.S. Government Printing Office, 1880–1901), series 3, vol. 1 (hereafter *OR*), also contains some important documentation on the UDC. See Wool to Scott, 4/23/61, and other subsequent correspondence and documents relevant to the subject. Most of the sources cited under New York in *Bibliography on Northern States* treat the committee with varying degrees of detail and quality.

4. The outstanding book on the governors during the Civil War is Hazeltine, *Lincoln and the War Governors.* See also William B. Weeden, *War Government, Federal and State in Massachusetts, New York, Pennsylvania, and Indiana, 1861–1865* (Boston: Houghton, Mifflin, 1906). For background on the evolution of the governors' power in the nineteenth century, see Leslie Lipson, *The American Governor from Figurehead to Leader* (Chicago: University of Chicago Press, 1939), pp. 1–25; Arthur N. Holcombe, *State Government in the United States,* 2d ed., rev. (New York: Macmillan, 1926), pp. 280–336; and James W. Fesler, ed., *The 50 States and Their Local Governments* (New York: Alfred A. Knopf, 1967), pp. 39–59. Daniel J. Elazar's work is also helpful in this regard: see *The American Partnership: Intergovernmental Co-operation in the Nineteenth-Century United States* (Chicago: University of Chicago Press, 1962).

5. Compared with those for other states, the secondary sources on Massachusetts during the Civil War are not outstanding. However, an enormous amount of exceptionally detailed information, frequently down to the village level and usually unanalyzed and undifferentiated, is available in print. Of the volumes listed in *Bibliography on Northern States,* I have found these to be the most helpful: George L. Austin, *The History of Massachusetts from the Landing to the Present Time* (Boston: B. B. Russell, 1884); James L. Bowen, *Massachusetts in the War, 1861–1865* (Springfield, MA: Clark W. Bryan and Company, 1889); Oscar and Mary Flug Handlin, *Commonwealth: A Study of the Role of Government in the American Economy: Massachusetts, 1774–1861,* 2d ed., rev. (Cambridge: Harvard University Press, 1969); Henry G. Pearson, "Massachusetts to the Front (1860–1861)," pp. 499–515, and Thomas G. Frothingham, "Massachusetts in the Civil War (1861–1865)," pp. 516–51, in *Commonwealth History of Massachusetts,* vol. 4, *Nineteenth Century Massachusetts,* ed. Albert B. Hart (New York: Russell and Russell, 1966); P. C. Headley, *Massachusetts in the Rebellion: A Record of the Historical Position of the Commonwealth, and the Services of the Leading Statesmen, the Military, and Colleges, and the People in the Civil War of 1861–65* (Boston: Walker, Fuller, and Company, 1866); Henry G. Pearson, *The Life of John A. Andrew, Gover-*

nor of Massachusetts, 1861–1865, 2 vols. (Boston: Houghton Mifflin, 1904); and Robert H. Whitten, *Public Administration in Massachusetts: The Relation of Central to Local Authority* (New York: Columbia University Press, 1898).

6. It is nearly impossible to get two sources to agree on the number of men in military service from a state. Official federal figures are provided in *OR,* ser. 3, 4: 1264–1270; composite figures are on p. 1269. These figures are conveniently reproduced in Fred Albert Shannon, *The Organization and Administration of the Union Army, 1861–1865,* 2 vols. (Cleveland, OH: Arthur H. Clark Company, 1928), 2: 277–78. See also U.S. Bureau of the Census, *Historical Statistics of the United States: Colonial Times to 1970* (Washington, DC: U.S. Government Printing Office, 1975), pt. 2, pp. 1141–43. Many of the volumes cited in *Bibliography on Northern States* on Massachusetts give total numbers for the state; I have used the figures that seem most reliable and consistent.

7. Albert W. Niemi, Jr., *State and Regional Patterns in American Manufacturing, 1860–1900* (Westport, CT: Greenwood Press, 1974), provides a detailed analysis of state, regional, and national manufacturing in the late nineteenth century.

8. See Chapter 4.

9. The secondary sources on New York during the Civil War are much better than those for Massachusetts. The most important and helpful are Robert G. Albion, *Square-Riggers on Schedule: The New York Sailing Packets to England, France, and the Cotton Ports* (Princeton: Princeton University Press, 1938), and Albion, *The Rise of New York Port* (New York: Charles Scribner's Sons, 1939); Sidney D. Brummer, *Political History of New York State During the Period of the Civil War* (1910; reprint, New York: AMS Press, 1967); David M. Ellis et al., *A History of New York State* (Ithaca, NY: Cornell University Press, 1967); John A. Fairlie, *The Centralization of Administration in New York State* (1898; reprint, New York: AMS Press, 1969); Alexander C. Flick, ed., *History of the State of New York,* vols. 7–8 (New York: Columbia University Press, 1935); Philip S. Foner, *Business and Slavery: The New York Merchants and the Irrepressible Conflict* (Chapel Hill: University of North Carolina Press, 1941); John B. Lossing, *The Empire State: A Compendious History of the Commonwealth of New York* (Hartford, CT: American Publishing Company, 1888); Stewart Mitchell, *Horatio Seymour of New York* (1938; reprint, New York: Da Capo Press, 1970); Margaret G. Myers, *The New York Money Market,* vol. 1, *Origins and Development* (1931; reprint, New York: AMS Press, 1971); Henry G. Pearson, *James S. Wadsworth of Geneseo: Brevet Major General of the United States Volunteers* (London: J. Murray, 1913); Frederick Phisterer, comp., *New York in the War of the Rebellion, 1861–1865,* vol. 1 (Albany, NY: J. B. Lyon Company, State Printers, 1912); James A. Rawley, *Edwin D. Morgan, 1811–1883: Merchant in Politics* (New York: Columbia University Press, 1955); Don C. Sowers, *The Financial History of New York State: From 1789 to 1912* (1914; reprint, New York: AMS Press, 1969); Stevens, ed., *UDC;* and James Sullivan, ed., *History of New York State, 1523–1927,* vols. 3–4 (New York: Lewis Historical Publishing Company, 1927).

10. See note 6 for relevant sources on state contributions to the Union army.

11. Niemi, *State and Regional Patterns in American Manufacturing.*

12. Indiana benefits from a number of good-quality state histories. Among the most helpful are Donald F. Carmony, ed., *Indiana: A Self-Appraisal* (Bloomington: Indiana University Press, 1966); William A. Rawles, *Centralizing Tendencies in the*

Administration of Indiana (1903; reprint, New York: AMS Press, 1968); Kenneth Stampp, *Indiana Politics During the Civil War* (Indianapolis: Indiana Historical Bureau, 1949); George W. Starr, *Industrial Development of Indiana* (Bloomington: School of Business Administration, Indiana University, 1937); W. H. H. Terrell, preparer, *Indiana in the War of the Rebellion,* vol. 1 (1869; reprint, Indianapolis: Indiana Historical Bureau, 1960); Emma Lou Thornbrough, *Indiana in the Civil War Era, 1850–1880* (Indianapolis: Indiana Historical Bureau, 1965); William E. Wilson, *Indiana: A History* (Bloomington: Indiana University Press, 1966); and Writers' Guide Program of the Work Projects Administration in the State of Indiana, *Indiana: A Guide to the Hoosier State* (New York: Oxford University Press, 1941).

13. Stampp, *Indiana Politics,* p. 13.

14. Besides the sources listed in *Bibliography on Northern States,* the following are useful for banking in Indiana: Fritz Redlich, *The Molding of American Banking: Men and Ideas,* 2 parts, 2d ed., rev. (New York: Johnson Reprint Corporation, 1968), consult index; James Roger Sharp, *The Jacksonians versus the Banks: Politics in the States After the Panic of 1837* (New York: Columbia University Press, 1970), pp. 200–208; and Hugh Rockoff, *The Free Banking Era: A Re-Examination* (New York: Arno Press, 1975), pp. 98–100.

15. See note 6 for relevant sources on military manpower.

16. Thornbrough, *Indiana,* pp. 362–97; Wilson, *Indiana,* pp. 137–38; and U.S. Bureau of the Census, *Historical Statistics,* pt. 1, pp. 512–20.

17. Niemi, *State and Regional Patterns in American Manufacturing;* Carmony, *Indiana,* pp. 66–68; and Starr, *Industrial Development of Indiana,* pp. 9–75.

18. Secondary sources on Iowa are nowhere near as accomplished as those on Indiana; nonetheless, several are quite helpful: S. H. M. Byers, *Iowa in War Times* (Des Moines, IA: W. D. Condit and Company, 1888); Dan E. Clark, *Samuel Jordon Kirkwood* (Iowa City: State Historical Society of Iowa, 1917); Olynthus B. Clark, *The Politics of Iowa During the Civil War and Reconstruction* (Iowa City: Clio Press, 1911); Cyrenus Cole, *Iowa Through the Years* (Iowa City: State Historical Society of Iowa, 1940); Federal Writers' Project of the Work Progress Administration for the State of Iowa, *Iowa: A Guide to the Hawkeye State* (New York: Viking Press, 1938); Earl S. Fullbrook, *Sanitary Fairs—A Method of Raising Funds for Relief Work in Iowa During the Civil War* (Iowa City: State Historical Society of Iowa, 1917), and Fullbrook, "Relief Work in Iowa During the Civil War," *Iowa Journal of History and Politics* 44 (April 1918): 155–274; Benjamin T. Gue, *History of Iowa: From the Earliest Times to the Beginning of the Twentieth Century,* vol. 2 (New York: Century History Company, 1903); Ivan L. Pollack, *The Iowa Civil War Loan* (Iowa City: State Historical Society of Iowa, 1917), and Pollack, "State Finances in Iowa During the Civil War," *Iowa Journal of History and Politics* 44 (January 1918): 53–107; Morton M. Rosenberg, *Iowa on the Eve of the Civil War: A Decade of Frontier Politics* (Norman: University of Oklahoma Press, 1972); Leland L. Sage, *A History of Iowa* (Ames: Iowa State University Press, 1974); Elizabeth D. Leonard, *Yankee Women: Gender Battles in the Civil War* (New York: W. W. Norton, 1994), pp. 51–103, 227–39; Cyril B. Upham, *Equipment of the Iowa Troops in the Civil War* (Iowa City: State Historical Society of Iowa, 1917), and Upham, "Arms and Equipment for the Iowa Troops in the Civil War," *Iowa Journal of History and Politics* 44 (January 1918): 3–52.

19. For banking in Iowa, in addition to *Bibliography on Northern States,* see Redlich, *American Banking,* consult index, and Bray Hammond, *Banks and Politics in America, from the Revolution to the Civil War* (Princeton: Princeton University Press, 1957), pp. 614–17, 623–24.

20. See note 6 for relevant sources on troop mobilization.

21. Niemi, *State and Regional Patterns in American Manufacturing.*

22. The secondary sources I have consulted indicate no financing or support for war financing by banks, individuals, and the like in Missouri and the Nebraska Territory. Such support is only implied for Minnesota, and I have not researched California and Oregon because of their isolation.

23. Duane Lockard, *The New Jersey Governor: A Study in Political Power* (Princeton, NJ: D. Van Nostrand Company, 1964), pp. 6–8.

24. My research has turned up no explicit study of power within any state, let alone the collective states, of the North. However, numerous sources do implicitly support the elite interpretation simply by indicating sources of financing, the governor's background and staff, and so forth. Moreover, from the discussion of elite patterns that preceded the Civil War and that take place after hostilities, it would be extraordinary if not impossible to find anything but elite mobilization patterns during the war. One of my major theses is that war tends only to exaggerate and make more manifest peacetime trends rather than creating new ones. What is fascinating, however, is the way the Civil War mobilization systems so explicitly reveal which groups dominated society, elite strategies and divisions over how to maintain mass loyalty, and changes occurring in the elite during a period of dramatic change in the nation's overall structure. These matters, of course, could be studied without the Civil War, but mobilization for the war makes the process much easier. However, it is critically important to keep in mind that the elites are most visible at the state, not the federal, level.

For a fully authenticated study, scholars must be much more thorough and systematic than I have been. Research in primary sources will also be necessary since the existing secondary sources either do not provide enough information or have presented it in a way that is unhelpful. Focusing on a few representative states, instead of all states (which would be a daunting task), would go far to achieve the type of study I have suggested. The limited nature of my work, however, does not create any great uncertainty on my part about my conclusions on the elite nature of American society. Nonetheless, more work from others would be welcome, regardless of their methods and conclusions.

In exploring further secondary sources on power patterns before and during the Civil War, I examined a host of available studies, most of which involve New England and some of which cover the Middle States. I have included these volumes and articles in *Bibliography on Northern States* and have indicated which works, other than those cited in the notes, appear to make a contribution to the study of power in America.

25. The analysis of welfare activities for soldiers' dependents is based on various state studies. For Massachusetts, see Austin, *Massachusetts;* Bowen, *Massachusetts;* Pearson, "Massachusetts to the Front," and Frothingham, "Massachusetts in the Civil War," in Hart, ed., *Massachusetts,* vol. 4; Headley, *Massachusetts;* and Pearson, *Andrew,* 2 vols. For New York, see Ellis et al., *New York State;* Flick, ed., *State of New York;* Lossing, *Empire State;* Phisterer, *New York;* Rawley, *Morgan;* Stevens, ed., *UDC;* and

Sullivan, ed., *New York State,* vols. 3–4. For Indiana, see Stampp, *Indiana Politics;* Terrell, preparer, *Indiana,* vol. 1; Thornbrough, *Indiana;* and Wilson, *Indiana.* For Iowa, see Byers, *Iowa;* Clark, *Kirkwood;* Cole, *Iowa;* Fullbrook, "Relief Work in Iowa During the Civil War," and *Sanitary Fairs.* For other states, see the sources listed in *Bibliography on Northern States.* See also Robert H. Bremner, *The Public Good: Philanthropy and Welfare in the Civil War Era* (New York: Alfred A. Knopf, 1980), pp. 72–90.

The sources on this subject are not particularly good, with much of the information being anecdotal rather than systematic or quantitative in nature. Nonetheless, a few studies previously cited have some sound coverage; and works on all the states combined provide a reasonably accurate picture of events.

Washington in 1862 enacted a federal pension system for disabled and deceased soldiers and their dependents. The program had its greatest impact after, not during, hostilities. The nature and impact of the Civil War pension system is imaginatively examined by Theda Skocpol, *Protecting Soldiers and Mothers: The Political Origins of Social Policy in the United States* (Cambridge: Harvard University Press, 1992). Additionally, see Megan J. McClintock, "Binding Up the Nation's Wounds: Nationalism, Civil War Pensions, and American Families, 1861–1890" (Ph.D. diss., Rutgers University, New Brunswick, 1994)—the author discusses pre–Civil War pension systems and cites sources on mid-nineteenth-century attitudes and policies toward social welfare.

26. For poor-relief practices before the war, see Bremner, *Public Good,* pp. 14–34, and Michael B. Katz, *In the Shadow of the Poorhouse: A Social History of Welfare in America* (New York: Basic Books, 1986), pp. 3–109.

27. The same sources that deal with the home-front welfare activities in note 25 also treat with soldier-relief efforts. For Bremner, *Public Good,* see pp. 54–71.

I have found no record of soldiers'-aid societies in Kansas and West Virginia. Perhaps this lack stemmed from the extreme conditions these states faced during the war and the fact that the U.S. Sanitary Commission and the Western Sanitary Commission were active in each state.

28. Allan Nevins, *The War for the Union,* vol. 2, *War Becomes Revolution* (New York: Charles Scribner's Sons, 1960), pp. 478–79.

29. The casual and flawed records kept by Iowa during the war make it difficult to assess with full confidence the state's performance in aiding the troops.

30. The single best source on the USSC is the official history: Charles J. Stille, *History of the United States Sanitary Commission: Being the General Report of Its Work During the War of the Rebellion* (Philadelphia: J. B. Lippincott and Company, 1866). See also U.S. Sanitary Commission, *The Sanitary Commission of the United States Army: A Succinct Narrative of Its Works and Purposes* (1864; reprint, New York: Arno Press and the New York Times, 1972). The one monograph on the subject is also helpful: William Quentin Maxwell, *Lincoln's Fifth Wheel: The Political History of the United States Sanitary Commission* (New York: Longmans, Green, 1956). See also Laura Wood Roper, *FLO: A Biography of Frederick Law Olmsted* (Baltimore: Johns Hopkins University Press, 1973), pp. 156–232, and Elizabeth Stevenson, *Park Maker: A Life of Frederick Law Olmsted* (New York: Macmillan, 1977), pp. 195–246. George M. Fredrickson, *The Inner Civil War: Northern Intellectuals and the Crisis of the Union* (New York: Harper and Row, 1965), pp. 98–112, provides an insightful essay on the

commission. A fresh, critical analysis of the USSC is presented by Rejean Attie, "'A Swindling Concern': The United States Sanitary Commission and the Northern Female Public, 1861–1865" (Ph.D. diss., Columbia University, 1987). See also Bremner, *Public Good,* pp. 35–46, 49–71, and Fullbrook, "Relief Work in Iowa During the Civil War," pp. 155–76. Nevins, *War for the Union,* 4 vols., includes quite a bit on the USSC; consult the index (full citations for these volumes appear in Chapter 6). *OR,* ser. 3, 1–2, and U.S. War Department, *Report of the Secretary of War to the President, 1861–1865,* also contain some information on the USSC and the Medical Department (full citations for the secretary of war's reports appear in Chapter 6.) Numerous general works at least treat briefly with the Sanitary Commission; for example, see Russell F. Weigley, *History of the United States Army* (New York: Macmillan, 1967), pp. 224–26. Some of the volumes on New York state history also include quite a bit on the USSC; see *Bibliography on Northern States.* Obviously, such an important organization still is in need of more attention.

31. Some of the best sources on the Medical Bureau are Mary C. Gillett, *The Army Medical Department, 1818–1865* (Washington, DC: Center of Military History, 1987), pp. 155–299; James A. Huston, *The Sinews of War: Army Logistics, 1775–1953* (Washington, DC: Office of the Chief of Military History, 1966), pp. 168, 240–52; George Worthington Adams, *Doctors in Blue: The Medical History of the Union Army in the Civil War* (New York: Henry Schuman, 1952); and Frank R. Freemon, "Medical Care During the American Civil War" (Ph.D. diss., University of Illinois, Urbana-Champaign, 1992). See also Stephen B. Oates, *A Woman of Valor: Clara Barton and the Civil War* (New York: Free Press, 1994).

32. The statistics are from Nevins, *War for the Union,* 1: 283–84; Stille, *USSC,* Appendix 8, lists the monographs on sanitation and the like.

33. For the list of monographs, see Stille, *USSC,* Appendix 8.

34. Huston, *Sinews of War,* pp. 251–52; and Weigley, *U.S. Army,* pp. 224–26.

35. Stille, *USSC,* pp. 487–90.

36. Regrettably, there is no monograph on the WSC. The following sources have been helpful: Maxwell, *Lincoln's Fifth Wheel,* pp. 97–106, 111, 131–32, 185, 194, 219; Bremner, *Public Good,* pp. 57–62, 69–70, 95–96, 99; Stille, *USSC,* pp. 138–65; and Fullbrook, "Relief Work in Iowa During the Civil War," pp. 187–96. Some of the state histories of Missouri also devote considerable attention to the WSC; see *Bibliography on Northern States.*

37. The USCC has also been neglected by scholars; no monographic treatment exists. I have consulted Maxwell, *Lincoln's Fifth Wheel,* pp. 97–106, 111, 131–33, 185, 194, 219; Bremner, *Public Good,* pp. 57–62, 69–70, 95–96; Stille, *USSC,* pp. 138–65; and Fullbrook, "Relief Work in Iowa During the Civil War," pp. 176–87.

38. Nevins, *War for the Union,* 3: 321–23, and Bremner, *Public Good,* pp. 65–69.

39. Stille, *USSC,* pp. 150–51.

40. Ibid., p. 58.

CHAPTER SIX. UNION WAR AND NAVY DEPARTMENTS

1. Many of the works cited for this chapter deal with the War Department before and after the declaration of war. The most detailed study is that of A. Howard Meneely,

The War Department, 1861: A Study in Mobilization and Administration (New York: Columbia University Press, 1928), pp. 13–114.

2. *The War of the Rebellion: A Compilation of the Official Records of the Union and Confederate Armies* (Washington, DC: U.S. Government Printing Office, 1880–1901), series 3, vol. 1 (hereafter *OR*), deals with the period from November 1, 1860, through March 31, 1862, and is a remarkably rich source of correspondence, orders, and reports on the administration of the Union army. It covers federal-state relations, important statistics, bureau operations, and so forth. Especially enlightening are the queries from the states that often went unanswered, and the fact that Thomas A. Scott, the assistant secretary, not Cameron, appeared to be handling most business from the secretary's office after Scott's appointment in August. See also U.S. War Department, *Report of the Secretary of War to the President, 1861,* Sen. Ex. Doc. 1, 37th Cong., 1st sess., 7/1/61, pp. 19–83 (*Annual Report of the Secretary of War,* hereafter *ARSW*); U.S. War Department, *ARSW, 1861,* Sen. Ex. Doc. 1, 37th Cong., 2d sess., 12/1/61; U.S. Congress, Senate, *Report on Contracts for the Army,* Ex. Doc. 17, 37th Cong., 2d sess., 1/16/62; and U.S. Congress, House, *Report on War Department Contracts for the Year 1861,* Ex. Doc. 101, 37th Cong., 2d sess., 4/24/62.

Secondary sources are legion; an introductory list includes Erwin S. Bradley, *Simon Cameron, Lincoln's Secretary of War: A Political Biography* (Philadelphia: University of Pennsylvania Press, 1966); Brooks M. Kelley, "Fossildom, Old Fogeyism, and Red Tape," *Pennsylvania Magazine of History and Biography* 90 (January 1966): 93–114; Burton J. Hendrick, *Lincoln's War Cabinet* (Boston: Little, Brown, 1946); Harry J. Carman and Reinhard H. Luthin, *Lincoln and Patronage* (New York: Columbia University Press, 1943). See also James A. Huston, *The Sinews of War: Army Logistics, 1775–1953* (Washington, DC: Office of the Chief of Military History, 1966), pp. 159–252; L. D. Ingersoll, *A History of the War Department* (Washington, DC: Francis B. Mohun, 1880), pp. 328–69; Samuel R. Kamm, *The Civil War Career of Thomas A. Scott* (Philadelphia: University of Pennsylvania Press, 1940); Meneely, *War Department;* Allan Nevins, *The War for the Union,* vol. 1, *The Improvised War, 1861–1862* (New York: Charles Scribner's Sons, 1959); Erna Risch, *Quartermaster Support of the Army: A History of the Corps, 1775–1939* (Washington, DC: Office of the Quartermaster General, 1962), pp. 333–452; Fred A. Shannon, *The Organization and Administration of the Union Army, 1861–1865,* 2 vols. (Cleveland, OH: Arthur H. Clark, 1928); Russell F. Weigley, *History of the United States Army* (New York: Macmillan, 1967), pp. 197–264; and Lloyd M. Short, *The Development of National Administrative Organization in the United States* (Baltimore: Johns Hopkins University Press, 1923), pp. 236–41.

3. Cameron to Morgan and Cummings, 4/23/61, and other correspondence, *OR,* ser. 3, 1; Lincoln to Senate and House of Representatives, 5/26/62, and other correspondence, *OR,* ser. 3, 2; U.S. Congress, House, Select Committee on Government Contracts, *Report on Government Contracts,* House Rep. no. 2, 37th Cong., 2d sess., 12/17/61, part 1: Report, pp. 54–68, 137–47 (intermittent), part 1: Testimony, pp. 1–1109 (intermittent) (hereafter referred to as the Committee on Contracts). In its publications, the committee almost simultaneously refers to itself as both a "select" and a "special" committee; I have used the first designation.

4. U.S. Congress, House, *Report on Purchase of Small Arms,* Ex. Doc. 67, 37th Cong., 2d sess, 3/5/62, pp. 1–27; *Report on War Department Contracts for the Year 1861;* Committee on Contracts, *Report on Government Contracts,* part 1: Report,

pp. 1–2, 34–54, 137–47 (intermittent), part 1: Testimony, pp. 1–1109 (intermittent), and part 2, pp. I–II, XXXIII–XXXVIII, XLVI–XLVII, L–LII, LVI–LXXVI, i–xiv (intermittent), 1–1611 (intermittent); care must be taken with these publications because the reports are combined with the testimony and varying and confusing pagination is used; Committee on Contracts, *Report on Government Contracts—Final Report*, House Rep. no. 49, 37th Cong., 3d sess, 3/3/63, pp. 1–2, 5–24, 25–29 (intermittent); Ripley endorsement to Callender letter, 9/25/61, *OR*, ser. 3, 1; U.S. Congress, Joint Committee on the Conduct of the War, *Report, Part III: Department of the West*, Sen. Rep. no. 108, 37th Cong., 3d sess., 4/6/63, pp. 3–279 (hereafter cited as Committee on Conduct of War). There are only six pages to the report; the remainder is attached testimony and related documents.

5. Most of the preceding sources are relevant for Stanton as well as for Cameron. The biographies of Stanton include George C. Gorham, *Life and Public Services of Edwin M. Stanton,* 2 vols. (Boston: Houghton, Mifflin, 1899); Frank A. Flower, *Edwin McMasters Stanton: The Autocrat of Rebellion, Emancipation, and Reconstruction* (New York: W. W. Wilson, 1905); Fletcher Pratt, *Stanton: Lincoln's Secretary of War* (New York: Norton, 1953); and Benjamin P. Thomas and Harold M. Hyman, *The Life and Times of Lincoln's Secretary of War* (New York: Alfred A. Knopf, 1962).

6. Commission on Ordnance and Ordnance Stores, *Report on Ordnance and Ordnance Stores,* Sen. Ex. Doc. 72, 37th Cong., 2d sess., 7/17/62. The commission at times worked with or shared its work with the Committee on Contracts and the Committee on Conduct of War. Portions of its 595-page report appeared in the publications of those committees and others were published separately; for example, see U.S. Congress, House, *Report on Interest of Members of Congress in Government Contracts,* Ex. Doc. no. 151, 37th Cong., 2d sess., 7/17/62, pp. 1–7.

7. The discussion and analysis of the structure and operations of the Quartermaster Department are based on *OR,* ser. 3, 1–5, covering the years 1860–1866, which is an outstanding primary source on the evolution and activities of the Quartermaster Department. From this source it is possible to trace the Quartermaster Department and other bureaus through the confusion of 1861, to the growing proficiency of 1862, to the efficient handling of supply from 1863 forward. At times the *ARSW* and annual reports of the various bureaus to the secretary of war will be found in the *OR.* For some examples of important documents in it, see Meigs to Cameron, 10/30/61, 1; Meigs to Stanton, 8/13/62, 2; Meigs, "Sketch of the campaign and review of the military situation," [ca.] 8/63, 3; Meigs to Stanton, 2/2/64, 4; and Meigs to Stanton, 11/8/65, 5—this is the fullest and most complete annual report of the Quartermaster Department that I have located in print; it includes reports from most of the subdivisions and is 274 pages in length. What becomes fully evident from the various volumes of the *OR* is not only how well supplied the Union armies were but also the enormous amount of waste that grew out of ignorance, inexperience, and casualness on the part of officers and men alike. Another invaluable source on the Quartermaster Department is the *ARSW.* In these reports, the secretary of war often summarized and presented condensed versions of the bureau's reports, included his own analysis of the situation, and placed the quartermaster's operations within the larger context of the total war effort. See *ARSW, July 1861; ARSW, December 1861;* U.S. War Department, *ARSW, 1862,* House Ex. Doc. no. 1, 37th Cong., 3d sess., 12/1/62; U.S. War Department, *ARSW, 1863,* House Ex. Doc. no. 1, 38th Cong., 1st sess., 12/5/63;

U.S. War Department, *ARSW, 1864,* House Ex. Doc. no. 83, 38th Cong., 2d sess., 3/2/65; U.S. War Department, *ARSW, 1865,* House Ex. Doc. no. 1, 2 vols., 39th Cong., 1st sess., 11/22/65; and U.S. War Department, *ARSW, 1866,* House Ex. Doc. no. 1, 39th Cong., 2d sess., 11/14/66. Reports from and about the Quartermaster Department to Congress are also a valuable source of information; see *Report on War Department Contracts for the Year 1861;* U.S. Congress, House, *Report on Contracts Made by the Quartermaster's Department,* Ex. Doc. no. 84, 38th Cong., 2d sess., 3/3/65; and various reports by the Committee on Contracts and the Committee on Conduct of War already cited. See also extracts from Meigs's journal in *American Historical Review* 26 (1920-1921): 285–303.

Secondary sources are plentiful. Almost all the volumes cited in notes 2 and 5 provide needed information on the Quartermaster Department. The most important are Risch, *Quartermaster Support,* pp. 333–452; Huston, *Sinews of War,* pp. 168–86, 215–52; and Russell F. Weigley, *Quartermaster General of the Union Army: A Biography of M. C. Meigs* (New York: Columbia University Press, 1959), pp. 57–326.

Good overviews of the economy before, during, and after the Civil War are presented in Harold F. Williamson, ed., *The Growth of the American Economy,* 2d ed., rev. (Englewood Cliffs, NJ: Prentice-Hall, 1951), pp. 90–334; Lance E. Davis et al., *American Economic Growth: An Economist's History of the United States* (New York: Harper and Row, 1972); N. S. B. Gras and Henrietta M. Larson, *Casebook in American Business History* (New York: F. S. Croftsand Company, 1939), pp. 682–705; and Chester W. Wright, *Economic History of the United States* (New York: McGraw-Hill, 1949), pp. 234–447. For works dealing with manufacturing in general, see J. Leander Bishop, *A History of American Manufactures from 1608 to 1860,* 3 vols. (Philadelphia: Edward Young and Company, 1868); and Victor S. Clark, *History of Manufactures in the United States,* 3 vols., 1 and 2 (Washington, DC: Carnegie Institution, 1929).

8. There is no monograph on the Subsistence Department during the Civil War. Basic developments can be traced through the *OR,* ser. 3, 1–5, and *ARSW, 1861–1866.* Various reports of the Committee on Contracts also touch upon the department's operations. Several secondary sources are also helpful; see Risch, *Quartermaster Support,* pp. 382–87, 451–52; Huston, *Sinews of War,* pp. 168–85; and Nevins, *The War for the Union,* 1 and 2, *War Becomes Revolution* (New York: Charles Scribner's Sons, 1960), and 3, *The Organized War, 1863–1864* (New York: Charles Scribner's Sons, 1971).

9. Land transportation other than railroads, including wagons, draft animals, and the like, is the subject of numerous reports, documents, and correspondence in *OR,* ser. 3, 1–5, and is covered extensively in *ARSW, 1861–1866.* The Committee on Contracts expended a great deal of effort on the subject in general and particularly on the purchase of draft animals. See *Report on Government Contracts,* 1: Report, pp. 69–71, 83–99, 128–30, 137–47 (intermittent); 1: Testimony, pp. 1–1109 (intermittent), and 2, pp. XXXIII–XXXVIII, LVI–LXIV, i–xiv (intermittent), 1–1611 (intermittent). The Committee on Conduct of War also investigated some aspects of land transportation; see *Report, Part I: Army of the Potomac,* pp. 150–60, and *Part III: Department of the West,* pp. 3–279 (intermittent). The best secondary source on the subject is Risch, *Quartermaster Support,* pp. 373–82, 420–26. Edward Hagerman, *The American Civil War and the Origins of Modern Warfare: Ideas, Organization, and Field Command* (Bloomington: Indiana University Press, 1988), relates supply transportation to com-

bat in a particularly impressive way. Weigley, *Meigs,* also includes much useful information on land transportation in his analysis of the Civil War.

10. *OR,* ser. 3, 1–5, contains valuable information on inland water and ocean-going transportation. For just a sampling of the documents, see Cameron to Tucker, 5/8/61, 1; Stanton to Jeffrey, 4/1/62, 2; Parsons to Allen, 6/23/63, 3; Parsons to Meigs, 12/23/64, 4; and Meigs to Stanton, 11/8/65, Quartermaster Corps' Annual Report, pp. 225–30, 5. *ARSW, 1861–1866* are also good primary sources. Congress made queries and conducted various investigations regarding water transportation; see U.S. Congress, Senate, *Report on Vessels Purchased or Chartered for the Use of the War Department,* Ex. Doc. no. 37, 37th Cong., 2d sess., 3/27/62; *Report on War Department Contracts for the Year 1861;* Committee on Contracts, *Report on Government Contracts,* 1: Report, pp. 2–34, 137–47 (intermittent), 1: Testimony, pp. 1–1109 (intermittent), 2, pp. II–XIV, XL–XLII, i–xiv (intermittent), 1–1611 (intermittent); Committee on Conduct of War, *Report, Part III: Department of the West,* pp. 310–13.

For secondary sources, see Risch, *Quartermaster Support,* pp. 368–73, 405–19; Huston, *Sinews of War,* pp. 211–14; Gorham, *Stanton,* 1: 289–299; and Flower, *Stanton,* pp. 162–65. Meneely, *War Department,* Weigley, *Meigs,* and Kamm, *Thomas A. Scott,* include important information on water transportation scattered throughout their volumes.

11. The discussion and analysis of the railroads during the Civil War are based on a rich collection of primary and secondary sources. *OR,* ser. 3, has a great many documents on the railroads, particularly in the last years of the war. For examples, see Scott to Sibley, 7/12/61, 1; Secretary of War Order, 8/19/62, 2; Parsons to Meigs, 6/22/63, 3; McCallum to Stanton, 11/27/64, 4; Meigs to Stanton, 5/19/65, 5; and McCallum to Meigs, 5/26/66, 5. Policy, activity, and developments involving the railroads are regularly covered in the *ARSW, 1861–1866.* Congress also sought information about and investigated the railroads; see Committee on Contracts, *Report on Government Contracts,* 2, pp. XIV–XXXIII, LII–LIII, i–xiv (intermittent), 1–1611 (intermittent); Committee on Conduct of War, *Report, Part I: Army of the Potomac,* pp. 370–86, 681–87, and *Part III: Department of the West,* pp. 427–30; and U.S. Congress, Senate, *Report of the Secretary of War,* Ex. Doc. 34, 38th Cong., 2d sess., 3/3/65.

Secondary sources are of critical importance for basic information about and an understanding of the railroads during the Civil War. See Thomas Weber, *The Northern Railroads in the Civil War, 1861–1865* (New York: King's Crown Press, 1952); Kamm, *Thomas A. Scott;* George E. Turner, *Victory Rode the Rails: The Strategic Place of the Railroads in the Civil War* (New York: Bobbs-Merrill, 1953); Edwin A. Pratt, *The Rise of Rail-Power in War and Conquest, 1833–1914* (London: P. S. King and Son, 1915), pp. 14–102; James A. Ward, *That Man Haupt: A Biography of Herman Haupt* (Baton Rouge: Louisiana State University Press, 1973), and Ward, *J. Edgar Thomson: Master of the Pennsylvania* (Westport, CT: Greenwood Press, 1980); John Westwood, *Railways at War* (London: Osprey Publishing, 1980), pp. 17–54; John F. Stover, *History of the Baltimore and Ohio Railroad* (West Lafayette, IN: Purdue University Press, 1987), pp. 99–117; William E. Bain, ed., *B & O in the Civil War: From the Papers of Wm. Prescott Smith* (Denver, CO: Sage Books, 1966); Risch, *Quartermaster Support,* pp. 361–66, 394–404; and Huston, *Sinews of War,* pp. 198–211. Most of the other secondary sources cited in notes 2 and 5 also treat with the railroads in varying degrees.

Nevins, *War for the Union,* 1, 2, 3, and 4, *The Organized War to Victory, 1864–1865* (New York: Charles Scribner's Sons, 1971), offers good information on the railroads, as does Weigley, *Meigs.*

12. Haupt's first name is usually anglicized as "Herman" in secondary sources; primary sources sometimes use the Germanic "Hermann." I have used the first form.

13. The telegraph system in general during the Civil War, and the U.S. Military Telegraph and the Signal Corps in particular, are also treated in both primary and secondary sources. Once again, *OR,* ser. 3, has a number of good documents on the subject: see Sanford to Snyder and Burns, 8/9/61, 1; General Orders no. 38, War Dept., Adjt. General's Office, 4/8/62, 2; Stanton to Lincoln, 12/5/63, pp. 1137–38, 3; Nicodemus to Stanton, 10/31/64, 4; and Fisher to Stanton, 10/20/65, 5. *ARSW, 1861–1866* are also useful. Contrary to its usual practice, Congress largely left alone the telegraph system, the USMT, and the Signal Corps, perhaps because they did not generate much controversy and were not the subject of charges of inefficiency or corruption.

Secondary sources are both important and substantial. See Robert L. Thompson, *Wiring a Continent: The History of the Telegraph Industry in the United States, 1832–1866* (Princeton: Princeton University Press, 1947); William R. Plum, *The Military Telegraph During the Civil War in the United States,* 2 vols. (1882; reprint, New York: Arno Press, 1974); and J. Willard Brown, *The Signal Corps, U.S.A. In the War of the Rebellion* (1896; reprint, New York: Arno Press, 1974). More general accounts are found in Dulany Terrett, *The Signal Corps: The Emergency* (Washington, DC: Office of the Chief of Military History, 1956), pp. 9–10; Meneely, *War Department,* pp. 126–32, 246–51, 372; Risch, *Quartermaster Support,* pp. 366–68, 458–59; and Huston, *Sinews of War,* pp. 195–96. Kamm, *Thomas A. Scott,* and Thomas and Hyman, *Stanton,* treat the telegraph system throughout their volumes. See also Edwin Gabler, *The American Telegrapher: A Social History, 1860–1900* (New Brunswick, NJ: Rutgers University Press, 1988); Paul Israel, *From Machine Shop to Industrial Laboratory: Telegraphy and the Changing Context of American Invention, 1830–1920* (Baltimore: Johns Hopkins University Press, 1992); and Menahem Blondheim, *News over the Wires: The Telegraph and the Flow of Public Information in America, 1844–1897* (Cambridge: Harvard University Press, 1994).

14. See Chapter 4.

15. The small-arms industry and the Ordnance Department between 1840 and 1860 are treated in Felicia J. Deyrup, *Arms Makers of the Connecticut Valley: A Regional Study of the Economic Development of the Small Arms Industry, 1798–1870* (Northhampton, MA: Smith College Studies in History, 1948), pp. 115–74; David A. Hounshell, *From the American System to Mass Production, 1800–1932: The Development of Manufacturing Technology in the United States* (Baltimore: Johns Hopkins University Press, 1984), pp. 44–50, 61–65; Gene S. Cesari, "American Arms-Making Machine Tool Development, 1798–1855" (Ph.D. diss., University of Pennsylvania, 1970), pp. 230–370; Merritt R. Smith, *Harpers Ferry Armory and the New Technology: The Challenge of Change* (Ithaca, NY: Cornell University Press, 1977), pp. 219–335; and Alfred D. Chandler, Jr., *The Visible Hand: The Managerial Revolution in American Business* (Cambridge: Harvard University Press, 1977), pp. 72–78.

16. The discussion and analysis of the Ordnance Department during the Civil War is based on *OR,* ser. 3, which is exceptionally rewarding about ordnance matters, par-

ticularly in the first few years, including foreign purchases and operations as well as domestic ones. For representative documents, see Ripley to Cameron, 6/10/61, 1; Ripley to Stanton, 11/21/62, 2; Watson to Cooper, Hewitt & Co., 1/12/63, 3; Adjt. General's Office, General Order no. 193, 5/7/64, 4; and Dyer to Stanton, 10/20/65, 5. *ARSW, 1861–1866* are also valuable primary sources on all aspects of ordnance operations. The Commission on Ordnance and Ordnance Stores, *Report on Ordnance and Ordnance Stores,* is a gold mine of information on arms purchases. Congress spent a great deal of time and energy on the Ordnance Department and its functions; see *Report on Purchase of Small Arms; Report on Interest of Members of Congress in Government Contracts;* U.S. Congress, House, *Report on National Armory,* Report 43, 37th Cong., 2d sess., 2/28/62; Committee on Contracts, *Report on Government Contracts,* Part 1: Report, pp. 34–52, 137–47 (intermittent), Part 1: Testimony, pp. 1–1109 (intermittent), Part 2, pp. I–II, LXIV–LXXXIV, i–xiv (intermittent), 1–1611 (intermittent); Committee on Conduct of War, *Report, Part III: Department of the West,* pp. 3–279 (intermittent); *Report, Part II: Heavy Ordnance,* Sen. Doc. 142, 38th Cong., 1865, Rept., pp. 1–7, Testimony, pp. 8–179.

Secondary sources are numerous but not outstanding. There is no one comprehensive, solid study of the Ordnance Department during the Civil War. Numerous volumes of varying quality offer some general or detailed information about Ordnance or some aspect of its wartime operations. See Carl L. Davis, *Arming the Union: Small Arms in the Civil War* (Port Washington, NY: Kennikat Press, 1973); Deyrup, *Arms Makers,* pp. 175–201; Robert V. Bruce, *Lincoln and the Tools of War* (Indianapolis: Bobbs-Merrill, 1956), pp. 22–58, 69–74, 99–117, 118–30, 167–69, 192–93, 222–24, 260–67, 286–99; Donald A. MacDougall, "The Federal Ordnance Bureau, 1861–1865" (Ph.D. diss., University of California, Berkeley, 1951); Constance McLaughlin Green, Harry C. Thomson, and Peter C. Roots, *The Ordnance Department: Planning Munitions for War* (Washington, DC: Office of the Chief of Military History, 1955), pp. 16–18; Marvin A. Kreidberg and Merton G. Henry, *History of Military Mobilization in the United States Army, 1775–1945* (Washington, DC: Department of the Army, 1955), pp. 127–28; Meneely, *War Department,* numerous entries; Huston, *Sinews of War,* pp. 188–95; Nevins, *War for Union,* 1: 342–69 and various other entries in 1–4; Shannon, *Union Army,* 1: 107–48; and Weigley, *U.S. Army,* pp. 235–39. See also the other secondary sources cited in notes 2 and 5.

17. The arms scandals are treated in one way or another in most of the primary and secondary sources cited in note 16. See also Sanford J. Ginsberg, "Corruption and Fraud in Government Contracts During the Civil War" (Master's thesis, Columbia University, 1940), pp. 20–24, 36–42, and 45–46, and R. Gordon Wasson, *The Hall Carbine Affair: An Essay in Historiography* (Danbury, CT: privately printed , 1971).

18. Davis, *Arming Union,* p. 64.

19. Of the secondary sources cited in note 16, Bruce, MacDougall, Huston, and Shannon are severe critics of Ripley and the Ordnance Department. Davis and Weigley are more supportive of the person and the institution without being apologists. Davis offers far and away the most detailed, thorough, and enlightened study of the subject.

20. Arthur P. Van Gelder and Hugo Schlatter, *History of the Explosives Industry in America* (New York: Columbia University Press, 1927), pp. 115–20. Some of the studies of the Du Ponts can also be helpful; see John K. Winkler, *The Du Pont Dynasty*

(New York: Blue Ribbon Books, 1935), pp. 108–16; William S. Dutton, *Du Pont: One Hundred and Forty Years* (New York: Charles Scribner's Sons, 1942), pp. 87–103; William H. A. Carr, *The du Ponts of Delaware* (New York: Dodd, Mead, and Company, 1964), pp. 163–72; Gerard Colby, *Du Pont Dynasty* (Secaucus, NJ: Lyle Stuart, 1984), pp. 65–94; Leonard Mosley, *Blood Relations: The Rise and Fall of the du Ponts of Delaware* (New York: Atheneum, 1980), pp. 52–63; and Norman B. Wilkinson, *Lammot Du Pont and the American Explosives Industry, 1850–1884* (Charlottesville: University Press of Virginia, 1984), pp. 1–122.

21. Kreidberg and Henry, *Military Mobilization,* pp. 123–29; and Weigley, *U.S. Army,* pp. 249–50.

22. Huston, *Sinews of War,* pp. 171–73. See also the sources cited in notes 2 and 5.

23. The discussion of the Union command system is based on a number of sources. The standard works on the subject are Kenneth P. Williams, *Lincoln Finds a General: A Military Study of the Civil War,* 5 vols. (New York: Macmillan, 1949–1959); T. Harry Williams, *Lincoln and His Generals* (New York: Grosset and Dunlap, 1957); Herman Hattaway and Archer Jones, *How the North Won: A Military History of the Civil War* (Urbana: University of Illinois Press, 1983); and Archer Jones, *Civil War Command and Strategy: The Process of Victory and Defeat* (New York: Free Press, 1992). An excellent, brief analysis is found in Weigley, *U.S. Army,* pp. 240–53. Many of these ideas and others are expanded further by Weigley in *The American Way of War: A History of United States Military Strategy and Policy* (New York: Macmillan, 1973), pp. 128–52; Weigley, "Military Strategy and Civilian Leadership," in *Historical Dimensions of National Security Problems,* ed. Klaus Knorr, pp. 38–77 (Lawrence: University Press of Kansas, 1976); and Weigley, "The Necessity of Force: The Civil War, World War II, and the American View of War," in *War Comes Again: Comparative Vistas on the Civil War and World War II,* ed. Gabor Boritt, pp. 225–47, 265 (New York: Oxford University Press, 1995). See also Allan R. Millett and Peter Maslowski, *For the Common Defense: A Military History of the United States of America* (New York: Free Press, 1984), pp. 154–210, 214–30; relevant chapters of Joseph T. Glatthaar, *Partners in Command: The Relationships Between Leaders in the Civil War* (New York: Free Press, 1994); and Gabor Boritt, ed., *Lincoln's Generals* (New York: Oxford University Press, 1994).

24. Once again, *OR,* ser. 3, 1–5, is a valuable primary source. For representative documents, see Dennison to Lincoln 4/15/61, 1; Stanton to Halleck, 5/1/62, 2; Fry to Stanton, 11/17/63, 3; Prov. Mar. General's Office, Circular no. 28, 7/25/64, 4; and Rathbone to Fry, 11/1/65, 5. *ARSW, 1861–1866* are also helpful in tracing the evolution and operation of wartime manpower policies.

Most secondary sources treat in some way with the raising of armies, including Eugene C. Murdock, *One Million Men: The Civil War Draft in the North* (Madison: State Historical Society of Wisconsin, 1971); John K. Mahon, *History of the Militia and the National Guard* (New York: Macmillan, 1983), pp. 97–107; Iver Bernstein, *The New York City Draft Riots: Their Significance for American Society and Politics in the Age of the Civil War* (New York: Oxford University Press, 1990); James W. Geary, *We Need Men: The Union Draft in the Civil War* (DeKalb: Northern Illinois University Press, 1991); Kreidberg and Henry, *Military Mobilization,* pp. 83–123; Shannon, *Union Army,* 1: 15–50, 151–323, and 2: 11–260; John Whiteclay Chambers II, *To Raise an Army: The Draft Comes to Modern America* (New York: Free Press, 1987), pp. 41–65; Weigley, *U.S. Army,* pp. 198–201, 204–16; Russell F. Weigley, *Towards an American Army: Military Thought from Washington to Marshall* (New York: Columbia University Press, 1962), pp. 54–99; Craig L. Symonds, "An Improvised Army at War, 1861–1865," in *Against All Enemies: Interpretations of American Military History from Colonial Times to the Present,* ed. Kenneth J. Hagan and William R. Roberts, pp. 155–71 (New York: Greenwood Press, 1986); Nevins, *War for Union,* 1–4, various entries; James M. McPherson, *Ordeal by Fire: The Civil War and Reconstruction* (New York: Alfred A. Knopf, 1982), pp. 165–73, 251–52, 350–60, 409–10, 486; and J. G. Randall and David Donald, *The Civil War and Reconstruction,* 2d ed., rev. (Lexington, MA: D. C. Heath, 1969), pp. 192–93, 310–19, 392–93, 537–38. Various essays in Maris A. Vinovskis, ed., *Toward a Social History of the American Civil War: Exploratory Essays* (Cambridge: Cambridge University Press, 1990), deal imaginatively with the war and manpower mobilization. Reid Mitchell, *Civil War Soldiers* (New York: Viking, 1988), includes some important material on manpower mobilization. See also notes 2 and 5.

25. The analysis of the Navy Department is based on both primary and secondary sources. See Howard K. Beale, ed., *Diary of Gideon Welles, Secretary of the Navy Under Lincoln and Johnson,* 3 vols. (New York: W. W. Norton, 1960), and Robert M. Thompson and Richard Wainwright, eds., *Confidential Correspondence of Gustavus Vasa Fox, Assistant Secretary of the Navy, 1861–1865,* 2 vols. (New York: De Vinne Press, 1920). On the whole, the annual reports of the secretary of the navy are excellent and generally better than those of the secretary of war. Lengthy documents, they contain full and detailed information on almost every aspect of the navy's operations, including ships built, bought, or leased; contracts let; and new and modified policies, procedures, and developments. See U.S. Navy Department, *Report of the Secretary of the Navy to the President, 1861,* Sen. Ex. Doc. no. 1, 37th Cong., 1st sess., 7/4/61 (hereafter *Annual Report of the Secretary of the Navy [ARSN]*); *ARSN, 1861,* Sen. Ex. Doc. 1, 37th Cong., 2d sess., 12/3/61; *ARSN, 1862,* House Ex. Doc. 1, 37th Cong., 3d sess., 12/1/62; *ARSN, 1863,* House Ex. Doc. 1, 38th Cong., 1st sess., 12/7/63; *ARSN, 1864,* House Ex. Doc. 1, 38th Cong., 2d sess., 12/4/64; *ARSN, 1865,* House Ex. Doc. 1, 39th Cong., 1st sess., 12/4/65; and *ARSN, 1866,* House Ex. Doc. 1, 39th Cong., 2d sess., 12/3/66. See also Committee on Contracts, *Report on Government Contracts,* Part 1: Report, pp. 20–34, 137–47 (intermittent), Part 1: Testimony, pp. 1–1109 (intermittent), and Part 2: Report, pp. II–III; U.S. Congress, Senate, *Report on Purchase of Vessels for the Government,* Ex. Doc. 15, Parts 1 and 2, 37th Cong., 2s sess., 1/15/62 and 1/20/62; U.S. Congress, Senate, *Report, Prevention, Etc., of Frauds in Making Contracts,* Misc. Doc. 105, 37th Cong., 2d sess., 1/20/62; U.S. Congress, House, *Report on Contracts Made with Bureaus Connected with the Navy Department,* Ex. Doc. 150, 37th Cong., 2d sess., 7/15/62; U.S. Congress, House, *Report on Supplies for the Navy,* Ex. Doc. 40, 38th Cong., 1st sess., 2/17/64; U.S. Congress, Senate, Select Committee on Naval Supplies, *Report on Contracts for Naval Supplies,* Rept. 99, 38th Cong., 1st sess., 6/29/64; Committee on Conduct of War, *Report, Part III: Light-Draught Monitors,* Rept., pp. I–IV, Testimony, pp. 3–120; U.S. Congress, Senate, *Report of the Secretary of the Navy on Contracts for Vessels of War,* Ex. Doc. 18, 39th Cong., 1st sess., 1/31/66; U.S. Congress, House, *Report on Ordnance and Ordnance Stores,* Ex. Doc. 16, 39th Cong., 2d sess., 12/16/66; and U.S. Bureau of the Census, *Historical Statistics of the United States, Colonial Times to*

1970 (Washington, DC: U.S. Government Printing Office, 1975), 2: 1114–16, 1140–43.

Secondary sources on the Navy Department during the Civil War are neither as numerous nor as good as those on the War Department. Nonetheless, they are critically important for tracing and understanding wartime developments. See Richard S. West, Jr., *Gideon Welles: Lincoln's Navy Department* (New York: Bobbs-Merrill, 1943), and West, *Mr. Lincoln's Navy* (New York: Longmans, Green, 1957); William C. White and Ruth White, *Tin Can on a Shingle* (New York: Dutton and Company, 1957); David B. Tyler, *The American Clyde: A History of Iron and Steel Shipbuilding on the Delaware from 1840 to World War I* (Newark: University of Delaware Press, 1958), pp. 3–25; Bern Anderson, *By Sea and by River: The Naval History of the Civil War* (New York: Alfred A. Knopf, 1962); Edward W. Sloan III, *Benjamin Franklin Isherwood, Naval Engineer: The Years as Engineer in Chief, 1861–1869* (Annapolis, MD: United States Naval Institute, 1965); Leonard A. Swann, Jr., *John Roach, Maritime Entrepreneur: The Years as Naval Contractor, 1862–1886* (Annapolis, MD: United States Naval Institute, 1965); Charles O. Paullin, *Paullin's History of Naval Administration, 1775–1911* (Annapolis, MD: U.S. Naval Institute, 1968), pp. 249–307; John Niven, *Gideon Welles: Lincoln's Secretary of the Navy* (New York: Oxford University Press, 1973), and Niven, "Gideon Welles, 5 March 1861–4 March 1869," in *American Secretaries of the Navy, 1775–1913,* ed. Paolo E. Coletta, 1: 320–61 (Annapolis, MD: Naval Institute Press, 1980); William J. Sullivan, "Gustavus Vasa Fox and Naval Administration, 1861–1866" (Ph.D. diss., Catholic University, 1977); Paolo E. Coletta, *The American Naval Heritage in Brief* (Washington, DC: University Press of America, 1978), pp. 116–36; Dana M. Wegner, "The Union Navy, 1861–1865," in *In Peace and War: Interpretations of American Naval History, 1775–1984,* ed. Kenneth J. Hagan, pp. 107–25 (Westport, CT: Greenwood Press, 1984); James C. Bradford, ed., *Captains of the Old Steam Navy: Makers of the American Naval Tradition, 1840–1880* (Annapolis, MD: Naval Institute Press, 1986); Robert V. Bruce, *The Launching of Modern American Science, 1846–1876* (New York: Alfred A. Knopf, 1987), pp. 287–312; Spencer C. Tucker, "U.S. Navy Gun Carriages from the Revolution Though the Civil War," *American Neptune* 47 (Spring 1987): 108–18; William N. Still, Jr., *Monitor Builders: A Historical Study of the Principal Firms and Individuals Involved in the Construction of USS Monitor* (Washington, DC: Department of the Interior, 1988); Robert M. Browning, Jr., *From Cape Charles to Cape Fear: The North Atlantic Blockading Squadron During the Civil War* (Tuscaloosa: University of Alabama Press, 1993); and Thomas J. Legg, "Quest for Glory: The Naval Career of John A. Dahlgren, 1826–1870" (Ph.D. diss., College of William and Mary, 1994). See also William M. Fowler, Jr., *Under Two Flags: The American Navy in the Civil War* (New York: W. W. Norton, 1990); Ivan Musicant, *Divided Waters: The Naval History of the Civil War* (New York: HarperCollins Publishers, 1995); Herman F. Krafft and Walter B. Norris, *Sea Power in American History* (New York: Century Company, 1920), pp. 181–296; Dudley W. Knox, *A History of the United States Navy* (New York: G. P. Putnam's Sons, 1936), pp. 191–316; George R. Clark et al., *A Short History of the United States Navy* (Philadelphia: J. B. Lippincott, 1939), pp. 238–405; George T. Davis, *A Navy Second to None: The Development of Modern American Naval Policy* (New York: Harcourt, Brace, 1940), pp. 8–15; Robert G. Albion and Jennie B. Pope, *Sea Lanes in Wartime: The American Experience, 1775–1945,* 2d ed., enlarged (New

York: Archon Books, 1968), pp. 148–73; Harold and Margaret Sprout, *The Rise of American Naval Power, 1776–1918* (Princeton: Princeton University Press, 1946), pp. 151–64; E. B. Potter et al., *The United States and World Sea Power* (Englewood Cliffs, NJ: Prentice-Hall, 1955), pp. 294–382; Fletcher Pratt and Hartley E. Howe, *The Compact History of the United States Navy* (New York: Hawthorn Books, 1962), pp. 119–72; Millett and Maslowski, *Common Defense*, pp. 210–14; and Short, *National Administrative Organization*, pp. 299–305. See also the recently published surveys on naval history, Chapter 4, n. 43.

26. Paullin, *Naval Administration*, p. 261.

CHAPTER SEVEN. UNION CIVILIAN ORGANIZATION

1. The analysis of Civil War financing is based on J. W. Schuckers, *The Public Services of Salmon Portland Chase* (New York: D. Appleton and Company, 1874); Frederic C. Howe, *Taxation and Taxes in the United States Under the Internal Revenue System, 1791–1895* (New York: Thomas Y. Crowell, 1896), pp. 50–213; Albert B. Hart, *Salmon Portland Chase* (Boston: Houghton, Mifflin, 1899); Wesley C. Mitchell, *A History of the Greenbacks: With Special Reference to the Economic Consequences of Their Issue, 1862–1865* (Chicago: University of Chicago Press, 1903); Ellis P. Oberholtzer, *Jay Cooke: Financier of the Civil War*, 2 vols. (Philadelphia: George W. Jacobs and Company, 1907); Robert A. Love, *Federal Financing: A Study of the Methods Employed by the Treasury in Its Borrowing Operations* (New York: Columbia University Press, 1931), pp. 74–117; Henrietta M. Larson, *Jay Cooke: Private Banker* (Cambridge: Harvard University Press, 1936); Joseph Dorfman, *The Economic Mind in American Civilization, 1606–1865* (New York: Viking Press, 1946), 2: 956–87; Paul Studenski and Herman E. Krooss, *Financial History of the United States: Fiscal, Monetary, Banking, and Tariff, Including Financial Administration and State and Local Finance* (New York: McGraw Hill, 1952), pp. 137–60; David Donald, ed., *Inside Lincoln's Cabinet: The Civil War Diaries of Salmon P. Chase* (New York: Longmans, Green, 1954); Robert P. Sharkey, *Money, Class, and Party: An Economic Study of Civil War and Reconstruction* (Baltimore: Johns Hopkins University Press, 1959); Irwin Unger, *The Greenback Era: A Social and Political History of American Finance, 1865–1879* (Princeton: Princeton University Press, 1964), pp. 3–40; Fritz Redlick, *The Molding of American Banking: Men and Ideas*, 2 parts, 2d ed. (New York: Johnson Reprint Corporation, 1968), 2: 1–174; Bray Hammond, *Sovereignty and an Empty Purse: Banks and Politics in the Civil War* (Princeton: Princeton University Press, 1970); Paul A. David and Peter Solar, "A Bicentenary Contribution to the History of the Cost of Living in America," in *Research in Economic History: An Annual Compilation of Research*, ed. Paul Uselding, pp. 1–80 (Greenwich, CT: JAI Press, 1977); Gabor S. Boritt, *Lincoln and the Economics of the American Dream* (Memphis, TN: Memphis State University Press, 1978); Frederick J. Blue, *Salmon P. Chase: A Life in Politics* (Kent, OH: Kent State University Press, 1987); John Niven, "Salmon P. Chase and the Republican Conventions of 1856 and 1860: Bolingbroke or Sincere Reformer?" in *A Crisis of Republicanism: American Politics in the Civil War Era*, ed. Lloyd E. Ambrosius, pp. 55–72 (Lincoln: University of Nebraska Press, 1990); Robert Stanley, *Dimensions of Law in the Service of Order: Origins of the Federal Income Tax, 1861–1913* (New

York: Oxford University Press, 1993), pp. 27–42; John Niven, *Salmon P. Chase: A Biography* (New York: Oxford University Press, 1995); and John Niven et al., *The Salmon P. Chase Papers*, vol. 1, *Journals, 1829–1872* (Kent, OH: Kent State University Press, 1993). See also Chester W. Wright, *Economic History of the United States*, 2d ed. (New York: McGraw-Hill, 1949), pp. 430–47; Lewis H. Kimmel, *Federal Budget and Fiscal Policy, 1789–1958* (Washington, DC: Brookings Institution, 1959), pp. 61–82; Paul B. Trescott, *Financing American Enterprise: The Story of Commercial Banking* (New York: Harper and Row, 1963), pp. 16–63; Herman E. Krooss and Martin R. Blyn, *A History of Financial Intermediaries* (New York: Random House, 1971), pp. 91–116; Sidney Ratner, James H. Soltow, and Richard Sylla, *The Evolution of the American Economy: Growth, Welfare, and Decision Making* (New York: Basic Books, 1979), pp. 344–72; and Larry Schweikart, "U.S. Commercial Banking: A Historiographical Survey," *Business History Review* 65 (Autumn 1991): 621–28. Basic statistics are available in U.S. Bureau of the Census, *Historical Statistics of the United States: Colonial Times to 1970*, 2 parts (Washington, DC: U.S. Government Printing Office, 1975). See also U.S. Congress, Joint Committee on the Conduct of the War, *Report, Part II: Red River Expedition*, 38th Cong., Rept. pp. III–XLIX, Testimony, pp. 3–401 (hereafter Committee on Conduct of War).

2. Several volumes provide a great deal of detail on Lincoln's cabinet and its dynamics; see Burton J. Hendrick, *Lincoln's War Cabinet* (Boston: Little, Brown, 1946); Harry J. Carman and Reinhard H. Luthin, *Lincoln and the Patronage* (New York: Columbia University Press, 1943); Howard K. Beale, ed., *The Diary of Edward Bates, 1859–1866* (Washington, DC: U.S. Government Printing Office, 1933); Tyler Dennett, ed., *Lincoln and the Civil War in the Diaries and Letters of John Hay* (New York: Dodd, Mead, 1939); James A. Rawley, *The Politics of Union: Northern Politics During the Civil War* (Hinsdale, IL: Dryden Press, 1974); and Philip H. Burch, Jr., *Elites in American History: The Civil War to the New Deal* (New York: Holmes and Meier Publishers, 1981), 2: 15–26. The biographies and studies of various secretaries and their departments are also helpful concerning the cabinet and its functions; see Chapter 6, nn. 2 and 5, and 25, and note 1 of this chapter. Several biographies of Lincoln and other general studies of the Civil War have also proved helpful; see James G. Randall, *Lincoln the President*, 4 vols. (New York: Dodd, Mead, 1945–1955); Benjamin P. Thomas, *Abraham Lincoln: A Biography* (New York: Alfred A. Knopf, 1952); Stephen B. Oates, *With Malice Toward None: The Life of Abraham Lincoln* (New York: Harper and Row, 1977); Gabor S. Boritt, ed., *Lincoln, The War President* (New York: Oxford University Press, 1992); Mark S. Neely, Jr., *The Last Best Hope of Earth: Abraham Lincoln and the Promise of America* (Cambridge: Harvard University Press, 1993); Phillip S. Paludan, *The Presidency of Abraham Lincoln* (Lawrence: University Press of Kansas, 1994); Merrill D. Peterson, *Lincoln in American Memory* (New York: Oxford University Press, 1994); David H. Donald, *Lincoln* (New York: Simon and Schuster, 1995); James M. McPherson, *Ordeal by Fire: The Civil War and Reconstruction* (New York: Alfred A. Knopf, 1982), McPherson, *Battle Cry of Freedom: The Civil War Era* (New York: Oxford University Press, 1988), and McPherson, *Abraham Lincoln and the Second American Revolution* (New York: Oxford University Press, 1991); J. G. Randall and David Donald, *The Civil War and Reconstruction*, 2d ed., rev. (Lexington, MA: D. C. Heath, 1969); William R. Brock, *Conflict and Transformation: The United States, 1844–1877* (Baltimore: Penguin Books, 1973); and articles by Phillip

S. Paludan, Harold H. Hyman, and Hans L. Trefousse on Lincoln in Ambrosius, ed., *A Crisis of Republicanism.*

3. Allan Nevins's analysis changes in nature and emphasis from volume to volume: see *The War for the Union,* vol. 1, *The Improvised War, 1861–1862* (New York: Charles Scribner's Sons, 1959), pp. 202–6; vol. 2, *War Becomes Revolution* (New York: Charles Scribner's Sons, 1960), pp. 362–65; vol. 3, *The Organized War, 1863–1864* (New York: Charles Scribner's Sons, 1971), pp. 221–22; and vol. 4, *The Organized War to Victory, 1864–1865* (New York: Charles Scribner's Sons, 1971), pp. 62–63. See also Russell F. Weigley, *Quartermaster General of the Union Army: A Biography of M. C. Meigs* (New York: Columbia University Press, 1959), pp. 217–18. On the National Academy of Sciences and its origins, see A. Hunter Dupree, *Science in the Federal Government: A History of Policies and Activities to 1940* (Cambridge: Harvard University Press, 1957), pp. 135–48.

4. Sources in note 2 on the cabinet are helpful in terms of executive-legislative relations. Other secondary sources of importance include John Y. Simon, "Congress Under Lincoln, 1861–1863" (Ph.D. diss., Harvard University, 1960); Hans L. Trefousse, *The Radical Republicans: Lincoln's Vanguard for Racial Justice* (New York: Alfred A. Knopf, 1968); Harold M. Hyman, *A More Perfect Union: The Impact of the Civil War and Reconstruction on the Constitution* (New York: Alfred A. Knopf, 1973); Michael L. Benedict, *A Compromise of Principle: Congressional Republicans and Reconstruction, 1863–1869* (New York: W. W. Norton, 1974); Allan G. Bogue, *The Earnest Men: Republicans of the Civil War Senate* (Ithaca, NY: Cornell University Press, 1981), and Bogue, *The Congressman's Civil War* (New York: Cambridge University Press, 1989); Christopher Dell, *Lincoln and the War Democrats: The Grand Erosion of Conservative Tradition* (Cranbury, NJ: Fairleigh Dickinson University Press, 1975); Alfred H. Kelly, Winfred A. Harbison, and Herman Belz, *The American Constitution: Its Origins and Development,* 6th ed. (New York: W. W. Norton, 1983), pp. 299–327; and Mark E. Neely, Jr., *The Fate of Liberty: Abraham Lincoln and Civil Liberties* (New York: Oxford University Press, 1991).

5. U.S. Congress, House, Select Committee on Contracts, *Report on Government Contracts,* 1, 2, and *Final Report,* 37th Cong., 2d and 3d sess., 1862–1863, includes both reports and testimony. Many secondary sources cite the committee's work, such as Fred A. Shannon, *The Organization and Administration of the Union Army, 1861–1865,* 1 (Cleveland, OH: Arthur C. Clark Company, 1928). Secondary sources on the committee itself are few. For those that have been written, see Sanford J. Ginsberg, "Corruption and Fraud in Government Contracts During the Civil War" (Master's thesis, Columbia University, 1940); Virgil C. Stroud, "Congressional Investigations of the Conduct of War" (Ph.D. diss., New York University, 1954), pp. 36, 138–64; and Bogue, *Congressman's Civil War,* pp. 81–88, 103–9. See notes in Chapter 6 for congressional documents and reports relating to the oversight function involving the armed services.

6. The reports and hearings of the Joint Committee on the Conduct of the War are contained in numerous volumes, most of which have been cited here and in Chapter 6: Committee on Conduct of War, *Report,* I–III, S. Rept. 108, 37th Cong., 3d sess., 1863; *Report, Fort Pillow Massacre,* S. Rept. 63, 38th Cong., 1st sess., 5/5/64, with appended S. Rept. 68, 38th Cong., 1st sess.; *Report,* I–III, S. Ex. Doc. 142, 38th Cong., 2d sess., 1865; and *Supplemental Report,* 2, S. Ex. Doc. 142, 38th Cong., 2d sess., 1866.

Nearly all sources on the Civil War in one way or another at least touch upon the Joint Committee, as is the case with most of the sources cited here and in Chapter 6. Nonetheless, the first full-scale study was done by T. Harry Williams, "The Committee on the Conduct of the War: A Study of Civil War Politics," 2 parts (Ph.D. diss., University of Wisconsin, 1937). Williams followed up his dissertation with a series of articles and a book on the subject: "The Committee on the Conduct of the War," *Journal of the American Military Institute* 3 (1939): 139–56; "Benjamin F. Wade and the Atrocity Propaganda of the Civil War," *Ohio State Archaeological and Historical Quarterly* 48 (January 1939): 33–43; "The Attack upon West Point During the Civil War," *Mississippi Valley Historical Review* 25 (December 1939): 491–504; "Andrew Johnson as a Member of the Committee on the Conduct of the War," *East Tennessee Historical Society's Publication* 12 (1940): 70–83; and *Lincoln and the Radicals* (Madison: University of Wisconsin Press, 1941). Although Williams did not originate the highly negative view of the committee, he authenticated and popularized it through his study and publications. His interpretation is reflected closely in more recent work: Stroud, *Congressional Investigations,* pp. 32–36, 49–137, and Elizabeth Joan Doyle, "The Conduct of the War, 1861," in *Congress Investigates: A Documented History, 1792–1974,* ed. Arthur M. Schlesinger, Jr., and Roger Bruns, 2: 1197–1232 (New York: Chelsea House Publishers, 1975).

A much more positive, and in my view balanced, interpretation is found in William W. Pierson, Jr., "The Committee on the Conduct of the Civil War," *American Historical Review* 23 (April 1918): 550–76, and Hans L. Trefousse, "The Joint Committee on the Conduct of the War: A Reassessment," *Civil War History* 10 (March 1964): 5–19. Trefousse cites the works of other historians in reference to the committee. See also Marshall E. Dimock, *Congressional Investigating Committees* (Baltimore: Johns Hopkins University Press, 1929), pp. 111–12. Also relevant to the topic are David Donald, "The Radicals and Lincoln," in *Lincoln Reconsidered: Essays on the Civil War Era,* ed. Donald, pp. 103–127, 2d rev. ed., (New York: Vintage, 1956); Donald, "Devils Facing Zionwards," and T. Harry Williams, "Lincoln and the Radicals: An Essay in Civil War History and Historiography," in *Grant, Lee, Lincoln and the Radicals,* ed. Grady McWhiney, pp. 72–117 (Evanston, IL: Northwestern University Press, 1964). See also Albert G. Riddle, *The Life of Benjamin F. Wade* (Cleveland, OH: William W. Williams, 1887), and Hans L. Trefousse, *Benjamin Franklin Wade: Radical Republican from Ohio* (New York: Twayne Publishers, 1963).

7. Several articles on nineteenth-century federalism and politics are worthy of note: William R. Riker, "The Senate and American Federalism," *American Political Science Review* 49 (June 1955): 452–69; Daniel J. Elazar, "Civil War and the Preservation of American Federalism," *Publius: The Journal of Federalism* 1 (Winter 1972): 39–58; see also Elazar's *American Partnership: Intergovernmental Cooperation in the Nineteenth-Century United States* (Chicago: University of Chicago Press, 1962), in which he develops further some of his major ideas; Carl N. Degler, "The Nineteenth Century," in *Theory and Practice in American Politics,* ed. William H. Nelson, pp. 25–42 (Chicago, IL: University of Chicago Press, 1964); and Wallace D. Farnham, "The Weakened Spring of Government: A Study in Nineteenth-Century American History," *American Historical Review* 68 (April 1963): 662–80.

8. Eric L. McKitrick, "Party Politics and the Union and Confederate War Efforts," in *The American Party Systems,* ed. William N. Chambers and Walter D. Burnham,

pp. 117–51 (New York: Oxford University Press, 1967). Rawley, *Politics of Union,* expands upon McKitrick's ideas in his book-length study. See also Joel H. Silbey, *A Respectable Minority: The Democratic Party in the Civil War Era, 1860–1868* (New York: W. W. Norton, 1977).

9. Claudia D. Goldin and Frank D. Lewis, "The Economic Cost of the American Civil War," *Journal of Economic History* 35 (June 1975): 299–326. I have put together some comparative statistics on various wars: *The Military-Industrial Complex: A Historical Perspective* (New York: Praeger Publishers, 1980), pp. 106–8. For basic statistics, see U.S. Bureau of the Census, *Historical Statistics,* 1: 8; 2: 1106–8, 1114–18, 1140–43. For interesting discussions on the economics of the Civil War, other periods of hostilities, or both, see Chester W. Wright, ed., *Economic Problems of War and Its Aftermath* (Chicago: University of Chicago Press, 1942); Curtis Nettels, "Economic Consequences of War: Costs of Production," and Chester W. Wright, "The More Enduring Economic Consequences of America's Wars," *Journal of Economic History* 3 (December 1943): Supplement 1–26; Milton Friedman, "Price, Income, and Monetary Changes in Three Wartime Periods," *American Economic Review* 42 (May 1952): Part 2, 612–43; Marshall A. Robinson, "Federal Debt Management: Civil War, World War I, and World War II," *American Economic Review* 45 (May 1955): Part 2, 388–401, 409–14; Richard N. Current, "God and the Strongest Battalions," in *Why the North Won the Civil War,* ed. David Donald, pp. 15–32 (Baton Rouge: Louisiana State University Press, 1960); Herman E. Krooss, *American Economic Development* (Englewood Cliffs, NJ: Prentice-Hall, 1959), pp. 447–79; Harry N. Scheiber, Harold G. Vatter, and Harold U. Faulkner, *American Economic History* (New York: Harper and Row, 1976), pp. 181–88; W. Elliot Brownlee, *Dynamics of Ascent: A History of the American Economy,* 2d ed. (New York: Alfred A. Knopf, 1979), pp. 255–65; and Ratner, Soltow, and Sylla, *American Economy,* pp. 344–72.

10. Russell F. Weigley, *History of the U.S. Army* (New York: Macmillan, 1967), pp. 252–53.

11. The scholarship on this subject is already substantial: see Charles A. and Mary R. Beard, *The Rise of American Civilization,* 2 vols. (New York: Macmillan, 1927), 2: 52–121; Louis M. Hacker, *The Triumph of American Capitalism: The Development of Forces in American History to the End of the Nineteenth Century* (New York: Simon and Schuster, 1940), pp. 339–73; Robert E. Gallman, "Commodity Output, 1839–1899," in *Trends in the American Economy in the Nineteenth Century,* vol. 24 of *Studies in Income and Wealth,* Conference on Research in Income and Wealth (Princeton: Princeton University Press, 1960), pp. 13–71; Thomas C. Cochran, "Did the Civil War Retard Industrialization?" *Mississippi Valley Historical Review* 48 (September 1961): 197–210; Ralph Andreano, ed., *The Economic Impact of the American Civil War* (Cambridge, MA: Schenkman Publishing Company, 1962); David T. Gilchrist and W. David Lewis, eds., *Economic Change in the Civil War Era* (Greenville, DE: Eleutherian Mills–Hagley Foundation, 1965); Harry N. Scheiber, "Economic Change in the Civil War Era: An Analysis of Recent Studies," *Civil War History* 11 (December 1965): 396–411; Robert E. Gallman, "Gross National Product in the United States, 1834–1909," in *Output, Employment, and Productivity in the United States After 1800,* vol. 30 of *Studies in Income and Wealth,* Conference on Research in Income and Wealth (New York: National Bureau of Economic Research, 1966), pp. 3–90; Stanley L. Engerman, "The Economic Impact of the Civil War," in *The*

Reinterpretation of American Economic History, ed. Robert W. Fogel and Engerman, pp. 369–79 (New York: Harper and Row, 1971); Jeffrey G. Williamson, "Watersheds and Turning Points: Conjectures on the Long Term Impact of Civil War Financing," *Journal of Economic History* 34 (September 1974): 636–61; Peter Temin, *Causal Factors in American Economic Growth in the Nineteenth Century* (London: Macmillan, 1975); Robert E. Gallman, "The United States Capital Stock in the Nineteenth Century," in *Long-Term Factors in American Economic Growth,* ed. Stanley L. Engerman and Gallman, vol. 51 of *Studies in Income and Wealth* (Chicago: University of Chicago Press, 1986), pp. 165–213; Patrick K. O'Brien, *The Economic Effects of the American Civil War* (Altantic Highlands, NJ: Humanities Press International, 1988); Roger L. Ransom, *Conflict and Compromise: The Political Economy of Slavery, Emancipation, and the American Civil War* (New York: Cambridge University Press, 1989); Richard F. Bensel, *Yankee Leviathan: The Origins of Central State Authority in America, 1859–1877* (New York: Cambridge University Press, 1990); Stuart Bruchey, *Enterprise: The Dynamic Economy of a Free People* (Cambridge: Harvard University Press, 1990), pp. 254–80; and J. Matthew Gallman, *The North Fights the Civil War: The Home Front* (Chicago: Ivan R. Dee, 1994), pp. 99–108, 181–97. Several authors summarize and evaluate this scholarship in addition to citing and discussing other sources not cited; see Susan P. Lee and Peter Passell, *A New Economic View of American History* (New York: W. W. Norton, 1979), pp. 223–39, and Barry W. Poulson, *Economic History of the United States* (New York: Macmillan, 1981), pp. 185–90. The work of other scholars is also relevant to the topic; see Emerson D. Fite, *Social and Industrial Conditions in the North During the Civil War* (New York: Macmillan, 1910); Douglass C. North, *The Economic Growth of the United States, 1790–1860* (Englewood Cliffs, NJ: Prentice-Hall, 1961); Paul W. Gates, *Agriculture and the Civil War* (New York: Alfred A. Knopf, 1965); and Phillip S. Paludan, *A People's Contest: The Union and the Civil War* (New York: Harper and Row, 1988).

12. Glenn Porter and Harold C. Livesay, *Merchants and Manufacturers: Studies in the Changing Structures of Nineteenth-Century Marketing* (Baltimore: Johns Hopkins University Press, 1971).

13. Scheiber, "Economic Change in the Civil War Era."

CHAPTER EIGHT. ECONOMIC MOBILIZATION IN THE SOUTH

1. The analysis of the Southern economy on the eve of the Civil War is based on Gavin Wright, *The Political Economy of the Cotton South: Households, Markets, and Wealth in the Nineteenth Century* (New York: W. W. Norton, 1978), and Wright, *Old South, New South: Revolutions in the Southern Economy Since the Civil War* (New York: Basic Books, 1986); Eugene D. Genovese, *The Political Economy of Slavery: Studies in the Economy and Society of the Slave South* (New York: Pantheon Books, 1965), and Genovese, *The Slaveholders' Dilemma: Freedom and Progress in Southern Conservative Thought, 1820–1860* (Columbia: University of South Carolina Press, 1992); James Oakes, *Slavery and Freedom: An Interpretation of the Old South* (New York: Alfred A. Knopf, 1990); Victor S. Clark, *History of Manufactures in the United States, 2, 1860–1893* (Washington, DC: Carnegie Institute, 1929), pp. 41–53; Lester J. Cappon, "Government and Private Industry in the Southern Confederacy," in *Humanis-*

tic Studies in Honor of John Calvin Metcalf, University of Virginia Studies, 1: 151–89 (New York: Columbia University Press, 1941); Fred Bateman and Thomas Weiss, "Manufacturing in the Antebellum South," in *Research in Economic History: An Annual Compilation of Research,* ed. Paul Uselding, pp. 1–44 (Greenwich, CT: JAI Press, 1976), and Bateman and Weiss, *A Deplorable Scarcity: The Failure of Industrialization in the Slave Economy* (Chapel Hill: University of North Carolina Press, 1981); Laurence Shore, *Southern Capitalists: The Ideological Leadership of an Elite, 1832–1885* (Chapel Hill: University of North Carolina Press, 1986); Mary A. DeCredico, *Patriotism for Profit: Georgia's Urban Entrepreneurs and the Confederate War Effort* (Chapel Hill: University of North Carolina Press, 1990); Albert W. Niemi, Jr., *State and Regional Patterns in American Manufacturing, 1860–1900* (Westport, CT: Greenwood Press, 1974); Robert C. Black III, *The Railroads of the Confederacy* (Chapel Hill: University of North Carolina Press, 1952); Larry Schweikart, *Banking in the American South from the Age of Jackson to Reconstruction* (Baton Rouge: Louisiana State University, 1987), and Schweikart, "U.S. Commercial Banking: A Historiographical Survey," *Business History Review* 65 (Autumn 1991): 618–28; Douglass C. North, *The Economic Growth of the United States, 1790–1860* (New York: W. W. Norton, 1966), pp. 61–215, and North, Terry L. Anderson, and Peter J. Hill, *Growth and Welfare in the American Past: A New Economic History,* 3d ed., rev. (Englewood Cliffs, NJ: Prentice-Hall, 1983), pp. 80–89; Chester W. Wright, *Economic History of the United States* (New York: McGraw-Hill, 1949), pp. 430–47; Lance E. Davis et al., *American Economic Growth: An Economist's History of the United States* (New York: Harper and Row, 1972), pp. 369–417; Harry N. Scheiber, Harold G. Vatter, and Harold U. Faulkner, *American Economic History* (New York: Harper and Row, 1976), pp. 175–89; Susan P. Lee and Peter Passell, *A New Economic View of American History* (New York: W. W. Norton, 1979), pp. 154–239; Sidney Ratner, James H. Soltow, and Richard Sylla, *The Evolution of the American Economy: Growth, Welfare, and Decision Making* (New York: Basic Books, 1979), pp. 131–55, 208–49; and William J. Cooper, Jr., and Thomas E. Terrill, *The American South: A History* (New York: McGraw-Hill, 1991), pp. 183–383 (this text includes a recent, thorough bibliography). See also Chapter 3 with notes 10–11 on Southern agriculture and Chapter 4, nn. 3 and 22, on banking in the South and elsewhere.

2. The discussion of class dynamics in the South draws upon Gavin Wright, "'Economic Democracy' and the Concentration of Agricultural Wealth in the Cotton South, 1850–1860," *Agriculture History* 64 (January 1970): 63–93, and Wright, *Political Economy of Cotton South;* Genovese, *Political Economy of Slavery;* Lee Soltow, *Men and Wealth in the United States, 1850–1870* (New Haven: Yale University Press, 1975), and Soltow, *Distribution of Wealth and Income in the United States in 1798* (Pittsburgh, PA: University of Pittsburgh Press, 1989); Robert E. Gallman, "Trends in the Size Distribution of Wealth in the Nineteenth Century: Some Speculations," in *Six Papers on the Size Distribution of Wealth and Income,* ed. Lee Soltow, pp. 1–30 (New York: National Bureau of Economic Research, 1969); Peter H. Lindert and Jeffrey G. Williamson, "Three Centuries of American Inequality," in Uselding, ed., *Research in Economic History,* pp. 69–123; Bell I. Wiley, *The Plain People of the Confederacy* (Baton Rouge: Louisiana State University Press, 1943); Frank L. Owsley, *Plain Folk of the Old South* (Baton Rouge: Louisiana State University Press, 1949); Paul D. Escott, *After Secession: Jefferson Davis and the Failure of Confederate Nationalism* (Baton Rouge:

Louisiana State University Press, 1978); George C. Rable, *Civil Wars: Women and the Crisis of Southern Nationalism* (Urbana: University of Illinois Press, 1989); Shore, *Southern Capitalists;* Bateman and Weiss, "Manufacturing in South," and *A Deplorable Scarcity;* Lee and Passell, *Economic View,* pp. 154–239; Scheiber, Vatter, and Faulkner, *American Economic History,* pp. 175–81; Ratner, Soltow, and Sylla, *American Economy,* pp. 142–48; Emory M. Thomas, *The Confederate Nation, 1861–1865* (New York: Harper and Row, 1979), pp. 1–16, 44–45; Eric H. Walther, *The Fire-Eaters* (Baton Rouge: Louisiana State University Press, 1992); David S. Heidler, *Pulling the Temple Down: The Fire-Eaters and the Destruction of the Union* (Mechanicsburg, PA: Stackpole Books, 1994); Ralph A. Wooster, *The Secession Conventions of the South* (Princeton: Princeton University Press, 1962), Wooster, *The People in Power: Courthouse and Statehouse in the Lower South, 1850–1860* (Knoxville: University of Tennessee Press, 1969), and Wooster, *Politicians, Planters and Plain Folk: Courthouse and Statehouse in the Upper South, 1850–1860* (Knoxville: University of Tennessee Press, 1975); W. Buck Yearns, *The Confederate Governors* (Athens: University of Georgia Press, 1985); Malcolm C. McMillan, *The Disintegration of a Confederate State: Three Governors and Alabama's Wartime Home Front, 1861–1865* (Macon, GA: Mercer University Press, 1986); Lacy K. Ford, Jr., *Origins of Southern Radicalism: The South Carolina Upcountry, 1800–1860* (New York: Oxford University Press, 1988); and Daniel W. Crofts, *Reluctant Confederates: Upper South Unionists in the Secession Crisis* (Chapel Hill: University of North Carolina Press, 1989).

3. The analysis of the Confederate states is based on May S. Ringold, *The Role of the State Legislatures in the Confederacy* (Athens: University of Georgia Press, 1966); Yearns, *Confederate Governors;* Wooster, *Secession Conventions;* McMillan, *Disintegration of a Confederate State;* Richard C. Todd, *Confederate Finance* (Athens: University of Georgia Press, 1954), pp. 37–39, 65, 116, 133–34; Wayne K. Durrill, *War of Another Kind: A Southern Community in the Great Rebellion* (New York: Oxford University Press, 1990); Richard D. Goff, *Confederate Supply* (Durham, NC: Duke University Press, 1969); Rich Halperin, "Leroy Pope Walker and the Problems of the Confederate War Department, February–September, 1861" (Ph.D. diss., Auburn University, 1978); William A. Albaugh III and Edward N. Simmons, *Confederate Arms* (Harrisburg, PA: Stackpole Company, 1957), pp. viii–ix, 3, 47–96, 137–61; Escott, *After Secession,* pp. 19–274; DeCredico, *Patriotism for Profit;* Robert H. Bremner, *The Public Good: Philanthropy and Welfare in the Civil War Era* (New York: Alfred A. Knopf, 1980), pp. 47–49, 62, 72–78, and 91–110; H. H. Cunningham, *Doctors in Gray: The Confederate Medical Service* (Baton Rouge: Louisiana State University Press, 1958), pp. 139–45; Francis B. Simkins and James W. Patton, *The Women of the Confederacy* (Richmond, VA: Garrett and Massie, 1936); Mary E. Massey, *Ersatz in the Confederacy* (Columbia: University of South Carolina Press, 1952); Donna R. D. Krug, "The Folks Back Home: The Confederate Homefront During the Civil War" (Ph.D. diss., University of California, Irvine, 1990); Frank L. Owsley, *State Rights in the Confederacy* (Chicago: University of Chicago Press, 1925); Charles H. Wesley, *The Collapse of the Confederacy* (1937; reissue, New York: Russell and Russell, 1968), pp. 62–68; Charles W. Ramsdell, *Behind the Lines in the Southern Confederacy* (Baton Rouge: Louisiana State University Press, 1944); E. Merton Coulter, *The Confederate States of America, 1861–1865* (Baton Rouge: Louisiana State University Press, 1950); Curtis A. Amlund, *Federalism in the Southern Confederacy* (Washington, DC: Public

Affairs Press, 1966), pp. 94–128; Clement Eaton, *A History of the Southern Confederacy* (New York: Free Press, 1954), pp. 250–68, and Eaton, *Jefferson Davis* (New York: Free Press, 1977), pp. 220–30; Richard E. Beringer et al., *Why the South Lost the Civil War* (Athens: University of Georgia Press, 1986), pp. 203–35; and Gabor S. Boritt, ed., *Why the Confederacy Lost* (New York: Oxford University Press, 1992).

CHAPTER NINE. CONFEDERATE WAR AND NAVY DEPARTMENTS

1. The discussion of the War Department is based on Rembert W. Patrick, *Jefferson Davis and His Cabinet* (Baton Rouge: Louisiana State University Press, 1944), pp. 103–81; Frank E. Vandiver, *Rebel Brass: The Confederate Command System* (Baton Rouge: Louisiana State University Press, 1956); Richard D. Goff, *Confederate Supply* (Durham, NC: Duke University Press, 1969); Burton J. Hendrick, *Statesmen of the Lost Cause: Jefferson Davis and His Cabinet* (Boston, MA: Little, Brown, 1939), pp. 178–85, 324–29; George G. Shackelford, *George Wythe Randolph and the Confederate Elite* (Athens: University of Georgia Press, 1988); Emory M. Thomas, *The Confederate Nation, 1861–1865* (New York: Harper and Row, 1979), pp. 74–76, 148–49, 191–92, 218–19, 286–87, and Thomas, *The Confederacy as a Revolutionary Experience* (Englewood Cliffs, NJ: Prentice-Hall, 1971), pp. 67–71; and Eli N. Evans, *Judah P. Benjamin: The Jewish Confederate* (New York: Free Press, 1988), pp. 115–36.

Two recent surveys of the Confederacy offer little on economic mobilization in general and the War Department in particular, but they provide a great deal of information on Confederate leaders: see William C. Davis, *"A Government of Our Own": The Making of the Confederacy* (New York: Free Press, 1994), and George C. Rable, *The Confederate Republic: A Revolution Against Politics* (Chapel Hill: University of North Carolina Press, 1994). Richard N. Current et al., eds., *Encyclopedia of the Confederacy,* 4 vols. (New York: Simon and Schuster, 1993), present articles on practically every subject involving economic mobilization. These volumes are an extraordinarily valuable source that tap nearly the entire scholarly community working on the South.

2. Sources on the Confederacy's Quartermaster Department, unlike that of the Union's, are very limited. Without Goff, *Confederate Supply,* even an outline of corps activity would be impossible. Other sources that are helpful include Charles W. Ramsdell, "The Control of Manufacturing by the Confederate Government," *Mississippi Valley Historical Review* 8 (December 1921): 231–49; Lester J. Cappon, "Government and Private Industry in the Southern Confederacy," in *Humanistic Studies in Honor of John Calvin Metcalf,* University of Virginia Studies, 1: 151–89 (New York: Columbia University Press, 1941); Vandiver, *Rebel Brass,* pp. 79–126; Frank E. Vandiver, *Their Tattered Flags: The Epic of the Confederacy* (New York: Harper and Row, 1970), pp. 54, 242–43; Thomas, *Confederate Nation,* pp. 133–34; E. Merton Coulter, *The Confederate States of America, 1861–1865* (Baton Rouge: Louisiana State University Press, 1950), pp. 209–18, 253–54; Clement Eaton, *A History of the Southern Confederacy* (New York: Free Press, 1954), pp. 138–40; Wilfred B. Yearns, *The Confederate Congress* (Athens: University of Georgia Press, 1960), pp. 233–34; and Mary A. DeCredico, *Patriotism for Profit: Georgia's Urban Entrepreneurs and the Confederate War Effort* (Chapel Hill: University of North Carolina Press, 1990), pp. 47–71.

3. Goff, *Confederate Supply*, pp. 92, 132.

4. The discussion of horses and mules is based on Charles W. Ramsdell, "General Robert E. Lee's Horse Supply, 1862–1865," *American Historical Review* 35 (July 1930): 758–77; Goff, *Confederate Supply*, pp. 17, 24, 60, 72–74, 141–42, 207, 212–13, 237–38, 240–41, 247, 251; and Vandiver, *Rebel Brass*, pp. 101–7.

5. Vandiver, *Rebel Brass*, p. 104.

6. The analysis of the Confederate railroads is based on Charles W. Ramsdell, "The Confederate Government and the Railroads," *American Historical Review* 22 (July 1917): 794–810; Ramsdell, *Behind the Lines in the Southern Confederacy* (Baton Rouge: Louisiana State University Press, 1944); Robert C. Black III, *The Railroads of the Confederacy* (Chapel Hill: University of North Carolina Press, 1952); Augus J. Johnston II, *Virginia Railroads in the Civil War* (Chapel Hill: University of North Carolina Press, 1961); John Westwood, *Railways at War* (San Diego, CA: Howell-North Books, 1981), pp. 17–54; George E. Turner, *Victory Rode the Rails: The Strategic Place of the Railroads in the Civil War* (Indianapolis: Bobbs-Merrill, 1953); Jeffrey N. Lash, *Destroyer of the Iron Horse: General Joseph E. Johnston and the Confederate Rail Transport, 1861–1865* (Kent, OH: Kent State University Press, 1991); Allen W. Trelease, *The North Carolina Railroad, 1849–1871, and the Modernization of North Carolina* (Chapel Hill: University of North Carolina Press, 1991); Eaton, *Southern Confederacy*, pp. 148–50, 243–49; Coulter, *Confederate States*, pp. 269–83; Vandiver, *Tattered Flags*, pp. 243–51; Yearns, *Confederate Congress*, pp. 129–31; and Charles B. Dew, *Ironmaker to the Confederacy: Joseph R. Anderson and the Tredegar Iron Works* (New Haven: Yale University Press, 1966), pp. 35–37, 50–52, 126–28, 266–75.

7. Westwood, *Railways at War*, p. 18.

8. Black, *Railroads of the Confederacy*, p. 63.

9. For the Confederate use of the telegraph system, see Robert L. Thompson, *Wiring a Continent: The History of the Telegraph Industry in the United States, 1832–1866* (Princeton: Princeton University Press, 1947), pp. 373–79, 413; William R. Plum, *The Military Telegraph During the Civil War in the United States*, 2 vols. (1882; reprint, New York: Arno Press, 1974), 1: 134–36, 2: 106–21; J. Willard Brown, *The Signal Corps, U.S.A. in the War of the Rebellion* (1896; reprint, New York: Arno Press, 1974), pp. 43–45, 205–24; Curtis A. Amlund, *Federalism in the Southern Confederacy* (Washington, DC: Public Affairs Press, 1966), p. 73; Coulter, *Confederate States*, pp. 283–84; and Vandiver, *Rebel Brass*, p. 17.

10. Goff, *Confederate Supply*, provides the most complete and balanced account and assessment of the Subsistence Department. Other sources are essential for understanding wartime developments, but many tend to be biased against Northrop. See Vandiver, *Tattered Flags*, pp. 53, 238–39, 242; Coulter, *Confederate States*, pp. 239–54, 463–65; Eaton, *Southern Confederacy*, pp. 140–43; Shackelford, *George Wythe Randolph*, pp. 115–16, 123–26, 143–50; Thomas B. Alexander and Richard E. Beringer, *The Anatomy of the Confederate Congress: A Study of the Influences of Member Characteristics on Legislative Voting Behavior, 1861–1865* (Nashville, TN: Vanderbilt University Press, 1972), pp. 163–65; Johnston, *Virginia Railroads*, pp. 127–38; and Yearns, *Confederate Congress*, pp. 116–25.

11. Goff, *Confederate Supply*, p. 168.

12. The Ordnance Department is treated in Frank E. Vandiver, *Ploughshares into Swords: Josiah Gorgas and Confederate Ordnance* (Austin: University of Texas Press,

1952); Sarah W. Wiggins, ed., *The Journals of Josiah Gorgas, 1857–1878* (Tuscaloosa: University of Alabama Press, 1995); Goff, *Confederate Supply;* Dew, *Ironmaker to the Confederacy;* Maurice Melton, "Major Military Industries of the Confederate Government" (Ph.D. diss., Emory University, 1978); Charles S. Davis, *Colin J. McRae: Confederate Financial Agent* (Tuscaloosa, AL: Confederate Publishing Company, 1961), pp. 13–33; William A. Albaugh III and Edward N. Simmons, *Confederate Arms* (Harrisburg, PA: Stackpole Company, 1957), pp. viii–ix, 3, 47–96, 137–61, 195–277; Giles Cromwell, *The Virginia Manufactory of Arms* (Charlottesville: University Press of Virginia, 1975); Vandiver, *Rebel Brass,* pp. 7–8, 85–88, 98–99, 111–21; Vandiver, *Tattered Flags,* pp. 53, 239–42; Rich Halperin, "Leroy Pope Walker and the Problems of the Confederate War Department, February–September, 1961" (Ph.D. diss., Auburn University, 1978); Shackelford, *George Wythe Randolph,* pp. 69, 97–98, 110–14; Coulter, *Confederate States,* pp. 199–209; Yearns, *Confederate Congress,* pp. 125–29; Thomas, *Confederate Nation,* pp. 133–34, 206–14; Eaton, *Southern Confederacy,* pp. 131–38; Cappon, "Government and Private Industry in the Southern Confederacy," pp. 151–89; Ramsdell, "Control of Manufacturing by the Confederate Government," pp. 231–49; DeCredico, *Patriotism for Profit,* pp. 24–46; John C. Schwab, *The Confederate States of America: A Financial and Industrial History of the South During the Civil War* (New York: Charles Scribner's Sons, 1901), pp. 268–71; and Fritz Redlich, *History of Business Leaders: A Series of Studies,* 1, *Theory: Iron and Steel, Iron Ore Mining* (Ann Arbor, MI: Edwards Brothers, 1940), p. 84.

13. Eaton, *Southern Confederacy,* p. 132.

14. For the Medical Department, see H. H. Cunningham, *Doctors in Gray: The Confederate Medical Service* (Baton Rouge: Louisiana State University Press, 1958); Glenna R. Schroeder-Lein, *Confederate Hospitals on the Move: Samuel H. Stout and the Army of Tennessee* (Columbia: University of South Carolina, 1991); Frank R. Freemon, "Medical Care During the Civil War" (Ph.D. diss., University of Illinois, Urbana-Champaign, 1992); Coulter, *Confederate States,* pp. 428–39; and Vandiver, *Tattered Flags,* pp. 114–16.

15. The analysis of blockade running is based on Stephen R. Wise, *Lifeline of the Confederacy: Blockade Running During the Civil War* (Columbia: University of South Carolina Press, 1988); Richard I. Lester, *Confederate Finance and Purchasing in Great Britain* (Charlottesville: University Press of Virginia, 1975); Warren F. Spencer, *The Confederate Navy in Europe* (University: University of Alabama Press, 1983); Frank L. Owsley, *King Cotton Diplomacy: Foreign Relations of the Confederate States of America,* 2d ed., rev. (Chicago: University of Chicago Press, 1959); Howard Jones, *Union in Peril: The Crisis over British Intervention in the Civil War* (Chapel Hill: University of North Carolina Press, 1992); Goff, *Confederate Supply,* pp. 15–16, 34–35, 43–47, 52–55, 65, 68, 118–25, 129, 133–39, 140–41, 144–47, 152–53, 158, 175–84, 202, 210–11, 218, 224–25, 229, 235, 237, 241, 244, 247, 249–51; Samuel B. Thompson, *Confederate Purchasing Operations Abroad* (Chapel Hill: University of North Carolina Press, 1935); Frank E. Vandiver, ed., *Confederate Blockade Running Through Bermuda, 1861–1865: Letters and Cargo Manifests* (Austin: University of Texas Press, 1947); Davis, *Colin J. McRae,* pp. 35–88; Coulter, *Confederate States,* pp. 285–307; Louise B. Hill, *State Socialism in the Confederate States of America* (Charlottesville, VA: Historical Publishing Company, 1936); Stanley Lebergott, "Through the Blockade: The Profitability and Extent of Cotton Smuggling, 1861–1865," *Journal of Eco-*

nomic History 61 (December 1981): 867–88, and Lebergott, "Why the South Lost: Commercial Purpose in the Confederacy, 1861–1865," *Journal of American History* 70 (June 1983): 58–74; David G. Surdam, "Cotton's Potential as Economic Weapon: The Antebellum and Wartime Markets for Cotton," *Agricultural History* 68 (Spring 1994): 122–45; and Richard E. Beringer et al., *Why the South Lost the Civil War* (Athens: University of Georgia Press, 1986), pp. 53–63.

16. Coulter, *Confederate States,* p. 204, and Eaton, *Southern Confederacy,* p. 235.

17. For Confederate strategy and command, see June I. Gow, "The Old Army and the Confederacy, 1861–1865," in *Against All Enemies: Interpretations of American Military History from Colonial Times to the Present,* ed. Kenneth J. Hagan and William R. Roberts, pp. 133–154 (Westport, CT: Greenwood Press, 1986)—this is among the best and most suggestive work on the subject; T. Harry Williams, "The Military Leadership of North and South," pp. 33–54, and David M. Potter, "Jefferson Davis and the Political Factors in Confederate Defeat," pp. 91–112, in *Why the North Won the Civil War,* ed. David Donald (Baton Rouge: Louisiana State University Press, 1960); Beringer et al., *Why the South Lost the Civil War;* Archer Jones, *Civil War Command and Strategy: The Process of Victory and Defeat* (New York: Free Press, 1992); Joseph T. Glatthaar, *Partners in Command: The Relationship Between Leaders in the Civil War* (New York: Free Press, 1994), relevant chapters; Vandiver, *Rebel Brass,* and Vandiver, *Tattered Flags,* pp. 88–89, 158–63, 273; Steven E. Woodworth, *Jefferson Davis and His Generals: The Failure of Confederate Command in the West* (Lawrence: University Press of Kansas, 1990), and Woodworth, *Davis and Lee at War* (Lawrence: University Press of Kansas, 1995); Allan R. Millett and Peter Maslowski, *For the Common Defense: A Military History of the United States of America* (New York: Free Press, 1984), pp. 163–65, 207–10; Yearns, *Confederate Congress,* pp. 102–15, 140, 227–28; Eaton, *Southern Confederacy,* pp. 111–31; Clement Eaton, *Jefferson Davis* (New York: Free Press, 1977), pp. 242–50; Coulter, *Confederate States,* pp. 333–73; Shackelford, *George Wythe Randolph,* pp. 59–150; Richard M. McMurray, *John Bell Hood and the War for Southern Independence* (Lexington: University Press of Kentucky, 1982); Gerald A. Patterson, *Rebels from West Point* (New York: Doubleday, 1987); and William J. Cooper, Jr., "A Reassessment of Jefferson Davis as War Leader: The Case from Atlanta to Nashville," *Journal of Southern History* 36 (May 1970): 189–204.

Two excellent biographies dealing with Davis and Lee include complete bibliographies on their subjects and treat sensibly the major controversies surrounding them: William C. Davis, *Jefferson Davis: The Man and His Hour* (New York: HarperCollins Publishers, 1991), and Emory M. Thomas, *Robert E. Lee: A Biography* (New York: W. W. Norton, 1995).

18. The analysis of military manpower mobilization in the South is based on Albert B. Moore, *Conscription and Conflict in the Confederacy* (New York: Macmillan, 1924); Coulter, *Confederate States,* pp. 308–32, 440–81; Thomas, *Confederate Nation,* pp. 152–55; Vandiver, *Tattered Flags,* p. 242; Amlund, *Federalism in Southern Confederacy,* pp. 74–76, 105–6; Eaton, *Southern Confederacy,* pp. 87–110; and Lebergott, "Why the South Lost," pp. 58–74. See also Kenneth Radley, *Rebel Watchdog: The Confederate States Army Provost Guard* (Baton Rouge: Louisiana State University Press, 1989), and sources on class antagonisms in Chapter 8, n. 2, and on conscription in notes 19 and 20 of this chapter. See also Reid Mitchell, *Civil War Soldiers* (New York: Viking, 1988).

19. John W. Chambers II, *To Raise an Army: The Draft Comes to Modern America* (New York: Free Press, 1987), pp. 41–67, quotation, p. 46. The same point is made by Yearns, *Confederate Congress,* p. 88. See also the discussion on Union manpower mobilization in Chapter 6.

20. Alexander and Beringer, *Anatomy of Confederate Congress,* pp. 106–38, quotation, p. 197.

21. For the Confederate Navy Department, see Tom H. Wells, *The Confederate Navy: A Study in Organization* (University: University of Alabama Press, 1971); Joseph T. Durkin, *Stephen R. Mallory: Confederate Navy Chief* (Chapel Hill: University of North Carolina Press, 1954); Patrick, *Jefferson Davis and His Cabinet,* pp. 244–71; Hendrick, *Statesmen of the Lost Cause,* pp. 363–86; William N. Still, Jr., *Confederate Shipbuilding* (Athens: University of Georgia Press, 1969), and Still, *Iron Afloat: The Story of the Confederate Armorclads* (Nashville, TN: Vanderbilt University Press, 1971); William M. Fowler, Jr., *Under Two Flags: The American Navy in the Civil War* (New York: W. W. Norton, 1990); Frank J. Merli, *Great Britain and the Confederate Navy, 1861–1865* (Bloomington: Indiana University Press, 1970), and Merli, "The Confederate Navy, 1861–1865," in *In Peace and War: Interpretations of American Naval History, 1775–1984,* ed. Kenneth J. Hagan, pp. 126–44, 2d ed., rev. (Westport, CT: Greenwood Press, 1984); Wilbur D. Jones, *The Confederate Rams at Birkenhead: A Chapter in Anglo-American Relations* (Tuscaloosa, AL: Confederate Publishing Company, 1961); Thomas, *Confederate Nation,* pp. 76–77, 128–32, 139; Eaton, *Confederate Nation,* pp. 170–86; Vandiver, *Rebel Brass,* pp. 14–15, 63–74; Yearns, *Confederate Congress,* pp. 99–101, 125, 128, 141–45, 230; Halperin, "Leroy Pope Walker," pp. 42–75; Melton, "Major Military Industries of the Confederate Government," pp. 131–294; Dew, *Ironmaker to the Confederacy,* pp. 105–7, 115–23; Cappon, "Government and Private Industry in the Southern Confederacy," pp. 151–89; and Goff, *Confederate Supply,* pp. 32, 56–59, 119–20, 137–40. See also relevant citations in note 15 on blockade running; the most recent publication on naval aspects of the Civil War, Ivan Musicant, *Divided Waters: The Naval History of the Civil War* (New York: HarperCollins Publishers, 1995); and recent naval surveys cited in Chapter 4, n. 43.

22. Wells, *Confederate Navy,* p. 47.

CHAPTER TEN. CONFEDERATE CIVILIAN ORGANIZATION

1. The analysis of Confederate finances is based on Douglas B. Ball, *Financial Failure and Confederate Defeat* (Urbana: University of Illinois Press, 1991); Richard C. Todd, *Confederate Finance* (Athens: University of Georgia Press, 1954); John C. Schwab, *The Confederate States of America: A Financial and Industrial History of the South During the Civil War* (New York: Charles Scribner's Sons, 1901); John M. Godfrey, *Monetary Expansion in the Confederacy* (New York: Arno Press, 1978); James F. Morgan, *Graybacks and Gold: Confederate Monetary Policy* (Pensacola, FL: Perdido Bay Press, 1985); Larry Schweikart, *Banking in the American South from the Age of Jackson to Reconstruction* (Baton Rouge: Louisiana State University Press, 1987), and Schweikart, "Secession and Southern Banks," *Civil War History* 31 (June 1985): 111–25; Gary M. Pecquet, "Money in the Trans-Mississippi Confederacy and the Con-

federate Currency Reform Act of 1864," *Explorations in Economic History* 24 (April 1987): 218–43; George K. Davis and Gary M. Pecquet, "Interest Rates in the Civil War South," *Journal of Economic History* 50 (March 1990): 133–48; David G. Surdam, "Cotton's Potential as Economic Weapon: The Antebellum and Wartime Markets for Cotton," *Agricultural History* 68 (Spring 1994): 122–45; Rembert W. Patrick, *Jefferson Davis and His Cabinet* (Baton Rouge: Louisiana State University Press, 1944), pp. 203–43; Burton J. Hendrick, *Statesmen of the Lost Cause: Jefferson Davis and His Cabinet* (Boston: Little, Brown, 1939), pp. 188–232; Wilfred B. Yearns, *The Confederate Congress* (Athens: University of Georgia Press, 1960), pp. 123–24, 166–70, 184–217, 229–30; Charles W. Ramsdell, *Behind the Lines in the Southern Confederacy* (Baton Rouge: Louisiana State University Press, 1944); Judith F. Gentry, "A Confederate Success in Europe: The Erlanger Loan," *Journal of Southern History* 36 (May 1970): 157–88; Richard N. Current, "God and the Strongest Battalions," in *Why the North Won the Civil War,* ed. David Donald, pp. 15–32 (Baton Rouge: Louisiana State University Press, 1960); Stanley Lebergott, "Why the South Lost: Commercial Purpose in the Confederacy, 1861–1865," *Journal of American History* 70 (June 1983): 58–74; Thomas B. Alexander and Richard E. Beringer, *The Anatomy of the Confederate Congress: A Study of the Influences of Member Characteristics on Legislative Voting Behavior, 1861–1865* (Nashville, TN: Vanderbilt University Press, 1972), pp. 201–35; Curtis A. Amlund, *Federalism in the Southern Confederacy* (Washington, DC: Public Affairs Press, 1966), pp. 51–64, 123–28; Emory M. Thomas, *The Confederate Nation, 1861–1865* (New York: Harper and Row, 1979), pp. 72–74, 136–38, 148–50, 264–65, 286; E. Merton Coulter, *The Confederate States of America, 1861–1865* (Baton Rouge: Louisiana State University Press, 1950), pp. 149–82; Clement Eaton, *A History of the Southern Confederacy* (New York: Free Press, 1954), pp. 224–49, and Eaton, *Jefferson Davis* (New York: Free Press, 1977), pp. 196–208; and Charles B. Dew, *Ironmaker to the Confederacy: Joseph P. Anderson and the Tredegar Iron Works* (New Haven: Yale University Press, 1966), pp. 197–209.

2. There is no good scholarly study on the dynamics of the Davis administration. The one full-scale monograph by Patrick, *Jefferson Davis and His Cabinet,* treats more with the individual departments than with the executive as a whole. Hendrick, *Statesmen of the Lost Cause,* though useful, is much too erratic and idiosyncratic in his approach. The following volumes provide varying levels of coverage and insight involving the enormous complexities of the subject: Coulter, *Confederate States;* Eaton, *Southern Confederacy,* and Eaton, *Jefferson Davis;* Frank E. Vandiver, *Ploughshares into Swords: Josiah Gorgas and Confederate Ordnance* (Austin: University of Texas Press, 1952), Vandiver, *Rebel Brass: The Confederate Command System* (Baton Rouge: Louisiana State University Press, 1956), and Vandiver, *Their Tattered Flags: The Epic of the Confederacy* (New York: Harper and Row, 1970); William C. Davis, *Jefferson Davis: The Man and His Hour* (New York: HarperCollins Publishers, 1991), and Davis, *"A Government of Our Own": The Making of the Confederacy* (New York: Free Press, 1994); George C. Rable, *Confederate Republic: A Revolution Against Politics* (Chapel Hill: University of North Carolina Press, 1994); Joseph T. Durkin, *Stephen R. Mallory: Confederate Navy Chief* (Chapel Hill: University of North Carolina Press, 1954); Steven E. Woodworth, *Jefferson Davis and His Generals: The Failure of Confederate Command in the West* (Lawrence: University Press of Kansas, 1990); Richard D. Goff, *Confederate Supply* (Durham, NC: Duke University Press, 1969); Thomas, *Confeder-*

ate Nation; Eli N. Evans, *Judah P. Benjamin: The Jewish Confederate* (New York: Free Press, 1988); Frank L. Owsley, *King Cotton Diplomacy: Foreign Relations of the Confederate States of America,* 2d ed., rev. (Chicago: University of Chicago Press, 1959); D. P. Cook, *The North, the South, and the Powers, 1861–1865* (New York: John Wiley and Sons, 1974); Lynn M. Case and Warren F. Spencer, *The United States and France: Civil War Diplomacy* (Philadelphia: University of Pennsylvania Press, 1970); and the various articles in Donald, ed., *Why the North Won the Civil War.* In one way or another, most of the works cited here and in Chapters 8 and 9 contribute to understanding the collective successes and failures of the Davis administration. For a suggestive essay on Confederate wartime administration, see Paul P. Van Riper and Harry N. Scheiber, "The Confederate Civil Service," *Journal of Southern History* 25 (November 1959): 448–70.

3. For this interpretation, see Louise B. Hill, *State Socialism in the Confederate States of America* (Charlottesville, VA: Historical Publishing Company, 1936); Raimondo Luraghi, "The Civil War and the Modernization of American Society: Social Structure and Industrial Revolution in the Old South Before and During the War," *Civil War History* 18 (September 1972): 230–50, and Luraghi, *The Rise and Fall of the Plantation South* (New York: New Viewpoints, 1978); and Richard E. Beringer et al., *Why the South Lost the Civil War* (Athens: University of Georgia Press, 1986), pp. 215–18.

4. George G. Shackelford, *George Wythe Randolph and the Confederate Elite* (Athens: University of Georgia Press, 1988), pp. x–xi.

5. Richard F. Bensel, *Yankee Leviathan: The Origins of Central State Authority in America, 1859–1877* (New York: Cambridge University Press, 1990), offers a rich and suggestive analysis along the lines of state-building. However, by focusing on theory more than practice, the author's analysis and conclusions are often questionable.

6. More and better work has been done on the Confederate Congresses than on their Union counterparts, perhaps because of the fascination over a "lost cause," the novelty of a political system operating without parties, or the fact that the Southern legislatures were smaller than those of the North and in a sense less complex. See Yearns, *Confederate Congress;* Alexander and Beringer, *Anatomy of the Confederate Congress;* and Ezra J. Warner and W. Buck Yearns, *Biographical Register of the Confederate Congress* (Baton Rouge: Louisiana State University Press, 1975). See also Coulter, *Confederate States,* pp. 134–48; Eaton, *Jefferson Davis,* pp. 209–19; and Davis, *Jefferson Davis,* pp. 444–55, 582–85. Eric L. McKitrick's brilliant essay is among the most insightful on the politics of the Confederacy: "Party Politics and the Union and Confederate War Efforts," in *The American Party Systems,* ed. William N. Chambers and Walter D. Burnham, pp. 117–51 (New York: Oxford University Press, 1967). Rable, *Confederate Republic,* challenges McKitrick's analysis and presents an alternate interpretation. Rable and Davis, *"Government of Our Own,"* deal extensively with the South's political culture and thereby enlighten congressional operations, legislative-executive relations, and states' rights versus nationalism. Since their volumes are essentially narratives, the information and insight are scattered throughout the text.

7. Eaton, *Jefferson Davis,* p. 217.

8. Alexander and Beringer, *Anatomy of the Confederate Congress,* p. 342.

9. Ibid., p. 341.

10. The reference, of course, is to David Donald, "Died of Democracy," in Donald, ed., *Why the North Won the Civil War,* pp. 79–90.

11. Ramsdell, *Behind the Lines,* pp. 85–99. Ramsdell's other pathbreaking articles on Confederate mobilization already have been cited in Chapter 10 and in Chapters 8 and 9 and are also cited in a bibliography of his scholarly work appended to *Behind the Lines,* pp. 123–36.

12. For example, see Eaton, *Jefferson Davis,* pp. 196–97.

13. Eaton, *Southern Confederacy,* pp. 67.

14. One of the clearest and best known is Current, "God and the Strongest Battalions," in Donald, ed., *Why the North Won the Civil War,* pp. 15–32.

15. The most recent example is Beringer et al., *Why the South Lost the Civil War,* pp. 424–42. See also Coulter, *Confederate States,* pp. 566–67, and Eaton, *Jefferson Davis,* pp. 231–41.

INDEX